Des Rubens on The Wand (V,5), Creag Meagaidh – 26 March 2015. Photo: Geoff Cohen.

THE SCOTTISH MOUNTAINEERING CLUB JOURNAL

Vol. XLIII **2015** **No. 206**

EDITORIAL

SITTING IN THE SCHOOL library during what was known as a study period I was attracted by a series of red bound volumes and surreptitiously took one down. The SMC Journal fell open at the page on which WH Murray describes his wonderful traverse of Liathach. I was enthralled. I had already climbed Liathach with a school party under the watchful eye of Archie Hendry who taught French and German and became SMC President. We had stayed at the Ling Hut. I was just 15 at the time and not expected to do very well at school. Little did I think that I would one day write for the Journal, far less, be honoured by becoming its 16th editor.

Since 1992 I have contributed articles for three different editors: Ken Crocket, Charlie Orr and Noel Williams; they were all very different in style and each had his special strength. One of the things they had in common with each other and, I'd guess, with the other twelve editors, is that they all took the responsibility of maintaining our Journal with great seriousness. An example I hope to follow.

I also hope that members and the wider mountaineering community will go on contributing the articles, short stories, scholarly pieces, photographs, artwork and poetry which go to make up the gloriously unique content of the Journal and will remain as a rich record of our way of life for succeeding generations.

I would particularly like to thank Noel Williams, a most meticulous editor, for all his patient help and instruction without which his apprentice would have struggled even more than he has.

THE HILLS ARE ALIVE...

By Ian Crofton

HERE I AM AGAIN, perched on a snow step at the foot of some iced-up buttress, shivering and shaking and shifting from foot to foot. You'd think at my age I'd know better. I try, and fail, to exercise patience, flicking kinks out of the ropes draped down the slope below. So many times, over so many years, I've found myself here, or places like it. So many times over so many years – I've found that time, and the years, compress, fold over on each other, the patterns repeating with subtle variations. It is like a pibroch, with neither beginning nor end. And all the city days, weeks, months, in between, vanish, as if they had never happened.

The first pre-echo came the year I started climbing. For most people of a certain age, 1968 is remembered for other things: the Tet Offensive, the Paris *événements*, Soviet tanks on the streets of Prague, Martin Luther King and Bobby Kennedy assassinated. As for me – awkwardly poised at the end of that year on the edge of adolescence – I found myself perched on a bucket cut into the slope at the start of NC Gully, dreaming of a girl I'd just partnered at a Christmas dance. A girl I'd never see again, but whose name I still, strangely, remember.

What was more concrete, as I shivered and shook and shifted from foot to frozen foot, was the all-too-present chill in my bowels. Somewhere above me, Mr Stewart – who taught me violin at the school and climbing in the holidays – was cutting steps. He was, as I remember it, tucked away from view, somewhere up round a corner. But I could hear the reports of his progress. Chop. Tinkle. Chop. Tinkle. Tinkle tinkle. Patter, patter whirrrr. Again and again, for what seemed like the full length of a December afternoon.

Then a different sound. Bong. Bong. Bang, bang, tang ting ting ping. The rising chimes – though I didn't know it then – of a piton being hammered into a crack. The rope ran out, as did the daylight. You'll never forget your first time at the top of a winter climb looking out west across the silver slither of Loch Linnhe in the aftermath of a sunset, towards the darkened hills of Ardgour. The long way down was lit by sparks as crampons hit rock, the night filling with the stench of sulphur.

This time, this year, we're on Milky Way in Coire an Lochain. Quite enough for us at our age, Bob says, at the start of the season. So it would seem, as the ropes slow down, stop. Stay stopped. Then the sound rings down the years. Bong. Bong. Bang, bang, tang ting ting ping. The rising chimes that cheer, and reassure. And then, at last, the rope starts to run.

In my ridiculous teenage years, I was all but deaf to the music of the hills. What I heard in my head, as I (in my own eyes at least) battled heroically on the heights, were thundering symphonies – Beethoven, Sibelius, and, most especially, Bruckner. Big Romantic symphonies,

Unknown party on The Milky Way (III), Coire an Lochain. *Photo: I. Crofton*

music full of *Sturm und Drang* that seemed to tell the story of my own apotheosis in the crucible of peak and blizzard. Thus my imaginary love life was a film, and Ludwig and Jean and Anton provided the soundtrack. The snow blew, the wind howled, the hero struggled down the cruel mountain – until, at last – is that a light in the darkness? A candle in the window of the lonely cabin? A door that opens? And, silhouetted against the firelight, is it, could it be, the most lovely...? Yup, we are such stuff as dreams are made on. Wet dreams.

Bruckner still has his power to evoke a feeling of elemental struggle, but it was disillusioning to discover in my twenties that the landscape that Bruckner had in mind when composing his symphonies was not the rugged scenery of the Alps, but the pretty meadows and quiet woodland glades of northern Austria, far from the mountains. There may even have been milkmaids and Bambis involved. So why did I hear only rockfall and storm, avalanche and thunder?

If they'd been invented in those days I would have tramped the hills and clambered up the crags plugged into an iPod, got myself high on the intra-aural fix of pre-packaged emotion that only music can deliver. Even without an iPod, there was often music running through my head, some welcome or unwelcome ear worm wriggling in time to my breath. But as the years passed I found such distractions created a barrier between myself and the natural world. If I quietened myself, rid my mind of human music, muted that song beating through my head, I could sometimes hear other kinds of music in the hills, music that might or might not have been in time with the beat of the human heart.

There's birdsong, of course. In the higher hills the most you're likely to hear is the quiet *tseep* of a meadow pippit, the belch of a ptarmigan, the rasping deep *caw* of a raven. On the lower slopes in May, among the scattered birches and oaks, you may hear a distant, insistent cuckoo, and, closer by, the falling liquid cadences of willow warblers. On the summer moors, there is the sweet melancholy cry of the curlew, the ringing *crwee* or *coor-li* that gives it its name, followed by the bubbling trill of its lovely drawn-out song. The first time I became aware of the beauty of this song was as a young man, climbing at the Whangie after too many weeks trapped in the city. All through the long May afternoon, as we grappled with the gnarly unreliabilities of the rock, the curlews drew their cries across Stockie Muir and Thief's Hill, lost souls looking for lost lovers.

In such places too you may hear the *pee-wee* of the lapwing, a sound that haunted Robert Louis Stevenson while in exile in faraway Samoa:

Be it granted me to behold you again in dying,
Hills of home! and to hear again the call;
Hear about the graves of the martyrs the peewees crying,
And hear no more at all.

West Kip, East Kip and Scald Law in the Pentland Hills
Robert Louis Stevenson's 'hills of home', where, from his exile in the South Seas, he remembered above all else the call of the peewits. Photo: I.Crofton

Also on the moors, and even up on the ridges, wheatears sometimes take a break from their curt *chack chack* to make brief attempts to imitate the skylark. But no bird can live up to the latter in terms of the endless joyful energy of its song, belted out at full tilt while it hovers high above the grass.

There are other less distinct musics in the hills: the hum of bees in the heather, wind sighing through the tops of the pines, the patter of rain on a flysheet, the roar of stags on an October hillside, the howl of a winter storm buffeting around the high corries. Then there is the extraordinary metallic whine of a stone skimmed across a frozen lochan – a sound so satisfying that one February in Snowdonia, having traversed the small but perfectly formed Cnicht with my daughter Claire, we paused at the northeast end of the ridge by the ice-covered Llyn yr Adai and span stone after stone, listening for the descending scale of tonks as the pebbles scampered across the white surface.

All these are comforting sounds, but there are some noises to be heard among the hills that are less certain, more sinister. One June long ago I was camping alone on the shore of Loch Beinn a' Mheadhoin in Glen Affric. Sleep was long deferred by the lingering midsummer light and by the plaintive *twee-see-see* alarm call of a sandpiper. Eventually the light dimmed and the sandpiper settled on her nest. Just as sleep seemed at last a possibility, the silence of the woods above me was broken by a heart-stopping cry. It was something like a high-pitched bark – but not quite. The hair on the back of my neck stood to attention, every nerve and sinew tensed. Then the cry came again. My blood turned to ice, my spine to jelly.

It might have been a roe deer, I told myself. It might have been a fox. But there is no such thing, as Napoleon once observed, as one o'clock-in-the-morning courage – especially when you are on your own in the dark in the wilds. So my imagination got the better of my rational self, conjuring up all kinds of shapeless, ungraspable horrors lurking in the wildwood beyond the road.

But the wild can also smile. Ten years or more ago, on a February trip to Torridon, I found myself on Slioch, the day after a strenuous traverse of the snowy crest of Liathach. There was a premonition of spring in the air, a warmth in the sun, although patches of hard snow still clung to the upper slopes. At one point I became, I think intentionally, separated from my companions. Contentedly I found my own way in the mild sunshine, clambering from rock to rock up the steep slope below Coire na Sleaghaich, while numerous trickles of water tinkled all around me. As I climbed I found myself feeling lighter and lighter, gently caught up by the water music, and by an indefinable happiness.

I thought then, and often do to this day, of a story told by Showell Styles. One summer long ago, he was climbing with two companions in Arctic Norway, looking for a new route up the east side of Stortind, a

The view towards Beinn Eighe from Slioch, 10 February 2003, the day of the water music. Photo: Ian Crofton.

seriously jagged peak in an area that was not then fully mapped. Faced with overhanging buttresses of rotten rock and insurmountable bergschrunds, they failed to find a way to the summit. There then followed a long retreat across a difficult glacier, and then down snow-covered ledges and unstable, steep moraine, until they reached the birch-filled, boulder-crowded valley bottom. Styles was some way ahead of his friends. Exhausted after fourteen hours of continuous effort, much of it made through the sunlit midsummer night of the far north, he rested for a while with his back against a rock. The valley, he says, was still, and yet there were voices – the river below him, waterfalls somewhere high above, a breeze occasionally soughing round the mountainside. He found himself lulled into a half-sleep, and then became conscious of the sound of music. He held his breath as wind and water merged into a harmony, as if, he is certain, an orchestra was playing.

Styles says he was sure he was not dreaming. He even hit his fist against the rock to make doubly sure. And then, on a sudden waft of the breeze, he heard what he described as 'a noble melody'. It seemed to him, he said, that he was hearing the horns of Elfland.

Styles wrote down the theme, a four-note phrase: F (quaver), B flat (crotchet), D (quaver), C (breve). Strangely, he later learnt that that very same melody was used as a theme by Wagner – who scored it for the horns. The tune is simple enough, possibly simple enough for some strange combination of natural sounds to come together to produce – or at least to evoke in the passive, receptive mind of an exhausted body – a sensation of melody. Of course, humans are great projectors of patterns onto nature, from seeing faces in the shapes of rocks to hearing the sound of the waves in a seashell held up to the ear.

I have never forgotten this story of the horns of Elfland, and have, from time to time when out in the hills, lain down tired on a grassy sward by a rushing mountain stream and closed my eyes against the sunshine, and let what comes, come. And it is more likely to come, I've found, if you've succeeded up some tricky, perhaps even scary, climb. The day will have been long, and the tiredness you feel involves all your muscles, and also your brain, purged of thought after the concentration and the nervous uncertainty and the fear.

If there are no other distractions (a blister, a chatty companion, a pressing need to consume a Mars Bar), it is sometimes possible to experience an overwhelming sensation of wellbeing. The music of the babbling water is crucial – the bass notes, the middle tenor, the gurgling, ever-changing descant. Perhaps, after hard exercise, the endorphins – the body's natural opiates – also play their part, kicking in with a dose of quiet euphoria, reinforced by the regular, directionless, trance-inducing rhythm of a mountain stream going calmly, purposelessly about its business, to become part of the sea, and then the clouds, and then the rain, and then itself again, flowing once more down the mountain to the sea. Just as the water surrenders itself to an endless cycle, with no sense of time or intention, so I too (I persuade myself) can become part of the universe I'm in, rather than a spectator looking at the world through a TV screen, chewing popcorn, scratching that itch, locked out from the inside.

But then the sun goes behind a cloud, the midges rouse themselves, and I'm off down the hill as fast as my tired legs will carry me. The bubble bursts, and my mind is filled instead with the thought of the froth on top of that first pint.

A PATCHWORK OF PATEY

By Mike Dixon

All humans are unique but some humans are more unique than others.

APPROACHING THE SPRAWL of Westhill one Saturday in May 2013, I don't mind admitting I felt apprehensive. The person I had arranged to meet was only nine when his father was killed. Waiting for the door to open I had a preconceived notion of who I would see. Tousled black hair, lantern jawed, heavily lined face, fag clenched between lips, a young Humphrey Bogart look-alike but without the world weariness. However, my host displayed none of these features though he says he most resembled his father when both were youngsters. He remembers being taken up Ben Mor Coigach by him, an outing he later repeated with one of his daughters for her first mountain in the North-West Highlands.

Tom Patey tests a MacInnes axe while Hamish looks on, April 1968 *Photo: John Cleare*

During the following five hours I was given a sample of the extensive material he has on his computer relating to his father. Ian is proud of his father's achievements and so he should be. Few have had such a varied array of talents: academic, climbing, literary, musical, entertaining. Few were legends in their own lifetime. Thomas Walton Patey undoubtedly was.

Thankfully, researching Patey was not going to be a study of 'phantoms and dust, the mere echoes of echoes.' Of course I was too late for some significant figures but there were four men with intriguing nicknames who Patey crossed paths with: 'Fred the Ted', 'Zeke' and the 'Gay Lothario' were all tracked down and visited.

'ROGOCOMOCO – Robert Gordons College Mountaineering Company assembled at the door of the Luibeg Bothy, 7 Jan 1949. Bob Scott's "Horrible Hielanders..." Left to right I. Rettie (complete in kilt), D. Haston, A. Gill, B. Falconer and Me! (What a horrible dockside tough!) – I had not washed for six days. The picture was taken in pouring rain on the day of departure. The owner of the sullen face protruding through from the bothy is Bill Brooker, one of the best young rock climbers in Aberdeen (17 years old). Next door is the stick shed where we slept on Sunday night. "Ah, bitter chill it was" (Keats).' Patey at age 16. Photo: I. Patey Collection

'Sticker' (Alex Thom) has lived in Canada for 40 years so e-mail had to do. A member of the Kincorth Club of Aberdeen, he knew Patey in his student days and made this observation about him: 'I admired Tom in every way in the hills and the pub he had great talent. Tom was very much a one man band, so I did not like climbing with him, he was too serious, too driven for me, took chances.'

The next person I met was Joe Brown. His friendship with Patey began on the 1956 Mustagh Tower expedition and was a close one for 14 years. 'There was no one who came anywhere near him for having a good time whether you were in a pub or on a mountain.' Joe didn't initially have a favourable opinion of Patey. His maintenance of the medical supplies was slipshod (sand in some of the syringes) and he was not particularly sociable. I spent two concentrated hours with Joe reminiscing and viewing his scanned images from that trip. A four man team successful on the most technical route in the Himalaya at the time. Joe's trips to Norway with Patey were new information to me. Whenever they climbed together the important thing was to try and do new routes with atmosphere, the grade being irrelevant. They were in Romsdal in 1967 when a strong French team including Patrick Cordier established a new diretissima on the Troll Wall which had taken fourteen days of climbing to complete. Joe and Tom passed the jubilant team just as they reached the rim. The French knew about Brown's prowess and thought they must have climbed the British Rimmon Route on the Wall, still a big undertaking then and climbed two years earlier. Enquiring what time they started Joe answered '7 a.m.' 'Which day?' 'This morning,' he replied before they scuttled off, leaving the French speechless. In reality the fresh-looking pair had completed a gigantic scramble well away from the Troll Wall with a pitch of Grade III to finish which Brown had to persuade Patey to put the rope on for.

Tom Patey's life falls roughly under five headings: pre-university, university, foreign trips to the Alps and Himalaya, time with the Marines and life in Ullapool.

The first and fourth were sparse on information. 92 year old Ellon resident May Forbes was a saviour for the former. She still attends St Mary's on the Rock, the Episcopalian church where Patey's father was minister. She herself taught Tom at Sunday school. The Reverend Thomas Maurice Patey, according to May, had a caring attitude to all local residents, even cutting logs for one lady not one of his parishioners. This inclusiveness was shared by Tom, one of his nicest features according to Martin Boysen. The musical influences can be traced to his mother who played the organ in church. There is a picture of the 14-year-old Tom on Tap o' Noth near Rhynie with a mouth organ in his hand.

From the school and student days I met Gordon 'Goggs' Leslie who knew Patey at Robert Gordon's College before both entered Aberdeen University together. By all accounts, Goggs was endearingly eccentric and was very keen on the Teutonic dimension in mountaineering. This fed into Patey's creative imagination in his writings. Goggs was also the co-author of Scotland's first Grade V, after he and Patey took seven hours to cut their way up the final 200 foot headwall of *Douglas Gibson Gully* on Lochnagar, tunnelling a formidable cornice. 'We shook hands. I was very proud. It was so beautiful with a bright moon shining…he knew he had really done something.'

Alan Will, who with Patey and George Macleod did the first big line on the Central Gully Wall of the Dubh Loch, *Vertigo Wall*, remembers Patey's speed of movement. He found it difficult to keep up with him on approaches despite being a champion athlete at Robert Gordon's. He recalls staying with Patey in the delightfully named 'vermin villa' just outside Braemar. Patey arrived with a dixie of boiled potatoes and no other food or utensils whatsoever. 'The way he climbed he was very much an individual, looking after number one. He virtually always led, he chose the line. Anyone climbing with him was just a supporter.'

Patey fondly described the mountains and companions that nurtured his skills in 'Cairngorm Commentary' and the song 'Aiguilles des Cairngorms.' The memorable third verse of the latter lampoons the great Chamonix guide Armand Charlet. It was written after an Alpine trip blighted by poor weather in 1954. But Charlet nearly had the last laugh. The following year Freddie Malcolm and Patey were on one of Charlet's most famous routes the north face of the Aiguille du Plan where they narrowly escaped obliteration by serac collapse. 'Patey never eats, drinks, shits till he gets to the top.' After nine hours of virtually continuous effort they reached the summit. 'He was a wonderful companion on the mountain if you could keep up with him.'

Patey on accordion, Tom Weir on drums, in the Fife Arms, Aviemore, New Year 1955/6. Photo: Ian Patey Collection

Rakaposhi in the Karakoram was a mountain requiring endurance rather than the technical skills demanded of Mustagh Tower. In 1958 Patey was in the Marines and enjoying a free expedition at the expense of the military. Richard Brooke was the only team member I could trace. In March 1962 he was up in Scotland for a profitable week with Patey. It began at Creag Meagaidh with the first ascent of the *Post Horn Gallop* and a failure to straighten out the *Centre Post*. They also attempted the

Cuillin Ridge in what Patey dismissed as not true winter conditions but which, on viewing Richard's slides, I have no doubt modern climbers would accept. In Richard's diary he notes bedding down at the Laggan Hotel prior to another major new route on Creag Meagaidh. No early night for Tom who 'went off to spend a riotous evening at Carrbridge and got back in the small hours – what energy.' The next day they made the first ascent of *Last Post*.

It was John Barry who helped initially in tracking down Patey's peers from his national service days. John himself is one of the few successors to Patey in terms of being able to write humorously about climbing. He provided contacts for Sam Bemrose whom Patey nicknamed the 'Gay Lothario' and who appears in his two Norway essays. I was curious as to how someone as individualistic and with such a disregard for his appearance as Patey would have fared in the military. I wondered how I'd get on meeting men who were trained to be killers in their day but I couldn't have met a group more hospitable, generous hearted, genuinely interested in people and not afraid to express their emotions. Working as a team when you and your peers' lives depend on it makes most other forms of cooperative work seem shallow. Sam made it quite clear he wasn't gay in the modern sense and said I could have any drink I fancied even including tea.

Sam felt Patey was slightly wasted as he wasn't using his full range of medical skills. The same afflictions kept cropping up in the Marines: bruises, breaks (which were dealt with at a hospital), foot rot, crutch rot and VD. Everybody was very fit. However Tom was respected as a doctor. On one occasion his quick diagnosis and evacuation of a Marine in Norway who'd had a brain haemorrhage helped minimise the long term damage to the man.

The only time Sam saw Patey upset was when he was leaving the service. There was a speech of thanks for his mountaineering and medical contribution to the unit then the NCOs presented him with a wrapped up vest and underpants which they'd died black.

Heading further south I made a diversion to photograph *Wrecker's Slab* at Cornakey on the north coast of Devon. Approaching it in brilliant weather it looks harder than VS. In fact it is technically easy now the current line has been pruned of loose rock. What it must have been for Patey, John 'Zeke' Deacon and Admiral Keith Lawder, was an adventure, a line with atmosphere, a trait highly valued by Tom wherever he climbed. Just south of here is the cliff Henna where Mick Fowler, a modern prophet of the Patey school of adventure, found that very essence on the disintegrating shale of these highly unconventional lines.

Zeke had a reputation as one of the best Marine rock climbers of his era with quality lines like *Bishop's Rib* at Chair Ladder, *String of Pearls* and *Green Cormorant Face* at Bosigran amongst his first ascents. His nickname comes from a Zane Gray western character, a sharp shooting, good guy cowboy. He lives in a beautiful house looking down on Sennen in Cornwall, a place he retired to with its many happy associations. I arrived for elevenses which at Zeke's was a couple of Glenmorangies. 'My doctor says I shouldn't but at my age...' As to Wrecker's Slab he remembers the holds on pitch 1 coming out like drawers in cupboard. On one occasion on a Scottish winter training course in 1960 he had flu symptoms. They were in tents on a training stint in the hills. Patey examined him and took his temperature and said I don't think you should go out today. Zeke said he was actually feeling a bit better. But Patey was adamant about him resting for two whole days in his sleeping bag while the rest of his group were patrolling around the Lairig Ghru and Braeriach. Zeke was puzzled as to Patey's insistence but it soon became clear:

'You're not yourself, you're not well but not only that I want you on Saturday.'

'What do you mean on Saturday?'

'I've got something in mind, North Post.'

Thus a plan was being hatched for another foray to Creag Meagaidh, a happy hunting ground for Patey.

Patey: pen and ink drawing by Helen Forde after a photo by Douglas Scott

'You never get a day off in a small place like Ullapool,' stated Donnie Smith who was head of the police rescue team based in Dingwall in the sixties. He climbed regularly with Patey and was very aware of how he protected his image and privacy in the community. Patey preferred Donnie to pick him up in Ullapool so his car wouldn't be seen at Inverlael, Braemore Junction or Dundonnell. Patey would cut things fine when it came to surgery timings. They were sitting at the summit of Beinn Dearg at 1.30 p.m. on a winter's afternoon after climbing a gully. Tom realised what day it was, uttered a torrent of expletives and announced he had to be back for surgery at 3 p.m. So they ran down the ridge above Gleann na Sguaib and got back to Ullapool with five minutes to spare. That afternoon Patey conducted the surgery in boots, breeches and heavy jersey. The latter was several sizes too big and Patey looked on it as a kind of plaid. It had an earthy smell which would have been masked by the fact that back then doctors could perform consultations while smoking.

Patey the master of comic deflation and characterisation in his articles and songs was something I wished to explore further. Take Graeme Nicol, a medical student three years younger than Patey. Looking at a photo of the first winter ascent of *Scorpion* on Càrn Etchachan in 1952 I'm reminded of Tom's description of the young man, driven to succeed for the fatherland: 'Graeme was desperate to bivouac on the route.' Of course it's exaggerated for effect but Graeme gave me some background. The Patey group would address themselves in mock teutonic manner and discuss routes with the fervour of the Austro-Germanic climbers of the thirties. To express weakness was to invite rebuke. The fact that Graeme is blue eyed and was blond haired gave more ammunition for Patey's characterisation of him as a fully paid up member of the Munich School.

Patey's abilities as musician and entertainer were as important parts of the man as his climbing. A magnet for folk singers and climbers in the sixties was Temple Cottage at Balmore outside Glasgow, still the home of Mary Stewart. It was an open house where Royal Robbins, the Boningtons, Whillans, The Incredible String Band, Hamish Imlach and of course Patey all spent time. The main room has a rustic cosiness and in Mary you'd be pushed to find a kinder host. She talks fondly of that era in a gentle voice. Mary commented that musician Hamish Imlach and Patey got on very well. The older Imlach was virtually the size of a Munro so mountaineering was not a common link with Tom. Imlach's most famous comic song was 'Cod Liver Oil and the Orange Juice.' The ingredients were certainly two items which never featured prominently in either man's diet.

Surprisingly the SMC has no Patey images in its archive. His peg hammer and doctor's desk from Ullapool are now housed in Mick Tighe's Scottish Mountain Heritage collection. As well as photographs and correspondence another key archive made available to me was the guest book for the bothy behind the house in Ullapool. It reads like a who's-who of British mountaineering in the sixties. The first entry exemplifies the hospitality:

> 29/2/64 Arrived at hut 20.00 hrs. Guardian & family very friendly. Drank Glenmorangie with Guardian until 02.00 hrs. Dr A.G. Nicol was carried to bed by the Guardian and one of the party. Much song.

Some significant first ascents are recorded such as *Penguin Gully* on Beinn Dearg, climbed by Patey, W.H. Murray and Norman Tennant in 1964 in a style probably never repeated. The words are Patey's:

> 30th March
>
> To round off the SMC Easter Meet at Inchnadamph a Presidential first ascent was made with aides de camp Tennant and Patey. This was a 1000ft ice gully. Still in perfect conditions (despite the poor winter)... Named Penguin Gully from the characteristic attitude of two members of the party throughout most of the climb. Step cutting on hard ice all the way – 5 hours.
>
> Both senior members had forgotten their crampons and did not of course have any rock or ice pitons, the junior member had forgotten his boots, gloves and anorak. Improperly equipped and poorly shod and clad the party nevertheless forced a passage by sheer SMC grit, classic rock belaying and hewing mighty bucket steps...

On the day of Patey's accident there were four fellow climbers as well as three female onlookers who went along for the boat trip out to the Maiden stack off Whiten Head: Brian Fuller, Paul Nunn, Clive Rowland and Dave Goodwin. Dave abseiled next to last. Patey gave him a safety rope then followed. The brutality of witnessing Patey's plummet 100 feet onto his back on the stack's plinth left 20-year-old Dave traumatised. He stopped climbing for three years. Like Dave, one of the women, Di Cundy had met Patey for the first time the evening before at Sheigra and had therefore known him for less than 24 hours. On returning to the campsite she remembers the poignancy of seeing his accordion in the tent.

When I started the project the only snatches of Patey's voice I'd come across were from the Old Man of Hoy broadcast in 1967. Joe Brown provided me with a recording of 10 songs performed by Patey in the flat above Joe's first shop in Llanberis in 1967. Three of them do not appear in *One Man's Mountains*. Then Dave Goulder who ran Glen Cottage in Torridon in the late sixties gave me a tape of a radio programme broadcast in 1971 to commemorate Patey, Jim McArtney and Ian Clough. It was a delight to hear the voices of Bob Scott, Bill Brooker, Whillans, Mike Taylor and McArtney. Everyone I've met knew there was something special about Patey. I'll leave the last words to Joe Brown:

'I look back and it's Tom that I always miss the most…Life would be so much better if he was still around.'

(I would like to thank Ian Patey for allowing me access to material connected with his father and the SMT for providing a grant towards the research.)

MERCURY FALLING

A humorous tour of deep water soloing around Scotland

By Julian Lines

I AM SURE THAT EVERYONE will agree that deep water soloing in Scotland seems a ridiculous idea, but then again, so are other Scottish fixations such as tossing logs, deep-fried Mars Bars and perhaps, to some, even the notion of Independence.

Temperature or the feeling of hot and cold is all in the mind; in the physical it is just a column of mercury in a tube. In any case, cold water only makes you pull harder, hold on tighter, for longer, and makes you swim faster if you happen to fall in. When you get out (assuming that you ever do), you shiver enough to burn off any excess body fat. Then, on your next attempt, you'll be lighter and therefore more likely to levitate and succeed. But that's a dietary secret, and if it leaks out, every Cosmopolitan reader will be seeking out the shores of Scotland rather than jetting off to the Caribbean to achieve that slimline look, and I'll be seeking out the Editor for a proportion of their augmented margins!

The Scottish coastline is vast, does not host any great white sharks to my knowledge, has immense variety in geology, and harbours some of the best DWS in the World, most of which have yet to be found. So here are a few to help you on your way.

Since the sun rises in the east, we will begin with *Lean Meat* (F6b+ S1) at Craig Stirling, a few miles south of Aberdeen. This cunning, overhanging flake crack bursts its way across a squiggly chunk of overhanging schist. Step off the psych-up ledge and fidget for a while with the initial flake, before moving up to grab the perfect (footless) handrail. Your heart will now be thumping hard; if you are made of lean meat, then this traverse will be boring and a foregone conclusion. However, if you are not so lean, then things become far more interesting because you will be pumped and when you realise that you are not going to make the monster jug on the arête, you can smile, fall off and tuck yourself tightly into a bomb. Having done so, you will be safe in the knowledge that the headlines in the paper the following morning will read, 'Norway hit by tsunami of unknown origin'. On a more pleasant note, this route has been climbed in a complete birthday suit – the perpetrator wishes to remain anonymous.

Next up is Longhaven, so head into a tangle of jams in the Granite City, and then exit towards a stark, treeless coastline twenty miles further north. Here you need to search out The Red Tower where there is a collection of finger-frying paths of tenuous complexity. *Hole in the Wall* (F7a+ S1) is the supposed classic. It is one of the most sought after E5 leads on the east coast. A roped ascent is like losing your virginity; on completion, you smile with relief, feeling elated, but also wondering what all the fuss was about. Attempting it without a rope is a different encounter altogether, you feel a mixture of nerves and vulnerability, yet also excited and cheeky. It's more akin to performing outdoors, forever expecting to get caught. If that didn't excite you enough then you should try *Jacala* (F7c+ S3), a vague line of improbable ergonomics up the right side of the wall. It requires both gross negligence and the biggest springs of the year and there is still a high chance of receiving a barnacle back scratch if you fall off. Sounds great, doesn't it? Okay, I haven't been that fair so for those who don't have Cumberland sausage fingers or Kevlar skin then try *Neanderthal Woman* (F6a S1) on the adjacent wall. It traverses out from the neck and follows the lovely runnel above with only one 'Oh shit I might get wet!' move at 20ft. Sounds better doesn't it?

Sweeping round onto the Moray coast, you will reach the town of Cullen, home to both Cullen Skink, which could either be a lizard or a hallucinatory product if you are dyslexic, and Logie Head, which is a most friendly spine of Sandstone that wades into the sea and finally truncates in the shape of *Dark Star* (F6a S0). If you like tomfoolery then wait for a group of climbers to be climbing above the platform on the popular east facing wall, then step off the end of the platform, above a small, square-cut bay of floating kelp. You will now be burrowing your hands up some lovely overhanging cracks, and, since you are out of sight, you can make all sorts of extremis grunts. They will think you are a little unhinged and will be reaching for their phones to call the coastguard.

After sampling a bowl of warm haddock soup continue along the Moray Coast – the land of the rain shadow and dust storms to reach the sunny village of Cummingston. Here you will find some sandstone, sea stacks, caves and pebbly beaches. In amongst the caves is the shy, 25ft high hanging arête of *Bunny Boiler* (F7a+ S2/3) which is a little dubious because of the way the beach level changes beneath it. Rule of thumb: a sandy base and 6ft of water at high tide is the best you are going to get. If you are up for it, first practice the art of the armchair landing. If you need a demonstration, ask Mike Robertson, but don't follow if he jumps from 60ft; 5ft will suffice. Once you have mastered that, access the base of Sidle, drop down and let rip your best simian swings along a line of fragile looking razor-edged pancakes and honeycombs, all very healthy, to reach the base of the arête. The holds are a little sandy, so stay cool. Dare to be different?

If you have survived thus far then continue through the highland capital of Inverness and up the non-compliant (for dws) east coast to take the ferry across the Pentland Firth to Orkney. There is so much more to the islands than a graveyard of battleships in Scapa Flow, Highland Park whisky, Pictish Stones and a 500ft rotting sea stack – there is, of course, the bullet-hard sandstone of Yesnaby and a good playground to experience what single figured sea temperatures are all about. If you are not confident

The author on Lum Crack (F6a+ S0), Orkney *Photo: Scott Johnston*

sans rope then it may help to climb lathered in duck fat or wear a dry suit, or both. Firstly, try out *Lum Crack* (F6a+ S0), not really a crack, although good craic if you manage to remain attached to this flowing piece of climbing up the left side of the Gardyloo Wall.... However if you like the cold, think you can emulate Jesus by walking on water and curl into the lotus position viewed only by the sea birds, then *Tantric Sex* (F6c+ S1) is a must. Firstly you have to abseil down the headland facing the Castle of

Yesnaby sea stack. Untie, and traverse into the cave. Now comes the tricky bit. If the tide is too high then you will have to wade or swim; at lowish tide you have your chance to mimic the son of god himself. Gain the ship's prow pillar where you begin with the stork impression, standing on one leg at a time to don boots. Fire up through the roof of the cave; swing right to get your well-earned rest on the 'lotus ledge'. Make sure you have reawakened from your yogi trance before embarking on the leg-flexing overhung groove above. You will now be wearing a big smile in the knowledge of having just completed the second best deep water solo in Scotland.

After the cold waters of Orkney, the Gulf Stream on the northwest coast might purvey slightly kinder temperatures. Driving down this part of the highlands you will notice the gargantuan – black (sandstone) and white (quartzite) – primordial pieces standing defiant on their game-board of gneiss. By the time you are passing the pawn of Stac Pollaidh, you will need to be falling out of your thoughts and psyching up for your one hour walk across boggy terrain to reach Baby Taipan Wall. The obvious, long, low level break of the wall that is *Land of Milk and Honey* (F6b S0) isn't really at all like milk and honey; it's more like jams, slopes and rising heartbeats. So if there aren't any heart problems in your family then you should give it a bash. It is close to the water, in fact too close, so you can do silly things like cut loose and break wind. From the twisting descent slab at the northern end of the wall, swing round the arête and check out the line; it's obvious – like a set of cat's eyes. Continue until you reach the pebbly beach – there is no easy way out, so it is best to reverse or wait for a St Bernard to arrive in a dinghy, by which time you may have died of pneumonia and become a fossil.

If the bog hasn't swallowed you, and the midges haven't driven you out of the country, then continue a little further to the Achiltibuie peninsula, adjacent to the Summer Isles. If you have a large wad of notes in your pocket then take the tourist boat to the southern tip of Tanera Beag, if you haven't then you will have to muscle your way across in a kayak; or if you are completely insane then swim across with the Orcas; it's only two miles! The Cathedral Cave is the place to be if you like to spend most of your time upside down, or in the water with the jellies, or both. The hanging left arête of *Ambergris* (F7a S2) is well positioned and easy at the start. If you think you are good at wrestling hippos then roll up your sleeves and set to the hanging groove with muscles busting off the bone. If you survive, move up to a rail rest and continue... Don't look down! It's a long way and you really don't want to punch a hole through the tourist boat, which has by now probably crept in unawares.

Whilst you are on the Summer Isles, it may be prudent to flag down the ferry to Stornoway as it passes. Head over to the west coast of Lewis and take the bridge over to the isle of Great Bernera. Snoop round the headland until you see something resembling the bow of the Amoco Cadiz

The author on Mega Tsunami, prow finish (7b), Isle of Lewis. *Photo: Joanna George.*

punching out across the Atlantic. This is *Mega Tsunami*. At bang on 60ft high, it's a challenge for those who have no cells in the left side of their brain (or right side for that matter). My advice to you is wear foam padded underwear, and don't solo alone, preferably don't solo it at all. Just look at it, beat your chest and imagine yourself up there being... err...brave. However, if you fancy it, firstly make sure the sea isn't beating the gneiss to a pulp before gaining the perfect right-angled arête. At half height, make use of the 'solitary confinement' ledge; it doesn't do anything for the confidence though. Trust me! Climb upwards further into no man's land; at this point if your mates are scaring you with pterodactyl noises, then gibber your way up an overhanging crack on the right side (F7a S2). Contrarily, if you want to scare your mates, then tackle the overhanging prow direct with sloth like technique although hopefully immeasurably faster than said creature for the best deep water solo experience in the country (F7b S2).

Returning to the Isle of Lewis head past Mangersta in search of a small tooth of rock protruding out of the sea. If there is a prevailing south-westerly (common) then you may never find this tooth as it will be under the waves. If calm, strip down, don dry bag and swim the narrow channel. The race is now on; squeeze into a Gollum type niche, change, traverse hard left to the left arête of the wall: *The Last Pirate in Persia* (F5+ S0). Shake your way up this with cold, jump in and swim ashore. By now you will be shivering enough to be of benefit to the National Grid.

Continuing with the island hopping theme from Lewis to Harris and Harris to Skye; it's time to sniff out the chocolate coloured dolerite of Neist. Luckily the rocks don't melt in the sun. Head down under the lighthouse into Foghorn Cove. *Immiscible* (F6c S0) is one of those routes that look lovely but turn out to be really frustrating. Saunter up the lower arête believing that it will be plain sailing all the way to the top. Wrong… the arête becomes more subtle at half height, you can see the holds, feel them (small), but can't commit to them, always thinking that a better hold surely must materialise. My advice is: stop pissing around, because when you do decide to go, the tide will have gone out, which means the fall is twice as far and the water half as deep. Contort through the move and continue more easily realising that climbing is better than chocolate sometimes.

Finally, the tour wouldn't be complete without going to Mull and more specifically, Erraid, which leads us to Traigh Gheal, an old haunt of Robert Louis Stevenson. It's certainly a romantic place; however the off-width crack of *Brine Shrine* (6b S0) doesn't look so. Traverse down into a body bridge slot at the base – the brine shrine. Now, if you are a skeleton then you can chimney up the inside with ease, if you are dumb then you can try all your Kung Fu off-width skills and get spat out into the pure turquoise, or if you are of lateral thinking, you will find all the holds on the outside of the crack. Jumping from the top is obligatory. Then swim to the nearest harbouring yacht and use your best charm to cadge a lift to Eilean na Muc, a small island made of the most beautiful granite a little under a mile away. Here, on the south east tip of the island is a bijou hub for water rats. Teeter down a ramp and hop onto the overhanging wall; a topless flake seduces you onwards to a finger crack. If you are American then jam this painful atrocity with much glee; other nationalities can evade the aforementioned pain by making cool shapes on the chickenheads out on the left wall, fashioning your own *Origami* (F7a+ S0).

When you have done all the above, or at least one or two of them, congratulations, you can now dispense with your water wings, award yourself a deep fried Mars Bar, and who knows, Scotland might by then have become Independent. Of course my tongue is firmly in my cheek.

The alternative look at the S grade system for deep water soloing.

S0: Exciting if you can't swim.

S1: Good for a go if you enjoy tombstoning.

S2: For those who look good on camera whilst falling through the air.

S3: Do you not have any friends?

NO COUNTRY FOR OLD MEN

By Michael Cocker

IT IS JUST POSSIBLE that we were the first people ever to gaze into the huge canyons that form the upper reaches of the Tabo Nala; certainly no one has ever been there. Through shifting cloud we could see immense walls of greyish brown scree plunging into an abyss below. Beyond, a chaotic jumble of snow splattered peaks and glacial remnants receded into the distance. The scale was vast and formidable. You could hardly describe it as beautiful but it was certainly impressive. None of us had ever seen anything quite like it before.

Kamen Gyalmo *Photo: Mike Cocker*

We were standing on the rounded top of an outlying summit in the north east corner of Spiti, a remote province in the Indian Himalayas, trying to locate our main objective, Kamen Gyalmo, an unclimbed peak of around 6500m. The landscape was complex, arid and inhospitable. A high mountain desert riven by deep fissures with sources of water difficult to find once away from the Lingti Nala, the great gorge that divides the region. Around 55 million years ago it had been a sea bed and the presence of numerous fossils was a frequent reminder of this. Of the larger life forms only snow leopards, blue sheep, yaks and vultures now manage to survive here.

There are no passes giving access to the Tibetan plateau, but the region's proximity to the ill-defined border makes this a politically sensitive area. Until recently it was closed to all except the locals who, in the summer months, take their yaks a short distance up the Lingti Nala for grazing. Kamen Gyalmo had been recommended to us by the Indian mountaineer Harish Kapadia who, in 1983 and 1987, had led the only two expeditions to venture into this area prior to ourselves. Harish's exploration, however, had concentrated on the mountains to the west of the Lingti Nala, and only briefly entered the terrain to the east, where we were based, close to the Tibetan border.[1]

We were a team of five: Derek Buckle (leader), Dave Broadhead, Geoff Cohen, Hamish Irvine and me. Being a restricted area meant that we had to obtain permission from the Indian Ministry of Defence and request an X-Visa instead of the usual tourist one. In order to satisfy the requirement of these and other official bodies we had labelled ourselves with the misleadingly grand title, 'The 2014 British Spiti Expedition'. Anyone who has ever encountered Indian bureaucracy will have some idea of what we were up against, but on this occasion the system excelled itself. Despite having applied for permits eight months earlier, authorisation only came through two weeks before we were scheduled to fly to Delhi, leaving us barely enough time to get a visa. And then it was only for four, Hamish's name was not included, which, we later discovered during our meeting with the Indian Mountaineering Federation, in Delhi, meant that he would not be allowed to travel beyond base camp.[2]

Sorab Gandhi, our liaison officer, joined us in Delhi and, after acquiring an Inner Line Permit in Shimla, we continued by jeep along the legendary Hindustan Tibet road through Kinnaur to Spiti. A week after leaving Delhi we arrived at Lalung Village and the start of the Lingti Nala. Here we met up with the Nepali porters who would help carry our equipment to base camp and the village headman who arranged a local guide for us. He also suggested that we have a puja (ceremony) performed by their lama to ensure a safe passage in the mountains. Buddhism had been introduced to the area more than a thousand years ago and some of the artwork in the well preserved village gompa (temple) dates from this period, but much older animistic practises, dedicated to the local mountain gods, were also still evident. The puja was duly conducted the following morning and we were all given a length of blessed string to carry with us.

The trek to base camp took five days and was much harder than expected. Faint trails of loose shale and scree crossed three high passes, one over 5000m, with long descents into rocky canyons between. The lack of water made campsites scarce and one night, when there was nowhere we could safely pitch the tents, was spent under a rock overhang.

[1] H. Kapadia, *Himalayan Journal*, 40 (1983), 96–107 and 44 (1987), 96–101.

[2] This is a condensed and simplified account of these events. The full version would take a whole article!

Cohen and Buckle on Tangmor Plateau, Sisbang Peak on the right. *Photo: Mike Cocker*

On 7 September we established base camp (5130m) in the upper reaches of the Sheru Nala, one of the numerous deep canyons branching off from the Lingti Nala. It was a stark and barren place but, essentially, there was a small spring of good clean water. Not having a permit to venture beyond this point Hamish decided to return to Lalung with the local guide and porters and continue to Ladakh. We arranged to meet up again at Kaza, the main administrative town in Spiti, in three weeks.

We had not yet had sight of Kamen Gyalmo and had only a rough idea where it was located; researches on Google Earth before we left the UK had been of limited benefit as the images were vague and partially obscured by cloud cover.[3] The maps we had were also far from accurate, but did suggest that a long ridge may connect the rounded Cairngorm like summits at the head of the Sheru Nala with Kamen Gyalmo. The first few days were, therefore, spent exploring these peaks. During an early reconnaissance we climbed an interesting ice couloir leading up to the plateau, which we named *Fossil Gully* (WI 2). A high camp was then established at the edge of the snowline. Looking south from here we saw the passes we had crossed on the trek to base camp and an impressive rock peak called Sisbang.[4] To the west was the Lingti Nala. Immediately above our camp, to the north and east, was the snow covered plateau.

---

[3] Coincidentally since our return the satellite images for this area are much sharper.

[4] Sisbang Peak is also known as Chokula. The local tradition considers this mountain to be the physical manifestation of a wrathful deity called Chokula who controls their water supply – a vital commodity in this arid land. Centuries ago an 8-year-old child was annually sacrificed to Chokula. After the intervention of a Buddhist lama this was mitigated to a sheep or goat. The ritual continues today but a figure made of tsampa (roasted barley flour) is now used for the offering. Kishore Thukral, *Spiti Through Legend and Lore*, Mosaic Books, 2006, p. 43.

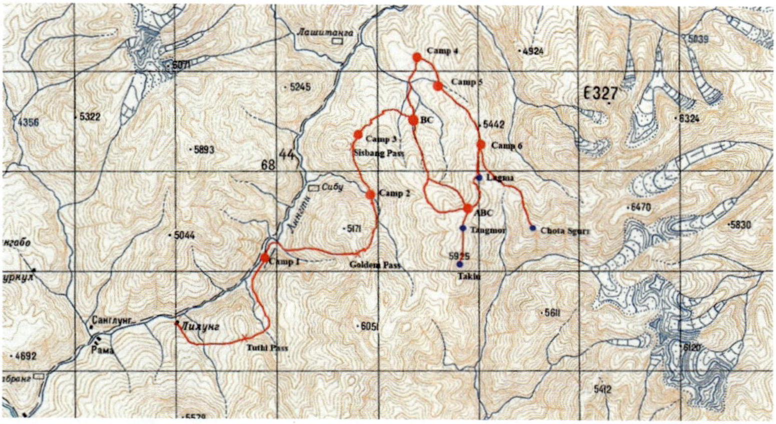

Map showing Camps and peaks ascended.

Over the next two days we surveyed this terrain and made the first ascent of Tangmor (5920m), the main peak at the centre of the massif, and a couple of other unnamed tops of similar height.

It was from one of these outlying tops that we got our first view into the upper reaches of the Tabo Nala, a vast and to date unexplored canyon running down to the Spiti valley. To the north east we could see two impressive peaks, the higher of which we eventually agreed must be Kamen Gyalmo, but there was no obvious way to reach it, for another ravine, the Talung Nala, appeared to cut us off.

We returned to base camp and, after considering our options, set out with food for a week to investigate the Talung Nala and attempt to access the peaks on the far side. Two days later Derek and I stood at the edge of a huge gorge looking down a thousand metres or more of steep rock and scree into a dry river bed below – there was no way we were going to be able to cross this. In the meantime Dave had been exploring the ground nearer the head of the gorge and had spotted a modest but attractive looking peak at the southern end of a long and difficult ridge leading up to Kamen Gyalmo. It was now clear that we didn't have enough time or supplies to make a serious attempt on our original objective, so, with the assistance of two of our high altitude porters, Tshring and Choder, we moved our camp to a point overlooking the head of the Talung Nala. It was around this time that Geoff, after noting that we were all pensioners, all now suffering from 'Spiti nose', an unpleasant state of crusty congestion resulting from the unusually dry air, expressed the opinion that he thought this harsh and barren environment was 'no country for old men'.

On 19 September we left camp early and, after a couple of hours crossing scree slopes, reached the start of the ridge leading up to the

The Team at Base Camp. *Photo: Mike Cocker Collection.*

unnamed summit Dave had noted earlier. The lower half of the ridge gave pleasant scrambling over broken rock, above which firm snow led easily up to the summit (5924m) and an impressive panorama. Dave was the first on top and also came up with the name Chota Sgurr which, in a mix of Hindi and Gaelic, roughly translates as small pointed peak. Although we carried a rope this proved unnecessary, crampons and a single axe being sufficient.

Two days later we were back in base camp where we relaxed for a day or so and waited for the porters. When they didn't arrive on the agreed date we began to wonder if they had found the terrain so arduous on the walk in that they weren't intending to return. As a consequence Derek, Sorab, the cook and most of the trekking crew left base camp with modest loads on the day we were scheduled to depart. Dave, Geoff and I, who had less pressing agendas, remained with three Sherpas. Much to our relief the porters arrived later the same day, the two parties having passed en route.

This time we planned to go directly down the Lingti Nala and reach Lalung in one long day. And what a day it was. It began with a knee-wrenching 2,000 metre descent on rough, unstable ground to the bed of the gorge. Once there steep walls and huge boulders frequently obstructed our passage, necessitating ten thigh-deep crossings of the icy, fast flowing river and exposed scrambling on the loose rock walls. Curiously, half way down the gorge we came across the body of a snow leopard that may have

Porters crossing Lingti Nala. *Photo: Geoff Cohen*

been killed by rock fall from above and, a little later, what looked like a pair of home-made wooden snow shoes. It was almost dark by the time we reached Lalung and we were all completely exhausted. The real stars of the day were, of course, the porters who managed all this with 25kg loads and at a pace I could barely keep up with.

The following morning, 28 September, transport was arranged to take us to Kaza, where we met up again with Hamish and the rest of the team. After a farewell party Derek, Sorab and most of the trekking crew departed for Manali, while Dave, Geoff, Hamish and I stayed on to make a two week trek through to Kinnaur.

It is unlikely that this remote corner of Spiti will ever become popular with trekkers or mountaineers, the terrain is too difficult and desolate, but for me it proved strangely attractive. The deep blue skies, the unusual clarity of light and air, the immense vistas over ground still largely uncharted and the sense of being in a place where humankind doesn't really belong are all rich impressions that I'll never forget. And long may it remain that way, an undisturbed realm where those two old adversaries, snow leopard and blue sheep, will be safe for all time.

Acknowledgements: The team are grateful for the generous financial assistance received from the Mount Everest Foundation, the Alpine Club and the Austrian Alpine Club. Excellent support services were provided by Rimo Expeditions based in Leh.

THE TREK – SPITI TO KINNAUR 2014

By Dave Broadhead

AT AN EARLY STAGE in planning for the 'British Spiti Expedition 2014' (described in the previous article), Mike Cocker, Geoff Cohen, Hamish Irvine and I decided to stay on for a couple of extra weeks trekking in the mountains. Inspired by 'Exploring Kinnaur & Spiti in the Trans-Himalaya' by Deepak Sanan & Dhanu Swadi, we thought that the Rupi-Bhaba wildlife sanctuary looked a suitable objective, described as 'the greenest corner of Kinnaur'. After almost a month in the harsh arid mountains of Spiti, we were looking forward to seeing some greenery and breathing moister air through long suffering noses. 'The expedition' part of the trip finally wound up in the town of Kaza (3650m), district capital of Spiti, where we were reunited with Hamish. After leaving us at base camp he had made his way to Ladakh where he climbed the popular trekking peak Stok Kangri (6153m), ran in the Leh Half Marathon, cycled up to the Khardung La (5359m) and trekked through the Markha Valley. Here we also said farewell to our fantastic cook team, our excellent liason officer Sorab and our tireless organiser and leader, Derek Buckle. They took back to Delhi large bags of our personal gear as we hoped to enjoy the trek with a minimum of encumbrance, though we kept hold of a climbing rope, ice-axes and crampons, in the hope of being able to climb a peak en route. As well as sorting out food and gear, three nights in Kaza enabled us to enjoy the comforts of the Sakya Abode Hotel and its excellent restaurant, with the help of products from the local 'bottle shop'. With time on our hands we took the opportunity to visit the nearby Buddhist gompas at Ki and Dhankhar. Both are located on dramatic hill top sites, giving spectacular views of the Spiti valley and of course a unique insight into the religion which still thrives in this part of India.

Happy to be on the move again, on 27 September we drove back down the Spiti River towards Lingti before crossing over and heading up its biggest tributary the Pin River. Not far beyond the confluence a huge landslide had swept down a side valley, creating a small temporary lake and a large problem for the road engineers. One can only marvel at the huge effort put into maintaining and improving the road system in this harsh terrain and welcome the benefits that it has brought to the local population, bringing in education, health care and of course tourists like ourselves, as well as providing an outlet to market for their lucrative apple and pea crops. In the mountains evidence of climate change was plain to see in the shrinking glaciers and disappearing summer snow beds and it was clear that this was not making life any easier in these remote valleys. Our destination was the village of Mudh (3770m) where most traffic stops, though the unrelenting extension of the road seemed to continue south up the west side of the valley, part of a scheme to establish an alternative link between Spiti and Kinnaur. We had planned to use all three of our High Altitude Porters but at the last moment Karma had to drop out. Fortuitously, a caravan of eight horses arrived from Kinnaur that afternoon with a party of trekkers and we were able to negotiate transport of some of our loads on their return journey starting the following morning. Leaving the village, the trail dropped down and crossed the river by a narrow suspension bridge then gradually climbed up the valley. After an overnight camp in a scruffy grassy hollow at Phaldar (c.4000m) we continued our steady climb soon after dawn, branching left into increasingly rugged terrain, heading towards the line of snowy peaks marking the Himalayan watershed. Our route was by no means obvious from a distance but the rough trail was easy to follow through moraine rocks and boulders until eventually a rising traverse across a snowfield lead at last to the cairns and prayer flags marking the summit of the Pin Bhaba/Wang Khango Pass (4865m). Late morning when we arrived, by now the cloud was rapidly building up on the surrounding peaks. Dropping more steeply down the south side we pitched our next camp near the junction of the Wangar River at Basha (c.3700m) where we paid and parted company with the horsemen.

Compared to our generally bleak and arid camps in Spiti, it was delightful to be surrounded by lush vegetation, albeit rather dried and faded with the onset of autumn. There were even a few small trees growing on the hillside opposite. Having decided to spend the next few days exploring the neighbouring valleys and hills, we left the tents and headed upstream and east for a recce with light sacs. Tshring and Choder came with us, though it was becoming clear that they were a bit uncertain of their role in what was clearly turning out to be not their usual sort of trip. Their limited grasp of English did not help, but they were always eager to please. Tshring seemed to be game for anything, while Choder had an air of Oriental inscrutability and although he always showed willing I often wondered what he really thought of us and our antics. After a couple of hours of rough undulating walking up the heavily grazed valley we reached Tiya (3795m) another wide flat river junction which seemed to offer various possibilities. In this situation the best strategy is to split up and spread out to explore in different directions. On the crest of the ridge directly above we could see a distinctive cairn which looked to me like a useful viewpoint. Despite a strenuous pull up steep grass and occasional rocks I reached my objective with twenty minutes to spare on my two hour turn-around time. Above me four enormous Griffon vultures were circling expectantly and my effort was rewarded with a fantastic view down into an attractive hidden valley. At the head of this valley stood the distinctive mountain we had seen from Basha and immediately called Twin Peak, for obvious reasons. Even more exciting, just before the afternoon clouds rolled across, I was sure I could make out a route to the summit which looked well within our limited capabilities. Descending to

Col Camp on Twin Peak *Photo: Mike Cocker*

Tiya via the hidden valley, no one else came up with any better suggestions, so by next morning we had agreed a plan and started moving up.

Tshring and Choder helped us carry our two tents up into the hidden valley then headed down with an order for supplies to purchase in Kafnu before returning to help us move back down in a couple of days. With our carrying muscle gone, the challenge next morning was to move the tents up the glacier above and hopefully find a campsite on the broad snowy col at the foot of the summit ridge. Groaning under our heaviest sacs yet, the crux of the route involved getting onto the glacier via a rubble-strewn rocky rib. Geoff and I managed the slithery scramble, the alarming sight of which persuaded Mike and Hamish to avoid the glacier completely and approach the col from the ridge above. In due course we were reunited and camped on the col (c.5000m) on comfortable gravel platforms, enjoying fantastic evening views as the afternoon cloud settled into the valleys below, leaving the surrounding peaks glowing in the moonlight.

With an early start the final summit ridge proved more pleasant than it looked. Following the rocks behind the elegant snow arête visible from below we reached the first summit of Twin Peak (c.5350m) less than two hours later and with some relief found ourselves looking down on the second, clearly lower summit. Feeling well pleased with ourselves, it was a pleasure just to sit in the sun and admire the magnificent views of the surrounding peaks. Below us to the north lay a huge glacier basin, the most extensive we had seen this trip while further east a long snowy ridge leading to a shapely higher peak looked very feasible if only we had been better supplied and a bit more ambitious. Soon back at our col camp we enjoyed a well earned brew before continuing down, splitting into two parties once again. Mike and Hamish thought they might be able to follow the rocky ridge all the way around towards my viewpoint cairn. In the event it turned out to be more straightforward to descend into the valley below the glacier, down which Geoff and I crunched in our crampons, relieved to find a much easier way down the nasty rocky rib by traversing below the evil looking icy snout. Reunited again, we picked up our spare gear and continued down to an idyllic grassy campsite at the mouth of the hidden valley. Next morning Tshring and Choder appeared bright and early, exactly according to plan and we moved down to Tiya where we spent the rest of the day tucking into newly purchased biscuits, washing ourselves and our clothes and generally relaxing.

For our final descent we each packed modest rucksacs of personal gear to carry, wondering how Tshiring and Choder would manage all the rest, but they seemed to have an endless supply of bits of string with which to tie extra bags on to their already substantial loads. From the river junction at Kara the rough trail dropped steeply and as we lost height the trees got bigger, an attractive mixture of birch and pine, particularly striking in their autumn colours. Our guidebook enthused about 'the enchanting meadows' at Mulling (3350m) but the heavy pressure of grazing animals and their untidy herders spoiled the effect for me. The forest rest house here turned out to be a solidly built Himalayan bothy which made for a sociable evening, though Mike and I eschewed the concrete floor and the nocturnal mice, opting to camp outside despite the rain. The dreich weather continued next morning, brightening up as we carried on down. With no evidence of any improvement in the rocky path we were not surprised to find a couple of scrawny cows had tumbled to their death in the ravine below, attracting an impressive number of vultures, many too gorged to fly off as we passed by. Our destination, the village of Kafnu received consistently unenthusiastic descriptions in the various guidebooks we had been able to consult, and we soon saw why. Situated at the end of the road, an important gathering point for the economically essential apple harvest, there was little more than a small bazaar beside an artificial lake, part of some sort of pump-storage hydro-electric scheme. We arrived in time for a late lunch at the garish green painted Lake View Resort. This was grungy enough to convince us to try the so called campsite above the lake, notable for its lack of facilities and an abundance of broken bottles scattered around. With the help of a few drams of 'Blenders Pride' we passed a not unpleasant night.

There were still a few days before our pick-up date which left us just enough time to trek up to Pandoshwar Meadows. Leaving yet more surplus gear at a neighbouring house, we followed a new road which left the main valley and lead in a few kilometres to the busy village of Yangpa. Soon the road reverted to a well graded footpath which eventually traversed into the next valley to the north, leading to the village of Surcho. We had intended to camp here but in the absence of a suitable site we enjoyed a memorable impromptu homestay with Mani Ram and his family. Highlight of the final climb up to the Meadows for me was the sight of several Impeyan Pheasants, flushed from their forest cover, flashes of irridescent colour gliding noisily down the valley. Our destination (c.3500m) turned out to be heavily grazed, with a shortage of flat spots for the tents, though we eventually found suitable sites with great views across the valley to distant peaks, beneath an impressive steep slabby crag. Finishing the 'Blenders Pride' we rounded off the day with a hilarious session of Scottish climbs charades which saw me almost reduced to tears of laughter. For our final day we explored further up the valley, at the head of which a rugged pass gave access to our previous camp at Tiya, according to our guidebook. There were clearly plenty of opportunities up here for interesting alpine style ascents up attractive rocky peaks. Meanwhile, my three companions focussed their attention on some of the impressive boulders scattered around. Bouldering in unsuitable footwear with the prospect of a twisted ankle resulting from an awkward landing discouraged me from joining in.

With time ticking by it was literally downhill all the way from here as we returned to Surcho and continued down to join the main valley at Katgaon where we spent a night in the comfortable Hydro Board Rest House. Tshiring and Choder nipped back up to Kafnu to recover our spare gear and leave word for our transport so that as planned we began the long drive back to Delhi on the Monday morning, sharing the road with lots of trucks loaded with apples going down and buses full of Bengali holidaymakers coming up. On my last visit to India, some thirty or so years before, there had been very few private cars to be seen. Now there are far too many, and the standard of driving is dangerously low, though thankfully the poor state of the hill roads encourages most to drive slowly. At Shimla we said an emotional goodbye to Tshiring and Choder, who were continuing their long journey back to Darjeeling on the overnight bus to Delhi. Practical and considerate as well as very strong and reliable, they had turned out to be good company and their efforts had gone well beyond the call of duty and made a big contribution to the success of our whole trip. Our drive continued the following morning in mist and rain and we came across several collisions resulting from the slippery road conditions. The long journey home continued according to plan and we were able to look back on a fantastic and varied trip, all the more enjoyable because we got on so well with each other and with our support staff.

A GRAPPLE FOR THE TEACHER

(In praise of Guidebooks)

By Ruth Love

Then the folk were sair pitten aboot,
An' they cried, as the weather got waur:
'Oh! Lord, we ken fine we ha'e sinn'd,
But a joke can be cairried ower faur!'
W.D. Cocker *The Deluge*

MY MISSION, SHOULD I choose to...was to get our friend Neal up The In Pin. It was the usual story for a non climber wishing to compleat his Munro round. 'Most Munro-baggers have to seek help from their rock-climbing friends or a Mountain Guide to get to the top of this one' it says in the SMC *Hill Walkers' Guide to the Munros*.

Neal is a friend and colleague of my husband Simon. They both teach. A family man with a busy life he has few opportunities to get away at weekends. With our various commitments the first weekend of July in the long school holiday (envy) was chosen as a suitable date for our adventure.

Meeting at Ratagan Youth Hostel in Kintail on Friday night the forecast was not at all promising: rain and gales were imminent. Still we set off for Skye the next morning hopeful of some let up in the weather and prayed that if there was not then we would just be able to deal with whatever was thrown at us. We checked in at the Glen Brittle Youth Hostel where we would be staying that night hopefully celebrating our glorious success and not just drowning our sorrows having near drowned throughout the day. It was at this hostel that Simon's parents met in 1957. They were both teachers (bit of a theme here) and keen hill walkers and I often wonder if Simon was conceived on a mountain side somewhere.

Our roles for the day were clear. Simon and I started climbing together but our mountaineering interests have diverged since then. I have pursued the more technical side with Scottish winter climbing being a particular passion whereas Simon has gained some of the Mountain Leader qualifications and enjoys taking school groups to the mountains at home and abroad. We try to pool our resources and find common ground. Today was certainly going to be a day for that with me designated to lead the climb and Simon to Ninja navigate through the slabs, gullies, buttresses and shelves on this Eilean a' Cheo, 'Isle of Mist'.

Despite pretty grim conditions we set off cheerfully taking the path on the south side of the Allt Coire na Banachdaich from the Glen Brittle Memorial Hut. The Parker guidebook suggests that: 'If a climbing party is afflicted by poor weather they can find solace in other parts of the "Magic Isle", which offers a wealth of varied excursions.' But there was only one excursion we were interested in and besides, all this rain enabled the Eas Mòr Waterfall to really show off. It was powering out water fantastically. I will not attempt to be poetic myself as Neal's subject is English. The conversation on the way up was suitably descriptive, literary and engaging. I hope that Neal does not read this article as it is sure to be red penned!

Between gaps in the cloud I was able to point out Window Buttress in the corrie. We could see through 'the remarkable hole which pierces its summit rock tower.' I had climbed this by the Mild Severe start (I now realise) which 'can be awkward in the wet' with seasoned SMC member 'Steady' Eddie Gillespie and it WAS in the wet. Eddie had trained me well for such an undertaking as this. I began recalling the many crazy, wet, windy climbs wearing big boots and with water streaming down inside the sleeves of my upward stretching arms, that I had done with him. 'Real mountaineering,' Eddie calls it. Later that day I was to be grateful for the toughening up that Eddie had helped me with.

Zigzagging up the final scree slopes to the cairned nick below the summit of Sgùrr Dearg, the weather remained wild and wet. Simon and I went through the notch first and dropped down the scree slope a little bit to wait for Neal. We had been here before and were not shocked by the plinth of gabbro looming ominously out of the mist. But Neal's face said it all as he popped through the notch and was confronted by this big frightening lump of slime– and that was just what he could see of it.

To escape from the full brunt of the wind we quickly travelled further down the slope to near the foot of the pinnacle's West Ridge. Simon and I exchanged glances: it was clear that we would be blown to our deaths if we continued with our intended East Ridge (Moderate) ascent. Although the easier route up, it is an exposed, narrow blade of rock with a particularly massive drop down one side and sideways on to the wind of the day. If we climbed at all it would have to be the relatively sheltered, steeper West Ridge. We broke the news to Neal. He had only climbed once, indoors at Ratho, and received some abseil training in Holyrood Park with Simon the week before! He totally understood the reduced options but declared that he did not think that he would be able to do it. Palpable disappointment on all sides as failure today could put Neal's compleation back a year or two. He was so close and this climb would mean a lot to him. We could but try, though I was not so sure that I would be able to lead it myself under these conditions. It looked seriously unprotected and I had only thrown my rock boots in as an afterthought. It was only a Diff, but damp and dark looking; I was definitely going to need them.

If I did succeed I knew I could be on the rock for a long time especially if Neal were to have a go. I donned lots of warm clothes and stuffed my pockets full of snacks. Like the Michelin Man I set off up the climb with Simon as my trusty belayer. I enjoyed the first steep, thuggish move which was up slightly overhanging rock and benefited from a visible first gear placement and Simon spotting for me. The next couple of moves weren't too bad either though quite steep. Thereafter it looked decidedly delicate and I felt most precarious just balanced on a narrow wet shelf contemplating the crux. With my last piece of protection below me and way out to the right, it did not appeal. According to J. Wilson Parker there is 'an awkward move between sloping shelves halfway up.' Noel Williams' *Skye Scrambles* gives the route as 'polished, and...quite tricky' for its grade and that's in the dry.

The crux seemed to involve a sort of mantelshelf into a very shallow sentry box. I was just below it and not sure what to do. I needed to be confident of making the move if I could not protect it. I thought it might be more possible from the left end but a fall would send me penduling and crashing on the ledges as I went. There then ensued a shuffle to the left, a long contemplative pause and then a shuffle to the right. Then (you've guessed it) a shuffle to the left again! I had a proper little Highland dance going on up there and in ballet terms, from what I remember, I think I was in position five! But it was not achieving anything. I hoped that my deliberations were not discouraging Neal who was watching closely. As a true gentleman, he was more concerned that I did not risk my life for the sake of his compleation. To a non-climber it might have seemed that way. 'You don't have to do this' were the cries from below.

I was quite prepared to back off if necessary but I wasn't going to do so without a full exploration of the possibilities. I did not want to let Neal down, except on abseil from the top later. Although I'm sure several pre-historic ages could have passed in the time I was taking, I felt no pressure or sense of impatience from Simon or Neal only appreciation and support. The day was still young and I suppose I was the only hope. Subconscious forces must have been at work for suddenly I spied a handful of grit at the back left-hand corner of the mantelshelf ledge. I scooped it away to reveal a tiny crack and thought 'Ah! That might take a small nut.' It did, but I'm sure the placement was purely psychological. Then more procrastination whilst I worked out how I was to perform the move. Some positive self talk and a decision to commit and suddenly I was up. Extremely relieved and feeling like there was now a chance I heard the teachers below awarding me A grades and double stars. 'Bloody, excellent!' I heard them say. Their hearts had been in their mouths of course– my husband does care about me really!

That part of the climb had afforded some shelter from the rage but stepping out onto the final, easier third of the climb I was well and truly blasted by the wind driven rain. Padding up the upper wet slabs I was fully exposed to the elements. Setting up the belay it was difficult to balance shelter and the need to cope with the changes in direction of the climb. I ended up safe, but out in the wind and rain.

Neal follows *Photo: Simon Love*

Simon moved out from the pinnacle as agreed to signal that Neal would start to climb, but after that I could not see or hear a thing. Over to Simon to hear how it went…

> Neal made a stab at the first move: he got off the ground, struggled but could not quite make the first ledge. He declared that he was sorry but he did not think he would be able to make the climb. I said that all tactics were fair in love and war and he could use my shoulder if he liked. I expected an affirmative response, and a chance to brace, but the next thing I knew a boot was weighing me down. Much to my

relief he made the ledge and I managed to straighten myself out. Neal's progress was tortured, and punctuated with repeats of his earlier declaration, each of which was met with an unyielding 'That's what you said last time and look at you now!' said with more conviction than I felt. I was heartily glad I was not in his boots. However, progress he made and I was having to re-ascend to the gap to keep an eye on him – he was disappearing into the same miasma that had swallowed Ruth.

After what seemed an interminable time, I detected a bit of movement in the rope and was able to take in. And so it went on. The weather was not getting any better but I was at least enjoying a good facial! At last the rope moved more freely. Neal must be approaching the slabs. Then his head appeared followed by the rest of him. He paused again. His face was a picture though I thought better of actually taking one. Totally white and exopthalmic: Neal's face at that moment I will never forget. Poor guy, this trauma was not meant to happen. It should have been so nice.

'Well done, nearly there.' I shouted. But before I could issue any further encouragement or instructions, Neal, in his terror, was hand over handing up the rope. I could not take in quick enough and the rope was very slack. I tried to call out about shock loading (we had briefed) but this man was determined to get to the top as quickly as possible. I just did what I could and hoped for the best and pretty soon he was beside me at the belay. What a supreme effort of will for a man who had not climbed before and in such outrageous conditions. I shook his hand and offered my heartfelt congratulations. But before he could accept them and descend, he wanted to make sure he had truly summited. Simon appeared again gesticulating. He pointed to behind us. The true summit's location is arguable but keeping Neal on belay I saw him up to, first the top of the East Ridge and then to The Bolster Stone. It would have been insane to actually stand on it that day but Neal was able to touch the top from the lower boulder. Job done but now to get down and away from this hell point.

I thought I'd better just check with Simon that he did not wish to come up as well but wisely he did not. No mistaking the gestures from below when I offered. He busied himself preparing for Neal's abseil. The Holyrood Park rappel training with Simon paid off in full. Neal executed the abseil in fine style and loved every second of it. It all ended in a big smile.

Now not being one to miss a tick, even if for the second time, I could not resist nipping up to touch the top of The Bolster Stone myself. I had spent all that time on the route (three hours it turned out) and it would have been rude not to even in those silly conditions.

Celebrating back at the hostel we got talking to a Mountain Guide. He had opted not to take his clients high on the hill that day and I do wonder if we were the only people on The Cuillin. After dinner I decided to take a look at the various guidebooks we had brought with us. I had not thought

The author abbs off *Photo: Simon Love*

it necessary before. J.R. Mackenzie's *Rock & Ice Climbs in Skye* describes the older, easier routes as 'Very highly polished and... treacherous in the wet.' The West Ridge is noted as being 'Extremely polished and horrific in the wet.'

As I write, Simon reports from a member of the Skye Mountain Rescue team he met on a Bushcraft course. Apparently a chunk of rock had broken from the West Ridge of The Pinnacle due to a lightning strike. This had contributed to making the route even more difficult and unprotected than I had expected. Perhaps, after all, we should have gone for that Solace in another part of 'The Magic Isle'.

THE HEIGHTS OF ALLUSION

By M.J. Cobb

'I canna change the laws of Physics for ye, Captain – but I can find ye a loophole'

(Chief Engineer Scotty of the Starship Enterprise)

WE HAD THOUGHT of camping but it was way, way too cold. Like the fields of Athenry, all the low, lying meadows were hard as iron so we drank too much Red Cuillin at the inn, found places in a bunkhouse and then had breakfast at noon under the cerebral hemispheres' pounding overhangs. Not a good climbing day, as usual in these parts. It was damp and grey-looking when we looked out of the window but, later, Aonghas wiped it with his sleeve and the condensation rolled down like tears and revealed the truth – blue skies and sparkling diamonds on the rashes. We set out for Brunch-nay-Frothed far too late, the challenge of the mountain not being enough. The ground was adamantly bone-jarring, the rock rimed with whiskers of refrigeration and the river Spiel was icy lumps and smoothen bumps, noiseless ovaloid bubbles squeezing along deeply-down like an overwhelmed lava-lamp.

Then Simpson suddenly appeared on the scene. Oh God, we thought we'd got away! We'd left him looking for his wallet, hunting through his holey trouser pockets in a panic while everyone else was sweeping and wiping to appease the warden. It seems he'd even found his manpurse – when the work was done.

'It was there after all, ah couldnae believe it.'

Typical. He even had the nerve to ask us why we were starting out so late and

'Would we consider revising our plans?'

Cheeky bastard. Threesome now – not a good number apparently, never worked on my ticket anyway, but what to do with only one rope? Simpson asked:

'Where's the other one then?'

'It fell off the top of my rucksack…if you remember? …and I went to look for it on my fruitless tod…if you remember? …so now this one's got a lonely heart.'

'Well, that's tough…I forget but did you tie it on properly?'

Obviously knot. Now it lies at the foot of the gully with a long-lost Friend, such is the brotherhood. I shouldered the pack of lies and we all mumbled off across that interminable, intractable, soulful moor by Meall-nan-Speallchaocher and up and up.

Pride aye comes afore a fall and Simpson was too pig-headed to be the first to call a halt to the proceedings. Even if he did, he'd been left so far behind that we barely heard his fragmented shouts so, for a while, things looked like they might be going pair-shaped again. But we couldn't shake him off. Meanwhile, the solitary rope was out and tied to my waist for the wee bitty scramble.

What do you want now? Yet another blow-by-blow description of how we tottered up from cramponstep to icehold and all that stuff? Use your imagination, you've been there or somewhere like it and should know what it's like. It wasn't too difficult, I can tell you that… it's just that it was getting on a bit and have I said that it was numbing our brass monkeys? Ice crystals hung in the air when we breathed out, like silver anti-missile chatter behind a Hercules plane in Iraq or Afghanistan.

At some point during those fifteen-hundred feet of climbing, probably as we traversed below the tottering Grand Gendarme – it's no' there any mair, fell into Coire a' Buster – we passed a critical point, not exactly of no return but when back-tracking becomes the least favourable option. Whether we realised it or not is a moot point but the simple fact is that, in our commitment to the cause we failed to make any rational assessment of our position. It's been said before by wiser men than me that experience is the sum of our near misses and, God knows, between us we had a plethora of those sitting on our shoulders and cawing in our lugs. By all sensible considerations we should have stopped and tried to retrace our steps but is not Adventure, at the risk of Punishment, born out of No Deals?

Those wise men, perhaps some lassies tae, were coming down off Nevis and the Buachaille and the Eunuch Earache at that very moment and heading for the Clenching and we were racing time going slow. The rope is a fork-tongued evil twister at times like this; morose when he's cold, deliberately dallying our progress, tangling us back and capriciously coating his bristly skin with snow, like a hoary old caterpillar. Its hibernating ex, not mine anymore, had been a smooth-talking new one, purple with red flecks, and as two-faced as a snake in the grass. Aren't they all, undermining your integrity with their reassurances?

I'll say one thing for Simpson though: he may be eighty-percent Homer but he doesn't waste time moaning. Like a statue of Buddha, he was hunched up in the snow over the top of his faded and ripped rucksack, stuffing jammy pieces and smoked mackerel into his gob. Aonghas watched in disgust and said that he wouldn't feed such muck to a horse if he had one. We had reached The Convoluted Ridge In The Sky, the sun was sinking lower and lower and unfeeling shadows were getting longer and longer. Over in the west, where the Harridan Sea was a frozen shiver, the great red orb thumped the world's rump and now the horizon was bruising livid orange then pink then black-and-blue. Ominously, there was also a moving curtain of cirrus clouds, pink bow-waves, harbingers of a mighty storm rippling its muscles. The mountains were getting ready to tuck themselves up in bed; the night wind thought it was time to come out to jeer and the powdery snow decided to join in, fed up with snoozing on its icy mattress. Little whirling dervishes were whispering warnings of trouble ahead but it was only another half-hour, I guessed, to the top.

Except we seemed to have a problem in the gloaming –

'What's that?'

'It's a cliff, a hundred feet of it, a straight drop…and boulders at the bottom…that's no' supposed tae be there.'

We looked at each other, shaking our heads, and then we both looked at Simpson.

'What, precisely, is the significance of the boulders?'

He couldn't answer; mouth full of woolly Dachstein-mitt leftovers, he just shrugged his shoulders and waited for a decision. Aonghas reckoned that we might be off-route, even on the wrong bit of mountain. How ridiculous is that? Now they were both looking at me…

'I thought you'd been up here before?'

'Aye, that's what you told Jimmy, ah remember it noo.'

'Funny thing, your memory.'

That shut him up. It was time for a show of strength and a morale-boosting rebuke.

'We're all in this together and now's not the time to start arguing. These buttresses all look the same in the snow and it's not a hundred feet. Okay, it's called the Deathtrap but it's just a wee step, we can climb down it and then quickly up to the cairn and then there's an easy slope and it's a doddle over Beinn Medium and then down to the glen. Look, there's Stub Copier nun Berth over there. I'll take a bearing; remember, the compass never lies. Now, be prepared, get your torches out.'

As I could have predicted, it seemed that Simpson had only an old bicycle lamp, claiming that a high-tech boost-mode LED headlamp, conned on eBay, had failed in its delivery. It was crucial that we negotiate the difficult step before it got dark and, with only one rope, it was too far for one abseil. Then, would you credit it, Simpson comes up with a mathematical solution to the problem –

'Um, I can't climb doon there, my crampon's just broken … but I've got a suggestion. You know how Floyd's algorithm provides the shortest paths between all pairs of vertices?'

'Oh yeah?'

'Aye. The rope will reach if we use it single so I can abseil and you can climb doon or if you don't fancy that you can abb tae and, as we won't need it again, we can leave the rope behind. Look, we'll jam the end in this crack here. I'll even go first now.'

And with that he manufactured a weird form of Turks-head and stuffed it into a snowy slot in the rock, pulled it down so that it sat in an icy narrowing and looked up in triumph whilst me and Aonghas can't come up with any other quick alternatives. He ties his battered old sac to the other end of the rope and chucks it over the edge, steps over the rope, hitches it over a shoulder and, without so much as a by-your-leave, disappears over the edge. For a few seconds all seemed to be going smoothly but then came a sudden series of jerks…and I'm not referring to the unexpected arrival of some of Simpson's pals. We watched in appalled horror as the knot gave a peristaltic hiccup and whipped into the air, only to disappear into the murk like a whippet's tail following its wag.

In the traditional folklore of European cultures, the Three Fates of Birth, Life and Death appear on the last day of a person's life and escort him from this world to the next. But Simpson wasn't quite there yet, although in hindsight, I might have given more consideration to the significance of the number three for between a trio of those boulders was a deep, narrow cleft full of soft snow and guess what? Yes, he found it headfirst like a spot-on Olympic diver from the high board. He was still there when we eventually down-climbed in our comforting pools of yellow light. It was the perfect bivouac spot to sit out the vile storm and Simpson was quick to point out that we were lucky that he had discovered the bleak wee hoosie. He had even coiled the wretched rope as if he owned it and was using it for a seat whilst he glugged from a battered hip flask. He must have been shaken up though, enough to make his alter-ego Smallweed envious –

'Oh my bones and back. Sorry, lads, I'd offer youse both a dram but I seem to have finished the whisky...rather a nice malt it wis tae. Tell you wit, though, it's mah roond when we get doon.'

No, I mean really shaken up. Especially when he later discovered in the pub that his wallet had fallen out of his jacket pocket, presumed lost in the snow under that duplicitous rope. It's probably still there if you want to go looking.

MATTHEW FORSTER HEDDLE: HUGH MUNRO'S HERO

By Hamish H. Johnston

PROFESSOR MATTHEW FORSTER HEDDLE (1828–1897) is best known as Scotland's greatest mineralogist, the author of *The Mineralogy of Scotland* (1901), still regarded as the bible of Scottish mineralogy. Less well known is that he was revered by Hugh Munro (1856–1919), who in 1897 wrote that Heddle's knowledge of the Scottish hills was unsurpassed and that he had climbed more Scottish mountains than anyone else.

Although the early years of Heddle's exploration of Scotland took place when most of the mountain terrain was still unmapped and transport was undeveloped, his knowledge was encyclopaedic. As a scientist he was driven to go in search of minerals, but as a man he loved the hills for themselves. 'If anyone could wander amidst the convoluted mazes of its [Sutherland's] hills without feeling his heart burning within him, it could only be from an utter want of sympathy with nature. The lungs play more freely, the stride gets longer, gravitation is an insignificant retardation, the big hammer's weight is scarce perceived; the whole man is improved in tone; even in the midst of nature's warfare, one feels altogether benignant, – so long at least she refrains from wrapping those grand hills in gloom.' Anyone who has escaped from workaday life to walk in the hills will instantly recognise these expansive feelings, and smile at Heddle's caveat regarding the weather.

For Heddle science was matched by aesthetics. He saw in the hills images of man and animals, and echoes of human experience of life. For him 'The ghastly cheek of Arkle is that of one who knows his next step – the grave,' while 'Stack Polly is a porcupine in a condition of extreme irascibility.' The neighbouring Cul Mòr, '...quietly reposing upon her back, teaches Jura a lesson in depicting lines of female loveliness.' Of Ben Loyal Heddle wrote 'Thinking of Scotland's Hills, we ever return to this as the Queen of All. For gracefulness, chasteness, versatility, and nobility of form, it stands pre-eminent.' Identifying a king gave Heddle problems but his choice was '...when viewed from the shoulder of Ben Yoss [Oss]; a hill, strange enough, of the same name, – Ben Laogh [Lui].'

Heddle's geological publications describe demanding long-distance cross-country walks undertaken to gather evidence. He listed the 80 peaks he climbed during the course of his Sutherland fieldwork in the vicinity of Torridon, Dundonnell, Kinlochewe, Assynt, Coigach and the Reay Forest, their collective height amounting to 177,020 feet. The most extensive accounts of Heddle's hill-walking activities are contained in the annual reports of the Royal Society of Edinburgh's Boulder Committee, for which Heddle undertook research every summer between 1879 and

1882. These reports reveal the thoroughness of his observations and the lengths to which he went to confirm or disprove his ideas. One year the Boulder Committee convener wrote that '...these extracts give no idea of the enormous amount of labour which the Professor has undergone in his boulder researches. During the summer and autumn of 1880, he must have walked several hundred miles, over districts many of which are not accessible to ordinary pedestrians. This is shown by the tracks of his surveys laid down by him on the ordnance maps, and by the names given in his notes of the hills and valleys visited.' Today one can read the reports and follow Heddle's routes on one's own maps.

Several of Heddle's mineralogist companions were founder members of the Scottish Mountaineering Club (SMC) when it was established in 1889. Of these the most regular was William Peyton (1830–1894), minister of the Free Church of St Lukes, Broughty Ferry, who accompanied Heddle on the expeditions described in his paper South West Ross, published posthumously in the SMC Journal in 1898. Heddle had long harboured a desire to climb the hills south of the Achnasheen–Lochcarron road, and had also contemplated '...nay, set my heart upon doing the whole length of the Mam Sodhail ridge in a single walk.' His 'great traverse', of some 45 miles and 14,000 feet of ascent, took four days, Heddle and Peyton staying overnight in the homes of shepherds and keepers. The route went from the Cluanie Inn northwards to Strathcarron. It ran against the grain of the land crossing four great east-west glens – Affric, Loch Mullardoch / Glen Cannich, Loch Monar / Strathfarrar, and Glen Carron – and involved climbing over, and often traversing along, the intervening mountain ranges. 'One of the hills was Sgurr na Lapaich (3778 feet). From the spongy nature of the grass it was the hardest climb I ever experienced. For about 1500 feet above Loch Mullardoch, the slope was at an angle of 47°...' wrote Heddle. Today the route cannot be followed exactly because Lochs Mullardoch and Monar were enlarged as part of post-war hydro-electric schemes.

A second SMC founder-member companion was Colin Phillip (1855–1932) a former student of Heddle's at St Andrews University who joined him on his 1880 Boulder Committee walks and provided the sketches. He also explored Knoydart with Heddle in the mid-1880s. William Inglis Clark (1856–1932) once wrote of a youthful ascent of Ben Nevis via Glen Nevis. When he and his companion emerged from a temperature inversion at the Càrn Mòr Dearg arête, they came across Heddle and Phillip, all four then ascending the Ben together.

One feature of Heddle's expeditions is his use of yachts to provide floating accommodation and access to the islands and otherwise inaccessible parts of the mainland. Heddle revelled in walking the island peaks, and traversing the tops of the mighty sea-cliffs of islands like Fair Isle, St Kilda, Foula and Mingulay. Minerals were always on his mind. He once attempted to climb the basalt-columned walls of Fingal's Cave

Matthew Forster Heddle in his 60s (1880s) *Photo: © National Museums Scotland*

to reach minerals visible in the roof. Heddle had a long acquaintance with the Cuillin of Skye. In 1871 he ascended Sgùrr a' Greadaidh, a peak first climbed the year before. In the glen Heddle met a shepherd who habitually told climbers that Greadaidh had not been climbed, so Heddle 'was rendered happy by the assumption that he had climbed a virgin peak.' A letter from 1888 describes an expedition from Loch Brittle with two companions. 'Both were astounded at the roughness of the place. Corry Laggan was the grandest bit of scenery I ever saw and it was the roughest bit of climbing I think I ever did, though perhaps the stiff hip had something to do with that. We never, or at least I never could have got down some of the places without the rope...we did 2 peaks and a shoulder, and were 13½ hours about it! One did not seem to have been done before, as it had no cairn. If you are ever back you really should go to the 2,500 feet shoulder of Sgurr Sgumain to look down into Corry Laggan.'

Although Heddle undertook countless expeditions in the hills there are only two full accounts from his own pen, both published in the SMC Journal. One, the unfinished 'South West Ross' (already referred to above) was stimulated by Heddle's irritation at reading a paper called 'Strathcarron as a Climbing Centre' by Lionel Hinxman (1855–1936), also a founder member of the SMC, and an assistant geologist with the Geological Survey. His paper in the 1895 SMC Journal concluded: 'To the south-east of Strathcarron lies the as yet unexplored country about the head waters of the Ling; and further afield still, the glorious mountain region of Loch Duich and Kintail.'

This claim annoyed Heddle who wrote, 'Mr Hinxman may be taken as here speaking as a mountaineer, and not as a geologist, when he uses the word "unexplored"; but I speak as both, when I say that with scarce an exception I have been at the top of every 3,000 feet peak of the district named, and that in almost every case with a 4-lb. hammer at my side, and a 14-lb. one over my shoulder; and that in the district named I have found several new localities of minerals, and several interesting rocks, now in the Museum of Science and Art, Edinburgh. This was done a considerable number of years ago, and I therefore hardly think that the district can be said to be "as yet unexplored."' In his note on the paper, Munro commented that '...this article was written by one who not only had an intimate acquaintance with the country, but was also able to add much, out of his own knowledge, to existing maps. The district described is one of the most interesting, if one of the least known, in Scotland; and there can be little doubt that the information given will prove of the greatest use to subsequent visitors.'

Earlier, in 1893, Heddle's Ben Avon appeared in the SMC Journal. It narrates two separate visits to the many tors, corries and cliffs of this extensive mountain in the Cairngorms. One of the walks was made in 1879. Heddle describes how his party met a keeper whose cooperation they secured by plying him with whisky and who then joined them on the first walk from the now ruined Lochbuilg Lodge. Heddle described the geological features they encountered – the double outflow from the loch, and erosion and potholes in the rocks caused by the wind – and recorded the keeper's amazement at his expertise. 'Noo, that's just extra-ordinar to hear ye, a gentleman who never set fut on the hill afore, tell me just what

I've stud here by the hour and wonerred at. The water ae day spin, spin, spinnin' in ae way, and on anither, jist the ither wey.'

Given the number and frequency of Heddle's excursions, many of which involved mineral collecting in difficult circumstances, it is surprising that Heddle managed to avoid serious injury or worse. Sir Hector Cameron, once a St Andrews' student, said that during his lectures Heddle would relate his '...miraculous escapes from death which he more than once had when, suspended by ropes he was collecting minerals from the face of some beetling precipice.' There must have been many slips and falls that came to nothing but he suffered a bad leg injury in 1880 when, descending Sgurr nan Gillean, he was struck by a boulder dislodged by a colleague behind him. This injury was to bother him in future years. Ironically Heddle had earlier told his friend and confidant Archibald Geikie (1835–1924) that the '...Rum hills very dangerous to climb– very much more difficult than Coolins– got a baddish fall– smashed nothing for I fell all along my side– looked as if I had photographed a rainbow for some time.'

It was on his way to Fort William that the 25-year-old Hugh Munro first met Heddle. Munro wrote that 'Together we shared the box seat of the mail from Kingussie to Fort-William on 15th October 1883. It was my first visit to Lochaber, and Professor Heddle was going to attend the opening of the Ben Nevis Observatory on the following day. What an agreeable travelling companion he was! What a fund of information, and how pleasantly he told it! One remark I have often thought of in subsequent years. He had been talking of the labour which so much mountain climbing involved: "But the hardest work is done in my own library, studying maps, piecing together routes, and planning walks."' Heddle was one of a party of more than one hundred people who left the Alexandra Hotel in Fort William and walked up the new pony track to the summit of Ben Nevis for the official opening. In the evening a dinner was held at which Heddle proposed a toast to the friends and promoters of the enterprise.

Heddle did not join the SMC when it was founded but his achievements and expertise were quickly recognised. 'It is a satisfaction to some of us who were members of Committee in 1893 to remember that it was decided to admit a limited number of Honorary Members to the Club, mainly because we desired to do honour to Professor Heddle,' wrote Munro. 'It is said that he appreciated this act of the Club as much or more than all the many distinctions which, in the course of his long and useful life, had been conferred upon him. In honouring him we honoured ourselves, by numbering him among our first Honorary Members.'

Heddle's name appears in articles in early editions of the SMC Journal as an authority on the height of mountains. Ever the scientist, he used his aneroid to record the height of every hill he climbed. In a talk to the St Andrews Literary and Philosophical Society in February 1891 Heddle said '...there were 409 hills in Scotland above 3000 feet high of which he had been at the top of 350, the total height of which was 1,183,000 feet.'

Soon after, in September 1891, Hugh Munro published his Tables of the 3000-Feet Mountains of Scotland. In these detailed Tables, Munro recorded 538 summits over 3000 feet in height, of which he regarded 283 as separate mountains and 255 as subsidiary tops. Munro had not climbed them all himself and had to defer to others for some of the heights. In the SMC Journal of September 1893 he published an article called 'Additions, Corrections, and Remarks' and wrote 'I have derived most valuable information from contributions to the Journal– notably from such articles as Dr Norman Collie's on the heights of the Cuillins and Professor Heddle's on Ben Avon.' Four Heddle measurements appear in a later paper by Munro about An Teallach.

Heddle certainly had the notion to climb all the Scottish 3000-foot peaks, and was competitive about it. In April 1891 he told Geikie that '...Peyton and I are going to mid Glen Lyon to do 5 3000ers others not get-at-ible from other points. I have now done 350 of the 409 3000ers. Peyton 270 – Phillip 260, others nowhere. These 5 will be my last I think. I can't get at most of the others on account of Wymans [sic].' William Winans was a wealthy American industrialist who had bought up leases of land, creating between Beauly and Kintail a huge deer forest to which he refused access.

By now Heddle's hill-going activities were hindered not just by access problems, but by deteriorating health, yet hillwalking was part of the cure. In July 1891 rheumatism had blighted a cruise and on his return '...I was advised to try exercise...I came here [Dollar] and have been climbing the hills in pain, torture at times.' A week later he reported that 'I believe the hill walking at the Ochils cleared it off but it was a most painful cure.'

Meanwhile, in August 1890, Peyton was on Bidean nam Bian, leading a party that included Rev. A. E. Robertson (1870–1958) who that month had begun a hill-walking career that would in 1901 see him become the first person to climb all the Munros. Peyton impressed Robertson with his energy, geological knowledge and the skill with which he guided the group.

If Munro had published his Tables even two years earlier it is possible that Heddle could have become the first Munroist. The determined Heddle would have solved the access problems and been fit enough to climb the few remaining hills, the number of which must have been quite small. Heddle had climbed 350 of Scotland's 3000-foot mountains, but as neither his list of 409 peaks nor his list of ascents have survived we do not know how far short of compleation [sic] of Munro's 283 separate mountains he was. We know that there were three Munros among the five mountains in Wester Ross that Heddle had not ascended. In contrast, by 1897, the year of Heddle's death, Rev. A. E. Robertson had climbed a mere 100 Munros.

After Heddle's death in 1897 Munro wrote a tribute in the *SMC Journal* in which he acknowledged Heddle's achievements. 'There can be little doubt that Professor Heddle had climbed far more Scottish mountains than any man who has yet lived...No district was unknown to him, and scarcely any high mountain unclimbed by him; and wherever he went there went not merely the trained geologist, but the truest lover and keenest observer of nature, and above all of the Scottish mountains...When in December 1896 I called to ask him to respond to the toast of 'The Highland Hills,' at the forthcoming dinner in Edinburgh, he told me that his climbing days were over, that he had no longer the physical strength or health requisite. His love of the mountains, however, was unabated. No one who was present at that dinner, and who listened to what, though not the principal toast, was undoubtedly the speech of the evening, will ever forget the graceful eloquence of that soul-stirring address, breathing the very spirit of the mountains. It is indeed a privilege to have heard it, and to have known Professor Forster Heddle.'

Sources and references

1) Information taken from the *Scottish Mountaineering Club Journal*:
1/6 (1891) pp276–314 (Munro's *Tables*),
2/5(11) (1893) pp225–34 (Heddle's *Ben Avon*)
2/6(12) (1893) pp330–36 (Munro's *Additions*, etc.),
3/13 (1894) pp10–18 (Munro's *An Teallach*),
3/16 (1895) pp218–22 (Hinxman's *Strathcarron*),
5/27 (1898) pp103–14 (Heddle's *South-West Ross*),
5/27 (1898) pp114–15 (Munro's note on Heddle).

2) Heddle's descriptions of Scottish peaks are from his 'Sutherland' in the *Mineralogical Magazine*, Vol. 4 No. 19 (1881).

3) Most of the Royal Society of Edinburgh's Boulder Committee Reports may be found online.

4) Heddle's count of the Scottish 3000' peaks is from the minute book (27th February 1891) of the St Andrews Literary and Philosophical Society (University of St Andrews Library Special Collections, UY8525/2).

5) Information on Rev A.E. Robertson is from Robin Campbell's *The Munroist's Companion* (1999).

6) I have quoted from Heddle's letters to Archibald Geikie (University of Edinburgh Library Special Collections, Coll-74/12/2) and to John Harvie-Brown (National Museums Scotland Library, Harvie-Brown Collection, Correspondence Box 26, files 422/3).

Readers wishing to identify detailed sources, including several not mentioned here, will find them in the author's *Matthew Forster Heddle: Mineralogist and Mountaineer*, published by NMS Enterprises Limited – Publishing, available from bookshops and from <www.nms.ac.uk/books>. ISBN 978-1-905267-98-9, £14.99.

THE PUBLIC BAR AT THE KINGS HOUSE

By Iain Smart

The mid-forties

THE FIRST TIME I entered the Public Bar at the Kings House was after a failed attempt on *Crowberry Gully*. I had got up the narrow cleft on the sixth pitch where I tore my coat – not a trivial matter as clothes were rationed. My companion was unable to follow. It was a long time ago, all of seventy years. It was some weekend in May of 1945 to be precise. The European war was over but the roads were still empty of cars and people. I remember the day clearly; it was cold, grey, windy and dingin on to rain. Kings House stood, as it does now, on bald moorland, but then it was a bleak shabby place, protected by a few trees, barely surviving the war. We approached along the old road, crossed the bridge and entered the Public Bar. This was a bold move; we were under-age drinkers when this was not yet the fashion. We entered a cheerless bare room. A small fire burned in a small grate on the right hand wall. A man crouched on each side of it absorbing what little heat it gave. They did not acknowledge us. We were eventually served half pints through a small aperture in the otherwise blank far wall. I have the feeling that the only two chairs in the place were occupied by the two 'semi-savage kerns or gallowglasses' crouched over the fire. (We had been revising Macbeth for our Highers and these terms were applied to his retainers – not by Shakespeare, but by one of the patronising commentators[1] on the text. I still have the original schoolbook with the speeches we had to memorise marked in pencil.) The two by the fireside lacked the dignity of shepherds or keepers and must have been down at heel itinerants on the way from somewhere to somewhere else. Appearances, however, can be deceptive. They were, perhaps, travellers rich in folklore awaiting the touch of Hamish Henderson to rescue the treasury of song and story that resided within their memory banks.

The mid-sixties

The second occasion that remains in my memory was some two decades later. Tom Weir and I came off the Buachaille one summer evening after climbing somewhere on one of the buttresses. This time the bar was packed with young people of both sexes. Youth and enthusiasm filled the air. Tom and I were definitely elderly. We stood at the edge of the throng pressed against the wall trying to look inconspicuous. The crowd started to sing Beatles' numbers: 'She loves you yeah, yeah, yeah', then 'It's been a hard day's night' and other early Beatles' songs. Everyone knew the

---

[1] If the commentator said that he was wrong: the kerns and gallowglasses were the servants of the 'merciless MacDonwald'. (Hon. Ed.)

words and joined in. It was exuberant. It was genuine contemporary folk.

It was also the mid sixties; it was still touchingly innocent. 'Maxwell's Silver Hammer' had yet to descend on the heads of Joan, the teacher and all the other pillars of stability. Rose and Valerie were not yet screaming from the gallery to set Maxwell free. Sid Vicious, Johnny Rotten and Dee Generate must have been little boys at this time. A few years later these profound thinkers would imprint an improved world view on the minds of their generation. As Bob Dylan, the gifted Pied Piper of the children of the sixties, pointed out 'the times they were a-changin.'

By contrast down the road at Lagangarbh in the sixties the real anti-authoritarian hard men had been deconstructing their environment for years. These fundamentalists had been grappling with the real reality of getting up uncompromising vertical rock and ice, unwatched by admiring crowds and therefore of no interest to astute financial operators. Success in this vertical field was appreciated by a small group of cold-eyed, Nietzschean cognoscenti and failure was a real flop, physically, psychologically and socially.

In Robin Campbell's classic article 'One Man's Meet' (*SMCJ*, 29/162 (1971), 351–5) Campbell gives a droll insight into the sociology of two relict populations that intervened between the hard men in Lagangarbh and the conventional youth singing Beatles' songs in the Kings House Bar, namely the gentlemanly, 'coffied and brandied' Old-Believers in the official SMC Meet in the Glencoe Hotel at the bottom of the glen and the culturally dispossessed losers in Dan MacKay's barn. This article is essential reading; it is a cameo of the period preserved in the amber of Campbell's prose.

Modern Times

The third occasion was in modern times. The bar was full but not crowded. There were tables and chairs and pleasant décor. A choice of exotic meals was on offer. Things like pizzas, lasagne, yogurt, Thai curries, ciabatta rolls and other exotica were available – things unheard of in earlier times but all commonplace now. The clientèle were well-dressed in colourful designer anoraks that looked functionally efficient as well as chic. Gore-Tex was the answer keeping out the blowing wind.

Rucksacks were no longer heavy and crudely serviceable military cast-offs but were now pleasing to the eye and replete with useful specialisations, exemplified by one sack that bore a pair of short axes with lean sinuous shafts and heads with an interesting reverse curve to the pick; the axes bracketed a pair of crampons with the functional beauty of tiger claws extended for the attack; they looked splendidly fit for a serious purpose.

The whole scene expressed good design and well dressed confidence. People at an adjacent table were comparing their GPSs and demonstrating the apps on their iPhones, iPads and iPods – able to snatch out of the air everything from birdsong to where you were on an OS map. Sophistication ruled. It was like being in an advertisement in a glossy magazine. Outside a multitude of cars of impressive sophistication compared to those of half a century ago shared the parking space with powerful motorbikes, wonders of compact engineering; they all ran on petrol costing what had once been a week's wages for each gallon. The times had been a-changing – very much for the better. I was sorry to have missed out on this Golden Age of living. If Mephistopheles had been passing by I would have tried to strike a deal with him. It was embarrassing to think of semi-savage kerns or gallowglasses. I felt like one myself; my table was even in the same position as the old fireplace.

CORVID'S LIST

By Graeme Morrison

That peak-baggin' magpie, Jay Rooke,
Compiled a most recondite book.
Friends who once crowed 'You're ravin'!'
Now a reprint are cravin'.
Corbett's choughed at the plaudits he took.

As a matter of interest, the surname Corbet or Corbett is believed to come from the French *corbet*, which in turn was derived from the Romance *corvetto*, a diminutive of the Latin *corvus* (= raven), so J Rooke Corbett truly was 'a little raven'.

THE CURIOUS INCIDENT OF THE DOG IN THE ICE

By John Spencer

'I'M OFF!' I EXCLAIMED, more out of surprise than anything else since, well, I wasn't expecting to fall. One of my axe placements in the less-than-ideal turf had ripped as I was thrutching up a short corner, my crampons scrabbling on not very much. In slow-motion I barn-doored, eyeballed the ice screw I'd placed a few feet below, let go of the other axe, and launched into space. But then, a second later: 'No I'm not!' as I realised I hadn't gone very far and was now dangling from the lanyard attached to the still-in-situ axe.

I was leading the second pitch of a route called *K9* on Lurcher's Crag in the Northern Cairngorms. It was our first real opportunity to get out onto something steep and white, not having had a dog's chance so far on account of the mild but wild and stormy start to the season. MWIS was reasonably optimistic: no precipitation forecast, a decent chance of cloud-free tops, maybe even some sun, and, most relevant to today's adventure, freezing levels down to 650 metres. We were three: myself, John and Robin. On account of it being the first weekend showing promise, we reasoned the hordes would be out to play and that the honeypots of Sneachda and Lochain would be hotching. None of us had climbed at Lurcher's before but others had told us that when it was 'in', bearing in mind its base is around 750m, there was good sport to be had and that it would also likely be quiet. It seemed like a good prospect.

A pleasant walk in the breaking dawn along the track from the Sugarbowl car park took us on a contouring line round the base of the Northern Corries from where, across the valley, we could see a steady stream of cars heading up to the main car park, seemingly vindicating our choice of venue. We passed through the Chalamain Gap, scene of one of the previous season's avalanche tragedies, and turned into the Lairig Ghru. Here the ambience changed, with a stiff breeze blowing and more of a 'big country' and serious feel to things.

Our original target was *Window Gully*, a single star IV/4, first climbed by Bill March with photographer John Cleare and Jonathan Bradshaw in March 1972. The highlight is climbing up behind an ice curtain, cutting a hole in it – the eponymous window – squeezing through and regaining the ice. It sounded fun, but when we finally located what we thought was the line on the craggy hillside it was clear there was no curtain. However *K9*, to the left, first climbed by Allan and Blair Fyffe in March 1996, looked to be well formed, with some interesting-looking ice high up. Also graded IV,4, it seemed worth a punt, so we thrashed our way up a steep snow slope to the start of the route.

Although we could make out a line we struggled to fit the route description to what we saw above us. It mentioned a 'lower icefall'

John Vaughan on pitch 1 of K9, Lurcher's Crag, January 2014. *Photo: J. Spencer.*

leading up to an overhanging wall; the latter was obvious, not so the icefall. Ah, well.

John led off up a corner, a mixed pitch of snow-covered rock, generally cruddy ice, and not-very-frozen turf, with little gear to boot. It was clear the freezing level was well above 750m. However the belay was good and Robin and I followed. My lead next. The route description said 'After a pitch trend left across mixed ground.' Hmm. This would avoid what looked to be the main challenge of the route, a splurge of ice breaching the left end of the roof. The 'mixed ground' was not appealing anyway, but neither was the very thin-looking continuation groove above the belay, which would have given direct access to the ice – this was our first route of the season after all. So I headed off on a bit of a dog-leg, moving rightwards up a snow ramp then back left towards the ice, protected now by a warthog hammered somewhat optimistically into a clod of turf. Twenty feet higher a solid-feeling screw in an icicle provided psychological protection to tackle the short turf-choked rock corner.

So anyway, there I was, gently swinging on my lanyards. I chuckled, part nervous laughter, part genuine amusement at this unexpected turn of events…but only for a couple of seconds as I was jolted back from slow-motion and reverie into real-time and reality. I wasn't that confident, either in the short stretch (literally) of elasticated fabric or the still-in-situ single axe from which I gently swung. So, with 'Take it steady, John' booming up from the belay, I hauled myself back onto the route, found the nice hook in a slanting crack I should have found first time round, took a deep breath and thrutched, not very gracefully, hands, knees and everything, up the corner. With a couple of satisfying thwacks, I found good placements with which to pull onto the ice. Phew! It seemed sensible to belay at this point. I placed two bomb-proof screws and a thread round an icicle and kicked a small ledge.

Safe now, I brought up the boys, just a little pleased to hear some huffing and puffing as they climbed the tricky corner, even the odd exhortation to me to 'Watch the rope!' Meanwhile, at last the sun had emerged, the sky was blue, and the views down the Lairig Ghru and across to Braeriach were magnificent – what a great stance. A party of two had arrived at the base of the route and were making their way up the first pitch.

After we'd sorted the dog's breakfast of tangled rope, John led off up a steep wall of ice leading into a cave beneath the roof, from the back of which sprouted an assortment of tat. Protected by this and a decent screw, he stepped down and out of the cave and onto an ice bulge. A chandelier of icicles loomed overhead, the ice below it all weird and bubbly from the constant drip and freeze of meltwater. Continuing leftwards and upwards, the angle eventually eased, although it still looked pretty 'out there'.

He made light work of the pitch. The pair below us had meanwhile grown tired of waiting, frustrated I imagine that we were taking a dog's age on the route – sorry guys, climbing as a threesome is always slow, especially when it's the first route of the season and if you're not simul-climbing, which we weren't, and they had moved into a groove system to our right; it looked quite pokey – a new route, we wondered? The freezing level had dropped over the course of the afternoon and by now everything, the belay, the rack and John's sac hanging from it, the rope

Bill March and Jonathan Bradshaw on the FA of Window Gully in 1972.

Photo: John Cleare.

and indeed himself, were coated in a thin veneer of clear water ice.

We were getting tired, it was cold and we'd had little sustenance since breakfast, other than a handful of nuts and raisins and a swig of water, so the chocolate biscuits produced from the depths of Robin's rucksack provided a welcome boost to both blood sugar and morale. I led off up a series of shallow icy grooves, with the occasional awkward step, leading up to a heathery and bouldery slope. The top pitch, described as 'the upper icefall running down a corner' was visible some 50 metres or so up and to our left, quite a way off the natural line. We scrambled up to its base. Although climbing it seemed rather contrived, and the light was beginning to fade and cloud was descending, it looked enticing – it had to be done.

I was pushed forward to the sharp end. The temperature drop had taken its toll, so to speak, and the ice was now rock-hard and brittle, thus placements required a bit more care and effort (or was it just that I was

Party on K9/Window Gully February 2014.

Photo: Simon Richardson.

tired?), and the ice was more easily shattered, thus the boys below were showered with chunks of ice of various sizes. All in all, a bit tougher than was at first apparent, and, as with the roof pitch, the grade felt more like technical 5 than 4.

The top. Customary handshakes, grunts of appreciation, sorting of gear and a refreshing slurping of a cup of lukewarm tea followed. It was cold, definitely heading for a two-dog night. Darkness had also fallen, and cloud was enveloping the summits – we were going to have to navigate off the hill. Robin led the way, our headtorch beams drilling into the darkness. The descent route was actually very straightforward, a trudge up to the ridge then a gentle stroll on more or less the same bearing, to avoid the Chalamain Gap, but on excellent crunchy névé.

We reached the almost-empty car park ten hours or so after setting off. A full-on day for sure, with a bit of everything thrown in for good

Bill March after emerging from the Window on the FA of Window Gully in 1972.

Photo: John Cleare.

measure. We dropped by Tesco in Aviemore where we purchased an armful of craft beers. When we got back to the hut, I slumped, dog-tired, in front of the fire, popped open the first bottle, and slowly slipped into that wonderful glazed post-full-on-winter's-day state of body and mind as the rest of the hut bustled, our fellow adventurers excitedly recounting their own stories.

None of us had heard of *K9* before our visit to Lurcher's. When we got home, browsing Simon Richardson's excellent scottishwinter.com blog, it transpired that just a week before our ascent, Andy Nisbet, partnered by Susan Jensen, had been on the route, forging a direct link between the top of the first pitch and the ice bulge through the roof, at V,5, the line I avoided (in their photo it looked as though it was a darned sight fatter!). However, the blog entry (<http://www.scottishwinter.com/?p=4163>, entitled 'A Dog's Life'!) also mentioned that on the FA of *K9* in '96 conditions had not been very icy and, crucially, the ice over the roof was not present, hence the traverse over mixed ground, and the attraction of the top icefall. By the by, Andy described a new line he and Jonathan Preston had climbed on New Year's Day (2014), up an ice column and ramp to the left of *K9* (*Robodog*, IV/5), as well as a line up the 'ribbed area left of *K9*' – perhaps the Fyffes' 'mixed ground'? – first climbed by Mark Griffin and Adrian Dye 'by accident' at III,4 and called *Far from the Madding Crowd*.

K9 then reappeared on the same site a few weeks later (one might say that every dog has its day) in an entry by Simon Richardson himself <http://www.scottishwinter.com/?p=4588>. The issue this time was speculation over whether *K9* and *Window Gully* were actually the same climb. In fact by the time of the writing of that blog, as later reported in the 2014 issue of the *SMCJ* (pp 257–8), John Lyall had carried out some canny and dogged detective work. The main evidence was a couple of photos taken by John Cleare showing Bill March emerging through the window on the first ascent of *Window Gully*. By the by, this is an iconic image in itself, capturing the ambience of cutting-edge winter climbing of the time, with March poised on front-points and brandishing a pair of Chouinard hammers. The photos clearly show similar features to all the recent photos of *K9* (and our own observations, to boot) and Lyall provided the answer: *K9* and *Window Gully* are indeed the same climb.

So how did the confusion come about? John Lyall's contention is that it arose from the fact that *Window Gully* was originally described, in the New Climbs section of the 1972 *SMCJ*, as being 'midway between North and South Gullies'; there was no mention of *Central Gully* although it had been climbed in 1970. Lurcher's Crag was not covered in several subsequent Cairngorm guides, neither the SMC comprehensive guides (including Bill March's 1973 and Strange and Dinwoodie's 1978 editions), nor Cicerone's winter guides (the first edited by John Cunningham in 1973 and revised by Allen Fyffe in 1981). However Fyffe and Nisbet's 1985 guidebook did feature Lurcher's, describing Window as lying between North and South Gullies, faithful to the *SMCJ* New Climbs entry, as did the 1995 SMC guide. However, by the time the current (2007) SMC guide was published, *K9* had been climbed, described as being midway between North and Central, with Window still described as being between Central and South Gullies. *K9* was described as linking a lower and upper icefall, the former leading to a narrowing 6m below an overhanging wall; whereas *Window Gully* climbed up 'lower slabs' for 75m to an overhanging wall 'from which ice falls in a screen'. A photograph of the south end of Lurcher's in the 2008 *SMCJ* accompanying the winter round-up (opposite p144) compounded the confusion, showing *Window Gully* high up and midway between Central and South Gullies. And as John Lyall pointed out in his e-mail (quoted on the scottishwinter.com blog), there is no position near the supposed line of *Window Gully* to get a photo like his or Cleare's. It seems that the route causing the confusion, lying high up the crag and between South and Central Gullies was in fact climbed by Ewan Clark and Andy Nisbet in 1984 at IV,5.

As an aside, it's worth reflecting on March's 1972 *SMCJ* entry: 'Midway between North and South Gullies a large ice-fall festooned with icicles hangs halfway up the face. This is the line of the climb. Climb quite steeply for 250ft to reach the foot of the overhanging wall from which the icefall hangs in a screen. Some objective danger was provided by a 40ft icicle hanging above these lower pitches (it fell off the next day). Stomach traverse and climb leftwards between the ice screen and the rock wall to the most substantial section of the ice. Cut a window in the ice curtain and climb through this onto steep ice which is climbed to easier ground (60ft). Continue up the gully over short ice pitches for 400ft to the top.' The general consensus seems to be that Window/K9 is IV/5, possibly V,5 in hard conditions (and apparently V,6 when climbed on the right); the first ascentionists graded *Window Gully* 'III'!

Meanwhile, the two routes are still listed as different in the UKC Logbook, and some of the entries make for interesting and amusing reading, what with tales of variable conditions, backing off, uncertainty about the line, inability to crawl through the cut window, and so on; clearly a route that has 'epic' potential! But there are also comments about the unusual nature of the route ('Unlike anything I've seen in Scotland'), and its quality, for example 'Amazing climb, worthy of stars…quality route.'

The suggestion was made in the 2014 *SMCJ* to rename Clark and Nisbet's 1984 'Window Gully' as 'Diamond Gully' since it was apparently climbed after a retreat (one of a series!) from *Tiara* in Garbh Choire Mhor on Braeriach. Whether the upper icefall should still remain part of *K9*, or, more logically, link with *Robocop* and other routes to the left will need to be decided. The next guidebook writer(s) will clearly have a bit of work to do to sort out and describe everything – there is now a plethora of other routes in the vicinity. Whatever, all seemed to agree, whether *K9* or *Window Gully*, it's a cracking route.

(A shorter version of this shaggy dog story was published in the Northumbrian Mountaineering Club's quarterly magazine *County Climber* in Spring 2014 and is published with permission of the editor; acknowledgements to Simon Richardson and Johns Lyall, Hall and Cleare for their advice and/or permission to use photographs.)

BALKANS REVISITED

By Graham Little

TEMPTING VIEWS INTO MONTENEGRO on my 2011 climbing trip to Albania were frequent and proved the catalyst for a family holiday in 2012. Montenegro (or Crna Gora – literally 'black mountain') is a compact and mountainous country with a population of around 650,000. It is currently an EU Candidate country and has already adopted the Euro. In addition to doing the tourist thing and climbing some splendid mountains, including the magnificent Bobotov kuk, 2523m, the highest peak wholly in Montenegro, we couldn't help but notice the wealth of rock climbing potential. So it came to pass that Jim Lowther, Ron Kenyon, Eric McKenna-Parker and I, the 2011 Albanian team, flew to Dubrovnik in mid June 2014 with a view to driving into Montenegro for a two week rock climbing holiday.

Eric on the excellent Centraina Kamin, Paklenica *Photo: Ron Kenyon*

Steady rain at Dubrovnik airport prompted scrutiny of the weather forecast which told of thunderstorms and heavy rain in the southern Balkans for the next five days. Ron suggested heading north to Paklenica. Having climbed there in 2006, I knew that it was as good a plan 'B' as any. After a strange night in Zadar, we established base camp in luxury apartments owned by the Dalmacija restaurant in Starigrad. Croatia became a full member of the EU in 2013 and although, in the short term, has retained its currency, the Kuna, most places already accept payment in Euros.

A glance at the Paklenica guide book reveals the brevity of the route descriptions and the need to scrutinize the topos – for example, the textual description for a 350m route reads 'A real nice experience on an open rock. The key length is long and demanding'! Although all the routes are bolted[1] (and these are maintained by the National Park Authorities using income from entrance ticket charges), it is easy to go off route. On our first day Jim and I did just that, doing four hard pitches on two different routes before abbing off. As it happened this error saved us from an epic on our intended route as an afternoon rainstorm battered the area. Day two saw us making up for lost time with an ascent of the four pitch Kamasutra (5b+)[2] and the 13 pitch D. Brahm (5c in the guidebook but the polished crux is at least 6a). Ron and Eric also had a good day, including an ascent of the excellent 7 pitch Centraini kamin (5a), and we duly celebrated in the Dalmatija – local wine and superb seafood. Day three took Jim and I back to our original objective, the classic Mosoraški (6a), a ten pitch route with a splendid, if polished, crux corner high up. A word of warning: on the third pitch the guidebook diagram is misleading – do not go left into a cave (with belay) but carry straight on up. Having experienced the rigours of the quick way down the previous day we carried on to the summit of Anića kuk, 712m. The pleasures of the day were enhanced on the descent by a close view of a pair of Golden Orioles. Jim and I had 31 pitches under our belt and with an improving forecast for Montenegro it was time to move on.

Now the most direct route from Paklenica to Žabljak, our first destination in Montenegro, is through Bosnia-Herzegovina and a quick Internet search revealed that the country's highest peak was near enough en route. So a plan 'C' was hatched! Leaving the end of the new motorway we immediately got lost. Now I can state with a high level of confidence that we were the first climbers to visit the tiny village of Grab in Bosnia-Herzegovina. Its only claim to fame, as far as I know, is a many fingered signpost pointing to such unlikely destinations as Tokyo, 12,029km!

Lunch in Mostar, with a visit to the famous medieval bridge destroyed during the Bosnian War in 1993 then rebuilt and reopened in 2004, saw us heading east to Gacko and then north to the Sutjeska National Park. After a night in a hotel reminiscent of 'The Shining', we took advantage of a short weather widow to climb Maglic, 2386m, a complex mountain with great buttressing defences. Clear skies for our drive through the

---

[1] Some routes are sparsely bolted. It's best to carry some traditional gear on all routes.

[2] Paklenica technical grades are somewhat inconsistent but as a general rule dropping one or two grades gives a British equivalent e.g. 5c becomes British 5b or 5a.

Admiring the Finger Post at Grab. *Photo: Graham Little*

forest (disturbing a dozing polecat) stayed with us for most of the ascent. Sadly, the cloud dropped as we neared the summit, depriving us of a magnificent view. After re-crossing the flower rich meadows below the mountain and entering the forest, a vicious hail shower caught us just before reaching the car.

The drive to Žabljak was full of contrast: the narrow twisting potholed road from Brod to Šćepan Polge (on the Montenegran border), to an exciting drive through the Piva Canyon, with its 50 plus tunnels, then the wonderful snaking mountain road on the south side of the Durmitor. Žabljak is a strange sort of town, slightly decrepit yet with a curious charm. The Luna restaurant, our 2012 eating and drinking haunt, had been given a makeover but still offered good value.

An attempt on the striking central rib of Prutas, 2393m, was our first foray from Žabljak but as the saying goes, if it looks too good to be true, it probably is! Several pitches on poor quality rock took us to a couple of pegs and an obvious abseil sling at under half height. Jim and I suggested retreat and Ron and Eric concurred. Feeling somewhat deflated, we debated on what to do with the rest of the day. A steep white slab not far from the road at the northern end of Lojanik came to the rescue. Covered in strange gill-like pockets it gave us four fine single pitch routes on excellent rock up to 5a.[3]

The following day we headed back up the mountain road, beyond the Seldo Pass, to walk into a crag high on the flank of Izmećaj (on the opposite side of the valley from Sedlena peak, 2227m). This area of the

[3] We used British grades for our new routes in Montenegro.

southern Durmitor undoubtedly has the best quality rock and some huge crags! Access to our crag was initially along a track, into a shallow valley (where we spooked a small heard of chamois), through ground hugging dwarf pines and then up over limestone pavements and rock steps. Our plan to climb the obvious slim buttresses was quickly revised as they looked like bolt protection terrain. Jim and I climbed the 100m rib on the right side of the crag (Severe 4a) and found a scrambling descent to the right of it, whilst Ron and Eric picked the plum, a flake and chimney on the left side of the crag (HVS 5a). Jim and I then tackled the chimney between the two slimmest buttresses which gave an exciting 100m (VS 4c) route with an obvious name – a chough sailed past as I tackled the crux! With the intention of checking out a buttress further up the valley, the four of us started to descend the strange karst terrain below the crag. Exactly how it happened I don't know but the unnatural wrenching angle between my lower left leg and foot brought instant pain. Cursing my carelessness, I limped back to the car. Employing a bag of frozen peas from the Žabljak supermarket as a compress and drinking lots of beer should have solved the problem but the following day my ankle was still in a bad way.

The principal objective of our trip was to climb Koplje (Spear), a 600m high pillar in the Prokletije Mountains of southern Montenegro. Reasoning that a day's rest would allow my ankle to recover, we drove south via the Tara Bridge, Kolasin (where I fell down a man hole!) and Andrijevica to Grusinje. Two great mountain flanked valleys run south from Grusinje: the Grbaja and the Ropojana, the latter leading to a high col in Albania where we'd camped in 2011. As with my 2012 family trip, we made base at the Eko Katun Grbaja (good value basic accommodation and food) at the Grbaja valley road-head. We all agreed that another non climbing day was in order and so Ron, Eric and Jim went for a long walk up the Ropojana valley whilst I read, bathed my still swollen ankle in the ice cold river, engaged with passing locals and admired a resplendent hoopoe.

With so few days left and a poor weather forecast, it was clear that any attempt on the Spear was out of the question. A plan 'D' was required! Although by no means the highest peak, Očnjak (Canine Tooth), 2185m, dominates the Grbaja Valley. A team ascent was clearly in order. Hoping to outpace the bad weather and with a well strapped ankle, an early start saw me hobbling after Jim, Eric and Ron as we searched for the faint path that heads up through the dense forest towards the mountain. After scrabbling up steep beech mast covered slopes we found the path which took us up through the dense undergrowth of a temperate rainforest. Eric and I caught sight of the silent flight of an Eagle Owl shortly before breaking out of the canopy onto more open mountain terrain. The steep final section of the ascent was by an unmaintained 'via ferrata', the rusting steel cables proving more of a handicap than a help. I reached the top first

The Matchstick Bridge into Albania. *Photo: Graham Little*

and quickly wrote my name in the summit book, the wind strengthening and clouds boiling up from the valley. The descent was painful and torrential rain soon added to my discomfort. We squelched back to the katun[4] at mid-day well pleased with our morning's effort.

There is a universal law that says expected short cuts rarely are: especially in Albania! To be fair, Ron was less convinced of the wisdom of our short cut than the rest of us. Our plan 'E' was to drive from Grusinje to the island of Hvar, via Albania, for some hot beach-based sports climbing. The scepticism of the Albanian customs officer, transcending the language barrier, should have been warning enough and the first bridge with its matchstick splintered decking a very big hint but no, we carried on. I have to say it was the worst drive of my life on a deep-rutted, boulder-strewn, rock-bulging nightmare of a track that went on and on and on! Even with Jim, Eric and Ron running alongside the car's ground clearance wasn't up to it. A friendly French guy eventually gave Ron and Eric a lift in his Landrover whist Jim scouted ahead removing the largest rocks before I coaxed our car over scree slopes and around huge potholes. After many hours of driving we reached the start of an under construction highway at Tamarë and I handed over the driving to Jim. Lots more rough driving, including a series of improbable hairpin bends, took us to a high pass and tarmac! Down to Lake Skadar we sped, back into Montenegro,

[4] Traditionally a summer hut in the mountains used by shepherds, but now also used to describe (sometimes small) chalet-type tourist accommodation.

round Podgorica (the capital), through Cetinje then down and down and down to the Gulf of Kotor and a night in the historic old town.

From Kotor, after some debate as we drove north on the busy coastal road, we implemented plan 'F', a visit to the semi-island of Peljesac. Although Peljesac is a peninsula it has all the character of an island. The recorded sports climbing there is underwhelming but from a base at Orebić we enjoyed the local wines and climbed Sv Ilija, 961m (the highest peak of the Croatian 'islands'), ascending from the west and descending to the east on paths alive with butterflies. That afternoon, Ron, Eric and I, took the passenger ferry to Korcula old town, thoroughly reinforcing our tourist credentials. An early start the following morning to catch the Dubrovnik to Edinburgh flight and the trip was over.

Although we hadn't even attempted our main climbing objective and the weather could only be described as mixed, we'd all had a great time. What made it so? We'd adopted a flexible and adaptable approach, making the best out of every situation: enjoying the countries we'd passed through, enjoying the company of friends, enjoying the chance encounters with strangers and wildlife. The journey became our objective and we were richly rewarded.

Some statistics: trip duration 14 days; team 4; countries visited 4; mountains climbed 4; total pitches climbed 73; new routes climbed 7; kilometres driven 2,500; locations stayed 7; sights seen innumerable; fall outs 0; injuries 1. (Back home in Scotland an X-ray revealed a fractured fibula and I spent four weeks with my lower leg in a plaster/brace.)

Postscript: on learning of my injury an old friend suggested that 'climbing is a dangerous activity and best left to the young and inexperienced'. I have to disagree; it is the very process of gaining experience, as we age, that enriches life. The risks we take are part of that vitality and are what makes climbing such a crazy yet fulfilling game.

SUNDANCE

By Guy Robertson

IN THE MIDDLE OF Beinn Eighe's apparently seamless Far East Wall, the mind's eye sharply converges into a single striking feature – a monstrous 'open book' corner running the full height of the crag. Given a strenuous E2 in summer, and with plenty of moss and dampness high up, *Sundance* was an obvious, if challenging winter target. Continuously overhanging, good gear, dirty, and with the promise of ice where the exposure explodes; it all added up to a most seductive possibility. For me, it created a deep and irresistible urge that I knew could not be resisted. Best of all, I wasn't sure I could pull it off. Es Tressider had tried it before – and he is no stumbling jelly-finger – failing on the summer crux in the face of a terminal lactate pseunami – 'Harder than anything I've been on before!' he'd pronounced emphatically. Es had climbed a number of grade VIIIs.

And so it was, mid-January, in the wake of a powerful westerly storm, Ian Parnell and I hooked up late one evening in a glistening Glen Torridon, after skidding our independent ways across a cryogenic landscape. 'Good eeeeevning Mr Robertson' he gestured, wryly as ever, in that slow, slightly loaded south-western English drawl. Despite his surprisingly un-athletic and perhaps even slightly rotund appearance, Parnell is an unstoppable winter climbing force. His enthusiasm and drive know literally no bounds, sending him regularly to the car hire shop – sometimes four or five times monthly – to fill another tank and steam north from Sheffield to pillage our sacred crags. With Ian, there's simply no danger of an easy day out, and on every occasion I've teamed up with him I've had to climb towards my limits. I had a strong gut feeling that this particular foray would continue that tradition.

As soon as we agreed on Beinn Eighe, our objective needed no discussion. We had shared fantasies about *Sundance* in the past, and both knew that only time and opportunity were in the way. The winter scene has boomed since the early '90s so it's highly likely that procrastination will only lead to your unclimbed dream being publicly paraded amongst the sycophantic hyperbole of the world-wide-web. It's a painful way to see a prized project fall.

As we pummelled pack-heavy up the south side of the mountain – deep snow, pitch black and foggy headed – a darting wind skelped our thoughts up and over the col and down to the crags, bouncing back tantalizing glimpses of what lay imagined up ahead. Would it be 'in'? Would we be fit enough? All the usual, inspiring uncertainties. When we got to the top, the clag descended, the wind picked up and our view was snatched away. A further half hour of teeth-rattling staggering southwards, down and along the crest, saw us flopping into the lee side for our first view of the cliff. Despite the thick clouds curling in titillation, we could see all we

Ian Parnell tackles the awkward introductory pitch of Sundance. Photo: Guy Robertson.

needed – the crag was sparkling white, the doors were open and the game was on.

Floundering up to our necks at the base of Far East Wall, the murk soon did the honourable thing and beat a hasty and comprehensive retreat. Above us towered the object of our desire, looming confident in its defence, yet sucking our eyes inexorably up over its natural beauty and aesthetic. I felt like a dirty Peeping Tom. It overhung dramatically throughout, and came complete with a set of quite preposterous icy fangs guarding salvation right at the top. My God it was steep!

Ian sharply dispensed with the 'introductory' pitch, quickly finding that it was indeed something of an 'introduction' and certainly no walkover; heavily iced, precarious, with less than convincing hooks and protection. Within a flash however I was locked into full-on battle mode, remembering instantly how arresting is the climbing on this mountain. Unlike other Scottish cliffs, there's often no time to think – just reach, then quickly slot or hook or torque or whack, then pull and repeat! Stopping for gear is a bit like lighting a fuse; as soon as the decision is made, there's a definite time-limit, so best to make sure you've chosen the right place. Fortunately, however, gear is one thing Beinn Eighe dishes out with gay abandon, and *Sundance* clearly wasn't about to prove an exception. After a good hour or so of strenuous fight, and a slight deviation to follow cracks on the left wall, some tenuous locks rightwards brought me to a good hook and shake-out at the base of a sharply

Ian Parnell on Pitch 3 of Sundance. *Photo: Guy Robertson.*

Ian Parnell makes further progress towards the overhang. *Photo: Guy Robertson.*

overhanging chimney. This was the summer crux, and a large in situ Hex a short way out of reach suggested it was also the site of a previous impasse. Mr Tressider must've packed his bags here, I quickly surmised. Feeling the pump beginning to simmer I pushed on rapidly past the Hex, knees high and feet threatening to disengage, before lodging my right side firmly into the crack. This was a strenuous position to hold. The unfortunate dimensions of the crack coupled with my less-than-ample frame precluded normal recovery through breathing. After another awkward nut was thrown in over my shoulder, and realizing it was highly unlikely oxygen would enter my lungs through my skin, I released from the crack into the frontal attack position, and made some assertive yarding movements to the sanctuary of a foothold. The crux was in the bag, and I hadn't held my breath for long.

Ian soon joined me on my commodious pedestal, his more-than-ample frame strangely affording him a bit more breathing space in the vicinity of the crux. 'I think the rucsack might've actually helped there!' he shouted, as I averted my gaze from his generous belly. He swung briskly into action, following some brief but very uncharacteristic mutterings about Christmas puddings, nasty cold viruses, and various other age old ploys created to evade one's climbing duties. This mettle hernia was short lived though, and before long he was galloping up the sheer wall overhead with all the vigour of a pedigree racehorse. Different climbers have different styles, and Mr Parnell's is quite unique. His progress is led by an impressively stout upper torso, so his moves are long and powerful, invariably preceded by a frighteningly confident 'bounce' on both axes, and followed by crampons that kind of assume their positions, rather than follow a set path.

But just as his galloping slowed down, the threat of nightfall crept round into the corrie. In mid-January, even with an early start and slick climbing, the snapshot days rarely yield to anything more than a stumble back in the dark. This day would be no different. I could already decipher that subtle but clear shift in air quality as day turns to dusk, as Ian's head abutted the underside of the final icy overhang. A twenty foot tentacle of fragile ice hung wickedly over his shoulders, clasping the lip of a three foot ceiling, while to his right the blank right wall of the corner plunged abruptly into dim space. A selection of unprintable expletives tinkled down through the air from up above me, suggesting that the exposure at this particular point was considerable. I looked up, eyeballing the tip of the fang, pondering the resulting aerodynamics should Ian decide to release it. 'Watch me here!' he demanded, so I did, but only with one eye if I'm honest. As he undercut right onto the wall and pulled up, despite repeated thrashings with the point of his left crampon, I was left unscathed by the fang and the route remained intact. In a surge of yelping adrenaline I soon joined him at the belay. Just one of those brief, unnecessarily awkward, steep and protection-less sections remained above the belay, before I found myself picking steps through broken ground toward the ridge and the top. We were back down at the sacks in a jiffy, munching cakes, stuffing sacks and slapping backs. 'One of Scotland's finest', we declared smugly in unison.

In time honoured fashion, we called the ladies back home, gloating over our prize as much as reassuring them of our safety. My other half was fully seven months pregnant with our second child, and being aware of the uncertainties she was audibly thrilled at our success. We shared the anticipation that by March at the latest my winter climbing endeavours would be cut short for the season, and knew a few feathers in the cap were important for domestic stability. I'd broken a finger in the Alps only four months previously, so for my first outing since then this was a resounding success.

For Ian it was homeward bound, and a date with his fiancé in a luxury Spa Hotel. Despite my dogged attempts to convince him that he could easily squeeze in another day and another route and make it back to Sheffield the following night, he was clearly sated and was having none of it. Some more garbled mutterings about too many puddings, nasty viruses and such like. For me, however, this was Day 1 of 2 and the forecast for the second had appeared distinctly perfect. A loose plan had been hatched, to hook up at a location still to be decided, somewhere in the North West Highlands, with none other than the legendary Mark 'Dr Death' Garthwaite.

THEY ALSO SAID OF ROBIN SMITH

By Jimmy Cruickshank

Robin Smth

Pen and ink drawing by Helen Forde, after the photo by Jimmy Marshall.

ROBIN WAS A MULTI-DIMENSIONAL bag of tricks, 'quite brilliant as a climber and the hardest man on this side of the border'[1], the youngest general committee member in SMC history, yet one whose nature 'attracted Guardian Angels and what that said about him'.[2] He died with Wilfrid Noyce on a joint British/Soviet expedition to Tajikistan's Pamir mountains in 1962, only six years after we climbed together when still at school. As I scouted around in the 1990s for material for his biography,[3] I encouraged potential contributors not to worry about undue expressions of nostalgia or emotion as excess could be edited out.

Almost sixty wrote to me. Only a limited amount of nostalgia was forthcoming even though 30 years had zipped by. Twenty more have since

[1] Letter to John Hunt (see 8), Pamirs expedition leader, from the SMC's Malcolm Slesser, his deputy, 17/10/61.

[2] Stated in a misplaced 1993 letter from Robin's senior Philosophy lecturer, Willie Stewart (*High Endeavours*, page 73).

[3] Published in 2005 by Canongate of Edinburgh as *High Endeavours: the Life and Legend of Robin Smith*.

come and gone, of course! A most memorable reaction came from Archie Hendry (died 2013), not long after I reappeared in his life for the first time since I was seventeen and he, an SMC climber and a teacher at our school, had been Robin's unofficial mentor for about two years. 'Somehow it's difficult to think of you as a grandfather, Jimmy,' he remarked, rather pensively, a reality that presses it home that Robin, had he been alive today (2015), would have been looking forward to his 77th birthday on 30 August.

As a grandfather too? Who knows? I raise this speculation only because I found it touching when two mothers talked of reciprocated empathy between Robin and their children. Furthermore, it neatly introduces the dreaded topic of emotions! In fact, contributors were most forthcoming about their reactions to the loss of Robin at the age of 23, although many snippets were not published. Inclusion would have stressed too numbingly often that he was dead. Sentimentality might have seemed maudlin and overdone, repeated sadnesses morbid. From another angle, over-frequent voicing of praise could have introduced a hagiographic ring.

Turning our backs on inhibitions, however, and for the moment ignoring fresh revelations of drama, let's start with input from WH Murray whose 'expectations of Robin were high indeed because on news of his death I felt devastated. He was already destined for the world stage.' Murray also detected that, 'like nearly all young climbers, Robin beheld his elders with a certain irreverence. At his age I too felt that men over thirty had one foot in the grave. A view that time evaporates!' Another octogenarian, kind 'Bee' (Elizabeth) MacNeill, informed me shortly before her sudden death in 1993, her sight gone, how she and her mother had looked after Robin for four years from 1946, in Crieff, far from his parents in Calcutta where he was born in 1938: 'My sister Kay and I often talked about him. With great joy! What might he have accomplished if spared?'

Like Bee, Robin's one-time girlfriend, the American June Hamilton, 'often thought of him', going on to reveal that 'Robin is frozen in my mind as a perpetual, bow-legged Peter Pan who brought an intense degree of aliveness to his everyday existence, a life he generously shared briefly with a lucky few.' Back on this side of the water John Cheesmond wonders typically: 'What might Robin have achieved, both on the hills and through his writing?' As if responding, Ted Wrangham, one of the last ever to be in Robin's company, on Pik Garmo, had no doubt that 'he would have made his mark on society, perhaps in a way none of us had foreseen'.

A film[4] based on one of Robin's new routes, *The Bat*, on Nevis (1959), was shot in 1979 by climbing cameraman Jim Curran who courteously obtained Robin's mother's approval and kept her updated: 'During the days spent camped under Carn Dearg Buttress we all felt very close to

[4] A piece about Curran's film, *The Bat*, appeared only in the paperback version of *High Endeavours*.

the spirit of the article ('The Bat and the Wicked') and hope that the film will do justice to the men, the climb, and the magnificent writing that inspired us in the first place.'

Dougal Haston, who shared in that success on *The Bat*, was working in Kent in July 1962 to finance his Alpine season. 'Stumbling out one bright clear Kentish morning, I made my way to the paper shop as usual,' he wrote in *In High Places*[5] ten years later. 'A great numbness came over me. It was the worst…so strange that I'd never see him again. So distant and so far away.'

Sheila Samuelson and Rosemary Brindle played supportive roles in Robin's and Haston's first British ascent of the Dolomites' Cime Ovest de Lavaredo in 1961. Upon return from the Alps a year later, Sheila met her father: 'As I climbed from the car, he said, "Your friend Robin Smith has been killed." I stared at him, stupefied. "He fell off a mountain in the Pamirs," continued father, getting it over with. "No," I said. "That's not possible. Robin never makes mistakes."' I also heard the news from my father, when I phoned him from within sight of Edinburgh's Salisbury Crags where Robin and I used to practice rock climbing. Thirty years later, prompted by Hendry, I felt drawn to the tricky task of capturing Robin in words.

Sheila could have believed it if an avalanche had taken him, or if he had stepped through a cornice in appalling visibility. 'For days I went around intoning, "Not Robin. What a waste. What a waste!"' Now, as she re-reads EUMCJ[6] articles by Robin, Dougal and Neil Macniven,[7] she is again struck by 'their wonderful, mad gallantry', and Binyon's words, even if hackneyed to some, still ring true to her: 'They shall grow not old, as we that are left…'

Gordon Greig, Robin's former lecturer in Logic (died 2006), also refers to a poem, Browning's *A Grammarian's Funeral*, which he and Robin had studied. 'I quote the closing verse, slightly altered [and now further condensed] to embrace both the Climber and the Scholar,' Greig wrote:

Here's the top-peak; the multitude below
Live, for they can, there:
This man decided both to Live and Know–
Bury this man here?

'Yes', Browning concluded of his Grammarian. So it was with Robin's comrades as they laid his poor battered body side by side with Wilf's in a crevasse on the ice shelf where they had been found. 'They were in age a generation apart,' John Hunt's diary chronicled of that day, 26 July 1962, two days after the accident. 'Each had attained high academic distinction;

---

[5] Haston, Dougal, *In High Places* (London: Cassell, 1973).

[6] Edinburgh University Mountaineering Club Journal.

[7] Three brilliant Edinburgh University climbers who all died young: Robin at 23, Haston at 36 and Macniven aged 21.

both were brilliant mountaineers. There they lay, in death united.' Hunt's letter to his wife on the 15th had said of Robin that 'he is hard to know, but I'm beginning to like him,' whilst Robin's to his mother on the 13th spoke well of the 53 year-old Hunt,[8] later teasing her with the quip that 'so far I'm on friendly terms with everyone, even those in our own party'.

Robin's fate ever to rest midst lofty heights might seem poetically inspiring, but he was nonetheless a hapless victim of rotten luck when chance factors coincided to provoke disaster. It had puzzled me why Anatoli Ovchinnikov, Robin's Russian rope partner for most of that fateful day, had used the word 'run' in a letter. I discovered the truth in the late 1990s from a member of Robin's party on Garmo, Ted Wrangham. He and Derek Bull were 2000 feet below at the bivouac when the accident happened. Bull saw the fall.

Ovchinnikov reported for *High Endeavours* that Noyce set off down the fatal Garmo slope on his own after the Russians stopped to fit crampons, and that he was almost a rope's length ahead before Robin could start to tie on to Sevastianov's end of the rope. As Robin followed, Wrangham disclosed, Noyce ran across a gully, and the sudden ensuing jerk on the taut, or near-taut, rope pulled both men off the mountain: hence the fall of some 4000 feet during the briefest of windows when Robin was helpless to provide protection or save himself. Never before had they been roped together. On hearing Wrangham's news, however, Robin's sister Marion and sister-in-law Claudie deemed it inappropriate for publication as long as Wilf's widow was alive.

Back in 1962, all-powerful, oppressive and irrational authorities in Moscow expected Soviet climbers to uphold USSR's international reputation by ensuring the safety of foreign visitors. Indeed, an instruction to Ovchinnikov from the 'upper leadership' was: 'In the mountains do everything the British want but you must ensure safety.' Yet the Brits turned out to be badly under-acclimatised, both Russians thought, and it was unknown that, at 6595m, Pik Garmo was 395m higher than records showed. Ovchinnikov wrote that two days (not one) would have been built in for the final push if the true height had been known in advance. At a late stage, indeed, they talked about taking an extra day, but that would have forced an unthinkable (for Soviets) late return to base. All agreed to stick with their goal: 1095m (c.3600 feet) above.

Hindsight shows just how flawed the U.K.'s media coverage was. No wonder! When I met Wrangham, he told me of a strictly 'need-to-know' pact of secrecy, doubtless thinking that I knew more than I did and perhaps relieved to share a burden. Even Malcolm Slesser of the SMC, the team's deputy leader, on another mountain that day, did not 'need to know'. Only six did: Wrangham and Bull; Russians Ovchinnikov and Sevastianov;

---

[8] In 1953 Hunt (later Sir John, then Lord Hunt) led the first successful Everest expedition. His letter was found at the Royal Geographical Society after publication of *High Endeavours*.

party leader John Hunt; and Eugene Gippenreiter, the expedition's Soviet Information Officer, a mountaineer who had to live with political intervention in sport. All associated with that pact are now dead, as is Slesser.

There seems little doubt that the pact's main thrust was directed at 'Moscow', which, in the Communist era, was capable of vindictive retribution towards its own people if shortcomings came to be publicised internationally. Its effect on surviving Brits, once home, was that their comments were necessarily evasive or vague.

In 1964 Malcolm Slesser dedicated his book *Red Peak*[9] to Wilf and Robin, referring to a 'bitter blow' even though the relationship with his fellow SMC member had been prickly before and during the expedition: 'Wilf [aged 44] had already given much to the world and was cut off at the peak of his creative life. Robin by contrast had given little. He undoubtedly had a brilliant mind and, once he had acquired experience of life, the impact of his brilliance would have been assured. His loss in some ways was the greater for that reason. He was a fearless and supreme master of his sport.'

Les Brown was still in the Alps that July when news reached Chamonix. 'It produced an enormous sense of loss in the community. Many just packed up and left,' the Lancastrian recalls. 'Robin was considered by everybody I knew as one of a very small elite of British mountaineers whose activities would have graced the mountaineering world for many years, not least because of his wonderful literary talents.' David Hughes from Leeds, Robin's partner on the first ascent of Yo-Yo in 1959, heard about the accident when returning from the Alps. 'I cried,' he confessed. 'With the confidence of youth I thought that Robin wouldn't, couldn't, fall. He gave such an impression of invincibility. How I wish he could have had half the pints I've had on the strength of that climb!' It was, though, Robin's affable trait that Robin Chalmers remembers: 'He was an easy and relaxed person to talk with and seemed to respect the climbing ability of anyone who enthusiastically took themselves into the mountains.'

Jimmy Gardner describes Robin's talent as 'monumental', adding that 'he thought big and had great determination. I was proud to have known him.' Trevor Jones said much the same when he wrote that it was 'a privilege' to have known Robin, whilst Jimmy Marshall once asserted, 'Everyone loved the man!', riled at the idea that anyone could think otherwise! A few, though, did fail to fall under Robin's spell, and if anyone feels that Robin Smith's canonisation seems all too imminent, they can always fall back on a few, potentially immortal words: 'He was part of a bad lot who left climbing huts in a right midden!' Even so, that kindly senior – Tommy Weir – could not but admire Robin.

Perhaps because I might have felt happier if he had not upset Weir by

[9] Slesser, Malcolm, *Red Peak* (London: Hodder and Stoughton, 1964).

unfairly classifying him as yet another elder who sat upon a self-made pedestal, I find myself relating to Robin via JM Barrie's Rectorial Address at St Andrews University in 1922, shortly after the carnage of the First World War. Barrie asked the students to envisage a play in which the parents of a soldier killed in the war enter a university to hand back a scroll presented to them in honour of their son. 'At first they had been enamoured to hear of what a scholar their son was, how noble and adored by all,' Barrie orated. 'But soon a fog settled over them, for this was not the boy they knew. He had many a fault well known to them; he was not always so noble; […] he sometimes made his father rage and his mother weep. They had liked to talk about such memories, and smile over them, as if they were bits of him lying about the house.'[10]

Barrie went on to advise youth, the students, to be wary of their supposed 'betters', of whom he was one. Had Robin read Barrie's piece, I've wondered more than once? We'll never know, but its title 'Courage' outlined the quality required for the 'great fight' that Barrie envisaged and advocated.

There again, we know, Robin responded positively to older people inclined to offer respect or kindness. Indeed, the SMCJ's reviewer of *High Endeavours*, spotted several such instances, like Willie Stewart, Robin's former senior Philosophy lecturer (died 1995), whose reward was a legacy of memories of someone whose 'sheer likeableness could shine so captivatingly', though it occurred to Gordon Greig, Stewart's friend and fellow lecturer, that 'sadly one wonders whether some never got past Robin's rough edges, and occasional gaucheries, to discover his charm and sympathetic, intelligent self.' We may suppose that, had he lived, Robin would have gone on to echo Willie Stewart's conclusion that 'Willie when young would not have suffered much of himself when old'! It distressed them, both emotionally and as academics, that their star student would not after all be taking up PhD studies at University College London. Nor would their advice ever again be sought.

Whatever it was about him, Robin is certainly not forgotten, as a person or as a climber. This was predicted by Jimmy Marshall when he wrote Robin's obituary for the 1963 *SMC Journal*, in words that will live on, such as when I cribbed them 42 years later for the conclusion of *High Endeavours'* epilogue.

Mark you, Marshall's words written specially for that book also touch me: 'I still recall him as if it were yesterday and warm to the remembrance of his uninhibited joy in the freedom of the wilder side of Scotland's bens.' As time passes, it perhaps becomes increasingly difficult to disagree with a complementary idea floated by Barrie at St Andrews, namely that 'memory' is a gift to older people, 'so that we might have roses in December'.

---

[10] Barrie's 1922 speech, titled *Courage*, was published under that name in booklet and hardback forms.

HIGHLAND APPRENTICESHIP

By Martin C. Cooper

WE LEANED BACK on our lanyards, facing each other at the apex of the pylon. Under Frank's watchful eye, I released the load on the pull lift and let the cradle swing free from the earth conductor, allowing it to hang from its new galvanised steel fixings – another part of the national grid was now fit for purpose for years to come. I looked at the old worn parts in my hand before putting them in my overalls, thinking they would make a fitting memento, representing a chapter of my life that was coming to an end. As is often the case, endings frequently lead to new beginnings. I had nearly completed my apprenticeship as an overhead linesman, but in a parallel world, I had recently set out on a completely different form of training – my Highland Apprenticeship.

Going back to a damp August morning sometime during the 1980s, I recall one of my early experiences.

4 a.m. 'I'm getting bitten'. 'Shut up and go back to sleep'. 'No, seriously, I am.' Silence. Every now and then, another bite and another and another. Annoying more than anything, but not conducive to sleep. Outside, windless. The only sound, that of very fine raindrops hitting the nylon flysheet. Another bite. 'I'm fed up with this.' I jumped up, unzipped the inner, stuck my head out and now completely unprotected, I was bitten with unbearable ferocity. My face contorted by the awful sensation of hungry insects feeding. Panicking now, I scrabbled for my boots preparing to escape my assailants. Tent door left wide open, rushing and tripping on untied laces as I ran. I paused on higher ground. The slightest breeze eased my suffering. As I looked down at our tent, all I thought was – 'they'll be up!' With the tent door left wide open, my two older companions were now at the mercy of these uncompromising assailants. Chris, accustomed to noon starts during term time at Cambridge University, was particularly unhappy at the hour and rudeness of his awakening. Malcolm, slightly more understanding but also none too pleased, joined him in uttering a range of expletives before and after my name – 'Cooper!'

I had experienced my first full-blooded encounter with the Highland midge, which along with heavy rain later that day brought our attempt at walking the West Highland Way to an end in Kinlochleven. It would not be the last time that rain and midges would thwart my plans, though a few years later (and now as a climber) I did consider these as significant factors to avoid when I decided to visit a glen west of Rannoch Moor to climb above Loch Etive.

Some great climbing stories have been told and retold about the renowned sweep of white granite on the south-east-facing slopes of Beinn Trilleachan. Here is one I really like, told of the days when the slabs were climbed using pegs. 'We were interrupted in our conversation around the coffin stone by the sound of iron mongery bouncing down the slabs towards us. It was a peg, and two of our number scurried around the base of the crag to claim it. Moments later the sound of something heavier was heard falling down the slabs from above. This time a peg hammer came our way and further members of our group set out to claim this latest prize. Next a shriek that sounded human caught our attention and upon looking up we saw a climber sliding, tumbling and falling down the rocks towards us!' The unfortunate climber had been properly introduced to the consequences of making a mistake on the Etive Slabs. The reputation of this venue goes before it – low angle, holdless, irreversible moves involving bold lonely leads interspersed by fierce overlaps that make up many climbs of great character and quality.

So having climbed and re-climbed *Spartan Slab* my questions were– what next? Did I believe there was anything I could climb next? All the other routes sounded really serious. 'Try Hammer,' said Andy. 'How bold is it?' 'Well the scoop is a bit goey, but the rest of it is OK.' Sounded reasonable and with my partner dispatched to climb the scoop (under the premise that the next pitch was harder) I sat back on my belay to witness firsthand what this bold Etive slab climbing was all about. Suddenly, I heard an awful scraping noise to my right. What sounded like a mixture of fabric, hardwear and maybe skin sliding down the slabs at an alarmingly fast pace. The noise ended with a thump and as I turned round I saw a fellow climber in a heap alongside his belayer. One of the slab's routes of great reputation – *Pinch Direct* had just expelled him from the notorious 'pinch pitch'. 'I just got my fingers on the edge of the pocket and my feet went,' he said. Not deterred another attempt was made, yielding the same result and this time with an injury that curtailed any further action. A self rescue was competently undertaken. I was not left with the impression that this was an incompetent team, rather two good climbers pitting their skill and nerve against one of the great classics. This place really did have reputation and at the time I was glad it was not me padding up to that elusive pocket. Our route (though much easier) went much more by the numbers. In time, further routes were added to my collection – *Pause*, *The Long Reach*, *Swastika*, *Jaywalk*, *Agony*…all brilliant, brilliant routes combining common characteristics with their own unique qualities. Each requiring elements of nerve and commitment that yield the reward of deep and lasting memories: the quartz band pitches, the Pause pitch, the Long Reach pitch, the prize of finding the corner pitches of Agony dry and the feeling all this climbing evokes: reading the line before committing and once underway no stopping, weight over the feet, no overreaching, keep breathing, be patient, feel the hairs stick up on the back of your neck and savour the moments when those rare and crucial holds are gained. On these slabs I began learning about a new and different aspect of the climbing game, one that relied on a cool head, judgement and technique. One where youthful strength could never be the solution to overcoming difficult cruxes.

Travelling from Etive to Skye, my learning context changed from solid low angle slabs, to the loose steep rock of the Old Man of Storr in the Trotternish Hills. This pinnacle is iconic not only in appearance, but also in the character of the man who first climbed it. A genuine inspiration to many young climbers – Don Whillans. With this information in my mind, I managed to entice my friend Jon away from the perfect gabbro of the Cuillin to try and climb this objective. 'I've walked around the base of it before, it looks hard but I think we can climb it, standing on the top would be amazing!' I said enthusiastically.

Whillans mentioned a bollard of rock at the start which he put a sling round and used for aid. I think we were in the right place but I did not find this feature – perhaps it had long since departed being part of the climb that Whillans referred to as 'like coal, rotten and loose'.[1] I climbed up to a bulge at 20 feet or so, managed to arrange protection in a disintegrating crack and fell off, then tried a few more times with the same results. With purism in mind for my ascent I lowered to the ground disappointed. Now it was Jon's turn. The bulge was too hard for him also. As Jon dangled on his ropes the young man in me was getting impatient – failure looked likely – 'Pull on the gear, aid it, who cares?' (I now just wanted to get to the top). Jon had also planned on a free ascent and besides he had come to Skye to climb great rock rather than engineer his way up this rarely climbed piece of decomposing basalt. He also lowered to the ground (probably wishing he was back in Coire Làgan). We discussed whether to aid this part of the route for a brief moment then agreed to give up. Reading Whillans' book later, I discovered that on his first ascent of the Old Man he used aid in the form of a peg to surmount the bulge we had both failed on. Once over this crux the angle eased and apparently the quality of rock improved. We failed where he had succeeded. Failure, as I was to discover is part of learning about climbing and this was by no means the last time the Highlands would get the better of me. Missing out on the opportunity to tread on this little frequented summit was disappointing and it still fills me with some regret today that we did not make it to the top. Pondering where we should invest our energy next to avoid wasting any more of the warm sunny day, I suggested a visit to Kilt Rock. 'The climbing is supposed to be fantastic, it is even written about in Extreme Rock' I said. Jon agreed, so we made the short drive north to this aptly named cliff that sits on Skye's east coast overlooking the Sound of Raasay and the Minch.

The highlight of our visit was *Grey Panther*: abseiling down this wonderful line to reach the base, I pondered whether my rack was big enough to accommodate all the great gear placements on offer. What

---

[1] Don Whillans & Alick Ormerod, *Don Whillans: Portrait of a Mountaineer* (London: Heinemann, 1971).

followed was a magnificent long pitch of safe, well protected climbing on perfect rock, each move was a delight – a far cry from our earlier experience of Storr. Jon enjoyed it so much he made another trip to this part of Skye during which he explored similar climbing just north of Kilt Rock at Staffin Bay.

Looking across to the mainland from Skye, it is possible to see a mountain that has perhaps taught me more about climbing in the Highlands than any other. The quantity, quality and variety of climbing to be found on Ben Nevis are in my view unsurpassed by any other Scottish mountain. I made my first ascent via the tourist path in the early 1980s. Curiosity drew me across the summit plateau to gaze down the precipitous north face and then stare over to the Càrn Mòr Dearg arête, which I had been told was an excellent ridge scramble. I spent time combing the observatory ruins looking for interesting artefacts and delighted in finding the summit spring, still upwelling beside what I later took to be the old wooden collecting tank used by the inhabitants of the observatory. The whole place impressed on me a deep presence of mountaineering and social history. I still feel this today, particularly, for some reason when climbing the final pitches of routes that culminate near the summit. On that first day it felt incredibly special and unique. It would only be a matter of time before I would explore some of this mountain's famous summer and winter climbs.

My first real climbing on Ben Nevis took place low down on its southern flanks above Glen Nevis. These initial experiences involved getting lost, more midges, rain, wet rock, following a guide book description for my chosen route up the wrong crag and spending a couple of unsuccessful hours looking for the wee classic route *Shergar* on Black's buttress. An acquired taste is perhaps required for this venue, but my experience here led me on a journey that introduced me to the delights of cragging in Glen Nevis. Linking the crags together from the foot of Pinnacle Ridge to the summit of Crown Buttress offers a great mini expedition giving many pitches of climbing. On a number of occasions I have enjoyed solo and roped excursions that have led me all the way to the top of Polldubh. Having discovered Glen Nevis, the focus of my attention inevitably led me to the other side of the mountain and on to its North Face. Here is how my earliest experience of this side of the mountain unfolded.

I did not quite make it to the hut and on my return I looked back and up to my right for the last time. A cliff bigger than my imagination towered above me, I felt very small and intimidated. I was four years old and unknown to me then, it was the Carn Dearg Buttress that stared down and across the Allt a' Mhuilinn at me. My parents knew of the spectacular cliffs that form the north face of Scotland's highest mountain and decided to take me on a walk to see them. My father had continued on the path as far as the CIC Hut, while my mother sat by the burn a few hundred metres lower down. Both were suffering the effects of very strong sun, I had drunk most of the water and felt ok. For a few minutes, I was out on a limb in this magnificent landscape, feeling that I was not directly under the supervision of either of them. It was a powerful moment that stayed with me when we returned home, but little did I realise then that one day I would attempt to tackle this huge north facing buttress as a climber.

Years later and again following in the footsteps of Whillans, my first visit to climb on the north face and in particular the Carn Dearg Buttress ended in failure. We set our tent up near the CIC Hut and made damp ascents of Tower and Castle Ridges while waiting for the great cliff to dry out. On day three heavy rain and gale force winds nearly flattened our tent. With time running out and no chance of dry rock, we retreated through the peat bogs that led from the hut down to the dam at the south west end of the Leanachan Forest. We would have to wait to climb *Centurion* another day. And probably fortunate we did, as with hindsight I doubt very much I could have made it up the route at that early stage in my life as a climber. Likely the second pitch would have proved too hard or I would have lost my way on the slabs leading to the 5a pitch near the top, or worse failed on that pitch and been unable to extract myself from the route. A couple of years later however, and in perfect spring weather, I found myself bridging up the second pitch. I shouted down to my partner that I was definitely climbing the pitch of my life – at that time I really was. This pitch and the route as a whole is a climb that I remember as one of my favourite (rock) climbs on the mountain – even better in my opinion than *Minus One Direct*.

Glissading down the spring snow in *Number Five Gully* at the end of my ascent of *Centurion*, I had no real idea (other than an ascent of *Castle Ridge*) of what winter on this mountain was all about. I had heard that people climbed ice on the north face, but had never tried it. I understood that there were some world famous winter routes on the mountain, but I could not understand how this rocky landscape could transform itself so radically in winter. I could tell from the scale of the cliffs that the routes might make tremendous adventures. I had to try. A logical progression from rock climbing and summer mountaineering was soon to follow. A new chapter in my Highland Apprenticeship was about to begin...

THE VAGABOND PROFESSOR: T. GRAHAM BROWN

By Peter Foster

Dr [sic] Brown appeals to me as a man possessed with the body of a respectable person and the soul of a vagabond[1]

PROFESSOR T. GRAHAM BROWN, F.R.S., (1882–1965) is probably best remembered for his part in the opening up of the Brenva face of Mont Blanc with a magnificent 'triptych' of routes (*Sentinelle Rouge*, *Route Major* and *The Pear*) in the late nineteen twenties and early thirties and for his bitter feud with Frank Smythe, who accompanied him on the first two climbs, regarding their respective contributions. During his climbing heyday between the Wars he was firmly of the establishment. In London, his natural habitat was the Royal Society, the Athenaeum and Alpine Club and he counted the reactionary E.L. Strutt (President of the A.C. and editor of the *Alpine Journal*) amongst his best friends. Following his retirement from the Chair of Physiology at Cardiff in 1947, he moved into a large, single room above his laboratory in the tower of the Institute of Physiology. The room overlooked the Bristol Channel and was filled with 'stacks of books, periodicals and papers, some of them physiological, most of them Alpine. Behind the stacks his camp bed and his belongings were invisible, and he himself (for he was of short stature) hardly to be seen until a visitor was close upon him.'[2] Each morning, dressed in an old but expensive three-piece suit and wearing a homburg hat, he would walk to a coffee-stall under the old railway bridge 100 yards away and breakfast with the labourers. In the same year he acquired a converted life-boat and took up cruising as well as continuing to climb in the Alps and Scotland. He was frequently absent from Cardiff and often incommunicado, his mail piling up at the Marine Hotel, Mallaig, and he claimed to be of 'No Fixed Abode', to the disbelief of H.M. Inspector of Taxes. What follows is an account of his vagabond years.

After ten years' absence, Graham Brown, aged 66, returned to the Alps in 1948. He had volunteered to participate in the inaugural, post-war Alpine Club meet to introduce a new generation of climbers to the Alps. Following a fortnight's poor weather in Kleine Scheidegg, he, Peter Lloyd, with whom he had been to Nanda Devi in 1936, and a promising novice, Neil Hanson, made their way to Courmayeur with ambitions to climb a route on the Brenva face. Walking along Val Veni, stripped to the

---

1 G. Basterfield, 'The Annual Me(a)lee', *Gritstone Journal*, 2/3 (1925–6), 5.

2 C. Evans, *Dictionary of National Biography 1961–70* (Oxford: University Press, 1981) 151–2.

Graham Brown in Glen Coe.

Used with the permission of the National Library of Scotland.

waist in the heat, Graham Brown appeared 'immensely enthusiastic',[3] revelling in his knowledge of the region and his rediscovery of it. Uncertain conditions dissuaded them from an attempt on Mont Blanc and instead they set out to climb the Aiguille Blanche de Peuterey. But after heavy snowfall overnight, they decided to retreat from the bivouac hut at the Brèche des Dames Anglaises. It started to snow again. Their route lay down a couloir which was swept by powder-snow avalanches. Progress was insecure and painfully slow. It took eight hours to descend the 1000ft to the Frêney glacier which they groped their way across in fading light. They bivouacked huddled around a candle which soon sputtered out and shivered their way through the night. The next day, they struggled to find a way up to the Col de l'Innominata; thick snow obscured the route and made climbing the rotten rocks even more precarious. They reached the col in the late afternoon and fought their way through waist-deep snow and a blizzard, down to the Gamba hut. The retreat had taken 36 hours.

[3] N. Hanson, 'Courmayeur 1948', *Alpine Journal*, 58 (1949), 26–36.

Years later Lloyd paid tribute to Graham Brown's indefatigability on this expedition, saying that he was 'a great companion and game to the end'.[4]

At Whitsun 1949, Graham Brown found himself the sole representative at a joint meet of the S.M.C. and Alpine Club, based at the Kings House Hotel. In search of climbing companions he appeared at the door of Lagangarbh which was occupied by Gordon Parish and Hamish Nicol. Parish, recently qualified in medicine and a founder-member of the Edinburgh University Mountaineering Club (E.U.M.C.), was serving in the R.A.F. and became the meets' secretary of the R.A.F. Mountaineering Association (R.A.F.M.A.). Parish and Graham Brown climbed together on Buchaille Etive Mor. Both men were out of training and Graham Brown expressed his frustration with his lack of form in 'luxuriant expletives'.[5] Their chance meeting led to friendship and Graham Brown's introduction to the E.U.M.C. and the R.A.F.M.A. whose members would provide him with climbing and sailing companions for the next few years.

Graham Brown began to attend E.U.M.C. meets regularly and developed an enthusiasm for his native mountains which were largely unknown to him. He travelled from Cardiff by train and bus for he never learned to drive. On one occasion he rode pillion on a motor-bike from Edinburgh to North Wales. He enjoyed the unruly atmosphere of the meets, campfires, singing and playing poker, although he was less comfortable when women were in the party. His company was actively sought by successive generations of students who held him in warm affection. (He was elected Hon. President of the club in 1951). He climbed to V. Diff./Severe standard, usually as second on the rope. In wet conditions he favoured wearing baggy shorts; a woolly balaclava was his trade-mark head-gear and he was inseparable from his pipe. He received numerous invitations from other climbing clubs to lecture on his exploits which he seemingly never refused, although sometimes his acceptance was conditional on being taken for a day's climbing.

In 1952, aged 70, he joined a university meet for what was to prove his last visit to the Alps. In stark contrast to his pre-War routine of dinner and billiards at the Athenaeum before boarding the boat-train, he spent the night on a bench in St James's Park and had an early breakfast at a Lyon's Corner House. He fared little better in Switzerland as the plans for accommodation were based on the youthful premise 'that sleeping out will not prove too uncomfortable. If it rains we can all crowd into Arthur's tent.'[6] Graham Brown climbed the Pigne d'Arolla and the Dent Blanche. Both routes resulted in long days. Going slowly and, at the end of the day, alone, he was forced to sleep out in fields in just his clothes. On the 25

---

[4] P. Lloyd Thomas, *Graham Brown 1882–1965* (Edinburgh: National Library of Scotland, 1982), 3–5.

[5] G. Parish, Conversation with Author 2/4/14.

[6] D. Mill, Letter to TGB 2/7/52; N.L.S. Acc 4338/11 (3).

July he made his first and only ascent of the Matterhorn, with a guide via the Hörnli ridge, in a very respectable time. This was his last climb in the European Alps, for although he made his way to Courmayeur, where he stayed with Una Cameron[7], rolling out his sleeping-bag in her garden, his extraordinarily ambitious plan to climb Mont Blanc via the frontier ridge of Mont Maudit and descend the *Route Major* was thwarted by bad weather.

Graham Brown also attended R.A.F.M.A. meets regularly, climbing with Gordon Parish, Johnnie Lees[8] and Mike Holton[9], all of whom played important roles in the development of the R.A.F. Mountain Rescue Service. At the beginning of 1951 Graham Brown was elected Hon. Vice-President of the association and six months later, he was dining Air Chief Marshal the Hon. Sir Ralph Cochrane[10] at the Athenaeum and offering his views on the future of the Mountain Rescue Service. He advocated that the R.A.F. should encourage young doctors into the service and identify recruits with mountaineering experience to be posted to the teams. Cochrane responded: 'We should more than welcome your activities as a Recruiting Sergeant throughout all your many contacts with Mountaineering Clubs.'[11] Graham Brown used this influence to the benefit of his young friends called up for National Service who soon learned that a word with 'Graham' could result in a more congenial posting.

While he was courting the R.A.F. top brass Graham Brown was falling out with the Alpine Club Committee over his editorship of the Journal and was eventually sacked under the pretext that his itinerant life-style made it impossible to communicate efficiently with him. In fact he was ousted as a consequence of an old-fashioned Club row, for he had upset Geoffrey Winthrop Young and his friends. But Graham Brown still enjoyed some influence within the Club and he proposed some of his young companions for consideration as members of the 1953 expedition to Everest. Lt. Col. H.W. Tobin, ex-Indian Army and a member of the Joint Himalayan Committee, wrote: 'Will you please tell me the names of the young climbers in Scotland that you would like to be given a chance' and, ignorant of the contemporary climbing scene, added,

---

[7] Una Cameron (1904–1987) climbed the *Sentinelle Rouge* and *Route Major* in 1935 and 1938, respectively, and was the first British climber to repeat these routes apart from Graham Brown who made the second ascent of *Route Major* in 1933.

[8] JR Lees (1927–2002). For a number of years he led the Mountain Rescue team based at R.A.F. Valley, Anglesey. In 1958 he received the George Medal for his part in a rescue on *Amphitheatre Buttress*.

[9] M Holton (1927–2006). Compiled the first R.A.F. Mountain Rescue manual.

[10] Sir Ralph Cochrane (1895–1977). Vice-chief of the Air Staff. During the war he commanded No 5. Group, Bomber Command, which included 617 squadron responsible for the Dambusters raid.

[11] R. Cochrane, Letter to TGB 21/5/51; N.L.S. Acc 4338/10 (2).

absurdly: 'Craig Dhu was one if I remember right.'[12] Although none of his Scottish nominees were selected, Charles Evans, who Graham Brown befriended after a fatal accident to Evans' partner on the Brouillard ridge in 1949, reached the south summit of Everest and wrote from Darjeeling to thank Graham Brown 'for starting the process that put me on this last expedition.'[13]

In 1947 Graham Brown acquired the converted life-boat, 'Marion of Lorne'. This was a joint venture with his old friend, Roy Stewart, with whom he had served in the Royal Army Medical Corps during the First World War, first at the shell-shock hospital, at Maghull, near Liverpool, and then for two and half years with the British Salonika Force in Macedonia. Stewart now lived at Taynuilt on the bank of Loch Etive where the boat was kept. From the start she was a source of trouble and expense. On her trial run she required pumping–out for half an hour and a further hour was needed to start the engine. Rotten timbers were discovered and it took over eighteen months to render her seaworthy, only for her to be damaged irreparably at her mooring in October 1950. Nevertheless, for two summers she provided Graham Brown and Parish with a base from which to explore Beinn Trilleachan. They noted the extensive granite slabs and recognised their potential and difficulty, but were first drawn to investigate the numerous gullies seaming the east flank of the mountain. They prospected a huge, twin-gully which they named Golden Eagle Chasm. A rocky rib between the easy left fork and the overhanging cleft of the right fork gave them some good climbing; one pitch necessitated proceeding à cheval along a knife-edged arête. The following summer they repeated the route with Lees and Dan Stewart, from the E.U.M.C., climbing a short steep wall which they had avoided the year before. Lees recalled: 'Dan, in vibrams, managed it nicely, and I soon followed, having to scratch one hold so that I could see it when I was five feet above it with my eyes, and get the edge of a tryke on it. Gordon didn't have much trouble either – it's Severe – but Graham needed a rather tight rope, and then came off it! He uses clinkers and couldn't get the right foot on at all, apart from having a reach roughly a foot shorter than us!'[14] Their return across the loch turned into a struggle with the temperamental 'Marion'. A mile from the anchorage, the engine cut out and the wind and tide proceeded to take them in the wrong direction. Lees tried unsuccessfully to restart the engine and ruefully observed: 'surprisingly enough Graham knows nothing whatsoever about engines.'[15] Stewart, Parish and Lees, who had trains to catch and a three-mile walk to the station, rowed ashore, abandoning Graham Brown to a rescue by a local farmer with a motor-launch.

[12] H. Tobin, Letter to TGB 25/9/52 N.L.S. Acc 4338/11 (3).

[13] C. Evans, Letter to TGB 19/8/53; N.L.S. Acc 4338/12 (2).

[14] J. Lees, Papers of Johnnie Lees; Mountain Heritage Trust GB 3075 JRL.

[15] Ibid.

Undeterred, Brown bought a replacement for 'Marion' which proved no less a liability. Originally the life-boat 'Cyril & Lilian Bishop' which had been used in the evacuation from Dunkirk, Brown had her converted and re-named her 'Thekla' in memory of a yacht of the same name, owned by his father. In July 1951, Graham Brown, with a crew of three, set out to sail her up the east coast from Wallasea, in Essex, to Edinburgh. On the second day out they ran into rough seas and took on water which failed to drain from the deck and also poured in around the centreboard despite packing with towels. The pump seized and they baled with buckets, eventually reaching safety in Yarmouth. Graham Brown took her in for repairs. The vendors of the boat who had also carried out the modifications pursued Graham Brown in court for unpaid bills but he countered that the conversion had been shoddy. The judgement went in his favour. Two years later, whilst anchored at Mallaig, 'Thekla' sprang a leak and almost sank and it was not until 1957 that Graham Brown embarked on major cruises around the west and north coast of Scotland and, in 1959, a three month round-trip to Tromsø, beyond the Arctic Circle. His crews comprised mainly Edinburgh University students. Given that some of them joined him more than once, it seems he was an amenable and generous skipper. His last cruise was probably in 1961. Robin Campbell poignantly recalls taking Graham Brown to view his boat a few years later and for the last time. 'He stared at it from the shore for a minute or so and turned away, unable to get aboard.'[16]

In 1961 Graham Brown moved from Cardiff back to Edinburgh, where he had purchased a Georgian flat in the West End of the city, less than a quarter of a mile from his birth-place. He occupied the ground floor in eccentric squalor and let the basement free-of-charge to members of the E.U.M.C. who have provided a vivid picture of Graham Brown reading and writing, seated in an over-sized armchair placed in front of an electric fire and surrounded by used matches, dottle and empty tins of tobacco, for he smoked almost continuously. By this time Graham Brown had given up climbing but he joined members of the club at their weekly meeting in an upstairs bar where he sipped a half-pint of beer and occasionally removed his pipe to contribute to the conversation. On his death in 1965, he bequeathed the flat to the university to provide accommodation for student members of the EUMC. The flat was sold in the 1990s but the university provided the club with a flat in Nicholson Street which still bears his name.

Between the Wars Graham Brown had gained a reputation amongst some of his colleagues at Cardiff and members of the Alpine Club for being a difficult and cantankerous man, wanting in tact and conciliation. He certainly pursued his feud with Smythe, obsessively. He was naturally reserved but could be a good companion and was capable of friendship.

[16] R. Campbell, Thomas Graham Brown 1882–1965 (Edinburgh: National Library of Scotland, 1982), 7–8.

Brown at sea.

Photo: National Library of Scotland.

However he could be prickly and he did not hesitate to break with friends if he perceived a slight. But after the War these traits were tempered by warmth and generosity and his reserve fell away. One tyro whom Graham Brown introduced to the Alps in 1950, recalls fondly 'the amount of time he spent in tutoring an alpine novice with kindness, wit and great good humour.'[17] While this change may have been partly the result of mellowing with age, the writing and publication, in 1944, of his book, Brenva, may have served as a catharsis. At last he could be assured that his version of the discovery and ascent of the climbs on the Brenva face would be appreciated and after Smythe's premature death in 1949, unchallenged. His reputation was secure.

Acknowledgements:
I wish to thank Gordon Parish, Bob Pettigrew and Robin Campbell for sharing their recollections with me and for commenting on the article. I am grateful to the National Library of Scotland and the Mountain Heritage Trust for permission to reproduce quotations from unpublished material in their possession.

[17] R. Pettigrew, Letter to Author 12/2/15.

ONE WEEK IN THE WEST

By Rob Archbold

A HEAVY SQUALL lashed more rain onto the far side of the tent. Looking across, in the half-light of a summer's night, I could see a shadowy figure crouched on hands and knees, staring in disbelief as a trickle of water flowed gently across the groundsheet. Little did we know that we would see the ingress of water on a somewhat larger scale before the end of our holiday.

My travel agent, Geoff Cohen, had tempted me with a Two-Centre Highland and Island Getaway Break, based in Torridon and Lewis. I was in charge of transport while Geoff was taking care of accommodation, although there seemed to be a curious mismatch between the size of the flysheet and the tent. The previous morning had seen us taking the long walk round to Coire Mhic Fhearchair, but after a bright start the sky had darkened ominously. As we neared the lochan, we were caught in a spell of heavy and persistent rain that seemed to rule out any prospect of climbing on the wonderful quartzite of the Far East Wall. A friendly gentleman in the car-park had recommended *Thin Man's Ridge* to us, mentioning that his son had taken part in the first ascent, so we started to traverse east, not fully realising just how far away it was. More rain, slippery rocks and vegetation forced a further change of plan: we would simply climb to the top of Ruadh-stac Mòr via a gully in its northern spur. This proved to be heavy going, and I made a mental note for the future to avoid pathless hillwalking with a bagful of runners on my back. But by the time we had reached the summit, the last of the rain clouds had disappeared and we were rewarded with fine views in the northerly directions.

As there was now no hurry, we lazed around for a while before heading south towards the main ridge, and as we approached the col, we looked across at the Far East Wall. Located on the clean grey pillar at the right-hand end was the attractive line of *Groovin' High*, which I'd climbed with Johnny Ingram and Greg Strange as a birthday treat almost a year previously. Further left was the line of *Sundance* which Geoff and I had climbed back in May, on the same day that Greg and Johnny had climbed *Sting*. We reminisced about the amazing holds, often invisible from below, that seemed to keep turning up on the quartzite; but still the penny didn't drop. Then a shaft of afternoon sunshine briefly lit the face and it suddenly dawned on us that maybe, just maybe, the cliff was drier than we'd thought.

It was past three o'clock by the time we stood under the damp slit cave in the middle of the grey pillar. Four hours and one more shower later, we stood at the top of *Birth of the Cool*, a natural twin to *Groovin' High* and subsequently to serve as the entry to the amazing overhang of *Ling*

Dynasty. The highlight was Geoff's bold lead of the short impending pitch below the bifurcation: some sustained jamming in the crack followed by determined jug-hauling on the wall above and right.

As the steamer pulled away from the quayside in Ullapool, I caught a glimpse of my rusty white sports-van looking a little forlorn at being abandoned on the mainland. We glided past the Summer Isles, enjoying fine views of Ben More Coigach and Beinn Ghobhlach. Our good intentions for taking the morning ferry had evaporated in a late start, followed by lunchtime beverages in Gairloch and an invigorating stroll along a glorious sandy beach.

It was almost nine o'clock in the evening by the time we had arrived in Stornoway and loaded ourselves onto the heavy-framed bikes. Greg Strange, who was away in the Pamirs as part of the Scottish contingent on the 1974 International Meet, had kindly lent me his bike for Geoff to use. My own steed was an ancient Hercules New Yorker, sporting a Sturmey-Archer 3-speed gear. Unfortunately, the middle gear kept slipping and so I struggled along in low gear while Geoff appeared to pedal effortlessly into the distance. I harboured dark thoughts: why hadn't I switched the bikes before Geoff had ever seen them?

The landscape had a striking simplicity, gently undulating and frequently interspersed with crofts and stacks of drying peat. We noticed several dry stream-beds and began to worry about finding a suitable campsite. After about ten miles, we turned left near Garynahine and in a few minutes crossed a shallow burn that was running towards the sea loch. As dusk fell, we pushed the bikes inland for about a hundred yards and found a perfect spot for the tent, right at the water's edge. But no sooner had we flung down the bikes and started to unpack the tent than three sinister figures in poncho capes and hats appeared from nowhere and quickly surrounded us. A frisson of anxiety rippled between us. Our friend Malcolm Nicolson of Stornoway had given us a lot of information about the island – could he have forgotten to tell us about the Lewis Mafiosi? After they'd been rifling through our gear for a couple of minutes, we eventually realised that they were water bailiffs, who thought they'd caught a couple of poachers red-handed. But as the nuts and karabiners hit the grass, they grudgingly came to accept that we really weren't planning to net the river after all. 'So okay to camp here then?' They laughed at our naivety and explained that it was out of the question – the boss, who was staking out another nearby beat, would never allow it. They became a bit more chatty; apparently, although it was hard to imagine during a drought, these west coast burns had some of the finest salmon beats in Scotland. Our new friends escorted us back to the road and we cycled on for a mile or so until we eventually found a scruffy pitch at the edge of a lay-by.

Next morning we cached the bikes near the head of Little Loch Roag. Geoff seemed anxious about the paucity of our rations for the next few

Creag Dhubh Dhibadail, Lewis *Photo: R.Archbold*

days and so we flagged down a passing motorist who told us that there might be a travelling shop back at the junction for Great Bernera. I hitched a lift back, only to find that the shop had indeed travelled. Another lift took me to Callanish, where I bought a few items in the village store before hitching back to Geoff. There was very little traffic, which maybe explains why the locals were so generous in stopping for strangers.

We trudged southwest at first, then west around the southern flanks of Beinn Mheadhonach. We took off our boots to wade the river in the shallow glen containing Lochan Lunadale and then climbed with mounting anticipation to the flat ridge between Mula Chaolartan and Cleite Fhidigidh for our first view of Creag Dhubh Dhibadail and the loch below it. The view was even more spectacular than the inspiring photograph that we'd studied in MacInnes's 1971 Constable guide. The big fault-lines of *Via Valtos* and *Solitude* were immediately apparent and between them lay the huge unclimbed wall. At one point a tongue of slabs rose up to the foot of the wall and way above it there was an obvious ramp leading diagonally right to the top of the crag. Our hope was to breach the wall by somehow linking these two features.

The weather held fair for the following morning. I led an easy pitch on the right-hand side of the tongue and then Geoff climbed a tricky groove where the slab steepened as it met the wall. He exited onto easier slabs and then had to traverse some way left to get a decent belay.

Having collected the gear and waited for a light shower to clear, I moved back into the middle of the wall and began to weave my way up as the holds dictated. When the wall began to impend, the only feasible option seemed to be an open groove running up on the left. It looked rather daunting, but on closer inspection revealed just enough in the way of holds and protection to allow steady progress, with an element of bridging keeping me more or less in balance. Nevertheless, I was more than happy when I eventually saw the chance to step back right and reach a perfect stance and belay. Geoff climbed a fine corner above on perfect black rock and continued up to another good belay.

We were making good progress, but knew that we were still a long way from the start of the ramp. The steep slabs above Geoff contained a shallow inset groove facing right. I climbed up on the right-hand side of this until it merged back into the steepening face and the holds gave out. It looked possible to traverse right to the profile some thirty feet away but what would lie beyond? I decided to look left instead. I climbed back down to the start of the groove and then all the way up on the left-hand side. Again, the holds seemed to peter out, or was it just the increasing angle of disinclination?

To save time, I used a nut in the groove to swing across to my previous high-point on the right and then I reluctantly started to traverse. I was heading off the line and there was no guarantee that things would improve beyond the profile. But after a short way, I realised that there might be another option. A thin crack headed straight up for a few feet before terminating in the bulging wall above. At this point a horizontal overhanging fold led back left. I fixed a runner in the crack and started to feel for underclings in the fold, peering down for any small footholds on the wall below. Teetering leftwards, I was heading for a curious slender block that was wedged between the fold and the beginnings of a small ledge. After a sequence of delicate moves, I reached the block, treated it with due respect, and then found good holds on the wall above, leading up to a grassy bay.

The way directly ahead looked blank, although there appeared to be some steep possibilities up and left. However, the easiest rocks led diagonally right into a fault-line leading up to an overhanging chimney crack. At this point, a narrow ledge led right, overhung by steep rock. Geoff made a difficult hand traverse, using footholds on the wall below, until he could launch up the bulging wall above. A sequence of determined pulls soon led him up to a good ledge on the left. I traversed right along an overhung wet shelf and then climbed a slab to easier ground. The cliff was beginning to ease back a little and the ramp was finally in view. It was nine o'clock. Geoff eyed up the big corner above on the left but in view of the time we decided to stick to Plan A. He headed towards the ramp: three pleasant pitches led us to the top by half past ten. We shambled down the hillside in the gloaming and celebrated with a midnight feast beside the loch.

Next morning I felt drained by all the efforts and uncertainties of our climb. Somewhat to my surprise, Geoff readily agreed to an easier day.

A youthful Geoff Cohen at Creag Dhubh Dhibadail *Photo: R.Archbold*

We climbed to the col between Teinnasval and Tamanaisval and spent a relaxing few hours strolling around the tops, with fine views to the western seaboard and south to Harris. We felt mentally and physically refreshed, ready to get back on the cliff for another climb. Fortunately, we made a much earlier start than usual.

The first pitch of *Via Valtos* went fairly smoothly. The final section of the crack appeared to overhang alarmingly, but a step rightwards onto the edge of the wall revealed some good holds. I made a few steep pulls and a quick stride back left before the bulging wall above could topple me off.

The second pitch was a tour de force by Geoff. He worked his way up the left wall and then climbed the overhanging section in fine style, eliminating four pegs for aid in one fell swoop. Early in the next pitch, I had to move up left into the main crack-line. There seemed to be two equally awkward ways to try it – a standard recipe for dithering. Then the first drops of rain arrived and I shot up like a scalded cat, running out the whole rope as fast as I could. By the time Geoff arrived the rain had really set in, but fortunately we were over the main difficulties. He quickly led the final pitch which was rapidly turning into a gurgling burn. We felt very lucky to have been able to repeat such a fine climb. If we had started much later, we would almost certainly have ended up either abseiling off or using a lot of 'initiative'.

The first few hours in the tent were pleasant enough, lolling about with brews, grub and chat. The rain grew even heavier and the first tiny rivulets appeared in the tent. By seven o'clock our sleeping bags were getting seriously wet and we realised that our position was rapidly becoming untenable. The whole hillside was awash and water was running through the tent; we would have to move fast to walk out in daylight. We packed as much as possible while still inside and then burst out to strike the tent and head back east. The river in the shallow glen had burst its banks and was now as wide as a football pitch – we kept our boots on and ploughed ahead right up to our knees.

Back at the road, we were lucky to find some shelter in an abandoned house. We made a brew and surveyed our sorry state. I had the bright idea of putting my cagoule and over-trousers back on before getting into my sodden pit. Equally futile was Geoff's attempt to dry his bag over the primus stove. He soon gave up and eventually wrapped himself in an old curtain. We dozed fitfully and rose at the first hint of dawn. By four o'clock in the morning we were on our way, pedalling furiously to try to get warm. We took a side trip to Callanish to see the amazing standing stones – hours ahead of the regular tourists. The sun came out and we commandeered most of the foredeck of the ferry, festooning every spare bench with our soaking gear. We basked in the warmth and gazed at the wonderful views of Suilven, Stac Pollaidh and the other mainland peaks. Our island adventure was almost over.

Postscript: I am grateful to Geoff for generous access to his diaries and photographs, and for many more good days on the hill. Regarding the hill names in Lewis, I have used those that we found in the map and guidebook at the time; more recent maps and books contain a variety of different spellings. After some editorial shenanigans, our new climb at Dhibadail was eventually named as *Joplin's Wall*. It fell into the latter stages of the Rowe-Tiso Moratorium and the *SMCJ* published only a very brief description. Some years later, it became apparent that *Panting Dog Climb* had repeated several sections of the route before finishing up the impressive corner system to the left of the ramp. We were pleased to find ourselves in such good company, and in the words of Jock Nimlin '...it was good to know that the joys of a first ascent should be shared by a larger number of people than might have been.'

A curious set of coincidences occurred one evening in February 2015 when I was writing part of this article. Taking a break, I noticed a picture of Robin Campbell in the *Press and Journal*, with a glowing citation for his Mountain Culture Award. Robin, of course, was Editor of the *SMCJ* in the early 1970s. A few minutes later I heard the unmistakable raw tones of Janis Joplin soaring high above an advert on STV: 'Take it, take another little piece of my heart...'

UP AND DOON THE WATTER

By Phil Gribbon

'TWO HOURS FOR YOU to get off our land. Get your stuff to the pier.'

We were being confronted by the guardian gatekeeper of the big house on the shore. He was a stocky tough brook-no-nonsense ex-army man clad in camouflaged clothing and he was laying down the law in no uncertain fashion. His two sidekicks leaned over their Landrover bonnet to give further support if need be to the boss man.

We tried some plaintive objections and then some gentle charm but to no avail: our bad-cop good-cop technique was a failure. These locals were uncommunicative well-trained automatons imbued with the ethos of their calling. Inwardly we fumed but knew the game was up, and started to make faltering gestures to gather our gear together. Light drizzle began to drift along the coast and began to soak into our flattened tents which they intentionally had collapsed on the ground.

We were the unwitting victims of a hard line approach being taken with any unwanted intruders. This seemed out of kilter with our expectation of some cooperation with the estate owner since after all we were a volunteer party that had just travelled from afar to ensure that his river footbridge was secure and safe. Surely this had all been arranged beforehand by our meticulous organiser. We began to wonder a teeny weeny bit if there had been some breakdown in communication.

Our link with the bridge went back to the time when we had become involved with a somewhat controversial repair on this old right of way bridge.[1] This had been done by Dave Meldrum and myself with much assistance from assorted professionals and willing helpers as a memorial project for two climbing friends who had died in a winter gully accident in Glen Coe. Recently word had filtered out that some minor repairs were needed and we had answered the call.

Let's look at the events leading up to this moment of our eviction. Very early a boat had picked us up and taken us up to the loch head. We had landed at the pier and had walked on until we found a level space to pitch our tents between the track and the sea. There we sorted out our bits and pieces; we were overwhelmed with a paraphernalia of possibly useful items, like wires and cutters, shackles and spanners, nails and hammers, bolts and nuts. Then, having made sure that we had packed our lunch pieces, we set off towards the bridge up the river.

When we veered too close to the hideaway of the landowner it was uncharacteristically proposed that we should not disturb him so we trotted off into the interminably tussocky bogland and trudged onwards until we were out of sight of the big house.

---

[1] For the original repair to the bridge see 'A Bridge for Troubled Waters' by Philip Gribbon, *SMCJ*, 32/173 (1982), 251–4. Ed.

When we reached the bridge we were surprised to find that there was little needing to be done. Dave and I began to ponder why we had been brought all this way for such trivial activity. All very strange, but perhaps there was more to this than met the eye. Don't ask any questions, boys; just do your job and keep mum.

Okay, let's forget it and go to work. We hauled tight the side stays that kept the bridge neatly aligned on the two support piers. Without much taxing of our brain power we concluded that there was a design flaw in the suspended structure because when the surrounding flat ground flooded and the river rose too high the planks got underwater and dragged the whole edifice sideways downstream and so loosened the stay wires. We replaced a few shackles, rearranged the walkway planks in a more tidy and symmetrical fashion, and in an exercise of unexpected strength hoisted the two main suspension hawsers back into their wooden beds.

What next? Let's take a walk upstream. How about visiting the big pool where, to our amazement in those days gone by, a majestic piscatorial object had erupted from the cool clear water to smack down on the rough inhospitable bedrock? Such an unexpected miracle was hard to believe, was it not?

There was a solitary figure perched at the pool edge and he was waving his long slender rod back and forth. What happened next was not any of our doing. We don't possess magical bewitching powers, but suddenly the fisherman was inflicted with frenetic tremors and, skittering over the rocks, he began to haul back on his curving rod.

He had hooked one of those fishy things but it was obvious he had not much idea about what to do next. After all most anglers only like indulging in the sensation of flipping a looping length of line artistically backwards and forward through the air. They must reckon the possibility of catching a poor fish is infinitesimally small.

We had not been noticed. He began to bawl for moral support but not being servants of the estate we hung back and admired his pantomime with respectful appreciation. An answering shout came from upstream and a sort-of-gillie man began to run down the far bank. He splashed across the river without stumbling and arrived to instruct the animated fisherman. With slow stealth and much careful coaxing the exhausted game fish at last was guided to within netting distance and then scooped heavenward in passionate exultation.

Here we were witnessing the laird's nephew or some such privileged guest catching his first salmon. This was the moment for us to creep forward and offer our congratulations while the bewildered young man was beside himself with joy and delight. We shook his hand, murmured appropriate words, touched our forelocks and backed off gracefully.

It was when we reached the campsite at the shore that we discovered that some vandals had made a rubbish heap of our overnight home, and it was not long before they returned in their vehicle and read the riot act.

We were soon herded onto the boat that they had to provide to get rid of us and chugged back doon the watter to a more friendly anchorage.

Once we had hauled our gear on shore we began to search in the damp gathering gloom for a place to pitch the tents. Luckily the slope of the hillside relented close to some trees and although engulfed in midge clouds we rapidly erected the tents and scampered inside to escape the tormenting insects. In joyful relief the primus was lit, a meal put on, the wine opened, and contentedly we ate until replete and lay listening to the rain pattering on the tent roof.

Music then began to waft up from the hostelry down by the shore. Loud shouting too, and in spite of the rain it seemed that some excessively enthusiastic revels had begun with loud words being bandied back and forth. What was the cause of those yells, bangs and thumps? It was all very peculiar and not being in the mood to investigate we snuggled down into our sleeping bags and gave up for the day.

We woke on a calm still morning, the midges had gone, and the sun was slanting across the water and sharpening up the rocky outcrops on the hills across the loch. Little wavelets whispered on the shingle beach, all was peace and quiet in the village.

We ambled off to thank the local who organised the boat that had taken us up the loch. He looked unslept and slightly haggard, his face drawn and listless, but he had good reason after his night before. But this was not a question of over indulgence but rather a long sleepless night guarding the home hearths from alien marauders. What we had heard but ignored had never been a high spirited cheerful ceilidh but rather a bad tempered brawl as the locals clashed with some outsiders. We had been in such deep sleep that we knew nothing about the eventual late arrival of the lawman to abruptly terminate their little local difficulty.

Now, this bright morning it was time to do something pleasant and satisfying.

What about the nice wee Corbett to take in behind the village?

Just the thing for a restful Sabbath day.

'AVALANCHES? NAE LADDIE, NAE IN SCOTLAND'

By John Hay

Avalanche debris in Coire Buidhe, 14 March 2015.

SUCH WAS THE PERCEIVED WISDOM of our elders in my young days. I had read of the loss of Gaick[1], but that was a quirk of the Fates. After all, for a man as hated as the Black Officer John MacPherson of Ballochroan, a notorious recruiting officer who chose to go a-hunting the wild deer and stay in a mountain bothy on the first day of the New Year in 1800, he got what was coming to him. This was a great avalanche that swept away the bothy and put an end to his sport and to the lives of MacPherson and his three companions sleeping inside. Moral no. I: Be careful where you choose to sleep after Hogmanay. Moral no. II: success in a-hunting the wild deer from a mountain bothy may be more in the hands of the Fates than the gun in your hands.

Forward 150 years. I had listened in awe to tales of my elder climbing companions being shot out of Douglas Gibson Gully like a champagne cork not in a cloud of delectable fizz but shrouded in that other white stuff

[1] 'Gaick', *SMCJ*, 14/82 (1917), p181.

peeling off the headwall. This was in the pre-Patey era when Douglas Gibson was classed 'Unjustifiable'. Moral no. III: attempting the 'unjustifiable' may be tempting the fates.

I even suffered the same result in a youthful venture into Raeburn's Gully. Fortunately the Fates were kind to a foolhardy youngster on his own: other than a bruised ego and a lot of snow down the back of my neck I suffered no ill effects and I learned a lesson – avalanches do occur in Scotland. Moral no. IV: don't always believe everything told to you by auld mannies.

Forward some six decades or so to a time when everyone knows we do have our avalanches in Scotland and we even have an official avalanche service. I was caught unawares by an avalanche. Again good fortune was with me, I was above it – in a helicopter counting deer – and not beneath it. The helicopter jaunt was courtesy of Forest Enterprise. I was in the back seat not really counting deer but enjoying the ride on a beautiful spring day when I suddenly saw this immense river of ice. Up to then I don't think anyone had seen it. It was frighteningly impressive: a great white tongue of ice snaking down towards the Loch. It went much further down the corrie than I would have thought possible, so next day I went up to photograph it.

The winter of 2014–15 had been especially wet in the west and on the higher ground there had been great accumulations of snow on the east-facing slopes. In Coire Buidhe, on the west side of Coire Domhain above Loch Mullardoch, the build-up of snow had cracked into tottering seracs before crashing down what in summer is a moderate grass and heather slope. I estimated that it began at the corrie lip at 2450ft (750m) and finished well beneath the snowline at 1300ft (400m) – a vertical drop of 1150ft (350m). The channel gouged out by the ice and rock was 20ft (6m) deep in places. Even at its snout some of the ice blocks were still the size of a car and as hard as good Cairngorm granite. Many other east-facing slopes in the area have suffered a similar fate. Moral no. V: even on fairly innocuous slopes dangerous avalanches do occur in Scotland.

Stalking note: for some reason I cannot fully explain, deer in summer love an old avalanche slope like this – but it is damned hard work to drag a culled carcase through the debris. Volunteers wecome.

Top: *More avalache debris in Coire Buidhe.*

Bottom: *Looking east along Loch Mullardoch with part of the 'great white tongue of ice' in the foreground. It reached within 900m of the Loch.*

Photos: John Hay.

AN RIABHACHAN

By Andy Nisbet

THE CRAGS ON An Riabhachan had intrigued me for many years. An Riabhachan is one of Scotland's most remote Munros, set between Lochs Mullardoch and Monar, and third going west in a group which often used to be climbed by boat up Loch Mullardoch, although I think the service has now stopped. It was only recently that I realised, thanks to John Mackenzie, that it was easier to approach by the private road up Glen Strathfarrar, and that the tarmac road went much further than I used to think.

There are some advantages of Munro bagging for climbers. When writing Northern Highlands Central, I had to include two routes at opposite ends of Creagan Toll an Lochain, a crag more than 1km long at the east end of An Riabhachan. My ignorance of the crag was obvious when I was trying to work out map references, so I decided I ought to pay it a visit, with the bonus of seeking out potential winter routes. But there were always nearer places to go, so it was some ten years before I made it. And the push was that I needed to bag the Munros, so why not walk up the corrie, look at the crag and then traverse the ridge, although it did mean going out to An Socach and back, so climbing An Riabhachan twice (only counting as one!).

Getting permission to drive the 16 miles up the road was the next issue. In summer the numbers of visitors and available days are limited, but you only have to turn up fairly early and sign in. You need to sign out by 7 p.m., so checking out the crag and doing the Munros put some pressure on the timescale, although the extra adrenaline saw me down more easily than I'd anticipated. The crag was most definitely of interest, with a number of possible routes photographed. There was a large wet area at the north end, and clearly where the icefall route *Redcoats Weep* (1998) goes. But left of it was a long wet groove which was of interest. Distant photographs were all I had time for, and two deep gullies particularly caught the eye, but then I reached the far end of the cliff and a somewhat hidden section got me quite excited. This was much better than I'd seen earlier, and the existing route *Spindrift Gully* (1969) was obvious. In winter you need to phone the MCofS and book your place; you need a membership number and car registration number.

So the cliff was on my list for the winter of 2013, with the required conditions being the road clear of snow (it would never be ploughed) and walking conditions good for quite a long approach. Climbing conditions ought to be good too, but this was much more likely on a high turfy cliff. But the winter was very cold and snowy with roadside icefalls in abundance, so little incentive for a long walk-in. And my winter had to end on 31 March, as I'd chosen April Fool's Day for a hernia operation, with the winter new routes bound to be over. Of course they weren't but I did climb eight days in a row before the op in a mad rush to get as much as possible done, so much so that they kept me in an extra day to explore unexplained dehydration. And the winter kept going until the end of April, and in retrospect I could have climbed on An Riabhachan.

2014 was very snowy high up but little lower down, so the road would be fine. But I kept waiting for the magical thaw and freeze, and then finally it arrived mid March. The only snag was that *Minus One Buttress* on the Ben was in perfect nick and I'd been waiting for 30 years to do it. And there was one day, after which the winter was forecast to end. Jonathan Preston would have gone for either, and we couldn't do both, so the new routes it was and the road was booked

It was a perfect day, 12 March, cold and sunny, and the walk-in was as good as you can get. Once we reached the corrie floor, there was perfect névé for the walk to the far end and a crag which could only be in great nick, the only snag being a cornice of large but uncertain size, as the scale was hard to estimate. At least there were plenty of huge chunks down in the corrie, a sign that it would have been impossible ahead of the thaw.

We decided to go for an easier looking line which was less steep and held loads of ice. This was roughly in the centre of this section of crag and not far left of *Spindrift Gully*. It was still a bit speculative just how good conditions would be so we started soloing up to see how far we'd get without the rope. Conditions were as good as we'd hoped so the rope only went on for the cornice pitch, which was pretty steep but not scary, as we reached a point where a big chunk had fallen off (*Bazinga* 180m III). The views from the top were stunning; this was a repeating theme but with rucksacks left below, at least the temptation to eat was missing.

We hurried down to the col between An Riabhachan and Sgùrr na Lapaich in order to descend back to the crag, and try a harder line. The steepest section of crag was left of where we'd just climbed but the vertical walls were bare (and smooth) so we decided on the first turfy line right of the steep walls. An exposed turfy ramp was a bit spooky with no gear but soon led to a terrace and another groove above. We were using a 60m rope with the idea of doing 30m pitches if the difficulty justified, but otherwise long pitches. This ploy is good because there's less weight on the walk-in and you rarely can be bothered being sensible and using the rope doubled. After this long pitch, Jonathan took over the steeper groove and unknown walls ahead. Fortunately there was more protection and the ground above became increasingly icy, leading on to the upper slopes and another cornice pitch which wasn't as bad as it looked (*Gatekeeper* 150m V,5). My energy levels were dropping but it was the last day of my season, so really there was no excuse for not squeezing in a last route. An easier gully at the left end of the crag was soloed to the same break in the cornice (*Bealach Gully* 140m II).

Steve Perry on Gotcha (V,5), An Riabhachan. *Photo: A. Nisbet.*

The walk out was even easier as our confidence in conditions had grown enough for us to walk across the frozen Loch Mor.

It was my best day of the winter, and quite hard not to be openly enthusiastic as there were more routes to do. Routine descriptions in the Journal and no write-ups on the internet would have to do.

Winter 2015 arrived with plenty of anticipation but the same requirements on roads and conditions. It's called patience and is not my forte. But come a very similar date (14 March) and conditions seemed similar, except the Ben wasn't in exceptional nick. Steve Perry and I were all set to go in to An Riabhachan when Brian Davison phoned to join us. The walk-in was remarkably similar, with me last as usual, but this time the crag was even icier and the cornice smaller.

A line just right of *Gatekeeper* had been spotted last time, with an apparently short overhanging corner and a wide crack needing a bit of good fortune. But looking from below, a white ice streak went straight through the corner and the line was on. An initial wall to gain the ice turned out to be tricky but once on the ice, there was nothing but first time placement delight until Steve took a purist's line at the top and announced he was in trouble with unfrozen turf in the back of a smooth V-groove. Still, he made it to the summit ridge and I bypassed his groove (*Gotcha* 150m V,5).

Now there was no point in having Brian there without pointing him at something harder, so long as we could second it. A steeper version of Bazinga had some tempting ice and a steep groove with a huge chockstone, but light underneath it which suggested a through route. As we soloed into the initial bay of *Bazinga*, it became obvious that the chockstone was a huge perched block instantly nicknamed the death chock but that getting past it presented more risk than difficulty. Brian made short work of the overhanging chimney underneath it, passed the chock easily without touching it and continued for a full rope length up easier ice. I knew Brian wouldn't think about belaying until all the rope was out, so Steve and I moving up from the belay was inevitable. But as always the call came just as we ran out of options, and we duly followed. The ice continued to join *Bazinga* near the top.

Steve and I joked that the competitive Brian would have to do one more route than Jonathan and I had done last year, so there never was any doubt we would be doing a third route. I caused some disapproval when I insisted on going down to the sacks for something to eat, and by the time I rejoined them, Brian was already halfway up the first pitch of an ice line which started part way up *Spindrift Gully*. Again the ice was perfect and I got perhaps the best pitch of the day (*Swag* 120m IV,4). Brian didn't even ask about a fourth route and again on a high, we walked out across the loch.

Brian and Steve both had to work the next week, but conditions were so good that I decided to revisit the crag on the Monday (after a rest day).

There were lots of easier options and some maybe not so easy, around the area of crag with *Redcoats Weep*. The groove left of *Redcoats Weep* was an obvious target, as was the rib right of *Spindrift Gully* on the previous section of crag. But other than that, I was free to choose. It soon became obvious that the gullies had their difficulties banked out and would be Grade I, but still useful as descents. I set off very early just in case the temperature warmed up during the day, reached the corrie by 9 a.m. but the crag base still took another hour. The nearer I got, the more obvious it was that every groove was filled with ice, and much of it was steeper than I'd expected.

I started off with an easier groove well left of the *Redcoats Weep* area and which just about made Grade III. After descending the Grade I gully, the next ice line to its left had a steeper section and made Grade III,4. I was now warmed up for the original target, which was definitely steeper but also III,4, although it did occur to me that the *Redcoats Weep* description was rather vague and could in theory have climbed this line. Soloing on ice doesn't take very long, although it is tiring, so the end was only going to come when I, rather than daylight, conked out. After a couple more routes left of the descent, separated by another Grade I gully, there was barely energy for the rib at the other end of the crag. Apart from the 'you won't get another chance' reason. The rib turned out to be very different, quite steep but remarkably helpful, with numerous flakes in the icy grooves. As a result, I managed to climb a more direct line than I'd expected and it left me very satisfied with the day.

Satisfaction only lasts until the next morning for the obsessive and 'you won't get another chance' only applies if you don't go back, so the phone call to the MCof S followed soon after. The Wednesday was as good a day as the rest and another four routes up the remaining lines which had caught my attention, plus one done by mistake, finally cured me. The most amusing point of the day was when I came across crampon steps with a different pattern to mine and worried I'd been beaten to it, before I remembered I was wearing different crampons the last time. It's great that there are still places like this in Scotland, although of course that was the last one!

Note: Route descriptions and topos are in the New Climbs section.

NEW CLIMBS

The deadline for sending route descriptions to the new routes editor is 30 June each year.

OUTER HEBRIDES

LEWIS SEA-CLIFFS, ARD MOR MANGERSTA, Upper Tier:
Rubik 10m E1 5a *. Andy Moles, Andrey Yakunin. 9 Aug 2014.
The slab and arete just left of *Inner Demons*. The gear is dubious in the upper half.

Ruble 10m E2 5a *. Andy Moles, Andrey Yakunin. 9 Aug 2014.
The slanting groove and slab just left of *Rubik*. Nice climbing but very little protection and some snappy holds.

Lady Mariposa 10m HVS 5a *. Andy Moles, Andrey & Anastasia Yakunin. 9 Aug 2014.
The next slanting groove left of *Ruble*.

ARD FEINIS:
Spicy Wall 10m E7 6c *. Dave MacLeod, Natalie Berry. May 2014.
At the right end of the crag is a smooth undercut wall. Move up underneath the overhang on large jugs to arrange protection on the right. Pull through the overhang leftwards with difficulty to a break (crucial cam slot on the left). Press on directly up the centre of the smooth wall with further tricky climbing to eventually gain good holds just below the top in the diagonal finishing crack of *Top Tackle Tips*.

DALBEG:
The headland bounding the north side of Black Geo contains a sea cave split by a striking vertical cracked groove system. Approach by abseiling down a slab to its base.

Wads Up There? 40m E5 6a **. Donie O'Sullivan, Crispin Waddy. Jun 2014.
Gain the line by a short bouldery traverse from the left. Go up to the roof. Move left to gain a juggy flake, then strenously back right above the roof. Finish direct. Steep and strenuous. Best left till the afternoon to dry out.

NORTH HARRIS, Creag Mo:
Stellar Crack 40m E3 5c **. Dave MacLeod, Calum Muskett. Apr 2014.
An excellent climb up the crack system at the right-hand end of the main wall, just right of an impressive 40m blank wall. Good protection and strenuous climbing with a worrying loose block near the top that can be delicately avoided, or maybe trundled by the next second.

Drive Station 40m E5 6a **. Calum Muskett, Dave MacLeod. Apr 2014.
An exciting and exposed line gaining a crack in the left side of the blank wall. Start right of the roof system below the crack-line in the wall above. Move left

into a small curving groove and climb this until it is possible to move rightwards with difficulty to the thin crack. Follow this to easier ground just below the top.

Last Resort 90m E5 **. Calum Muskett, Dave MacLeod. Apr 2014.
Another excellent route taking the big brown slab on the left side of the amphitheatre. Start below a grossly overhanging flake system in the left wall of the amphitheatre. Pull up on steep jugs and swing immediately left and up to gain a system of exciting steep flakes. Follow these to a good belay ledge at the top of the flake (40m 5c). Climb the 40m brown slab above, following left-trending lines of weakness with spaced protection to eventually pull over onto an easy finishing slab at the top (50m 6a). An intricate pitch on great rock.

Impact 85m HVS 4c. David Macmorris, Kevin Woods. 26 Jul 2014.
On the far right-hand side of Creag Mo. Start at foot of the buttress just right of some stepped overhangs. Take a grey wall direct up cracks and blocks to a grassy ledge (25m 4c). Move up and right through the line of least resistance to a traverse terrace. Follow this almost to its end and belay on a block. (20m 4a). Go to the end of the traverse (route is escapable here), then go straight up through a broad groove. Pull over to a grass ledge (25m 4b). Traverse right along the grass ledge and go up an easy vegetated groove (15m). Scramble to the summit.

PABBAY:
The crag accessed by walking from the camping to the opposite side of the beach, then heading left along the peninsula called Roisinis. The route ascends the centre of the wall direct, right of the existing route called *Plan B*.

The Perfect Mur D'or 20m E4 6a ***. Neil McCallum, Andrew McCallum, Mike Hutton, Josh Wright. 30 May 2014.
Climb the centre of the small but perfectly formed golden wall, with a good set of RPs for the hairline crack and tiny cams for the thin break. Start up *Plan B* and blast straight up the hairline crack and superb headwall. Could feel very spicy on a true on-sight (E5?); the tiny gear was inspected but not placed by abseil prior to the flashed first ascent.

The Poop Deck:
Poop, Left Finish 20m V.Diff *. Gary Latter. 14 Jun 2014.
The 6m square-cut corner left of the original flared groove finish.

Walking with Giants 35m E3 5c ***. Ed Nind, Gary Latter. 14 Jun 2014.
Superb sustained and well-protected climbing. Start from a belay on large ledge just over halfway up the easy corner of *The Stowaway*. Move up to the good flake on *Corncrakes for Breakfast*, then hand-traverse left on jugs to pull through the roof on *Thursday's Setting Sunrise*. Continue left more easily above the roof, stepping down to a steeper juggy traverse, exiting at the extreme left end of the cliff.

Head and Heart 25m E3 5c **. Gary Latter, Ed Nind. 14 Jun 2014.
A direct line up the crack and wall right of *Illegal Alien*. Climb the left side of the arete left of that route to the ledge, then the short wide crack. Continue up the wall above, past a good flakey break just before the top.

The Pink Wall:

Huffin' 'n' Puffin Direct 40m E6 6b ***. Sam Williams, Uisdean Hawthorn. 15 Jun 2014.
This version follows a more natural obvious line, avoiding the second hard pitch. Follow the original route to the break. Instead of traversing off left to the hanging belay on *The Bonxie*, make hard moves directly up to reach the crack system on *I Suppose a Cormorant's out of the Question Then?* Follow this to the huge undercut flake. Instead of going direct over this (crux of *I Suppose...*) hand-jam out right until possible to join the flakes of *The Ancient Mariners* and follow this to its belay. Finish up that route.

Hoofer's Geo:

Ankle Wrapper 25m E2 5c. Robert Taylor, Gary Latter. 23 Jun 2015
Climbs the wall then flakes 2m left of *Fracture Clinic*.

Banded Wall, South Face:

Shags Direct 30m E1 5c **. Masa Sakano, Patrick Hanlon. 22 Jun 2015.
Start as for *Shags and the City*. Follow the cracks direct all the way to the top through quadruple roofs, culminating at the final off-width crack.

MINGULAY, The Undercut Wall:

Kelvin and Hobs Direct 120m E3 5c ***. Gary Latter, Ed Nind. 10 Jun 2014.
1. 55m 5c From the 'projecting flake', continue slightly left, then direct on beautiful rock to gain the belay at the end of the original second pitch (45m). Move out right and climb wall to belay beneath a groove on a large clean ledge.
2. 50m 5b Continue directly up the fine groove (same as *Rayburnt* perhaps?), passing just right of prominent large triangular roof. This avoids the numerous birdy ledges encountered on the original third pitch.
3. 15m Scramble up rightwards to regain the abseil block.

The Secret's Out 95m E5 6a ****. Greg Boswell, Mike Shorter. 11 Jun 2014.
Start off a large step down on the left side of the ledge, just right of a quartz 'smile'.
1. 35m 6a Make a hard pull from a jug to reach a short crack. Step left and make powerful moves to reach then follow the rising rightwards crack-line. Belay at a ledge.
2. 35m 5c Move up directly from the ledge, weaving through some large roofs to belay at an obvious ledge.
3. 25m Scramble to the top.

The Ocean of Time 110m E5 6a ***. Sam Williams, Uisdean Hawthorn. 10 Jun 2014.
1. 45m 6a Start 3m left of *Taking the Hump*. Use black jugs and make a long move to a good spike (good gear). Move up to obvious corner above. Step left, gain a slopey rising hand-rail and lunge to a pocket. Continue straight up more steadily. Follow a quartz tongue to belay under the left end of the large roof.
2. 45m 5c Step left, then continue straight up, taking a hanging corner with interest.
3. 20m Scramble to glory.

Fine Lines 23m E5 6b ***. Gary Latter, Ed Nind. 10 Jun 2014.
Start a few metres left of *Hot White Spider*. Climb an undercut crack with difficulty to good holds at the base of a hanging right-facing corner. Climb this,then trend leftwards more easily to belay on a small bollard (shared with *The Aga Sanction*). Abseil off; sling and screwgate in-situ.

Geirum Walls :
Land Baby 10m E2 5c **. Masa Sakano, Patrick Hanlon. 17 Jun 2015.
Start as for *Water Babies*, but instead of going left on to the face, climb straight up the corner and surmount the roof via the corner-crack. Follow the continuation crack between *Water Babies* and *Mary Doune* with difficulty to the top.

INNER HEBRIDES AND ARRAN

EIGG, An Sgurr, Poll nam Partan (guide p75):
Raging Bull 16m H.Severe. Brian Davison. 29 Sep 2014.
The right-hand 50m of this crag (the one existing route is at its extreme right end) are out of the woods and more accessible than the remainder. At the left-hand section of cliff before it vanishes into the woods and before the footpath below passes through the gate, the crag reduces in height and becomes broken. About 10m right of this is a pillar detached from the crag at its top with a grassy and bramble covered recess to its left. Climb up the corner and into the narrow chimney behind the pillar to exit. A descent was made by climbing down the recess to the left.

COLL, Beginner's Slab:
The quartz vein rising up right is about Severe.

The Gully:
Hoghker Wall 10m VS 4b **. Andy Hyslop, Colin Moody, Billy Hood, Cynthia Grindley. 14 Jun 2015.
Start left of *Hogh* and climb up to finish up the hanging corner into which *Hogh* moves left.

Hoghdown 10m Severe **. Billy Hood, Cynthia Grindley, Colin Moody. 14 Jun 2015.
The crack right of *Hogh Hogh Hogh*, into which that route moves right.

The Sloch:
Bottleneck 8m Diff. Colin Moody, Billy Hood. 14 Jun 2015.
Right of the overhang of *Bold as Brass* is another overhang. Climb the weakness between them.

Submarine Rock:
Cracked Hull 9m E2 5b **. Andy Hyslop, Colin Moody, Billy Hood. 14 Jun 2015.
The crack right of *Depth Charge* gives overhanging moves.

Stephen Kennedy on the FA of Silkie (HVS,5a), Calgary, Mull. *Photo: ColinMoody.*

Note: Three routes were climbed by Billy Hood, Cynthia Grindley, Colin Moody, 13 Jun 2015. The left side and right side of the arete left of *Depth Charge* (both Severe but with long reaches) and the wall left of *Das Boot* at Diff.

An Caisteall:
Canada Wall 8m Severe *. Colin Moody, Andy Hyslop, Billy Hood, Cynthia Grindley. 14 Jun 2015.
The wall just right of *Greylag Wall* starting up a hairline crack. A step left was made at the top to avoid a slightly harder move.

MULL, Calgary:
Silkie 10m HVS 5a *. Steve Kennedy, Cynthia Grindley, Colin Moody. 18 Apr 2015.
Well right of *Campbell* is an easy chimney. Climb up to the base of the chimney, then move up left on the undercut slab. Finish up the cracks left of the slab.

Aird Dearg:
Unnamed F6b **. Colin Moody, Cynthia Grindley. 2014.
The pillar left of *Red Mullet*, moving right at the top.

Ardtun, East Wall:
Toe of Frog 15m E2 5c **. Gary Latter. 3 Sep 2014.
The finger crack just right of *Eye of Toad.*
Note: The approach is 30mins, (not 20) on very rough ground.

Kintra, Stile Crag:
There is a stile over the fence 100m south of Fish Box Wall. Above the stile is a steep west facing wall with an easy slab above. At the top of the hill is a south facing spike and other belays.

Stile Police 10m Severe *. Colin Moody, Cynthia Grindley. 27 Jun 2015.
Climb the corner-crack at the left side of the crag.

Kintra, Costa del Sol:
El Corazon 20m E5 6a ***. Gary Latter. 12 Oct 2014.
Superb climbing up the wall left of *El Niche*. Very sustained but very well protected on the upper section. Start just left of *El Niche*. Move up left to protection just above a seepage line, then up to the horizontal. Continue straight up to a wide break, then go direct to the leftmost and most defined of a series of intermittent cracks in the headwall. Step right and up to the rightmost crack, then climb direct with difficult sustained climbing to a horizontal break near the top. Pull directly up from here to mantel on a good incut ledge to finish.
Note: Two additional belay stakes were placed, left of the original one at the top of the crag. The finish of *El Niche* was cleaned; finish slightly leftwards, as opposed to 'finishing carefully onto a heather slope.'

FIONNPHORT, Grating Ramps:
Ferry Ahoy 10m E2 5c *. Jules Lines. 6 Apr 2015.
The wide crack to the right of *Grating Ramps*. Step left off the boulder into the line and continue up the widening crack.

Even Keel 9m E4 6a **. Jules Lines, Colin Moody. 16 Apr 2015.
Just to the right of *Ferry Ahoy* is a hanging flake and square-cut arete. Step off the boulder and move up to gain the flake that leads out to the arete, which is climbed in a great position.

Egg Boulder (NM 304 228):
Park as for *Grating Ramps* but head east across the flat bog for 400m. It is hidden from the road, facing east towards a knoll.

Archie 8m E5 6b *. Jules Lines. 16 Apr 2015.
Climb the smooth slab with a crux mantel to start, veering left under a slight overlap to climb the slab direct.

Note from Gary Latter: *Grating Ramps* is E1 5b (not E2)

Fidden:
Cheers 14m VS 5a *. Karen & Gary Latter. 11 Oct 2014
The corner and wide crack 2m left of the chimney of *Glad Tidings*.

Greetings 10m E2 5c **. Gary Latter. 11 Oct 2014.
Start as for *Count Jugular*, then climb the crack and small left-facing corner to the roof. Undercut left and pull through the roof to a good diagonal break. Finish up the final crack, as for *Merry Noel*.

Rusty Tractor Crag:
Cam Shaft 10m E4 6a. Jules Lines, Colin Moody. 16 Apr 2015.
The line of vague scoops between *Rocker Cover* and *Rust Bucket*.

ERRAID, Main Crag, Upper Tier:
Notes from Gary Latter: The final crack of *Chicken Out* is HVS 5a. *I Hear of the Red Fox* was climbed direct at E2 5c, avoiding the stretch right into *Walls without Balls*, but still shares holds with that route near the top (Gary Latter, Sep 2014)
Note from Colin Moody: *Trapezium* (p167) is in the wrong place in the guide (it was never written up). It starts at the arete right of *The Dead Pool* and goes up slightly left.

Main Crag, Lower Tier:
Kidnapped 12m E7 6c ***. Jules Lines (headpoint). 15 Apr 2015.
The main arete to the left of *Sentinel*. A bold and very technical lower section leads to an easier upper section passing a nice spiky jug.

Blurred Lines 9m E6 6b *. Gary Latter. 18 Apr 2015.
The thin diagonal crack emanating from the sharp left arete of the crag. Start up the left side (protection), then swing round the arete and continue with difficulty to join and finish up the groove of *Disingenuous*.

Disingenuous 7m E1 5b *. Gary Latter. 17 Apr 2015.
The crack and shallow groove in the left wall of *V Groove*.

The Long Way Around 8m E1 5b *. Gary & Karen Latter. 21 Apr 2015.
Twin cracks just left of *Weeping Corner*.

Note: *Spiral Arete* is worth 2 *, better than the adjacent *Prince of Thieves* and *Moody's Blues*, which are marred by a large ledge.

Mink Walls:
Iolaire 12m E2 5c **. Jules Lines. Sep 2014.
The clean wall and thin seams to the left of *Pond Filler*.

Dirty Washing 11m E2 5c **. Jules Lines. Sep 2014.
Start by the pond and take the flake to the break and the wafer thin flake in the arete above. Between *Pond Filler* and *Pond Life*?

Iris 7m VS 4b *. Jules Lines. Sep 2014.
The flake-line left of *Orbit*, taking the flake on the right at the branch.

Otter Walls:
Jules's Groove 18m E4 6a **. Gary Latter. 7 Sep 2014.
The undercut groove left of the corner of *Amphibian*. Climb the layback flake steeply to a good flange and undercut spike beneath the top hanging groove. Difficult moves to enter this soon lead to easier climbing. The base can be gained by a 25m abseil direct from a crack just above a large juniper ledge.

The Shellfish Gene 18m HVS 5a **. Karen & Gary Latter. 7 Sep 2014.
At the right end of the ledges, round right of *Gourmet Crab Crack*, are twin right-slanting cracks. Jam the left crack and bridge up to pull over bulge on good holds. Continue slightly right on good flakes to pull onto a sloping ledge by a good diagonal crack. Continue more easily above.

Notes: *Amoeba* is perhaps better described as a lead (low to mid-tide required) at E1 5b *. The crux is at the base (avoided if climbed as a DWS). Similarly, *Black Eye Rib* is E1 5c if climbed as a lead.

On an early repeat of *The Otter's Breakfast Table*, Gary Latter mistakenly climbed the obvious Direct Start up the prominent well-protected right-slanting groove at no change in the grade.

Erraid in the Woods:
Note: *Vicious* is VS 4c, definitely a grade easier than the 3 (HVS 5a) routes to the left.

Asteroid Chasm, North-North-East Face:
Time Warp 15m E3 5c **. Gary Latter. 8 Sep 2014.
The next crack left of *Venus*. Climb the crack to an off-width section near the top, then use a combination of this and the left-slanting dog-leg crack on the right to finish. Scramble up rightwards, then left to descend over the Asteroid.

Out of this World 28m E7 6b ***. Jules Lines, Gary Latter. 9 Apr 2015.
The unique and superb line of flakes up the centre of the chasm wall. Gain the middle of the three stepped ledges and step left off this onto a line of positive

flake holds that go up at first before curving up and right to gain a diagonal break. Go right along the break a metre or so until it is possible to pull into the base of a bold left-facing layback flake. Continue up this to finish at a finger of rock. The bottom 6m usually has a veneer of moisture and is serious; most of the route is run out apart from the distinct crux that is adequately protected with small wires.

South-South-East Face:
Shagged Out 25m E3 6a **. Gary Latter, Jules Lines. 9 Apr 2015.
The narrow left-facing groove and flake 3m right of *Space Traveller*. Move rightwards along shelves from below *Space Traveller* to gain the line. Follow it, then the flake, finishing up a crack in the headwall.

Notes: *Space Traveller* gives superb immaculate climbing, 3 stars and E1 5b is sufficient (not E2). *Venus* was thought worth E1 5b and 2 stars.

Beach Ball Wall:
Space Hopper 25m E4 6a **. Gary Latter. 8 Apr 2015.
The prominent diagonal line. Start 2m left of *Buckets in Spades*. Climb finger slots, then move up right to join *Buckets in Spades*. Continue along a right-slanting crack to finish up an easy-angled open groove.
Note: *Buckets in Spades* is E1 5b (Andy Hyslop thinks E2).

Strawberry Pig Slab:
Brambles 9m H.Severe 4b. Karen & Gary Latter. 8 Sep 2014.
The broken cracks up the left edge of the slab, just left of *Jo's Plums*.

ERRAID, Rubha Calachain (NM 29191 19221):
A sheltered bay with a tidal crag. Topo provided.

Mull it Over 30m Severe 4a. Gwilym Starks, Glen Howaston. 24 Aug 2014.
Go up a thin crack in a slab to a block come spike (optional belay). Traverse right along a ledge, crossing *Back to It* to climb a deep corner.

Back to It 20m V.Diff. Glen Howaston, Gwilym Starks. 24 Aug 2014.
Go up an easy wall and corners to the ledge as above. Follow obvious corner-cracks to the top.

Mullatov Cocktail 20m H.Severe 4b **. Andy Spink, Stevie Boyle. 24 Aug 2014.
Easy climbing leads to obvious twin cracks. Climb easily to a steep wall and climb the twin cracks.

Mariposa 20m H.Severe 4a. Stevie Boyle, Andy Spink. 24 Aug 2014.
Climb the flaked wall via a series of horizontal breaks and cracks. Finish up a bulging wall at the top.

New Slabs:
Second Hand 8m Severe 4a. Stevie Boyle, Andy Spink. 24 Aug 2014.
Right of *Nouvelle* up an arete and into an obvious slanting crack-line to the top.

EILEAN DUBH, Easter Island, South Face:
Sword of Damocles 15m E2 5c ***. Gary & Karen Latter. 7 Oct 2014.
The fine corner and crack, with a remarkable 6m long thin flake-crack wedged in its upper half. Climb a short jam crack onto a good ledge. Layback the wide crack above (Camalot 4 useful, though not essential) and continue up, hugging the flake.

The Dogs Doo Dah 15m E1 5b *. Gary & Karen Latter. 7 Oct 2014.
The prominent vertical crack above the left end of the large boulder at the base. Climb a diagonal flake to a good projecting block, then slightly left before moving back right to finish up the crack.

Note: *Eilean Doo* on the West Face is 15m (not 25m).

EILEAN NAN MUC, Sunset Walls South:
(NM 283 193) Alt 5m West facing
The southmost of three crags on the west side of the island, about 200m south of the sheltered landing bay.

Here Comes the Sun 8m E2 5c *. Gary & Karen Latter. 9 Oct 2014.
The central, slightly right-slanting crack, finishing steeply by a good flake.

Always the Sun 9m E3 6a ***. Gary Latter. 9 Oct 2014.
Fine well protected climbing on impeccable rock. The left-curving overlap, with difficult moves getting established in an improving flakey groove in the upper section.

ISLAY:
Creag an t-Saighdeir (Soldier's Rock):
West Face 20m HVS 5a. Tom Prentice, Simon Richardson. 13 Sep 2014.
This classically proportioned pinnacle is Islay's best-known sea-stack and gets its name from the prominent quartz band on its seaward side, reminiscent of a soldier's shoulder belt. The stack lies on the coast west of the abandoned settlement of Grasdale, approached from Kintra campsite at the south end of Laggan Bay. It was reached by a 100m swim. The stepped crack and corner on the West Face gave quality climbing on solid, well-protected rock.

The three pinnacles connected to the stack at low tide gave pleasant scrambly routes between Diff and V.Diff.

Cocked Hat Stack:
West Ridge 25m Diff. Tom Prentice, Simon Richardson. 14 Sep 2014.
The obvious stack in the bay to the north-east, south of Eilean Torrach, was reached by a 120m swim and climbed solo via its West Ridge.

ARRAN:
Note: *All Along the Watchtower* on Full Mead Tower is credited in the new guide to Andy Fraser & Robin McAllister. Mike Reed was also part of the FA team.

CIR MHOR, Upper East Face:
The Somnambulist 50m E7 6c **. Tony Stone, Iain Small (both led, pre-practised). 13 Jun 2015.

Creag an t-Saighdeir, Islay. *Photo: Tom Prentice.*

Tony Stone on the FA of Somnambulist (E7,6c), Cir Mhor, Arran. *Photo: Iain Small.*

Follows the left arete of the blunt prow forming the front face of the 'monolithic wall that flanks Sub Rosa Gully'. Both technical and bold, this route requires all your faculties for the bold, balancey upper arete. Beware of rope drag on the upper part and take doubles of Camalot 3 and 0.75. The initial section has some slightly friable flakes.

Scramble up steep broken ground to belay on a ledge below and left of the prow proper. Step up right to gain a short inset groove with a good crack. From its top, step left to undercuts, then awkwardly gain a higher crack leading up left to a good pocket (in-situ thread, Camalot 0.75 below). A hard section leads out right to a poor hold on the arete and a rockover to gain a pocket on the slabby right face of the arete (Camalot 0.75 in pocket to the right). Take the slab up to the roof above and from the flake on its right side, move out left to gain a sloping shelf running to the arete. Awkward moves from slightly left on the shelf lead up to cracks on the left side of the arete. Step back right to below a prominent long overlap. Reach over to a flake, then up to a large pocket in the slab) and pad up to the obvious break (Camalot 3). Move along this, back left, to the top arete. Start up this to gain a standing position in a pocket on the left side (in-situ thread). A bold technical section tackling the arete above eventually eases and a Camalot 3 can be placed in the rounded flake out right. Pull over onto the final slab and head initially rightwards, then back left to the long ledge. In-situ thread further right.

Skydiver Unstable Exit 40m E4 6a *. Tony Stone, Iain Small. 12 Jun 2015.
From the ledge at the top of *Skydiver*, an obvious intrusion runs up the steep wall above. Start below the intrusion. Gain the first break, then follow the intrusion exiting awkwardly onto the slab at the top. Surmount the short steep wall beyond at the obvious crack.

SKYE

SGURR A' BHASTEIR, North Face:

Smoked Salomon 60m III. Mark Francis, Murdo Nicolson. 17 Jan 2015.
Follow a line of thin turf through the middle of the left-hand side upper buttress.

Paramo Sapiens 50m IV,4. Mark Francis, Matt Barratt, John Smith. 19 Jan 2015.
Takes the icefall splitting the upper buttress.

Je Suis Charlet 95m III. Mark Francis, Murdo Nicolson. 17 Jan 2015.
Climbs an open corner with a bounding right wall, keeping right of an obvious groove.

Stormy Petzl 85m III. Mark Francis, Murdo Nicolson, Norman Macleod, David Bowdler. 1 Feb 2015.
Takes the left-hand icy groove from the same start as *Je Suis Charlet*. Belay on the obvious ledge, then exit through the top band via a turfy groove.

Lowe Supine 55m III,4. Murdo Nicolson, Mark Francis, Norman Macleod, David Bowdler. 1 Feb 2015.

Follow the obvious narrow slot at the left-hand edge of the crag.

Note: *Mike the Bhasteird* (2010) lies right of these routes on the lower tier.

North-East Face:
Twicicle 50m IV,4. Mark Francis, David Bowdler (left start); Mike Lates, Alex Anderson (right start). 30 Jan 2015.
Twin icefalls lie left of an obvious narrow gully coming down from the north-east ridge and above the wee lochan. Climb the right-hand icefall, or the steeper left-hand start. Exit left up icy slabs to belay at a low wall. Finish by easier ground taking a rising rightward traverse leading onto the north-east ridge (not included in length).

Farcicle 35m IV,5. Murdo Nicolson, Mark Francis. 7 Feb 2015.
This route is on the left wall of the narrow gully, just as it starts to narrow and just past an undercut wall. Starting at some ugly stacked blocks, climb the icefall in the corner. Finish by easier ground taking a rising rightward traverse leading onto the north-east ridge (not included in length).

SGURR A' MHADAIDH:
The four tiered buttress to the left of *Winter Gully*.

Sweetheart Buttress 300m III,4. Mark Francis, Gill Houlsby, Matt Barratt. 28 Dec 2014.
A good mountaineering route with an obvious line but easily escapable. Start just to the right of *South Gully*.
1. 30m Climb the turfy groove on the right.
2. 60m Follow slabs and grooves to the base of the undercut buttress.
3. 40m An easy walk up a ramp to the corner of the buttress and *Winter Gully*.
4. 30m A nice pitch onto the crest of the buttress.
5. 40m Easy along the crest to a steepening.
6. 15m Climb direct through, nice technical climbing on good gabbro.
7. 50m Easily to the last tier.
8. 40m Follow a steep, slim basalt chimney on the right and then weave your way up the face.
Follow the buttress to the bowl at the top, ending just below Bealach Glaic Mor.

SGURR A' GHREADAIDH, West Face:
Hidden Gully 130m V,6 ***. Steve Perry, Michael Barnard. 17 Jan 2015.
As for the summer route. The chimney pitch was very exciting back and footing up thickly verglassed walls using the well spaced chockstones as protection. Pitch 3 was sustained and absorbing with a lovely move right into the grooves. SP thought the grade was at least VI,6.
1. 30m Climb up to the base of the main chimney.
2. 30m Climb the chimney past chockstones and a through route.
3. 25m The chimney ends above. Climb a line of weakness just left of the obvious chockstone, then step right and follow grooves.
4. 45m Traverse right to a V-groove. Go up this and continue to easier ground.

SGURR NA BANACHDAICH, Sgurr nan Gobhar, Heart Buttress:
An obvious clean sheet of rock high on the northern flank of Sgurr na Gobhar above Coir' an Eich.

Techno Snob 40m E2 5c ***. Malcom Airey, Mike Lates. 3 Jul 2012.
Climbs the central fault line before breaking left to a more prominent crack. A fierce start (5b, hard to protect for the short) leads to a section of easier beautiful climbing on the wall above. Break left at 20m to the obvious parallel crack. Finish by small positive holds where this runs out to a poor block belay on the ledge above.

Oldest Raver in Skye Finish 35m E1 5b ***. Mike Lates, Lucy Spark. 10 Jul 2014.
The fierce rockover start to *Techno Snob* forms the crux of this easier variation. Continue direct where *Techno Snob* breaks left; easier but gives climbing of equally superb quality. Poor block belays above.

COIRE NA BANACHDAICH:
Banner Diction 165m III,4. Mark Francis, Murdo Nicolson, Ally Macaskill. 21 Jan 2015.
A deep recess lies 100m right of *Banachdich Gully*. This route starts below a steep icefall 20m left of this. Climb an iced rib to the foot of the icefall which is climbed on its left edge. Follow easier ice to some bulges to finish.

COIRE LAGAN, China Crag:
Taslim Ahmed 35m E1 5a/b *. Colin Moody, Cynthia Grindley. 14 Sep 2014.
Start between *Hueco* and *Aloo Gobi*. Go up towards the overlap and go past it on the right, then step left onto the ledge above the overlap. Make thin moves up then easier to join and finish up either the route on the left or right.

Howker 20m VS 4c *. Colin Moody, Cynthia Grindley. 14 Sep 2014.
The crack right of *Curver*.
Note: *Curver* (SMCJ 2014) is probably worth **.

SGURR ALASDAIR, South Face:
Central Route 20m V,6 **. Michael Barnard, Tim Oates. 24 Jan 2015.
As for the summer route, but starting up grooves on the left. Some useful ice on the first ascent.

Skye High 35m VI,7 *. Michael Barnard, Josh Fawcett. 1 Feb 2015.
An excellent pitch up the steep crack at the far left end of the crag.
1. 20m Climb the crack (pumpy and well protected).
2. 15m The deceptively difficult continuation fault. Either abseil off after this or continue up easier ground.

Con's Cleft 100m VII,7. James Sutton, Mike Lates. 1 Feb 2015.
Requires extreme weathering to come into winter condition.
1. 30m Gain the deep recess, place a high cam runner, then break out right, thin and strenuous, to gain the thin crack and eventual belay.
2. 10m Well protected but strenuous moves.

3. 40m A long pitch frequently requiring some big gear.

COIRE A' GHRUNNDA:
Here Today, Gone Tomorrow 50m IV,4 **. Tim Oates, Michael Barnard. 24 Jan 2015.
In good conditions a very prominent icefall forms left of *Vagabond Buttress*.

South Crag:
South Crag Gully IV,5. Michael Barnard, Josh Fawcett. 31 Jan 2015.
A winter ascent. Some ice is helpful (the more the better) but not essential.

Land of Plenty 55m III,4. Michael Barnard, Josh Fawcett. 31 Jan 2015.
A narrow chimney-gully up the right side of the very top buttress, gained from the gully on the right.

Owl Arete 48m VS 4b *. Steve Kennedy, Cynthia Grindley. Aug 2014.
The arete immediately right of *Owl Chimney*. Climb a short corner just right of the arete followed by a steep crack in the wall above. Move left onto the arete from the top of the wall. Climb the arete, sometimes on its left, avoiding the temptation to move into the chimney. Sparsely protected.

LOCH SCAVAIG, Improbable Wall (NG 482 189):
A wall on the far side of Loch Scavaig has a wide white streak down the middle of it. On the right side of this wall just to the left of the corner is a wide crack. This is the line of the following route.

Nose Lobe Smooth 30m E2 5c. Charlie Woodburn, Liam Lonsdale. 14 Aug 2014.
Follow the obvious crack all the way. A steep pull at 5m leads to fun climbing up to a pod below the top and a rest. Pull round this to the top. Jamming optional. Often wet in the upper section.

Around the blunt left rib of this wall the buttress turns up the slope. This wall is easier angled and has several crack-lines running vertically. There is a diagonal break running from left to right across this wall.

Rough with the Smooth 25m VS 4c. Dom Bush, Liam Lonsdale. 14 Aug 2014.
Follows this diagonal break finishing on the ledge above the wide white streak around to the right.

JMCS Buttress:
Whale Song 30m E2. Dom Bush, Gilly Mcarthur. 19 Aug 2014.
Start on the right side of the buttress at the obvious ledge. Follow the mid-height break from right to left with a long step down to reach a good hold where the crack becomes less defined and joins the route *Beached Whale* – 5b. Continue more easily along the continuation crack as it curves upwards (5a). Belay well back, as for *Beached Whale*.

Tumblehome 20m E5 6b. Charlie Woodburn (unsec). 18 Aug 2014.
Start just left of the boulder at the base of the wall, about 10m right of the hut.

Climb direct to the horizonal break of *Whale Song* – bold. Arrange good large cams and step right to below the left-trending diagonal crack above. Pull around the bulge following this crack to the top.

CORUISK, Sgurr a' Mhadaidh:

Note: Charlie Woodburn repeated *Skye Wall* on 19 Sep 2014. It's an absolute classic of UK trad, but the main difficulty of the route is getting there in dry conditions. This and a later repeat by Iain Small agreed on E7 6b.

Dubhs Ridge:

After topping out on *Old Mortality*, a lovely 25m slab lay directly ahead with a perfect crack running up the centre of the slab (on the left flank of the Dubhs Ridge).

The Cock Inn 25m Severe *. John Craven, Stuart Johnson. 3 May 2014.
The obvious slab just beyond the top of the gully normally used to start the Dubhs Ridge. Climb the crack in the centre of the slab.

GARBH-BHEINN, Winter Cliff:

Lies further up the corrie beyond the rock climbs on Creag Druim Eadar da Choire. Approach by Coire Selig is very wet so best to continue up the NNW ridge past the top of Creag Druim Eadar da Choire to approx. the 600m contour. Descend an enclosed but easy angled gully for 60m to reach the base of the cliff.

Yat for the Doh 60m II *. Mo Barclay, Stuart Leonard, Mike Lates. 4 Feb 2015.
A broad icefall leads up left from the foot of the descent gully. Climbed in two pitches staying close to the right wall rather than easier ground breaking left at the top.

Chockolates 80m V,6 **. Mike Lates, Mo Barclay, Stuart Leonard. 4 Feb 2015.
From the descent gully, traverse the foot of the cliff leftward for 40m. A rising leftward fault (25m) gives access to another ledge system. From here the most obvious break in the upper cliff is a steep narrow chimney slightly back right. Ascend vegetated snow slopes for 20m and belay below the fault.
1. 40m Climb easy but thin ice to the foot of the obvious chimney. Ice in the back was useful but not essential in the fight to reach the obvious chockstone. Belay 6m higher below the final huge chockstone blocking the way.
2. 40m Climb through a small hole behind the chockstone and continue with interest to reach a steep finish and block belay.

Making Memories 120m V,6 *. Alison Coull, Fiona Murray. 4 Feb 2015.
A gully line some 100m left of the above route.
1. 50m Follow the icy gully to belay under a roof.
2. 35m Traverse for 10m until a right-facing bulging corner can be gained. Climb this to its overhang. Pull over (crux) onto a turfy wall and climb up to a block.
3. 25m Move right to gain a left-facing corner. Follow this and easy ground to the top.

NEIST, Financial Sector:

Austerity Lite 25m E6 6b *. Dave MacLeod, Natalie Berry. 21 Jun 2015.

Good balancy climbing on the arete right of *Piggy Bank*. Make a few moves up the corner and arrange good cams in the overlap in the left wall. Stretch left to the rounded arete and make a series of balance moves on small edges leftwards around the arete to eventually reach a jug. Make another move up and left to gain the groove of *Piggy Bank* and finish up this.

An t-Aigeach:
Death Pirate, Davy Jones' Locker Start 35m E4 6a. Iain Small, Jules Lines. 20 Apr 2015.
A direct starting pitch from sea-level to link into *Death Pirate* giving a complete line up An t-Aigeach. Abseil to good ledges to the left of a recessed wide chimney. Follow the snaking crack on good clean rock to an overlap. Pull right into a crack and groove and where it becomes vegetated, step right onto the steep wall and climb into and up a wide groove to the big ledge at the base of *Death Pirate*.
Note: *Death Pirate* was climbed and was excellent with good clean rock. E6 6b,6b, fairly high in the grade. Pitch 1 is about 35m and not poorly protected (as in the original description) but the crux is run out. The crux was climbed more directly and in a fantastic exposed position by gaining a standing position on the hold on the arete, then climbing the right side of the arete to gain a sloping ledge and belay crack below the overhanging corner.

South of the Steps:
Note: The prominent crack of *Patsy Says* is very good but closer to 10m than 18m in length. The route was approached by abseil.

MINGINISH, Na Huranan:
A SW facing crag 200m on the north side of the Carbost to Talisker Bay road at its highest point. Park just before a big red shed on the saddle. A 15mins walk to the right end of the crag. The rock is compact and protection can be hard to find; it is worth carrying extra cams. The buttresses and routes are described from right to left, as one would approach.

Auld Dyke Buttress:
This is the very rightmost buttress. Beneath it and snaking down the hillside, is the remains of an ancient boundary wall. At the highest point of the crag a rather black and dirty large open scoop runs the full height of the buttress. It has a clean detached pillar sitting at half-height on its right and a block lying against the cliff base 5m to the left. Routes are described from right to left with reference to this groove.

Sun and Air 18m E1 5b. Paul Torode, Alan Hill, Brett Drinkwater. 1 Apr 2013.
Start 1m left of the block (at the second cracked groove left of the big open groove) and climb a deceptive groove with short wide crack section (crux). Move up and slightly right, then back left up a final groove.

The next three routes all start at the third cracked groove left of the big dirty open groove.

Rescue Dog Remedy 18m VS 4c. Stephen & Sally Reid. 9 Apr 2015.
Interesting climbing but be careful of detached blocks. Two metres left is a short

groove leading to a small block overhang (*A Boy Named Sue*). Climb the right wall of the groove to the right side of the overhang and make an awkward stretch up right to a detached block. Step back left over the top of the block overhang and climb up to the left side of a large detached block. Step back right over this, move up and then make a rising traverse back left to finish.

A Boy Named Sue 18m HVS 4c. Alan Hill, Paul Torode, Brett Drinkwater. 1 Apr 2013.
Climb the short groove with a small overhang at 3m. Move right to a vague ledge and good gear in a short steep corner-crack to the right. Move back left and onto a ledge, then finish leftwards.

Two Flew over the Cuckoo's Nest 18m VS 4c *. Stephen & Sally Reid. 9 Apr 2015.
Start left of the groove and climb a short wall to a ledge. Step right and make a hard move up a sharp rib using a hidden hold to gain a ledge on the right. Finish direct.

Uphill and some 12m to the left is a short dirty wide slot, where this section of crag is at its shortest.

Scratch Mahatch 15m HVS 5a. Alan Hill, Paul Torode, Brett Drinkwater. 1 Apr 2013.
Two metres left of the slot is a groove leading to a prominent hand crack.

Karate Kid 20m E2 5b *. Paul Torode, Alan Hill. 1 Apr 2013.
Four metres left is an obvious steep narrow V-groove below a large flake feature. Move up and right after the groove, finishing right of the flake. A large block at the top of the groove is balanced on a ledge.

The next route is up and left.

One Fell Swoop 12m HVS 5a. Alan Hill, Paul Torode. 1 Apr 2013.
Start on a blocky ledge below thin parallel cracks. Finish direct or up a left-hand corner.

SUIDHE BIORACH:
Toast 30m E7 6c ****. Dave MacLeod, Natalie Berry. 25 Jun 2015.
A brilliant climb taking on the horizontal roof and steep wall right of *Mother's Pride*.
1. 15m 5b Start about 6m right of *Mother's Pride* and climb the wall on big holds, moving left around a bulge and then traversing slightly right to a belay at the roof.
2. 15m 6c Arrange a couple of small cams in pockets in the roof and launch outwards using a positive undercut. Reach the next undercut and then gain jugs on the lip with difficulty. Continue directly up the pumpy steep headwall.

Note: *Tree Route Variation* at E1 5b is better than the original. At the large roofs, step left to tackle the obvious twin cracks. Huge holds make this remarkably easy. The continuation cracks stay left of the original route giving a more sustained challenge that needs some cleaning higher up. It is probably the same as the upper section of *Rapid Learning Curve*. Led by Francis Blunt on 20 Sep 2014.

RAASAY, Hidden Wall of Sithean Mhor:
The established routes here are at the right-hand end. Near the left side of the crag is a large, distinctly M shaped recess. Right of this is an obvious wide break slants from top left to bottom right across the crag. Two left-facing grooves lead into this break, the left one being very steeply undercut. The following route takes the right groove.

Desolation Roe 13m E1 5c *. Andy Moles, Ferdia Earle. 7 Jul 2014.
Gain the groove by a couple of steep pulls. Climb the groove to where it meets the main break at a ledge, then step left to finish up a short wall.

The Hardcôr-gi 15m E1 5c *. Ferdia Earle, Andy Moles. 7 Jul 2014.
A few metres right of the previous route is a triangular niche below the break. Gain the break via this recess, then follow the break left to a ledge. Finish more easily just to the right of the previous route. A very large cam would be useful, but is not essential. A poorly protected alternative is to gain the break at its lowest point off a boulder a few metres to the right.

Baby Missiles 15m E1 5c **. Andy Moles, Ferdia Earle. 7 Jul 2014.
The best line on the crag, straightening out the original *Route Seven*. Follow that route to the ledge, but continue in the same line up the steep crack. Safe and fun.

Ocean-Going Cliff:
Roe Is Me 7m E2/3 6a *. Ferdia Roe Earle, Andy Moles. 7 Jul 2014.
At the top left end of the crag, hidden behind a pinnacle block, is a short steep arete. Climb it without using the block. Micro, but fun climbing with good gear in the breaks.

Raucous Summer 13m E2 5c ***. Andy Moles, Ferdia Earle. 7 Jul 2014.
A brilliant technical route up the wall just right of the crag's central arete. Start at the base of the arete, just right of *Fingerlicker*, and move up and right onto the wall. Climb it directly by shallow grooves. Sustained but low in the grade (maybe).

Note: *Fingerlicker* was thought E1 5c **.

Sgurr nan Gall, Main Walls:
Ocean Between the Waves 25m E3 5c *. Andy Moles, Ferdia Earle. 8 Jul 2014.
This tackles the tapering red wall between *Fladda* and *Blood Test*. Climb thin cracks a few metres left of the shallow groove taken by *Blood Test* to the ledge. From an obvious curving crack, climb the wall above trending left then back right until forced into *Blood Test* at a distinct jutting flake. Finish up *Blood Test* or just to the left. Good climbing but not a fully independent line. A more direct version through the apex of the wall looks possible but very hard.

Collie Dread 25m VS 4c **. Ferdia Earle, Andy Moles. 8 Jul 2014.
Climb obvious flake-grooves up the wall between *The Tobacco Run* and *Oisinn McAulay*, with a couple of steeper crux moves through a large flake near the top.

Note: *Fladda* was thought E2 5b **, *Oisinn McAulay* HVS 5a **.

AIRD OF SLEAT, Creag Mhor:
The crag is only given a brief write-up in the Skye guide but Jamie Bankhead and others thought the crag well worth writing up. The routes have probably been done before but the crag is of good, clean south facing quartzite, with a lovely aspect. The routes are described from left to right, all approx 15m and climbed on 13 Sep 2014 by Jamie Bankhead, Seumas Mehan & Rich Parker. Bikes are recommended for the approach.

Leftward Leaning H.Severe 4a *.
Start up a crack, then move left to an arete. Climb this with no protection to the top.

Centre Ground V.Diff *.
Steady climbing with good protection.

No Guarantee HVS 4c *.
Attack the wall to the right, steep moves with poor protection.

Referendum Route Severe **.
Climb the steepening crack to the right on brilliant holds.

Devolution HVS 5a **.
Start up the thin diagonal crack before launching onto the apparently smooth wall above. This is climbed on small but positive edges with good Cam protection.

Suspicion V.Diff.
The diagonal crack throughout. Some dubious rock.

Fight for the Right H.Severe 4b *.
The short wall at the right of the crag. Tricky moves low down with poor protection lead to easier climbing.

NORTHERN HIGHLANDS NORTH

BEINN DEARG, Cadha Dearg:
Far East Gully 180m III *. Roger Webb, James Edwards. 17 Jan 2015.
At approximately NH 286 863, there is an easy descent gully splitting the cliffs at the east end of Gleann a' Chadha Dheirg. About 100m north of this the cliffs are split by a narrow gully. Climb this gully in four pitches; the penultimate pitch includes an excellent through route.

CONA' MHEALL, Coire Ghranda Face:
Imperturbable IV,6 *. Pete Macpherson, Neil Wilson, Roger Webb. 28 Dec 2014.
The Coire Ghranda face is wedge shaped, the thin end being to the north. Follow the face down and south-east to the first very obvious chimney gully; this is perhaps 300m north-west of *Spaghetti Gully*. Climb this feature in two pitches, always entertaining, always well protected.

ARDMAIR, Monster Buttress:
Tubby's Tremendous Trundles 35m E2 5b *. Ian Taylor, Tess Fryer. Jun 2014.
Start up the *The Raingoose*. Where that route pulls over a bulge into a corner, move right to good holds on the arete and climb up to the sloping ledge. Above is a right-slanting groove. Gain a ledge below this and go up a slab rightwards to easier ground (RPs needed). Finish up cracks.

CUL MOR, Coire Gorm:
The Greatest Show On Earth 180m X,10. Greg Boswell, Guy Robertson. 19 Jan 2015.
The first route to breach the big back wall of Coire Gorm, and a superb if somewhat death-defying route. The crux, unsurprisingly, is turning the great roof, and it is here that the protection is at its most sparse. Start at the biggest icefall just right of centre, below and right of large icicles hanging from a slight break in the roof. Above and slightly left of these icicles is a great soaring corner-groove, the centrepiece of the upper wall.
1. 40m Climb ice more or less directly up to the girdling break below the roof, then traverse this horizontally left for about 10m to belay by the icicles.
2. 20m Climb up the icicles, then work up and slightly right across the roof to the lip where a short hard traverse right allows a pull over onto the upper wall. Take a deep breath, then teeter up left to a ledge.
3. 20m Take the obvious line trending up and left to gain a cave by a little crest just right of the big groove.
4. 50m Step left into the groove and follow this with sustained interest to easier angled ground.
5. 50m Romp gleefully to easier ground below the summit of the mountain. It is probably easier and safer to continue to the summit before descending.

STAC POLLAIDH, West Buttress, South Face:
Non Compos Mentis 35m E3 5c *. Ian Taylor, Tess Fryer. 21 Jul 2014.
An alternative first pitch to *Felo de Se*. Start left of *Shadow on the Wall* and follow the easiest line up the narrow buttress until able to move left to a small rowan sapling in a corner. Go up the corner until able to pull right to an area of cleaned ledges. Climb directly above, finishing up a short crack, to belay on the ledge below the chimney pitch of *Felo de Se*.

Hank Marvin 30m E4/5 6a **. Ian Taylor, Tess Fryer. 5 Sep 2014.
From the belay on *Shadow on the Wall*, hand-traverse back right for 2m. Follow the crack above, through an overhang and continue up thin cracks to a junction with *Mid-Flight Crisis* at its niche. Go up a groove slightly rightwards until below some vegetation, move left and take flared cracks to the top.

Expecting to Fly Direct 48m E5 6a ***. Ian Taylor, Tess Fryer. 14 Jul 2014.
Start at a crack right of *Mid Flight Crisis* and just left of a short corner. Climb the crack (Camalot 3 and Friend 4 useful) to a ledge, then make a couple of moves up the right-hand of two cracks, to join the original line at a faded thread.

Note: *Shadow on the Wall* has been re-cleaned recently at 35m E4 6a **. A Friend 4 protects the crux making the original in-situ thread superfluous. *Plane Sailing* has also been re-cleaned and was thought to be E4 6a *.

West Buttress:
Virgil's Route 15m E3 6a. Tess Fryer, Ian Taylor. 3 Jul 2015.
The right-trending crack on the outer face of Baird's Pinnacle, starting up an easy corner.

WICKET GATE CRAG:
Pine Martens with Guns 15m E6 6b **. Ian Taylor, Calum Cunningham (both led). 5 May 2015.
Lies on the wall right of *Garden Path*. Start left of a big embedded flake and go up to a big break (Camalot 4), then up to another break. Move left along the break then go straight up the wall above (crux), heading for a small hanging groove. Finish more easily.

OSSUARY BLOCK:
The Ossuary Block aka Carragh Dearg (SMCJ 2009) is the obvious towering crag just south of the popular bouldering area known as Reiff-in-the-Woods. It is just above the east end of Loch Bad a' Ghaill and about 2km west of Stac Pollaidh (NC 091 093), 10mins. Zigzag down some steep slopes and go across rough ground. The excellent rough rock dries quickly.

There are two excellent highball boulder problems that start off the terrace on the left side of the crag. *The Beast's Lair* (6m Font 6B+) takes the blunt arete on the left above the big flake and *Vipe-out* (8m Font 7A) goes up the wall right of the dirty corner to an easier layback finish. Perhaps E5 6b in old money.

Find Meat on Bones 10m E7/8 6c ***. Iain Small. 2015.
This route finds a complex way up the challenge of the middle of the wall. Start off the stonemason's wall on the right. Headpointed above bouldering mats.

Under Reiff Wood 10m E6 6b **. Iain Small. 2014.
Takes the central arete between the highball wall and *Ossuary*. *Ossuary* (SMCJ 2009) is the obvious crack in the front face. Start from the right end of the upper ledge and step out to gain a big block in a large break. Strenuously arrange small wires in the hanging corner on right side of the arete, then pull out via a flake onto the left face before gaining small holds on the arete that allow you to swing over the corner and battle up the right side to sloping holds and a foot ledge. Bold moves above this in a great position lead to the platform top.

BEN MOR COIGACH, Creag Garbh Choireachan:
The Beast 20m E3 5c ***. John Mackenzie, Andrew McKenzie. 3 Jul 2015.
The obvious and most striking corner line on the top tier just right of the final pitch of *The Wild West*. It is sustained on clean rock with as much protection as you have the strength to put in. A fine combination of layback, jamming and bridging leads to a ledge and a final short crack.

Craicstone Grip 40m HVS 5a *. Andrew McKenzie, John Mackenzie. 3 Jul 2015.
The east facing walls and grooves rise above the right-bounding gully that borders the scramble of *West Ridge Direct*. A very obvious tongue of slab is met low down in the gully. Potentially good given a good brushing but climbed on-sight.
1. 35m 5a Climb the slab starting from a little alcove and go up the unprotected

and quite delicate rock to a step right, then back left to the upper slab before the steep upper walls. Move right to a deep corner-crack above some blocks and climb this, well protected, to a ledge.
2. 5m 4b Climb the short but steep corner above the spike belay, some loose but useful blocks.
Walk left to reach the left-bounding gully which is descended to a prominent niche on the left. This gains easy access to the ledge below the Upper Tier of the South Face and another descent to the right-bounding gully.

REIFF, Stone Pig Cliff:
Headstrong Direct 20m E5 6a **. Ian Taylor, Tess Fryer. 29 Aug 2015.
Start up the steep left side of the arete, pulling round right to join the original line at its crux.

Slab Inlet:
Old Buoy's Route 15m Diff. Michael Barnard. 24 Mar 2012.
At the back of the inlet is a deep cleft with a large chockstone at the top. Climb it.
Variation: V.Diff. Michael Barnard. 24 Mar 2012.
From near the top, move out to finish on the other side of the chockstone (bold).

Mermaid and Chips 12m E1 5a *. Michael Barnard, Rory Morris. 19 Apr 2015.
Climbs the narrow buttress between the deep cleft and the slab corner. Start in the cleft. Go up a short slab and swing round to gain the obvious ledge. Move up and right then back left to finish directly.

Bridge Over Troubled 12m HVS 5a *. Michael Barnard, Rory Morris. 19 Apr 2015.
Start as for the above before stepping right to climb the steep fault (the outside of the deep cleft of *Old Buoy's Route*). Finish direct over the capping roof.

The Slab, Landward End, Right-Hand Finish H.Severe 4c. Michael Barnard. 24 Mar 2012.
The obvious vertical corner.

QUINAG, Western Cliffs:
Jinky 120m V,5. Dave McGimpsey, Andy Nisbet, Jonathan Preston. 4 Feb 2015.
The gully left of *Balconic* (2013).

TARBET CRAGS, Foindle Crags, Big D Crag:
Described from the right-hand end of the crag.

Interrupted Slab 22m H.Severe 4b. John Mackenzie, Andrew James. 10 Apr 2015.
This is the clean reddish slab on the far right of the crag. Climb the left side via a shallow crack to a broken arete. Move right into a corner and finish up a short steep groove.

Jolly D 25m VS 4c **. Andrew James, John Mackenzie. 10 Apr 2015.
A very good climb following the left-slanting ramp line on the right side of the

Julian Lines on the FA of Statue of Liberty (E5,5c), Port Vasgo. *Photo: Andy Nisbet.*

Simon Nadin on the FA of Jacobite Gold (E4,6a), Ben Loyal. *Photo: Dave Allan.*

main crag. Well protected, exposed and fun. Climb the ramp moving around a bulge near the top.

BEN HOPE:

Tower Ridge Integral 470m V,6. Andy Nisbet, Steve Perry. 4 Mar 2015.
The ridge labelled in 'Highland Scrambles North' as *Tower Ridge* but including a lower continuation in the same line. It needs to be frozen but the upper part could be climbed alone at III,5. It may be possible to bypass the harder sections but as direct a line as was reasonable was chosen. Start at the base of the lower ridge, close to the gully on the right.
1. 100m Climb over short steps and an easier section, then more short steps to a steeper band.
2. 45m Climb this by a steep turfy fault leading to a terrace and the next tier.
3. 30m Climb a steep corner (crux) to step left on to a ledge. Traverse left, then go up left and back right to a ledge.
4. 50m Gain a terrace above and the next tier, climbed direct. Continue to another wall. Traverse left along a narrow ledge to regain the crest.
5. 75m Go along the crest to a smooth slabby section where the ridge bends right. Bypass this easily on the right, then return left to the crest and follow it to where the route up the rake joins.
6. 70m Take the best line up a slabby crest leading up to the tower. The intention was to climb the tower but it looks very hard. Follow the crest to the tower, then traverse right under it and climb a turfy corner ending with a difficult pull out of a niche.
7. 100m Regain the crest and follow it to easy ground which leads to the North Ridge.

BEN LOYAL, Sgor a' Bhatain:

Note: *Jacobite Gold* is E4 6a ***. Pitch 1 is 45m 6a; Pitch 2 is 30m 6a.

Sgor a' Chleirich:

Note: *Milky Way* Pitch 2 is 52m and better split at the optional belay at 20m.

Both routes are well worth seeking out.

CAITHNESS SEA-CLIFFS, MID CLYTH, Overhanging Wall Right:

A Fishy Pair 13m H.Severe 4b. Paul Torode, Alan Hill. 9 Aug 2014.
Traverse right past *Bonxie* to the arete and up this on its right-hand side.

Overhanging Wall Left:

Pelvic Thrust 10m HVS 5b. Alan Hill, Paul Torode. 10 Aug 2014.
Between *Psychedelic Wall* and *Slowboat*. Climb a thin crack through an overhang to a ledge. Go up the centre of the upper wall to a precarious finish.

SARCLET, Djapana Buttress:

The Grey Team 35m E2 5b **. Rob Christie, Charlie Macleod. 3 Sep 2014.
Five metres south of *Silver Surfer*, starting up a shoulder width chimney. Follow a corner left under a big roof. Exit right over the roof via the jammed block. Move up and left to rest, then right and up to gain a stance under the second roof. Exit left onto the wall, then up right to gain the prow on easy ground to finish.

East Face:

The Haar Bringer 35m E4 5c ***. Graham Tyldesley, Rory O'Hara Murray. 18 Apr 2015.

A line through the roofs left of *Groove Armada*. Start up *Time Bandit* and pass the 'protruding blob' on its right. Climb up and slightly right to a line of weakness in the roofs above. Follow this, stepping out right into a bridging rest before rejoining the line just above. A brilliant steep climb. A direct ascent would be a bit pumpier and maybe 6a.

ORKNEY, Rose Ness:

An update for the approach. Continue on from the cemetery and turn left following a sign for Upper Cornquoy. Park on the right in a good parking area just before the farm, ND 524 001. Go through a walkers' gate and follow a track to the cliff-top. Turn right and walk along the cliff past the impressive Hole of Ness to the crag (marked as Savernick on the 1:25,000 map), 15 to 20mins.

Route 0 HVS 5a. Jonathan Preston, Diana Preston. 1 Jun 2015.

The wall left of *Route 1*. Start up a jutting flake (left of centre on the wall). Follow this rightwards to finish direct up the centre of the wall on steep juggy holds.

Route 21 Severe. Jonathan Preston. 1 Jun 2015.

Further right from *Route 19*, around an edge and above rock pools. A fine looking corner with the crux right at the top (there is an escape ledge rightwards at half-height).

NORTHERN HIGHLANDS CENTRAL

BEINN A' MHUINIDH, Bonaid Dhonn:

Camino del Sol 60m VS 4c. Dan Moore. 22 Jul 2014.

Follow the lower approach via the goat track and just before the buttress starts turning round, there is a area of continuous steep rock about 50-60m high, with a wide open groove on the right leading up to some roofs and to the left of the arete are two parallel cracks in the middle of the buttress. This route takes the right-hand crack. Climb up carefully to the bottom of the crack which starts at the base of a shallow corner. Climb the crack which widens and then passes up and left through a steep bulge onto the easier angled slab above. Move up and right to climb a shallow groove just left of the arete and finish straight up. Continue scrambling to the top.

Losing my Edge 120m VS 4c **. Dan Moore. 23 Jul 2014.

This route climbs the prominent beak of rock described in the guide 5m above the path at the corner of the glen, right of *Route 1*. It effectively climbs the arete of the corner of the glen. There is an obvious nose/beak of rock with an overhung corner on its right side and containing a crack (clearly visible on the topo in the guide right of *Route 1*). Climb the arete on the right below the corner, until it joins the corner. Move steeply left round the overhang and follow the fault-line above for a few metres until below overhanging rock above. Move left and up to pull round on top of a big rectangular block (probably the one mentioned in *Route 1* description). Continue up the fault line above for a couple of metres, before traversing back right over the overhangs, spacewalking rightwards until possible to mantel up onto a ledge. Continue up a groove for a few metres to a good ledge and belay (40–50m). Continue up the slim V-groove above. Finish up the corner in the arete above.

Toblerone 120m V.Diff *. Ewan Lyons. 20 Apr 2014.
Start 20m left of the start to *Route I* and climb a triangular shaped leaning pillar to its finish. Climb the short, steep wall above (easier for the tall, watch out for loose block) or avoid on the right. Step left over one rib and gain another further left; follow this at an easy angle, crossing *Route II* to below the chimney. Step left to the foot of a right-angled corner, climb this, then step left again into another corner that leads to a blunt arete. Easy scrambling leads to a final steep wall. Topo provided.

BEINN A' MHUINIDH:

North-West Buttress 120m IV,4. Roger Webb, Simon Richardson. 13 Dec 2014.
The crag below the summit on the north-west face of Beinn a' Mhuinidh is disappointingly broken, however there is a steep buttress towards its right end at NH 029 662. This looks imposing from below but is cut by a deep right-trending fault.
1. 60m Climb easy snow and ice to the foot of the fault.
2. 30m Follow the fault and exit via a squeeze chimney to gain the right crest of the buttress.
3. 30m Climb cracks and short corners trending left to the top of the buttress.

STONE VALLEY CRAGS AREA, Meall an Triubhais Dhuibh:

Approach: Park at the car park by the green barn at NG 856 721. Follow a track north for a few hundred metres then head down to cross a burn and head towards a notch in the skyline, above which is a pond with many lilies. Visible from here to the north is the Lily Lochan Crag. The Main Wall is further round to the left and north.

Main Wall:

(NG 857 728) Alt 220m West facing
Gneiss Journey 45m HVS. Jeanie & Stuart Macfarlane. 19 Jul 2014.
Start at a corner at the right end of the lower tier and climb the full height of the crag.
1. 20m 4c Climb the corner and then move left onto the arete which is climbed to a heather ledge. Belay at a pine tree.
2. 25m 5a Climb up the crack just right of the tree to a heather ramp, then onto the wall above which provides thin moves to gain a heather ramp which is followed to an obvious corner. Climb the corner and then easier rock to the top.

Gneiss Wander 40m VS 4c. Stuart & Jeanie Macfarlane. 13 Sep 2014.
Towards the left end of the lower tier. Climb an obvious crack with a block at the top. Once the heather ledge is reached move up diagonally right to a crack left of the pine tree. Climb this and move right onto a heather rake. Follow this left until able to access upper tier, which is climbed to the top.

Totally Gneiss 35m VS 4c. Jeanie & Stuart Macfarlane. 13 Sep 2014.
Further up and left from *Gneiss Wander* is a left-facing corner. Climb up to the base of a wall just right of corner. Step left into the corner and climb up to a ramp coming in from the left. Continue up easier rock.

Arachnid 20m V.Diff. Stuart & Jeanie Macfarlane. 19 Jul 2014.
On the descent down the south side of the crag is a section of lovely rough gneiss. This route starts at a short corner and climbs straight up.

Bog Cotton Slab:
(NG 858 732) Alt 230m West facing
This crag is a few hundred metres north of the Main Wall and forms a runway of rough gneiss.

Left 25m Mod. Jeanie & Stuart Macfarlane. 13 Sep 2014.
Climb the left side of the slab.

Right 25m Mod. Stuart & Jeanie Macfarlane. 13 Sep 2014.
Climb the right side of the slab.

Lily Lochan Crag:
(NG 858 727) 210m South facing
This wall is few hundred metres south of the Main Wall.

Crack'n Slab 22m H.Severe 4b. Stuart & Jeanie Macfarlane. 13 Sep 2014.
Climb a crack on the lower tier to another crack on the next tier which is exited on the left to the slab above. Climb this to the top.

Flake Route 12m Severe. Stuart & Jeanie Macfarlane. 20 Jul 2014.
Start below an obvious flake and climb the flake.

Gneiss Arete 10m H.Severe 4c. Jeanie & Stuart Macfarlane. 13 Sep 2014.
The obvious arete at the left end of the crag. The start is a well protected boulder problem.

Red Wall 8m Diff. Jeanie & Stuart Macfarlane. 13 Sep 2014.
An immaculate red wall left of the arete.

Coot Crag (NG 862 728) 240m East facing, is about 5m high and varying lines can be soloed from Mod. to H.Severe.

LOCH MAREE CRAG:
Note: *Pagan Love Song*: The wet and dirty start can be avoided by climbing *Arial* for 10m, then moving left via a handrail. Any ivy re-growth is easily cleaned on lead. A little loose on the first pitch, but the second pitch is solid and sustained. Worth **.

CARNMORE AREA, Maiden Buttress, Carnan Ban:
Infamy 95m V.Diff **. Adam Archibald, Alex Murdoch. 13 May 2015
A fine sustained climb on excellent rock between *Dishonour* and *Tweedledum*.

1. 20m Climb near the right edge of the initial *Dishonour* slab to belay under the wall at its right end.
2. 20m Traverse left along the ledge and gain the top of the wall via the flake just around the far left end of the ledge (as for *Dishonour*). Traverse back right to belay above the previous belay.
3. 20m Climb the left-facing corner above to a further ledge.
4. 35m Climb straight up to the overhang and pull through this leftwards on magnificent jugs. Above, trend up and right on somewhat easier ground and belay at a large block.
Thereafter, either scramble up the grassy gully or finish as per one of the other routes.

GRUINARD BAY CRAGS, Post Crag:
Post-it Right-Hand Start 12m E2 5b *. Ian Taylor, Tess Fryer. 15 Aug 2014.
Start at *Scoobie Dubh* and follow the highest diagonal crack leftwards to join *Post-it* at half-height.

AN TEALLACH, Ghlas Tholl:
Low Riders 80m VII,8 **. Uisdean Hawthorn, Guy Robertson. 25 Feb 2015.
Takes a corner on the arete right of *Minor Rib*. At the top of the corner, move left across a steep wall to a ledge, then climb a line of small corners above to join *Minor Rib*.

FANNAICHS, Sgurr Mor, North-East Face:
Ma Larkin 220m III,4 *. Steve Kennedy. 21 Mar 2015.
Climbs the upper buttress left of *Easter Gully*. From a point about one third of the way from the foot of *Easter Gully*, move left and climb easy angled ice to a large snowfield below the buttress. Mixed ground via a scoop in the middle of the buttress leads to a terrace. Move left along the terrace then up leftwards to a short icefall. Climb the icefall leading to a snow bay on the left. Continue directly, finishing by a right-facing corner.

FANNAICHS, Coire nan Eun:
Twist 90m IV,4. Andy Nisbet, Jonathan Preston. 4 Jan 2015.
An icy fault well left of *Hawkwind* and near the left end of the East Buttress. Climb the fault via an icy ramp on the left to reach the top left of a bay (40m). Climb a groove above (the main fault is further right) to reach a terrace. Continue up via turfy ledges, short grooves and small zigzags to a ledge just below the top (40m). Traverse off left.

Jitterbug 90m III. Sandy Allan, Andy Nisbet. 26 Jan 2015.
Start about 10m right of *Twist* and climb turfy ground up to a short icefall in a right-facing corner. Continue up to a bay with a large block on the left and a flat block forming a thread (45m). Go up rightwards out of the bay, then return left to climb a steep turfy groove to the top (45m).

Twerk 110m V,5. Andy Nisbet, Jonathan Preston. 28 Dec 2014.
Some 20m right of *Slam* (West Buttress) is a left-rising bottomless ramp leading to the left end of a terrace. Climb the ramp to the terrace (45m). Traverse right along the terrace for 10m to a wide turfy fault. Climb this to a ledge and belay on

the left (35m). Traverse left and climb a left-rising ramp. Go right up a slabby corner to the top (30m).
Variation Start 80m V,5. Andy Nisbet, Steve Perry. 20 Feb 2015.
Start 6m to the right and climb a parallel ramp to a steep groove (which could be climbed if well frozen). Traverse right to a ledge (30m). Go up a slab to the terrace. Traverse right for 5m, then go up right and back left on turf to belay close to Twerk (50m). Finish up this route.

Samba 110m IV,4. Sandy Allan, Andy Nisbet. 26 Jan 2015.
Start some 10m right of *Twerk* and climb easily to a large block on a ledge (10m). Above is the first easy break to gain the main ledge mentioned in *Twerk*. Zigzag leftwards to reach the base of the right-hand of two parallel ramps (45m). Climb the ramp to its top (40m). Move left and climb a groove slanting left to finish (15m).

Bolero 90m V,5. Dave McGimpsey, Andy Nisbet. 15 Feb 2015.
The first icefall right of the rocky section of West Buttress. *Bunny Boiler* is the second icefall. Climb snow and easy ice to rock right of the icefall (20m). Climb the lower section of the icefall to below a steep corner (30m). Climb the steep iced corner to easier ice leading into a finishing gully (40m).

GLEN AFFRIC, Coire Ghaidheil:
(NH 092 221) Alt 650m South-East and East facing
Two main schistose crags. The main crag is due west of Lochan Coire Ghaidheil. There is an easy walk off south via the An Socach ridge or north via Bealach Coire Ghaidheil. Standard Moine schist climbing relying on cold icy conditions and frozen turf.

Faffricfossen 140m II. Dave Farnell, Andy Griffiths, Ric Hines. 25 Jan 2010.
A long wide open gully at the very back of the corrie with several steeper icy steps topping out right on the 921m summit.

Codeine Cuisine 90m II/III. Tom Davy, Ric Hines. 27 Nov 2010.
The deepest and longest gully cutting through the centre of the buttress due west of Lochan Coire Ghaidheil. Climb the gully passing icy and turfy steps taking the narrow right fork halfway up.

Stairway to Raigmore 50m II. Tom Davy, Ric Hines. 27 Nov 2010.
Climb the short deep gully 50m south of *Codeine Cuisine* via icy and turfy steps.

AN RIABHACHAN, Creagan Toll an Lochain:
Gotcha 150m V,5. Brian Davison, Andy Nisbet, Steve Perry. 14 Mar 2015.
An ice line right of *Gatekeeper* (SMCJ 2014). There was more ice on the crag than in 2014, and the cornice was much smaller, but the turf wasn't frozen in the back of grooves. Climb the short introductory tier as for *Gatekeeper* but head towards the right end of the lower band (20m). Climb a line of turf right of a short capped chimney and continue to gain the ice line, which forms down a defined fault (35m). Climb the fault to below an iced chimney (45m). Climb the chimney and trend slightly right to a rock band. Either climb a tricky V-groove or an easier ramp to its left (30m). Finish straight up, or wherever the cornice allows (20m).

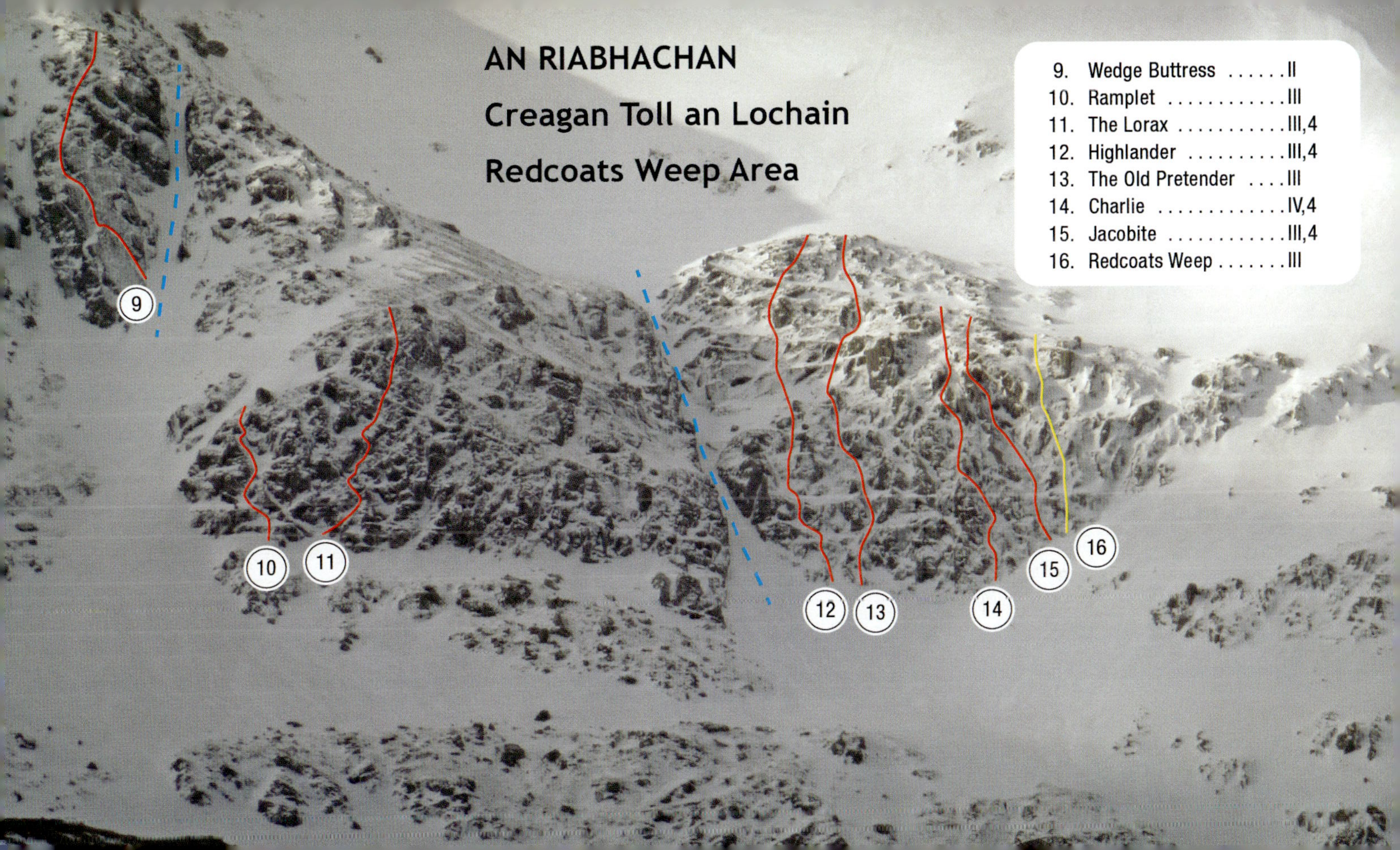
AN RIABHACHAN
Creagan Toll an Lochain
Redcoats Weep Area
9. Wedge Buttress II
10. Ramplet III
11. The Lorax III,4
12. Highlander III,4
13. The Old Pretender III
14. Charlie IV,4
15. Jacobite III,4
16. Redcoats Weep III
9
10
11
12
13
14
15
16

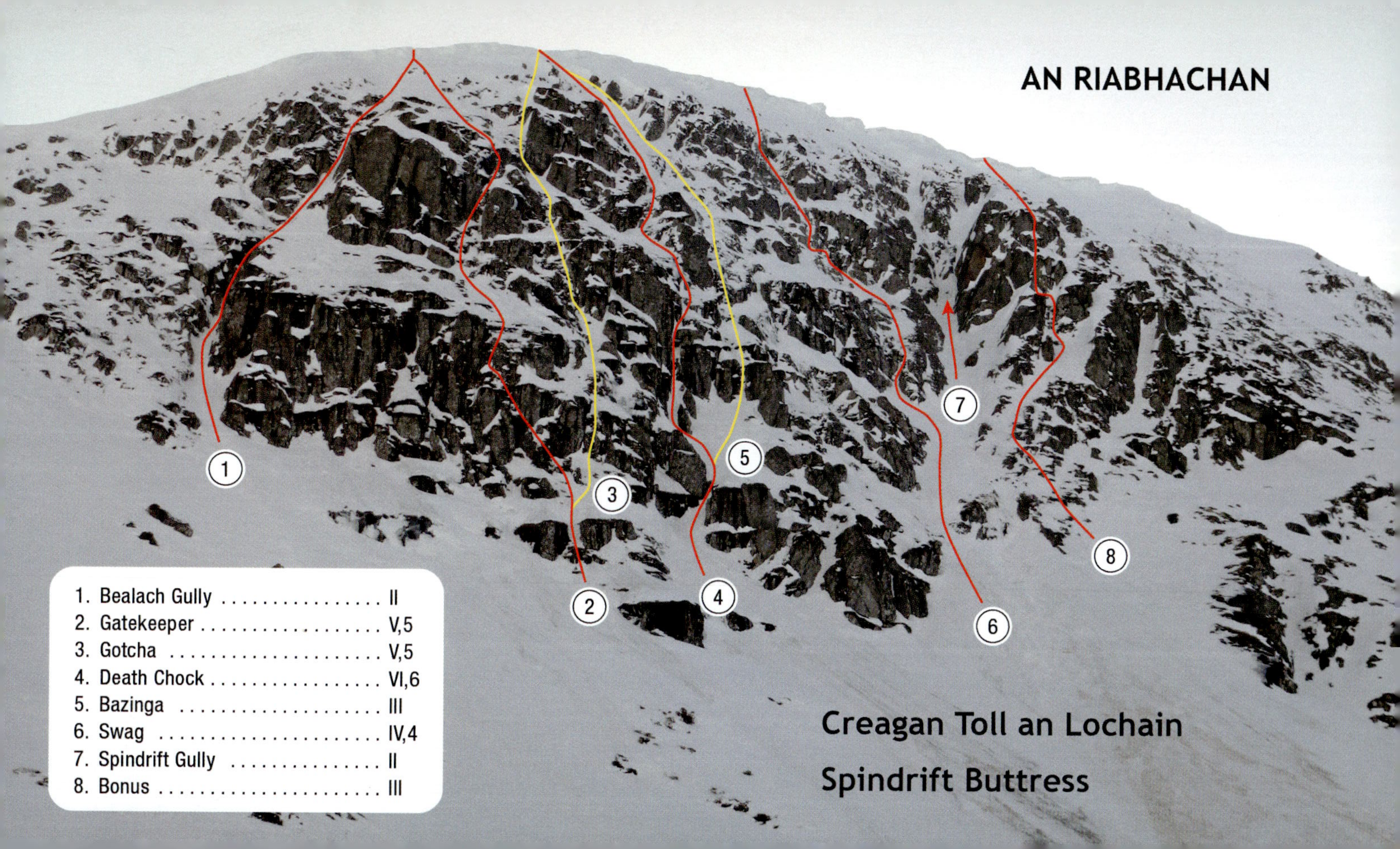
AN RIABHACHAN
1
2
3
4
5
6
7
8
1. Bealach Gully II
2. Gatekeeper V,5
3. Gotcha V,5
4. Death Chock VI,6
5. Bazinga III
6. Swag IV,4
7. Spindrift Gully II
8. Bonus III
Creagan Toll an Lochain
Spindrift Buttress

Death Chock 170m VI,6. Brian Davison, Andy Nisbet, Steve Perry. 14 Mar 2015.
A harder line left of *Bazinga*, but with the same start and finish. Gain the bay as for *Bazinga* but keep to its left side and go up a snow runnel to below a chimney which is overhung by a huge block (50m). Climb the chimney (technical crux), pass the block and continue to where a thinly iced slab gains snow leading up left (50m). Head back right on ice to the big fault line of *Bazinga* and climb its left edge to blocks on top of the rocks on its left (50m). Finish straight up (20m).

Swag 120m IV,4. Brian Davison, Andy Nisbet, Steve Perry. 14 Mar 2015.
An iced fault in the buttress between *Bazinga* and *Spindrift Gully*. Start up *Spindrift Gully* and move left to where an iced ramp leads up to below the fault line (not included in length). Climb the ramp, then go up on snow and ice to gain the base of the main fault (50m). Traverse left to an iced groove leading back right to the fault. Climb the fault to the upper snow band (55m). Finish straight up (15m).

Bonus 150m III. Andy Nisbet. 16 Mar 2015.
The ridge right of *Spindrift Gully* is helpful and has many flakes. Start right of the toe and move left on to the vague crest. Follow this to where a snow ramp leads up right (this lower part can bank up with snow). Follow the ramp until a left branch goes straight up. Go up this, then step left into a narrow groove on the crest and climb it to a ledge. Go up another groove to an easier upper crest leading to the cornice.

Right of this is a more broken section of cliff, then a wide shallow gully (Grade I, used for descent) before the next section of cliff which has several snowy grooves separated by shallow ribs. The first feature right of the gully is a groove with a ramp leading out left at two-thirds height to pass an overhang. Next right is a distinct groove which goes the full height of the cliff. These two routes and the Grade I gullies may have been climbed before. At the right end of this section is a well defined but shorter buttress with a slabby right face and flanked by gullies, the right gully being better defined.

Accidental Groove 200m II. Andy Nisbet. 18 Mar 2015.
The groove at the left end of this section. There are some short ice pitches low down and ice on the ramp leading out left.

Oggie 250m II. Andy Nisbet. 18 Mar 2015.
The well defined groove. There are two low angled 10m ice pitches low down and a short ice step to gain the main upper groove. The groove held icy neve and was about 50 degrees in angle.

Sauron 100m III. Andy Nisbet. 18 Mar 2015.
Left of the well defined buttress is a gully with a short steep ice pitch (unclimbed). Left again are iced slabs. Climb these to enter a deep left-facing corner, climbed on ice to easier ground. Climb the easier ground to the ridge (Grade I, not included in length)

Wedge Buttress 100m II. Andy Nisbet. 16 Mar 2015.

The well defined buttress. Start 15m up right from its toe and climb a turfy groove leading up left to the crest. Follow the easy crest.
Note: The gully on the right is Grade I and was used for descent.

Below and right of the above buttress is the rightmost area of cliff in the corrie. It is split into two sections by a snow gully, which will have a pitch in lean conditions but was Grade I on the day.

Ramplet 60m III. Andy Nisbet. 16 Mar 2015.
At the left end of the left section is a well defined slab ramp. Climb icy steps to gain and climb the iced ramp.

The Lorax 100m III,4. Andy Nisbet. 18 Mar 2015.
A mixed line with ice and turf up the steepest part of the left section. Start about 30m in from the left end at a small bay left of a rockfall scar. Take a ramp leading right (not the bigger and easier ramp further right), then pull up left into another ramp. Follow this rightwards to a small groove on the left which leads to a large pinnacle. Pull out left (crux) into another turfy ramp which leads right to the top.

The right section contains the route *Redcoats Weep* at its right end. Left of here is vague crest with two steep but thin icefalls to its left. Left again are two easier icefalls before reaching the snow gully.

Highlander 100m III,4. Andy Nisbet. 16 Mar 2015.
The leftmost ice line. Start at the bottom left corner of the section and climb ice steps before moving left to a short but steep ice groove. Climb this, then move left to icy steps which are followed to a snow terrace. Continue up thinly iced slabs to an easier finish

The Old Pretender 120m III. Andy Nisbet. 16 Mar 2015.
The second ice line. Start some 15m to the right and climb icy steps before a ramp leads up right to a big left-facing groove. Climb this to a snow terrace. Go up right from its right end and finish easily.

Charlie 100m IV,4. Andy Nisbet. 18 Mar 2015.
An ice line based on the crest. Start right of the crest and climb the first ice on its right before moving right into a ramp which leads left to the crest (the ramp could have been gained directly, slightly easier). Cross the crest (joining the upper part of the first thin icefall) and climb ice to easier ground.

Jacobite 90m III,4. Andy Nisbet. 18 Mar 2015.
The next ice line to the right leads into a big groove. Climb ice into and up the groove.
Note: It is unsure which line *Redcoats Weep* takes but there are two thicker ice lines to the right and which presumably form more quickly.

STRATHCONON, Loch Beannacharain:
(NH 237 503) Alt 400m
A prominent icefall on the north side of Meall Buidhe well seen from the road on the shore of Loch Beannacharain. Approach via Inverchoran, cross the bridge over

the Meig, turn right through a gate and skirt fields to reach a track on the north shore of the loch. Follow this for over 2km to the outflow of the burn adjacent to a wide clearing in the forest.
Descent: Unless conditions are good, the easiest is to follow the east ridge of the hill down to the track that leads back to Inverchoran.

Gift Horse 125m IV,5 *. Dave Broadhead, John Mackenzie. 22 Jan 2015.
On this ascent deep unconsolidated snow marred what could have been a good route. The obvious icefall screen has a junior relative lower down where the route starts.
1. 30m The right side of the scree was climbed to snow and a tree belay.
2. 30m Easy but deep snow led to a belay below the impressive screen.
3.30m The main screen was too fragile to climb so good ice was climbed a little to its right to an easing of the angle but an increase in the difficulties where a blank snow covered slab led right to a left-facing corner line which was followed to a recess.
4. 35m Move left to the centre of the fine icefall and climb up the middle over the top bulge in a good position to a snowy exit.

Creag Ruadh, North-East Face:
Feint Surprise 100m II. John Mackenzie. 15 Feb 2015.
Roughly in the centre of the face and prominent in lean conditions is a narrow snow gully. It curves first left, then straightens and steepens. It has a midway step of ice or turf and has three exits, the left easy but the centre and most interesting taken on this ascent via a narrow ramp under a rock overhang.

GLENMARKSIE CRAG, Small Wall:
Left of the gully lies Small Wall, with a rowan tree at its base. This is reached by a scramble up a short slab, 'The Hillary Step'. The crag is highest above some rock shelves that lie above a gully and it diminishes in height leftwards beyond the large rowan. The easiest descent or ascent is at the left-hand end where a rock ledge leads right to a pair of metal belay stakes and a large boulder. The routes are logically described from right to left. The first climbs start from the rock shelves above the gully. A good warm-up area or for those wishing to top rope.

Turf Wars 20m VS 4c *. Andrew James, John Mackenzie. 23 Jun 2015.
Takes the more broken ground to the right of *Botox Corner*. Start behind a broom bush at a footless overhang which commences proceedings. Continue up shelves and climb a slab below *Botox Corner*, then move up rightwards to another slab which gives a fine finish.

Botox Corner 20m E1 5b **. John Mackenzie, Andrew James. 2 May 2015.
This good route is both strenuous and then delicate. Start above the gully right of a thin crack and climb the wall to reach a niche. Step right to below an overhanging nose and pull over this to reach a shelf. Climb the narrow groove above to holds, then step right into the main corner and so to the top.

Skyfall 20m E2 5b **. John Mackenzie, Andrew James. 14 May 2015.
An excellent varied route that is both delicate and airy with adequate protection taking the roof-capped wall left of *Botox Corner*. Start from the rock shelves

below a thin crack. Climb to and up the sustained crack to reach a flake at the left end of the niche. From the crest of the flake, traverse left to below the roof and climb a thin crack in a shallow corner leading to the left end of the roof. Traverse right below the roof to the left arete of *Botox Corner*; move up then step back left to finish up the edge.
Variation: Direct Finish E3 6a/b *. John Mackenzie. 23 Jun 2015.
Rather than moving right under the overhang as for the original route, climb the overhang to finish more delicately (2 wires preplaced above the roof).

Pedestal Crack 10m HVS 5b. John Mackenzie, Andrew McKenzie. 21 Jun 2015.
The three routes from 1979 come next, then this route, which takes the thin podded crack squeezed in between *Staircase* and *Central Crack*. From the pedestal climb the tricky crack to stand in the pod. Continue up to a large ledge on the left and finish right of the big boulder.

Central Crack 10m Severe. John Mackenzie, Andrew James. 19 Mar 2015.
Climbs the left-slanting pronounced crack in the slabby wall left of *Staircase*.

One Small Step 10m HVS 5b **. John Mackenzie, Andrew James. 6 Apr 2015.
A fine little route with a delicate start and finish. Left of *Central Crack* is an overlap with a thin crack above. Reaching the crack is the first crux and the route finishes more thinly without stepping right into *Central Crack*.

Bog-jaaveled 9m HVS 5a *. John Mackenzie, Andrew James. 6 Apr 2015.
Another good line starting up the short left-facing corner with a small ledge on its right. Gain the ledge, then step left above, then immediately step back right to finish up the thin crack to a delicate exit.

BEN WYVIS, An Cabar:
Hut Custodian's Buttress 90m III,4 *. Andrew James, John Mackenzie. 21 Feb 2015.
To the right of *President's Groove* is a narrow buttress. This was started above the easier lower section to give some pleasant climbing with good hooks and positions.
1. 30m Climb *President's Groove* to a narrow ledge on the left wall by a large block and thread belay just below a steepening in *President's Groove*.
2. 30m Climb the right wall towards a small tree on the skyline to a block on the right, move right and up a short steep corner and up to easier ground.
3. 30m Above the easier ground is a wide groove. Climb the inset groove on its right over a short steep step and continue to the top.

NORTHERN HIGHLANDS SOUTH

BEINN FHADA, Coire an Sgairne:
Banshee 140m III. Andy Nisbet, Steve Perry. 27 Feb 2015.
This climbs the depression immediately right of 'the great black vertical wall'. Start in a bay right of the wall. Climb up to underneath the wall, then head right up a big diagonal ramp which goes to the top of the cliff. Leave this leftwards at

the first easy break and trend left up a short thinly iced slab (crux) into the twin upper fault. Take the left branch to the top.

Wolfman 200m IV,5. Andy Nisbet, Steve Perry. 27 Feb 2015.
Right of *Banshee* is another easy diagonal fault which goes the full height of the cliff. This takes a line crossing it. Start in a bay below and right of the fault. The right side of the bay is formed by a big smooth wall, possibly ice streaked, and the top is a steep groove. Climb the next groove left on ice, then traverse left on to turfy ground. Zigzag up this to below a narrow turfy groove (there is a bigger but harder groove to the right) – 40m. Climb the groove to reach the bigger groove and follow it to the diagonal fault (45m). Go up this until possible to head up left into a bay (50m). There are two steep faults out of the top of the bay but head rightwards to a narrow chimney on the right crest of the bay (25m). Climb the chimney, then trend right before finishing straight up (40m).

KYLE OF LOCHALSH, White Dyke:
Note: Andy Moles thinks that *Silver Sixpence* (SMCJ 2008) is actually the existing route *Shilling Corner*.

FUAR THOLL, Mainreachan Buttress:
Private Eye (The Big Sleep) 150m VIII,8. Iain Small, Murdoch Jamieson. 23 Jan 2015.
A steep, technical winter climb based loosely around the summer route but incorporating a different entry pitch and taking the obvious hanging ice smear and fault, before joining the original line. Start a few metres down from the summer start at an obvious left-trending ramp.
1. 40m Start up the ramp moving left to its end to gain a niche below a steep groove. Climb this (strenuous), then trend up and left over slabby ground to gain the ledge. Belay on flakes directly below the icy fault above (this is guarded by a steep compact wall).
2. 35m Step down and move right into a corner. Climb this (strenuous) to gain more helpful ground until a left-slanting slot can be gained. Move left up this to gain the ice at the start of the steep fault.
3. 35m Climb the steep icicle festooned fault (shattered rock) pulling right at the roof to a ledge. Continue straight up mixed corners to the girdle ledge below the final big open corner.
4. 40m Follow the big open corner, passing the occasional difficulty to the top.

BEINN LIATH MHOR, South Face:
Zeus 250m III. Sandy Allan, Andy Nisbet. 21 Jan 2015.
The second buttress from the left, so left across a big V-gully from *Artemis* (SMCJ 2009). Start up right from the toe of the buttress, just inside the base of the gully. Climb a long groove which leads to the crest. Follow the crest throughout to the top. The last section is avoidable on the left but worth doing.

McTwist 200m II. Sandy Allan, Andy Nisbet, Jonathan Preston. 22 Jan 2015.
At the right end of the higher section of cliff with the previous route is a well defined buttress with a big V-gully on its right. The steepest section, reached after two smaller tiers, was passed by a groove system on its left side.

Half Pipe Gully 200m II. Sandy Allan, Andy Nisbet. 21 Jan 2015.
Left of the central buttress with the roof and rock climbs in SMCJ 2011 is this fairly deep gully. It provided three short ice pitches and finished with a turfy corner straight up to an arete. Finish up the easy gully on the left.

Barbie 250m V,6. Sandy Allan, Andy Nisbet, Steve Perry. 25 Feb 2015.
A winter line based on the slabby rib right of *Half Pipe Gully* (*Doll Restoration*, 2011) but climbing turfy grooves and corners to the top of the cliff. Start below a deep groove just right of the rib and with a distinctive chockstone. Climb the groove, over the chockstone and up its continuation before moving left on to the rib where its angle eases (40m). Climb the rib for 6m before moving left into a corner. Climb this back on to the rib and go up across a terrace to below another tier (45m). Climb the tier on flakes on the crest and continue to a steep tier (40m). Move left into a corner and climb this to a final tier (35m). Climb this by a steep crack-line leading left and continue to easier ground (20m). Finish up the easier ground (70m).

Grey Vote 180m IV,5. Sandy Allan, Andy Nisbet, Jonathan Preston. 22 Jan 2015.
A slightly right-slanting fault line in the central buttress, parallel to and some 60m right of *Half Pipe Gully*. Start up a chimney which goes straight up into the fault line (30m). Climb a chimney in the fault line, then easier ground with icy steps to a terrace (40m). Continue up the fault line via an ice pitch (50m) and in the same line to easy ground (60m).

Note: The big gully right of these routes has been climbed before at Grade II.

MAOL CHEANN-DEARG, Creag Liath (North Face):

An Liath Beag 55m Severe. John Mackenzie, Andrew James. 11 Jul 2014.
Near the right end of the face before it turns right and immediately right of a broken groove is a clean rib above a squat pinnacle.
1. 25m 4a Climb the rib to an overhang, move left into a groove and belay above on the right by a large block.
2. 30m Move right and climb the face to easier ground and the grass terrace.

MEALL NAN CEAPAIREAN, North Face:

Mains Pressure 180m III,4 *. Ewan Lyons. 19 Jan 2015.
Start below the left-hand side of the big bowl (left of the existing routes) and climb to this via two icy steps. Cross the bowl moving slightly right to the wide girdling shelf. Move along the shelf right for a few metres then zigzag up left via turfy ramps to the left of steeper rock to the top of the buttress.

Isolation Valve 200m III. Ewan Lyons. 19 Jan 2015.
Start well over to the left of the buttress, 25m left of an icefall which is left of an area of steep rock. Climb up icy turfy grooves for 50m to a wide ledge. Traverse right along the ledge above the icefall, then over the bowl (crossing *Mains Pressure*). Move up left to finish up the higher and wider of two ramp lines.

SGURR A' CHAORACHAIN, Summit Buttress:

Flying Carpet 60m E3 **. Martin Moran, Robin Thomas (on-sight). 24 Jul 2014.

The route gains and climbs the deep groove in the overhanging section of cliff 20m right of the gully of *Excitable Boy*. Slow to dry, but worthwhile with some intricate and surprisingly helpful climbing in a serious ambience. Start at a short right-facing black corner under a roof.
1. 35m 5b Climb the corner for 5m, then bridge out left on to an obvious beak on the lip of the roof and continue to a break. Take the right-hand of the two grooves. Good steady climbing leads for 20m to a break under the roofs. Traverse 4m left and make a belay on a slabby rib just right of the main groove line.
2. 25m 5c Access to the main groove is barred by an overhang and dubious block. Instead, climb directly above the belay (RP runners) to a small spike which allows a swing left to enter the groove above the roof. Fine climbing up the groove and through final bulges leads to a grass ledge.
Abseil off or scramble 40m up left to the top of the cliff.

South-East Ridge:
Weer Zo'n Dag 300m IV,5. Dennis van Hoek, Marianne van der Steen. 24 Feb 2015.
An obvious big gully on the crag which faces north-east from the Corbett summit (not the radio mast). The aim was to climb it throughout but the base was loose and unfrozen. The name means 'One of those Days' in Dutch. Start well right of the lower part of the gully. Climb up left below a wide gully, then take a snow ramp up right to reach another gully. Climb this and one pitch up the subsequent buttress to a terrace. Traverse left along the terrace for about 100m to the main gully. Finish up this. Topo provided.

BEINN BHAN, Coire an Fhamair:
Messiah 240m IX,10. Greg Boswell, Guy Robertson, Uisdean Hawthorn. 2 Feb 2015.
Outstanding climbing up the great roof-capped groove immediately right of *Gully of the Gods*. Eyed by many, but usually dry and black, it takes uncommonly snowy conditions to bring this very steep line into what most climbers would agree to be acceptable winter. Start as for *Godzilla*.
1. 40m *Godzilla*, pitch 1.
2. 20m Step back down and left, then make a very exposed and rattling traverse horizontally left to belay below the great groove.
3. 25m Climb the groove direct to turn the first roof on the right, then continue up to belay before some very steep vegetation.
4. 35m Continue up the groove to an even bigger roof, then move left under this to gain a tiny hanging groove. Climb this to another roof where a difficult traverse right leads blindly into another groove. Climb this groove over bulges and on up to a terrace.
5. 25m Climb the continuation groove up trending slightly right to a final pull over onto the next terrace.
6. Follow the terrace easily round left, then up right to belay in the back right side of a big alcove (junction with *Outrage*).
7. and 8. Follow *Outrage* to the top.

BEINN DAMH AREA, Creag an Fhithich, Far Right Section:
Two small two-tiered buttresses lie to the right of the approach gully. The following routes take strong corner lines on the upper tier of the right-hand

buttress, well seen from the road. The routes are best approached by abseil (trees 50m back from top of the crag).

Wood Green Jam 8m E2 5c **. Michael Barnard, Alan Hill. 15 Oct 2014.
The fine left corner gives a good sustained struggle.

The Other One 10m E2 5c *. Michael Barnard, Alan Hill. 15 Oct 2014.
An obvious handrail leads into the right corner, with a thin move at half-height.

TORRIDON CRAGS, Rat's Crag:
(NG 898 566) South-South-West facing
The prominent steep wall down and slightly right of Creag nam Leumnach, 15mins.

Flight of the Rat 12m E3 5c **. Michael Barnard, Alan Hill. 15 Oct 2014.
A stern test up the fine thin crack at the right end of the crag. At the top of the crack, hand-traverse the lip to pull into the corner on the left.

The other two routes lie in the centre of the crag and require some care with loose blocks.

The Stag Stepped Out 10m VS 4b. Alan Hill, Michael Barnard. 14 Oct 2014.
The obvious right-facing stepped corner-crack.

Pressed Rat and Warthog 10m VS 4b. Michael Barnard, Alan Hill. 14 Oct 2014.
The crack and groove just left of the above.

Creag nam Leumnach:
The following routes lie on the wall at the far right end of the upper tier.

Toad 10m H.Severe 4b *. Michael Barnard, Alan Hill. 15 Oct 2014.
A fine vertical flake-crack (well seen when approaching the crag from the right).

Fern Gully 12m H.Severe 4b. Alan Hill, Michael Barnard. 14 Oct 2014.
Ten metres left of the above is a wide right-slanting flake-crack. Well seen from the top of *Warmer Cleaner Drier*.
Note: *Warmer Cleaner Drier* was thought worth 3 stars. Possibly E1 with a large cam in the top crack.

Diabaig, Red Wall:
In Crisis 20m E3 5b *. Michael Barnard, Alan Hill. 16 Oct 2014.
A memorable trip up the wall left of *An Offensive Man*. Four metres left of that route is a short vertical crack with a hairline crack above. Start just left of this and take a diagonal break to a heather clump. Move up to arrange protection, then step right and climb the wall to the niche and respite. Pull over the small overlap and continue directly to the top.

Nature's Way 20m E5 6a **. Michael Barnard, Ollie Mills. 23 May 2015.
Climbs the line of holds up the smooth wall between *Porpoise Pun* and *Batwing*. Bold and sustained in the lower half. Pre-practiced.

Note: The team thought the rock on the wall in general was excellent but that *Batwing* was very serious.

The Domes:
Yew Tree Wall 70m VS. Michael Barnard, Alan Hill. 12 Oct 2014.
Start up and right of *Hull Wall*, below a grey wall a few metres right of the yew.
1. 20m 4c Climb the wall via flakes and horizontal breaks; step left below the heather, then move up to belay.
2. 50m 5a Move right and go up the grassy bay to gain a shallow right-facing groove in the wall above. Climb this then break out left via flakes, with a thin move to gain a ledge on the left. Continue up the scooped corners above.

Dead Tree Crag (SMCJ 2009):
Small Black Flowers 20m VS 4c **. Michael Barnard, Alan Hill. 12 Oct 2014.
Variations on *Dead Tree Wall*. Start below a groove near the right end of the overhangs. Move up, then leftwards up a crack to reach the big flake. Continue as for *Dead Tree Wall* to below its crux, but instead finish out left along an excellent horizontal break.

Chock-a-block 10m H.Severe 4b. Alan Hill, Michael Barnard. 12 Oct 2014.
The arete left of the crag's grassy central corner, past a large block.

Rolling Wall:
Brave New World, Left-Hand Start. Michael Barnard, Alan Hill. 13 Oct 2014.
Equally good. Start as for *The Sea, The Sea*, then take the obvious diagonal crack through the bulge to join the route below its second crack. Grade is unchanged.

Rocking Wall:
Continuing left from *Alice's Overhang* leads to a short heather gully; over left from the top of this is a fine small dome split by a crack.

Rock 'n' Roll 8m VS 5a. Michael Barnard. 12 Jun 2015.
The crack on the right, finishing up the thin crack above.

The Pleasure Dome 8m HVS 5b **. Michael Barnard. 12 Jun 2015.
The main crack-line is sustained and well protected.

The other two routes take the slab on the left and are basically solos (though with the hardest moves at the start):

No-body's Rockin' 8m VS 5a. Michael Barnard. 12 Jun 2015.
Climbs the centre of the slab.

Adult Entertainment 8m HVS 5a. Michael Barnard. 12 Jun 2015.
Start as for the above but move rightwards above the lip to finish near *The Pleasure Dome*.

Pretty Crag:
We, the Drowned 10m E5 6b **. Gaz Marshall, Sarah Jones. 14 Jul 2014.
The blank slab into the obvious central hanging crack. Gain the port-hole feature

and place small wires in the insipient thin crack just above, then step right and tiptoe upwards to reach the safety of the main crack. Headpointed, later on-sight soloed by Jules Lines.

Virgin on Heat 10m E6 6b *. Jules Lines. 24 Jul 2014.
Start left of centre at an intrusion. Step up and move left into a hairline crack and climb it to its top and continue.

Note: The original routes there are undergraded by one grade. The map reference is reported as wrong.

SGURR DUBH, Creag Choire a' Cheud Chnoic:
(NG 96493 54989) Alt 450m North-West facing
This is a north-west facing quartzite crag which lies just to the south of Allt nan Corrag (named on the 1:25000 map) burn that drains the lochans on the west flank of the hill.
Approach: Follow the track past the Ling Hut and then cut up left near the southern bank of the burn to the crag. Allow 1hr plus over rough ground.
Descent: Move right to a rake that curves back to just beyond the crag.

The crag has a prominent right-facing central gully/corner that is capped by a wall. The following route takes the left arete and side wall above the gully.

Excaliber 35m VS 4b *. John Mackenzie, Andrew James. 27 Aug 2014.
Start at the base of the narrow gully and climb onto the arete and follow this edge until blocked by a large overhang. Step out right onto the sidewall and climb a narrow crack to much easier ground above. Continue over this to the top. A climb with good exposed positions lower down but take care with some loose blocks en-route.

Larch Tree Crag:
(NG 97632 55359) Alt 650m
This is a small but perfectly formed sandstone slab and sidewall that lies above the east corner of a delightful lochan. It is characterised by a mature larch tree that must be one, if not the, biggest specimen at its altitude in the NW Highlands, perhaps in Scotland. The front of the crag is a cracked slab and the left sidewall has a jamming crack next to the tree.
Approach: By any of the walking routes up the hill, all on rough ground, so allow 1.5 to 2hrs.
Descent: Move right to a hidden rake that curves right down an easy slab.

Larch Tree Slab 30m Severe 4a *. Andrew James, John Mackenzie. 27 Aug 2014.
Climb the pleasant central crack to exit up left via a wide V shaped crack.

Larch Tree Crack 25m VS 4c *. John Mackenzie, Andrew James. 27 Aug 2014.
On the left wall is an obvious jamming crack which is climbed to an easier wall above to join and finish up the V shaped crack as for the previous route. Not too arduous and very well protected.

Iain Small on the FA of Fascist Groove Thang, Direct Start (E5,6b), Beinn Eighe. Photo: Blair Fyffe.

Iain Small on the 2nd ascent of New World Order (E6,6b), Beinn Eighe. Photo: Blair Fyffe.

LIATHACH, Coire Dubh Beag:
West Buttress 300m II. Dave Broadhead, Stan Pearson. 3 Jan 2015.
Start at the bottom of *Hillwalk* gully and gain the buttress on the right. Meander up the buttress, following the most appealing line to reach the upper snow basin. Finish up a narrow chimney to the right (25m tech 4).

Coire na Caime, Northern Pinnacles:
Batman 160m VI,7. Andy Nisbet, Steve Perry. 13 Feb 2015.
The steeper right-hand face of the ridge with the route *Holy Ghost*. Conditions were very icy. Start at the base of the ridge.
1. 50m Climb leftwards up a fault line (not the one which starts at the base of *Trinity Gully Right-Hand*, although it could be an option) before returning right to climb a shallow chimney rightwards on to the right face of the ridge.
2. 25m Climb a wide crack (on ice on this occasion) into a big fault. Go up this until it steepens, then move right and make an awkward pull up right on to a ledge overlooking *Trinity Gully Right-Hand*.
3. 50m Pull up on to an inset slab, then step right to a wide crack. Pull up right (crux) on to an icy slab with some turf and climb this and a groove above to reach the ridge crest. Now joining *Holy Ghost*, go up to belay.
4. 35m Finish up the crest.

Pyramid Buttress:
Cheops 180m V,5. Andy Nisbet, Jonathan Preston. 5 Feb 2015.
A separate icefall some 30m left of *Pyramid Left Icefall*. Start below the line and climb two steps with snow between (30m). Climb a steep section using a corner on the left to reach another steep section (30m). Climb ice on the left and move right round a roof to continue over two bulges (30m). Traverse right for 10m and climb a shallow chimney before moving back left to turfy ground, climbed to easier ground (50m). Finish up the easier ground (40m).
Note: There were more direct versions of each of the three hard pitches, but on very steep ice (it was thawing on the day). There was an exceptional amount of (wet) ice.

BEINN EIGHE, Far East Wall:
New World Order 100m E6 6b ***. Murdoch Jamieson, Guy Robertson. 21 Jul 2014.
This follows the obvious corner which leads to roofs to the left of *Fascist Groove Thang*. Strenuous and well protected. Both first and second ascents thought top end of the grade.
1. 45m 5b As for *Fascist Groove Thang*.
2. 25m 6b Climb the corner with increasing difficulty, passing an overlap until it is possible to gain small edges on the left wall. Make moves up right to reach the base of the crack which leads to a roof. Turn the roof on its right to gain another crack. Follow this for a few moves (sting in the tail!) until possible to step right to a small ledge (immediately up left of 'the Fascist Groove').
3. 30m 5b Traverse left and up into the corner below the roof. Make airy moves out left to gain the arete. Follow this to the top.

Eastern Ramparts:
Note: *Turkish Delight*. Graham Tyldesley thought the crux was 6a and that linking pitch 3 with the steep crack of pitch 4 would be better (to avoid the uncomfortable belay). He also climbed a direct version to pitch 2. Halfway up the crag and just left of the line of the corner and crack is a long thin roof. A left-facing corner terminates at the right-hand end of the roof. After heading straight up to this corner expecting to climb it but on reaching it, it was more natural to step right and climb around it. A good pitch.

Boggle VII,8 ***. M. Moran, R. Thomas. 13 Dec 2014.
By the summer route.

CAIRNGORMS

COIRE AN T-SNEACHDA, Fiacaill Buttress:
Note: After starting up *Houdini*, Rob Adams & Fiona Murray climbed the final pitch of *Jailhouse Rock* at VI,8 on 28 Feb 2015. It would make a good direct finish to *Smokestack Lightning*. This would seem to have been done before by Adam Hughes & Matt Stygall on 15 Jan 2008.

COIRE AN LOCHAIN, No. 4 Buttress:
Banana Wall 55m XII,12. Greg Boswell, Masa Sakano. 25 Feb 2015.
1. 40m Start just right of *Fallout Corner* beneath the obvious steep wall. Climb up a big flake to reach the bulging wall and gain a small hanging niche/corner. Climb this, then past a blank wall trending slightly right to gain a roof. Go straight through the roof to the headwall, then up this to another roof and crack. Climb straight through to gain a sloping ledge direct.
2. 15m Climb straight up through the bulge to gain easier ground and to the top of the buttress.

MAM SUIM, Creag na h-Iolaire:
Storms of Life 40m III,4. Roger Webb, Simon Richardson. 11 Jan 2015.
The steepest climbing in the corrie lies on the wall left of the rib taken by the Richardson-Guerra and McKenzie-Ptacek-Savov routes. This route follows the most prominent line that arcs right under a series of capping grooves. Start on the left side of the wall and climb up to the start of the roofs, before traversing up and right in a series of unlikely positions to the steep finishing groove.

Fate is not an Eagle 40m IV,5. Simon Richardson, Roger Webb. 11 Jan 2015.
Start 10m right of *Storms of Life* and climb up and right to a steep short corner on the right side of the front face of the wall. Climb the corner, step right and continue steeply up, then left, to the final square-cut right-facing corner.

CREAGAN COIRE A' CHA-NO, Tower Buttress:
Punching Numbers 50m VI,7 **. Ally Swinton, Gav Swinton. 5 Dec 2014.
The obvious groove, corner and roof line to the right of *Mac's Crack*. Good gear and pumpy moves. Climb the first initial groove to a large ledge. Climb the large corner-flake. Pull out right and up into a small chimney. Climb wildly out the left

side of the chimney (stein-pull on left wall). Make one last awkward pull, then easy ground to the top.

COIRE NA SPREIDHE:

The Apron 300m II. Roger Webb, Simon Richardson. 8 Mar 2015.
A mountaineering line climbed up steep snow with short vegetated steps on the left side of the face. Start 50m left of *Central Couloir* and trend right, then left, to gain the upper snowfield. Follow this to gain the plateau just left of the steeper exits of *Central Couloir* and *Goulotte Cachee*.

SHELTER STONE CRAG:

The Spire (*Independent Start* – see SMCJ 2014), *Arete Variation*. Michael Barnard, Alan Hill. 27 Aug 2014
From the belay above pitch 1, move out right and climb the arete overlooking Steeple corner to the obvious ledge. Step back left to rejoin the route at the base of the upper vertical crack. Grade is unchanged.

Haystack, Haymaker Variation 45m E2 5c *. Michael Barnard, Alan Hill. 27 Aug 2014.
A good alternate pitch 3 for those looking for an additional challenge! Hand-traverse left from the belay to gain and go up a short right-facing corner to reach a thin crack (Friend 3.5 useful). Climb the thin crack with difficulty and continue up to gain the normal route at its right-slanting corner.

The Spire, Independent Start 120m E1 **. Michael Barnard, Alan Hill. 21 Jul 2013.
This start could also be used for *Haystack* or *Steeple*. It has a very fine second pitch. Start below the initial corner of *Haystack*.
1. 30m 4b Move up left onto the arete and continue up leftwards to climb a crack immediately right of a grassy fault. Trend up and right to belay near the right end of a grassy ledge (junction with *Haystack*).
2. 50m 5b Climb the right-hand crack up the slab; where this runs out, step right to continue up another crack leading into an obvious short corner. Move left along the ledge and go up a right-slanting corner (as for *Haystack*).
3. 40m Move up and right to gain a fault leading to the terrace (as for *Postern*). Step left to belay below the shallow groove.

Spire Direct 35m E3 6a **. Michael Barnard, Alan Hill. 30 Sep 2014.
A fine sustained line cutting through the penultimate pitch. Belay below a hard-looking corner just left of the big corner of *Steeple*. Climb the corner on slots to below a small overlap, then gain holds on the left (thin). Continue up and slightly rightwards to stand on a large flake. Now climb the vertical crack right of *Haystack* (occasionally using the next crack right again) to reach the ledge below the top pitch.

HELL'S LUM CRAG:

Diawl Bach, True Finish E3 6b. Michael Barnard, Alan Hill. 27 Aug 2014.
The final blank section of slab above the diagonal crack. Pre-practiced.
Note: *Diawl Bach* itself may be the direct start to *Kiwi Slabs*. *Kiwi Slabs* is only

given as a winter route in the guide but summer details are noted in last paragraph with the direct start at H.Severe.

666 12m E2 5b. Michael Barnard. 26 Jul 2014.
Climbs the blank grey slab right of the lower section of *Diawl Bach* (SMCJ 2014). Scramble off to the right or move left to continue up that route.

The following route lies on the short wall up and slightly left of the Lower Slab (left of Glasnost Slab):

Heaven Can Wait 30m E4 6a. Michael Barnard, Alan Hill. 27 Aug 2014.
The obvious blank section of slab, climbed via a series of small edges. Climb the first crux section to the break (good RPs), then continue up the slab (second crux) to the first smaller break. Step on this and reach for a good hold, then continue more easily. Pre-practiced.

CRAIG RAIBEIRT:
Gratuity 30m III. Jonathan Preston, Sarah Atkinson. 26 Dec 2014.
Start further up the right side of the buttress from *Typhoon Corners*, below a sapling. Climb up rightwards into a snow bay, then straight up to finish up a narrow turf filled V-groove on the right. Easy ground from the ledge above.
Note: The route lengths in SMCJ 2014 seem to include some easy ground.

Cold Turkey 60m III,4. Jonathan Preston, Sarah Atkinson. 26 Dec 2014.
A route on the next buttress right (across a short gully), the base of which is level with start of *Gratuity*.
1. 25m Start from a horizontal ledge at the base of the buttress. Climb a direct line up the centre of the buttress using flakes and turf to a large block on a platform (escapable from here).
2. 35m Traverse left from the col behind the block and climb a turfy groove to the top. Easy slopes above.

STAC AN FHARAIDH:
Well right of *Cold Turkey* is the vertical left wall of a more substantial buttress (the very left edge of the main Stac an Fharaidh crags).

Santa's Grotto 60m III,4. Jonathan Preston, Sarah Atkinson. 26 Dec 2014.
1. 35m Halfway up the vertical south-west facing wall of the buttress is a steep wide cleft; climb this up its left side with an awkward finish at the top on the right to a good platform.
2. 25m Finish more easily up a slabby left-facing corner on the left.

LURCHERS CRAG:
Shangri-La 135m IV,4 *. Andy Nisbet, Jonathan Preston. 3 Jan 2015.
A vague ridge which forms the left edge of the face left of the upper section of *Central Gully*. Start where a wide easy ramp leads out left from *Central Gully* (this is above the section with *Arctic Monkey*). The face above this ramp has a steep start but some 30m up the ramp is a deep groove. Climb the groove and a narrow chimney (on ice on this occasion), then easier ground to a steepening and big flakes (45m). Climb slabs with blobs of turf to the true start of the ridge and

continue up this slightly rightwards on slabby ground to a recess. Pull out left through this to a ledge above (45m). Continue up via a big right-facing corner to finish up blocky ground.

Beyul 80m III,4. Andy Nisbet, Jonathan Preston. 3 Jan 2015.
A line up the centre of the face. Start higher up *Central Gully* where a smaller ramp leads out left to the crest. Halfway up this ramp is a slabby depression. Start up this, then move left and back right to reach an overlap. Pull through this at a break at its left side and continue to a ramp which leads up left. Go part way up this, then climb a flaky groove and crack-line to the top.

El Dorado 90m III,5 *. Andy Nisbet, Jonathan Preston. 3 Jan 2015.
The right edge of the face, at times overlooking *Central Gully*, has two short overhanging sections on excellent hooks. Start just right of *Beyul* and move out right to a crest above *Central Gully*. Follow this blocky crest to the right side of the overlap mentioned above. Pull through this at a recess and continue to a steep wall. Move left to a slabby corner leading up right to a short blocky chimney (50m). Climb the corner and chimney to a platform overlooking *Central Gully*. Move left up a short steep groove to a crest leading left to the finish.

Beagle has Landed 140m V,4. Sandy Allan, Brian Davison, Andy Nisbet. 17 Jan 2015.
A big groove system right of *Dotterel*, between it and *Reindeer Ridge*. The steeper sections were climbed on thin ice with some turf. Right of *Dotterel* is a slabby area which dips into the main groove which is closer to *Reindeer Ridge*. Climb up on ice until a traverse right is made above a bulge. Go up a groove and over an ice bulge in to a long groove, climbed to its top (50m). Traverse left and climb on ice to the base of a deep groove. Step right and climb a ramp overlooking the groove to reach some more ice which leads to easy ground (40m). Go easily up a depression to finish up a steeper blocky buttress (50m).

Je Suis Charlie 150m III. Sandy Allan, Andy Nisbet. 8 Jan 2015.
Based on a groove system between *Reindeer Ridge* and *St. Bernard's Ridge*. Start on the right side of *Reindeer Ridge* and climb steeply into a ramp leading right into a bay; belay at its top left (40m). Climb icy slabs on the left, then a groove leading left before returning right to another bay (40m). A steep section above led to easier ground (40m). A system of slabby cracks (20m, could be avoided on the right) led to walking terrain and the summit of Creag an Leth-choin.

101 Dalmatians 160m VII,7. Sandy Allan, Brian Davison, Andy Nisbet. 19 Jan 2015.
A thin ice line up the left side of the depression between *St. Bernard's Ridge* and *Summit Ridge*. Thicker ice would drop the grade. Start well right of *St. Bernard's Ridge* near the rocks of *Summit Ridge*. Move left along a ledge to climb a tricky crack which leads to the ice line. Climb thin ice to a big ledge on the left (30m). Continue up the ice line over bulges to a slab bounded on the left by a right-facing corner. Go up this, then pull out left on to a ramp. Go up this and over a steep recess to easier ground (45m). Follow the easier depression to a headwall (60m). Climb a narrow chimney on its left side to an easier finish to the summit of Creag an Leth-choin (25m).

Blood Hound 180m VII,6 **. Steve Perry, Sandy Allan, Andy Nisbet. 9 Feb 2015.
A clean-cut left-facing corner formed in the left side of *Summit Ridge*. Start as for *101 Dalmatians* below and left of the corner where a ramp leads up right to the corner. Climb the ramp and corner (thin and bold), then an easier groove to near the crest of *Summit Ridge* (50m). Follow steps and corners left of the crest of *Summit Ridge* to the summit, pleasant but much easier.

Wallydraigle 240m III. Andy Nisbet. 24 Jan 2015.
The depression between *Dog Day Afternoon* and *Summit Ridge*. Start as for *Dog Day Afternoon* but continue up the left-diagonal fault into the base of the depression. Climb up the depression by a long easy-angled ice pitch, then walking with a couple of icy steps to a headwall. Climb this direct, passing right of a projecting block on a ledge. A line up a wide groove left of the block looks slightly harder.

Dachshund 100m IV,4. Sandy Allan, Andy Nisbet, Steve Perry. 9 Feb 2015.
The lower and left of two ridges which lead up left from the upper bowl of *Diamond Gully*. Start left of the crest and follow a turfy groove to the crest (50m). Follow the crest to a small col at the top of a gully between the two ridges, then go up, trending slightly right to give the best climbing to the top (50m).

Yappy 60m IV,6. Dave McGimpsey, Andy Nisbet. 16 Feb 2015.
A line of cracks on the same ridge but close to a vague crest on the front face (some 10m right of *Dachshund*). Climb fairly direct up cracks to the crest and follow this to join *Dachshund*, followed to the small col. Either descend rightwards for another route or finish up *Dachshund* (40m).

Snappy 60m IV,6. Dave McGimpsey, Andy Nisbet. 16 Feb 2015.
A further line of cracks some 6m right of *Yappy*. These are less steep but have a hard section low down. The crest is gained and followed to join the previous two routes and the same finishing options.

Schnitzel 50m IV,5. Dave McGimpsey, Andy Nisbet. 16 Feb 2015.
On the front face of the higher and right of the two ridges which lead up left from the upper bowl of *Diamond Gully*. This overlooks the gully between the two ridges. Start 5m left of the crest at a corner. Climb this for 6m until a fine crack leads left into a parallel fault line to the corner. Go up this until it is sensible to move left and take a diagonal line left above steep ground, before going straight up to the top.

Terrier 60m III,4. Andy Nisbet. 24 Jan 2015.
The higher and right of the two ridges which lead up left from the upper bowl of *Diamond Gully*. Start left of its base and climb left of the crest before moving right of the crest below a huge block. Go up right of the crest until a step left gains the crest, followed to easier blocky ground. Continue trending left up blocks to the top.

Soo 200m III,4. Sandy Allan, Andy Nisbet. 27 Jan 2015.
The depression between *Ptarmigan Ridge* and *Sweep*. Start left of *Ptarmigan*

Ridge and climb a gully slanting up right. After a tricky step, go back left into the depression and follow it easily over small icy steps to a headwall. Climb up the right side of this to join *Ptarmigan Ridge* over its small pinnacle and up the final crest.

COIRE GARBHLACH, Lower Corrie:
Seclusion 90m III. Jonathan Preston, Chris Duckett. 8 Dec 2014.
Start just below the 'prominent cave' (which in fact is no more than a shallow recess) right of *Hermit's Ridge*.
1. 10m Traverse easily right to an obvious turfy V-groove and climb this to a wide platform.
2. 30m Climb the slab above centrally by grooves until a short traverse left can be made to blobs of turf which lead to a block up and left.
3. 50m Finish more easily to another good rock belay on the left.

Upper Corrie:
Waive Wall 110m V,7. Andy Nisbet, Steve Perry. 2 Mar 2015.
The left edge of the buttress with *Curving Gully* (the rightmost buttress). Start up a short ice pitch leading into a snow runnel. This leads to turf steps and a steep wall (60m). Climb an overhanging flake-crack finishing over a chockstone (15m). Finish up a defined crest (35m).

Tau Volantis 110m II. Andy Nisbet, Steve Perry. 10 Mar 2015.
The centre of the same section (left of *Curving Gully*). Start at the cliff base at an easy left-slanting gully. Climb this to where it ends, then move right and go up on turf to an easing. Continue up through another steep turf band and finish up a snowy depression.

Necromorph 110m III,4. Andy Nisbet, Steve Perry. 10 Mar 2015.
The right side of the same section. Start up a big gully slanting right to reach an icefall on its left wall. Climb this with a steep start and continue left to reach a right-slanting fault. Go up this and finish easily up the rib left of *Curving Gully*.

ANGEL'S PEAK:
Angels and Demons 450m IV,4 **. Masa Sakano, Phil Ingle. 22 Mar 2015.
A fine mountaineering route that takes the longest line on the north face of the peak following snow or ice all the way, and finishes at the summit of the Munro. It is located at the leftmost edge of the north face buttress. The first two pitches (100m) involve some ice of tech 4, followed by 200m of snow. An ice wall straight above (15m, tech 4, crux), and finally an icy snow slope (90m). Topo provided.
Note: The top section has been climbed before in easier conditions.

BRAERIACH, Coire Beanaidh:
Rumbling Ridge 90m III,4. Roger Everett, Simon Richardson. 5 Dec 2014.
The south side of Coire Beanaidh contains a prominent rib.
1. 25m Start at the foot of the rib and climb a triangular wall and continue along the crest to the next steepening.
2. 35m Climb a steep corner-crack then traverse left (loose blocks) and make a steep pull onto the crest. Continue up short corners on the crest to below the final step.

3. 30m Surmount the final step easily on the left and continue easily to the top.

Coire Ruadh:
Anzac Day 70m IV,4. Simon Richardson, Sophie Grace Chappell. 25 Apr 2015.
A good line up the front face of the upper cliff. Climbed on ice but also possible under powder.
1. 30m Start midway between *Phantom Cracks* and *Anniversary Groove* and climb an icy groove to a triangular-shaped cave-impasse.
2. 20m Climb steeply through the right side of the impasse and continue up the ramp to its end.
3. 20m Climb the steep corner on the right and continue up the crest of the buttress (as for *The Apparition*) to the top.

Coire an Lochain:
Groove Sensation 100m III. Simon Richardson. 18 Apr 2015.
The well-defined V-groove to the right of *Ice Elation* fills with ice late in the season. Climb discontinuous icy slabs (awkward) to gain the foot of the groove and follow it to the top.

Left of *The Icefall*, the north wall of Coire an Lochain comprises an easy angled lower tier, a snow field and a steep headwall. Routes are described from right to left from *The Icefall.*

Waltzing Matilda 150m III. Simon Richardson, Sophie Grace Chappell. 25 Apr 2014.
Start 20m left of *The Icefall* and climb a recessed icefall to the snowfield. Climb up the right side of the headwall by traversing left and surmounting a steep mixed step to gain a funnel-shaped exit couloir.

White Cliffs of Dover 150m II. Simon Richardson. 18 Apr 2015.
Climb a broad snow couloir left of *Waltzing Matilda* to gain the open groove line on the left side of the headwall.

In the Mood 150m II. Simon Richardson. 18 Apr 2015.
Climb mixed ground left of *White Cliffs of Dover* and finish up the wide gully defining the left side of the headwall.

We'll Meet Again 120m II. Simon Richardson. 18 Apr 2015.
The buttress to the right of *The Icefall.* Start at the foot of *The Icefall*, follow a snow ramp up and right and climb through mixed ground trending left to a final snow crest leading to the plateau.

Coire nan Clach:
Tutor's Rib 80m II. Simon Richardson. 12 Apr 2015.
Climb the rib to the right of *Hey Teacher* by turfy steps just right of the crest to a small pinnacle and exit easily to the plateau.

Coire Odhar:
Westwand 400m II. Simon Richardson. 12 Apr 2015.
The fluted triangular west face has a distinctive low-angled gully that descends

low into the corrie and holds snow late in the season. Climb the gully taking the narrower left fork and climb up the continuation groove to a snow bay and exit left onto the ridge bordering Coire Dhondail.

BEN MACDUI, Coire Mor:

Tribute Day 80m II. Simon Richardson. 9 Nov 2014.
The narrow rib that starts up and left of *Memorial Rib*.

Honour Bound 80m III. Simon Richardson. 9 Nov 2014.
The rib between *Memorial Rib* and *Avalanche Rib*.

BEN AVON, Clach Bhan:

Torture HVS 5b. Graham Tyldesley, Dave Cowan. 18 Aug 2012.
A brilliant little climb if you like jamming gritty cracks. On the west side of the tor there is a bay housing a fine lagoon. This route climbs the crack up the centre of its back wall. Belay in the passageway which reaches the lagoon from the south. Gain the first crack. Traverse left with the water lapping at your feet to gain the second crack. Easy climbing up this crack brings you to an awkward few moves to escape. Could be shallow water soloed at F6a S3.

Meall Gaineimh (NJ 167 051):

There is a very attractive gritstone-like edge just below the summit of this NE top of Ben Avon. The routes are up to 10m long, face SW and are described left to right.

Left-Hand Crack H.Severe 4b. Graham Tyldesley, Mike Reading. 16 Jul 2012.
The left-trending crack left of *The Corner*.

The Corner Diff. Greg Strange. 21 Aug 2009.
This is the shallow right-slanting corner just left of the prominent S-shaped crack.

The S-Crack VS 5a. Greg Strange, Rob Archbold, Brian Findlay. 6 Sep 2009.
The obvious S-shaped crack towards the left side of the crag.

Torsion Balance E5 6b. Graham Tyldesley, Dave Cowan. 18 Aug 2012.
The cracked flake right of *The S-Crack*, and which finishes short of the top of the crag. Climb to the top of the flake. Rock out right to reach a break (gear). Mantel the break and finish directly.

Flaky Grit and Gritty Flakes E4 5c. Graham Tyldesley, Dave Cowan. 18 Aug 2012.
Start up the undercut flakes below and left of the top of *Personal Tibet*. Move up and then slightly right to gain a high break and finish up left to avoid the leftmost vertical crack of *Personal Tibet*.

(My Own) Personal Tibet E1 5b. Graham Tyldesley, Mike Reading. 16 Jul 2012.
The left-trending diagonal crack starting right of centre and ending in a pair of vertical cracks. Classic of the crag.

Tor Nessie E3 6a. Graham Tyldesley. 16 Jul 2012.

The rounded breaks up steep ground just right of the start of *Personal Tibet*. Biggish cams useful for the break below *Nessie*.

Chimney Crack Severe 5a. Brian Findlay, Rob Archbold, Greg Strange. 6 Sep 2009.
The chimney feature near the right end of the crag. It has a hard start.

V-Crack VS 5a. Greg Strange, Rob Archbold, Brian Findlay. 6 Sep 2009.
The second last short crack before the south end.

East Meur Gorm Craig:
Wear the Fox Hat 35m E2 5a. Graham Tyldesley, David Bird, 2 Aug 2013.
Further right from the square buttress with *Backslash* is a large, flake covered slab, bounded on the left by a chimney. There is a roof low down on the right. Climb a left-facing corner for about 5m to a heathery ledge. Move up left into a right-facing, left-trending groove. Climb this past some delicate flakes to the top.

99 E1 5b. Graham Tyldesley, David Bird, 2 Aug 2013.
Right of the large flaky slab wall is a buttress with a steep wall running up beside the gully on its right. A few metres up the gully a layback flake trends up rightwards. Climb the flake.

Magnum HVS 5a. Graham Tyldesley, David Bird, 2 Aug 2013.
Towards the top of the gully with *99* at its foot, steep cracks lead to a roofed niche with a crack in the roof. Climb to the niche and exit via the crack and a hold on the left wall.

The Aberdonian HVS 5b. Graham Tyldesley, David Bird, 2 Aug 2013.
The second buttress right from the large flaky slab buttress has a gully on its right-hand side. On the wall overlooking this gully is a right-trending grooved ramp. Climb a vertical corner for a few metres to the start of the ramp. Make hard moves right to get established on it. Follow it to its end and exit to the top of the buttress via a fine fist crack.

Clach Bun Rudhtair:
Climbing on this fantastic cluster of three sculptured tors was first recorded by Richard Frere in SMCJ April 1946, page 355.

Tax Avoidance H.Severe. Rob Archbold, Brian Findlay, Greg Strange. 12 Jul 2013.
The obvious crack on the slabby NW face of the North Tor. Start up a short corner and follow the crack until forced left to finish up another crack. Going straight up is E1 5c.

Tidy Package E1 5c. Rory Brown, Graham Tyldesley. 31 Jul 2013.
The direct finish to *Tax Avoidance*.

South Crack E2 5b. Greg Strange, Brian Findlay, Rob Archbold. 12 Jul 2013.
The enticing off-width crack on the south end of the Central Tor which leads to a minor detached pinnacle.

Neil McGeachy on the FA of Obscure Cleft (E4,6a), Ben Avon. *Photo: Rory Brown.*

Obscure Cleft E4 6a. Neil McGeachy, Graham Tyldesley, Rory Brown. 31 Jul 2013.
Start 10m left of *South Crack* on left-hand side of the gully wall. Climb three obvious snappy flakes until able to access the off-width to their left. Squirm up the crack, then follow a technical ramp line and groove leftwards to the top of crag. Very big cams essential.

Gritless Wonder HVS 5a. Brian Findlay, Rob Archbold, Greg Strange. 12 Jul 2013.
This is the west facing hanging crack just round left from the normal scramble to the top of the South Tor; it runs into a right-facing corner. Excellent climbing.

The Foot Masseuse E4 6b. Graham Tyldesley, Rory Brown, Neil McGeachy. 31 Jul 2013.
Positioned on the SE side of the Central Tor. A large chimney splits the tor. Just right of this is a good likeness of a 5m high foot. This route climbs the flaring crack defining its right-hand edge. Tricky but almost orthodox moves provide entry. Then swim upwards.

Back, Sack & Crack 15m VS 5a. Neil McGeachy, Donna Ryan. 31 Jul 2013.
Start down and right of *Time for T*. Climb the obvious corner-chimney to a monkey bum finish. A tight squeeze.

Time for T E3 5c. Graham Tyldesley, Rory Brown. 31 Jul 2013.
A stunning, flared and slightly off-width crack. On the upper tier of the South Tor this crack faces down into Glen Avon begging to be climbed! A steep hard start allows entry into the more amenable angle above. Deploy a range of udging manoeuvres to sustain upward progress. At its top move left along the ledge and make a committing move onto the slab above. Might be grit HVS, certainly no harder than 5.9. Large cams useful. Graded by crack climbing incompetents.

LOCHNAGAR, Southern Sector, Sunset Buttress:
Twilight Rib 90m III. Simon Richardson. 29 Mar 2015.
The crest of the rib climbed by *Mirk*. Start at the toe of the buttress (down and right of *Mirk*) and climb easily to where the rib becomes smooth. Traverse down and left and climb the line of turf over two steep steps to the col of *Mirk*. Follow the crest of the rib to the top as for *Mirk*.

Perseverance Wall:
Resolve 70m IV,5. Simon Richardson, Sophie Grace Chappell. 27 Feb 2015.
An elegant mixed route up the left side of Perseverance Wall. Start just right of *Forgotten Runnel* directly below a smooth slabby rib cut by a crack-line on its left-hand side.
1. 30m Climb through a short steep lower wall to gain the rib, and follow the crack-line to belay under the 'cheeseblock' – a distinctive protruding triangular block.
2. 30m Move up, then right through steep cracks to the top of the cheeseblock. Continue straight up two steep slabby sections to gain a deep wide twisting crack that leads onto the crest and junction with *Perseverance Rib*.
3. 10m Continue easily up *Perseverance Rib* to the top.

Remembrance Gully, Left-Hand Branch 80m II. Simon Richardson. 29 Mar 2015.
Remembrance Gully splits into three distinct lines. This route takes the left-hand exit from the central depression and finishes up mixed ground (just right of *The Handrail*) to a steep cornice exit.

Sinister Buttress:
Forsaken Gully, Right-Hand Branch 50m II. Simon Richardson. 29 Mar 2015.
Forsaken Gully is split at half-height by a rib. The narrower right-hand branch leads to the top of Sinister Buttress where there is less likely to be a cornice. Probably climbed before.

An t-Sron:
Boathouse Buttress 70m III,4. Simon Richardson, Ben Richardson. 26 Dec 2014.
The right edge of the small cliff situated at NO 291 843 just below the plateau of An t-Sron provides a short and easily accessible climb.
1. 20m Start 5m left of the right edge and climb an easy groove followed by a short slab and steep wall. Trend left and then climb steeply up to a good belay.
2. 15m Move left to second wall with a large sharp flake. Climb the right side of the flake and follow cracks trending right to the crest.
3. 35m Easy ground leads to the top.

CREAG AN DUBH LOCH, Broad Terrace Wall:
Range War (winter variation) 110m X,10 ***. Greg Boswell, Guy Robertson. 23 Jan 2015.
1. 40m Climb the turfy chimney to the leftward-slanting roof-capped corner. Go up this to belay off a huge block down and left of the *Range War* pedestal.
2. 30m Go up onto the pedestal and then ascend the wall and into the capping niche. Climb up and out of this to gain a jutting block on the right arete. Climb ice to a cave.
3. 40m Climb the ice to the top.

COIRE KANDER:
Kander Surprise 200m III. Russell Shanks, Alan Sewell. 7 Feb 2015.
This route climbs the first icefall on the left at the entrance to *Y-Gully*. Start below the overhanging roof and climb the ice bulge above on the right (easier options left). Break through this and continue to the snowfield above (50m). Easier climbing leads to the next icefall (50m). Go left to a narrow groove or further right, climb a short steep wall (50m). Easy snow slopes lead to the top (50m).

GLEN SHEE, Creag Dhearg:
(NO 122 735) Alt 500m
Creag Dhearg is a newly developed schist crag 500m uphill to the west of the A93, 3km north of Spittal of Glenshee. Protection is adequate on most routes and there is some lose rock in places. The lower crag consists of an obvious sharp ridge which is taken by *Valinch*, and the other climbs ascend its steep west flank, which cannot be seen from the approach. Descent is via a grassy gully below the west flank.

Valinch 120m H.Severe. Andrew Mallinson, Alan McIntosh. 31 May 2015.
1. 40m Ascend the obvious sharp ridge via slabs and pinnacles to an obvious block.
2. 80m The ridge gradually becomes a scramble which is followed to open hillside.

The following routes are on the west (left) flank of the ridge and all join *Valinch* at some point. Routes are described right to left when looking at the face from the grassy descent gully.

Blade Runner 80m HVS 5a. Andrew Mallinson, Sue Harper. 23 Jun 2015.
Climbs an obvious clean blade of rock 20m left of the start of *Valinch.* Exciting but poorly protected moves up the blade lead to the pinnacles on *Valinch*, which is followed to the top.

Old Friends 40m H.Severe. Andrew Mallinson, Sue Harper. 23 Jun 2015.
Climbs a clean small buttress 10m left of *Blade Runner* to the ridge of *Valinch*.

Redemption 30m VS 4b. Andrew Mallinson, Sue Harper. 23 Jun 2015.
Climbs the next clean slab to the left of *Old Friends* via pockets and edges. Finish along *Valinch*.

Happy 20m Severe. Andrew Mallinson, Sue Harper. 23 Jun 2015.
Climbs the bow shaped wall 10m to the left of *Redemption* via a series of pinch grips.

BOUSTIE LEY, Corrie of Clova:
On the walk up to Loch Brandy two prominent ridges can be seen dropping into Corrie of Clova on the west face of the Snub. The following route takes the left-hand of these which ends in a prominent, steep rock tower.

Boustie Buttress 90m III,4. Iain Young, John Higham. 13 Dec 2014.
Start at the lowest rocks and climb a right-slanting slabby slot. Step up and left at the top and continue to belay where the ridge lies back. Follow the crest, at first over rock then turf and snow to belay below the final tower. Take the central turfy groove (crux) exiting over a capping chockstone. Easy slopes lead to the plateau.

The following route takes the right-hand ridge.

The Snub 130m II. John Higham. 18 Dec 1999.
The lower part of the ridge consists of a rock buttress broken by a steep groove. Follow the groove and rock ridge above for about 50m. The upper part of the ridge consists of fine snow aretes interspersed with short rock steps followed by a steep snow finish.

Corrie of Bonhard:
Mystery Ramp 100m III,4. Simon Richardson, Ben Richardson. 20 Dec 2014.
Between *Chokestone Gully* and *Left Edge Route* is a prominent buttress high on the north-west wall of the corrie. Climb up to the foot of the easy angled gully formed in the depression to the left of the buttress.

1. 40m Climb the gully and exit right onto the broad ramp cutting across the steep front face of the buttress.
2. 30m Traverse right across the ramp until it narrows into a steep slanting groove. Climb the left side of the groove, transfer right after 5m (crux) and continue up the groove to easier ground.
3. 30m Move up to the headwall and follow the left-trending break in an exposed position to gain the top of the buttress. Easy slopes lead to the plateau in another 30m.

Cryptic Wall 100m V,6. Henning Wackerhage, Simon Richardson. 17 Jan 2015.
A good mixed route up the front face of the buttress climbed by *Mystery Ramp*. Start 40m right of *Mystery Ramp*.
1. 40m Climb a steep vegetated wall to gain the broad ramp of *Mystery Ramp* cutting across the buttress.
2. 35m Cross the ramp and climb a steep right-facing groove to its top. Move right up a ramp and step down into a steep V-groove that leads to an easier ramp and a stance on the edge of the buttress below the steep headwall (junction with *Mystery Ramp*).
3. 25m Climb the right-facing corner in the headwall to easier ground. Easy slopes lead to the plateau in another 30m.

GLEN CLOVA, The Bassies:
Bassies Way 250m II. George Allan, Billy Hood. 19 Jan 2015.
The ground immediately to the left of *Whitehaugh Gully*. Start at the left side of an obvious nose some way up the gully. Climb a short awkward corner then weave up the crest to easy ground. Go as you please climbing on the upper buttress leads to the plateau.

GLEN CLOVA, Coire Farchal:
Silver Threads Among the Gold, Direct Start 15m IV,6. Martin Holland, Ian McIntosh. 3 Jan 2015.
Forty metres below the normal start is a short buttress with an overhung base. Start below the central line of weakness of the buttress and make steep moves to gain the open V-groove. Step left and climb in to the deep cleft above and exit past a large chockstone. Easy ground above leads to the normal start.

Over the Hill 140m IV,4. Simon Richardson, Ben Richardson, Sophie Grace Chappell. 28 Dec 2014.
The line of weakness cutting through the barrier walls between *Brains Before Brawn* and *Elder Crack Buttress*. Start 20m right of *Brains Before Brawn* below a short 10m-high gully.
1. 40m Climb the gully, exit left and climb snow to a cave below the barrier wall.
2. 30m Climb up into a slot at the left end of the cave and continue up the steep groove above to exit on to a snow slope. Move up this for 20m to a good cave belay on the right side of a large diamond-shaped buttress.
3. 40m Continue up snow on the right side of the 'diamond' to its top then traverse up and left to a short corner cutting through the upper barrier wall. Climb this first on the left, then traverse right under a short roof and exit right. Belay on the large perched block above.
4. 30m Easy ground leads to the top.

GLEN CLOVA, Lower North-West Crag:
For a Handful of Beans 40m HVS 5a. Simon Richardson, Tim Chappell. 24 Aug 2014.
Good climbing up the centre of the wall between *The Beanstalk* and *Proud Corner*. Start at the foot of *The Beanstalk* and climb straight up the black cracked wall to a niche. Trend slightly right up the steep helpful crack above to a small ledge and junction with *Proud Corner* (just below its crux section). Arrange good protection here and take a deep breath, before stepping left and climbing the steep wall on the left on small positive holds. When the angle eases trend left to the second tree of *The Beanstalk*. Step right and climb the thin vertical crack past a third tree to the top.

GLEN CLOVA, Coire Fee:
Forestry Commission 350m V,6. Henning Wackerhage, Arno Alpi. 24 Jan 2015.
A climb on the large face to the right of *Look C Gully* in Corrie Fee and which covers some new ground (especially pitch 3). All pitches are close to 60m.
1. Start at the lowest point on the right of the face and climb the groove above. Exit and follow snowfields to a boulder.
2. Ascend the snowfield to belay to the right of a large open book corner.
3. Climb the crux groove just to the right of the open book corner. At the top climb an easier left-trending ramp to reach the upper snowfields. The crux groove can be avoided on the right.
4. Climb the snowfield and gully line to find a belay on the side of the buttress on the left.
5. Climb to below the top buttress. Aim for the notch and groove that separates the largest bulk of the buttress from the smaller buttress on the right.
6. Climb the groove and traverse to the right to reach easy ground that leads to the top.

Alphabet Soup, Variation Finish II. George Allan. 5 Feb 2015.
From the point overlooking *A-B Integrate* (SMCJ 2012), climb the buttress above instead of traversing away left up the snow fields.

GLEN ESK, Bruntwood Craig:
Reincarnation 130m IV,6. Andy Nisbet, Duncan Tunstall. 13 Dec 2014.
Based on the buttress left of *Avatar*. A spooky first pitch leads out to short technical sections. Start at a gully whose right wall forms a big ramp angling out to this buttress. Climb the gully to a tree (10m). Go up the gully for a further 10m before going diagonally right to a big ledge on the crest and below a bulging wall (50m). Move right and climb the wall at its weakest point to reach a tree (15m). Continue up the crest (25m). Reach the top of the ramp and climb an overhung chimney on the right (20m). Finish easily (10m).

GLEN MARK:
Note: There are crags on the south side of the glen at around NO 398 830. On 26 Dec 2014, Duncan Tunstall climbed a ridge (Grade II/III) left of the main crag, which has a long steep sidewall facing the ridge. Andy Nisbet found a way through the sidewall above half-height, then continued to the top (Grade III).

NORTH-EAST OUTCROPS

NIGG BAY TO COVE BAY:

Bridge of One Hair:

Stitch in Time 8m VS 4c. Greg Strange, Rob Archbold. 29 Jun 2011.
Start below *Lost Boys* and go up and left to climb a short impending crack on the crest between *Last Thread Wall* and the sidewall.

Long Slough:

Slinky Malinky 10m E1 5b. Greg Strange, Rob Archbold. 11 Jul 2011.
The crack and slim groove on the impending right wall of *Leaning Meanie*. Start 4m right of *Meanie* and climb up and right on to the edge of *Sneak*. Continue straight up.

Hidden Inlet:

(NJ 955 027) See UKClimbing
Deep Purple 10m E1 5b. Greg Strange, Brian Findlay, Rob Archbold. 6 Jun 2007.
The steep wall round left from *Yo-Yo Nicks*. Start up a short groove and use a good undercling to move up left onto the top wall.
Note: A direct finish to *Betty Swallocks* is HVS 5a.

Deceptive Wall:

The following two routes are on the dark north wall of Yawn Pillar which currently sports an old gas cylinder wedged at its foot. The rock is better than it looks.

Cylinder Wall 10m H.Severe. Greg Strange. 13 Sep 2013.
Start near the centre of the wall. Step over a gap and climb slightly rightwards, then trend left to finish close to the right-bounding corner.

Propane Edge 10m VS 4c. Greg Strange. 16 Sep 2013.
Start as for *Cylinder Wall* and climb up left to big quartz jugs. Continue steeply staying right of the left edge.

COVE BAY TO CLASHRODNEY, South Cove, Red Hole:

Procyon 35m E5 6b ***. Callum Johnson, Darren Wisniewski. 11 May 2015.
Climbs the second pitch of *Procrastination* but continues up the steepening corner-crack the whole way. Sustained but well protected. Belay as for *Orbital Ejection* and finish as for *Procrastination*. The first pitch of *Procrastination* was wet at the time of the first ascent so the route was accessed by abseil to the hanging belay at the end of P1. The inclusion of the first pitch would make a superb and sustained outing.
The FA was climbed first attempt after a quick inspection and clean on abseil.

Clashrodney:

Osiris 10m E3 5c. Michael Barnard, Chris Wilson. 16 May 2015.
Climb cracks and breaks right of *Onassis* to join its top section.
Note: *Stone Roses* (the normal way) was thought E3 5b. Committing, with potential for a bad ground fall and terrible landing.

THE COAST NORTH OF ABERDEEN, The Graip:

Phantom Edge 15m HVS 5b. Greg Strange, Brian Findlay, Stuart Smith. 12 Aug 1990.
Climbs the edge overlooking *Crick in the Neck* direct from the bottom joining *Phantom Graipist*. Good climbing. Missed out of current guide.

CRUDEN BAY TO NORTH HAVEN, Fulmar Wall:

The Shaft Direct 20m E1 5c. Greg Strange, Rob Archbold. 14 Jun 2013.
Start below the fall line of the hanging cleft. Climb a short crack to below a black overhang, then move up and right (crux) to gain the original line at a good foothold on the right edge. Continue up *The Shaft*.

Cornered Edge 20m VS 5a. Greg Strange, Rob Archbold. 30 Aug 2013.
This follows the short corner (with a little overlap below) on the wall right of *The Shaft*. Start at a triangular pedestal breaching the short impending wall right of the hanging cleft (as for *The Shaft*). Go up right and climb the corner direct to exit onto upper *Left Out Route*. If the crack in the corner is wet, go out right below the overlap, gain the edge, then step back left to the top of the corner (same grade).

Shadow Slab:

Twilight Zone 35m VS 4c. Rob Archbold, Greg Strange. 30 Aug 2013.
Traverse right above high water level for about 9m (as for *Route Two*), but just before an edge, go straight up to a prominent pale flake below smoother slabs. Follow a thin crack rightwards, then move up right through overlaps to easier ground. Finish up a left slanting crack.

COVESEA, Boulders Bay Area (NJ 176 708):

The guide approach description (NE Outcrops p332) is now out of date. A new cliff path goes east from the lookout well above the line of the old path and the 'steps' have been removed. The cliff-top path is still present but traffic will be needed to keep the gorse in check.

Note: *Zugzwang* is perhaps E4 on-sight. Runners were placed in the crack of *Private Dancer* on first ascent to protect the moves. A cam 000 can be placed from the ledge. Then straight up the arete with a good cam 00 at half height. An excellent line.

Special Brew 12m E1 5a *. John Hall, Sandy Paterson. 31 Aug 2010.
Start as for *Celebrate the Bullet*. Climb the wall directly between *C the B* and *Synthetic Pathway*. Good holds and good protection when found.

Better Together 12m E1 5b *. Steve Carter, John Trythall. Sep 2014.
Good climbing direct up the wall between *Past Imperfect* and *Not Gneiss*. Climb direct finishing through the pancake rock bulge with care at the top.

Not Gneiss 12m HVS 4c. John Hall, Sandy Paterson. 31 Aug 2010.
The cleaned crack to the right of *Past Imperfect*. Finish direct through the top niche – crux. Good pro but some suspect rock.

Notes: *Hacuna Mattata* has had a recent repeat with a direct start up the very sandy lower tier. A point of aid was apparently required to get to the original belay in the hanging corner. The top section was then thought to be very good. New grade not known.

The small crag mentioned in SMCJ 2010 at NJ 188 711 has been 'bouldered' on for many years and several of the routes have been done before. The Moray MC have coincidently just been re-creating two 1935 photos of climbers on *Preston South End* and *Prestonpans*.

12 Week Scan 14m E2 5c **. Steve Carter, John Trythall. Sep 2011.
Start as for *Sleepy Hollow* but move up and slightly right to tackle the right-hand side of the overhang direct (between *Sleepy Hollow* and *Family Affair*) and then finish up the wall above.

Notes: The local activists have addressed the problem of gorse at the route exits and they are all clear. The route *Paul Tax* that had suffered a rockfall is now established at E4 6a, and well protected.

MUCKLE CLEARY:
(NJ 489 689) Partially Tidal North-West facing
(The OS Explorer spelling is wrong.) Lookout Point is the headland immediately east of the harbour at Portknockie. On arriving in Portknockie on the A942 from either Cullen (east) or Findochty (west), make your way towards the harbour, but stay on the high-level road overlooking the cliffs and park in a lay-by at the top of a dirt track on Patrol Road leading down towards the harbour opposite houses that overlook the bay. To the right of the parking area looking out to sea is Muckle Cleary Bay. Lookout Point is the obvious promontory at the foot of the dirt track. A path leads out to the head of the promontory.

The crag has two climbing faces, Big Roof Wall and Other Steep Wall. Although partially tidal, it would be possible to climb here during a calm high tide.

Big Roof Wall:
Descent: At the top of Lookout Point is a small concrete structure. Big Roof Wall is accessed to the left of the concrete structure looking out to sea via an easy ramp system. Routes are described right to left.

Old Magician 15m Severe. Greg Strange, Paul Allen. 28 Sep 2008.
This short and pleasant route climbs the slab and easy fault via a small overlap to finish easily on good holds.

Adolescence 15m HVS 5a. Paul Allen, Greg Strange. 28 Sep 2008.
At the right-hand side of the big roof where the angle eases, this route starts up the crack which leads to small overlap beside a short groove. Surmount the overlap and climb slab up to a small overhang. Arrange protection and climb the overhang by good holds to find the top.

Crimson Red 10m HVS 5a. Greg Strange, Paul Allen. 28 Sep 2008.
At the left-hand side of the big roof wall, there is a ledge about 2m above sea-level. This route climbs the steep fault leading up and right to finish via improving holds near the edge.

Other Steep Wall:
Descent: Other Steep Wall is accessible from the eastward end of the wall by descending to just above sea-level and traversing to the foot of the crag.

Dreamer 15m HVS 5a. Paul Allen, Greg Strange. 28 Sep 2008.
The deceptive lower ramp running leftwards starting at a short corner. Climb up and left onto the ramp to finish at the top of the crag.

CULLEN AREA, Crathie Point (NJ 548 673):
This is the crag described as Unknown in SMCJ 2014. Immediately left of the 'clean grey slab' is the 'boulder filled gully' which leads into a chimney.

Gor Lum Me 12m VS 4b. Jonathan Preston, Diana Preston. 2 May 2015.
Climb the chimney.

Sloping Off 12m VS 4b. Jonathan Preston. 2 May 2015 .
A right-facing corner and overlaps left of the chimney.

Notes: There is a 10m V.Diff crack in the centre of the small buttress left of the previous two routes; Pete Amphlett, Dave Whalley, 2014. All routes on the clean grey slab are at least 15m rather than 12m.

Minestrone 15m V.Diff. Jonathan Preston, Pete Amphlett. 26 May 2015.
Left of *Lentils*. From the pointed block, step up and round to the left to climb the shallow left-facing corner and slab to the top.

Sweet Pea 15m VS 4c. Jonathan Preston, Pete Amphlett. 26 May 2015.
Start up *Split Pea*. At the split, continue diagonally right to the top right-hand corner of the slab in a fine exposed position.

The clean grey slab ends abruptly and overhangs a deep narrow geo. The far (west) side of this geo sports a steep greenish wall. Access at mid to low tide across the geo is via a barnacle encrusted rock or abseil (spike belays at top of cliff and thread further back). The following three lines are best viewed from below the clean grey slab.

Mange Tout 15m E1 5b *. Jonathan Preston, Pete Amphlett. 3 Jun 2015.
Start from a small black ledge at the left end of the wall (before it disappears into the depths of the geo). Move up slightly left, then climb straight up the obvious groove to the top.

Runner Bean 13m HVS 4c. Jonathan Preston, Pete Amphlett. 3 Jun 2015.
Start on a long sloping green ledge right of the previous route. Step up right and then up slightly left (crux) to climb a shallow groove just right of a smooth brown wall.

Chickpea 13m Severe. Jonathan Preston, Pete Amphlett. 3 Jun 2015.
Climb out diagonally right from the middle of the sloping ledge and follow a break more easily to the top.

REDHYTHE POINT, Redhythe West, The Black Wall:
Grey Ramp 15m VS 4c. Greg Strange, Brian Findlay. 12 May 2012.
Start about 6m right of *News Story* beside a small rock stack. Climb up and left to ledge. Traverse up right to gain and follow the grey ramp. Finish out right on black-streaked rock.

CLACH NA BEINN:
Note: Findlay Cranston climbed 3 short routes on 9 Sep 2014. All about Diff on clean rock. The first route is on the first pinnacle you come to when approaching from the east on the north side of the Slack of Dye gorge. It climbs behind the big spike up a chimney The latter two routes are on the furthest west pinnacle.

PASS OF BALLATER:
Low Squatta 10m E4 6c *. Jules Lines. Aug 2014.
Start as for *High Steppa* to the break. Go left to the arete and climb it.

Dysentery 15m E4 5c. Danny Laing, Jules Lines. 6 Jun 2015.
Start to the right of *The Terrorist*. Climb a blocky nose and a tiny left-facing groove to flat holds. Traverse right across the wall passing a broken flake to gain a pair of diagonal cracks. Finish direct.

Passing the Time 30m E1 5a. Michael Barnard, Ben Winter. 15 Jul 2014.
Climb the initial corner of *Convoy*; where that route traverses right, instead reach up for a crack just left of the small pine and pull onto the slab above. Step left and go up a short corner to below the top wall. Climb the light-coloured shallow groove in the arete, finishing on the right. The top wall is bold; finishing as for *Mandrax* would make the route VS 4c.

Drambo Direct 15m E6 6b **. Danny Laing, Jules Lines. Jul 2012.
Straightens out the line of *Drambo* taking a direct start up the wall on edges and sidepulls, making it an independent line from *Stoned Immaculate*, more sustained at the grade and without high side runners. The first ascent was climbed ground up, yo-yo style, placing gear on lead. The second and third ascent were soloed after pre-practice by Callum Johnson & Darren Wisniewski on 2 Nov 2014.

Warm Love 15m E5 6a ***. Jules Lines. 25 Mar 2015.
Start beneath the pod of *Cold Rage*. Slap out right for the arete and climb it via sustained slapping (gear easily placed in *Cold Rage*) to gain a shakeout. Continue up the upper arete on sidepulls in a wild position to pull out via the final flake-crack of *Anger and Lust*. High in the grade.

HIGHLAND OUTCROPS

New routes are not reported as the new guide is in production.

BEN NEVIS, AONACHS, CREAG MEAGAIDH

Indicator Wall:

Call me Ishmael 175m VIII,9. Uisdean Hawthorn, Iain Small. 16 Mar 2015.
Start to the left of *Psychedelic Wall* below the right-hand of the band of overhangs.
1. 55m Climb the rising traverse above the overhangs on thin ice and then step down into a steep iced corner. Climb this to the first belay of *Stormy Petrel*.
2. 60m Move right and climb the left edge of the large slab to an overlap. Make a committing move left through the weakness on thin ice onto a steep wall. Climb up and left to belay below the middle of the headwall.
3. 60m Climb a steep groove, then move left to gain the large obvious spike. Climb the groove to the right on good ice in an outstanding position to the top.

Tower Ridge, East Flank:

Tripod 65m VII,7 **. Dave MacLeod, Helen Rennard. 16 Mar 2015.
A direct start to the winter line of *Clefthanger*, taking a sustained and intricate crack-line, joining Clefthanger after 20m as it moves left.

The Piece Maker 80m VIII,9 *. Iain Small, Blair Fyffe. 10 Mar 2015.
A steep mixed and thin ice route taking the corner bounding the left-hand side of the the bay to the right of *Clefthanger*.
1. 30m Start below the corner of *Clefthanger*. Climb steep snow and a short corner to the left-hand end of a long snow ledge. Climb the steep corner above to a good flake then traverse left to gain a niche in a fault. Tackle the hard bulge above to gain a useful flake-crack and belay on a sloping ledge.
2. 20m Step up and left and climb a series of flakes to under an overhang below a thinly iced corner. Climb the corner to a big snow ledge and a good block.
3. 30m Traverse right to climb icy walls and steps to easier ground below the Great Tower of *Tower Ridge*.

Red Dragon 60m VIII,9 **. Dave MacLeod, Helen Rennard. 2 Mar 2015.
An exciting steep crack-line breaching the overhanging walls between *The Brass Monkey* and *The Urchin*.
1. 30m Start about 10m left of *The Urchin* below the crack which leads directly up the overhanging wall. Climb over the first bulge to an easier section and an awkward rest below a larger bulge. Poor protection unless the crack is free of verglas. Pull through the bulge on deep hooks to welcome good runners and continue with difficulty to reach easier ground which leads to a belay at small ledges.
2. 30m Climb short corners to steeper rock. Traverse left along a ledge and round into a large easy groove which leads to a block belay on *Tower Ridge*.

Douglas Boulder:

Inception 95m V,7. Steve Holmes, Duncan Curry. 18 Feb 2015.
Ascend *West Gully* of the Douglas Boulder for 15m. On the right wall and directly opposite the start of *SW Ridge* is a left-facing ramp. The first two pitches can be linked with careful rope management.
1. 15m Climb the corner direct, strenuous but well protected and belay below a broken chimney – superb.

2. 15m Climb the constricted chimney and steep upper corner to a large spike.
3. 45m Ascend a shallow cracked wall on the left, then continue over snow slopes on a rising rightward traverse aiming for a steep ice runnel. Climb the thin ice runnel for 6m and belay on the left before a short chimney
4. 20m The chimney and snow grooves on the left lead to *Tower Ridge*.

High Pressure Crack 170m VIII,9 ***. Dave MacLeod, Masa Sakano. 4 Mar 2015.
An excellent sustained battle up the steep crack-line looming over *Gutless*.
1. and 2. Climb the groove and chimney pitches of *Gutless* to the big ledge below the overhanging wall.
3. 30m Climb the right-slanting icy overhanging crack in the steepest part of the wall with sustained difficulty and good protection to a welcome resting niche above the lip of the overhang. Continue following left-slanting cracks to finally pull onto a large ledge.
4. 70m Climb more or less direct on easy mixed terrain to the top of the Douglas Boulder.

Secondary Tower Ridge:
Shear Fear 90m VI,5. Michael Barnard, John MacLeod. 14 Feb 2015.
The obvious icefall overlooking the easier upper gully of *1934 Route*, makes a good finale after *Vanishing Gully*. Often thin; would be at least a grade easier with thicker ice.
1. 60m Climb the main icefall and the short icy corner above. Continue up cracks in the buttress.
2. 30m Continue more easily up the rib to join *Tower Ridge*.

Goodeve's Buttress:
Sirius 160m V,6. Simon Richardson, Helen Rennard. 15 Mar 2015.
A parallel line left of *The Alpine Princess*. Start as for *The Alpine Princess* in a snow bay below the gully of *Hale Bopp Groove*.
1. 50m Move up the snow ramp of *The Alpine Princess* and take the first line of weakness on the left. This leads into a narrow V-groove that emerges at the top of the steep section of *Hale Bopp Groove*. Cross the gully and belay on the rib between *The White Line* and *Hale Bopp Groove*.
2. 50m Climb up to a small overlap in the gully line of *The White Line* and move left up a short icy ramp to gain the rib that lies between the two branches of *The White Line*. Follow the gully cutting into the rib (well seen from the corrie floor) passing to the right of a broad prominent spike to easier ground.
3. 60m Continue up ice and snow through a short mixed section to the plateau.

Creag Coire na Ciste:
Hans Solo 100m VIII,8. Guy Robertson, Uisdean Hawthorn. 11 Feb 2015.
Essentially an ice climber's version of *Storm Trooper*
1. 40m Follow *Storm Trooper*'s first pitch, which on this ascent was mostly thin ice.
2. 40m Directly above is a tantalising / terrifying ice streak (depending on your perspective). Gain this from the left and follow it very carefully (crux) to easier ground below the top.
3. 20m A short step, then over the cornice to the top.

Tenterhooks 160m VII,8. Simon Richardson, Roger Webb. 3 Jan 2015.
A steep and icy mixed climb tackling the impressive right wall of *Central Rib*.
1. 70m Climb the first section of *Wendigo*, them move up and right to below the final tower of *Central Rib*.
2. 35m Start up the final tower midway between *Wendigo* and *Tinkerbell* and climb a short mixed wall to a small snowfield. Cross this to join the left-facing icy corner of *Tinkerbell* and climb up to the snowy depression.
3. 30m Climb up to the steep icefall of *Tinkerbell Direct*, then bear left along the tapering ramp crossing the right wall of *Central Rib*. Where it fades, make a difficult series of moves past an undercut monolithic block to gain a steep hanging groove. Climb this to its top and exit right around a rib to a small stance.
4. 25m Continue up the icy groove above that runs parallel to the icefall of *Tinkerbell Direct* to reach easier ground. Exit up easy snow left of the final tower (as for *Tinkerbell*) avoiding the cornice on the right.

North Trident Buttress:
Scoop Wall, Direct Finish 15m E3 5c **. Michael Barnard, Alan Hill. 13 Sep 2014.
See SMCJ 2014. The obvious crack in the wall above the scoop belay. Bold, sustained and excellent.

Carn Dearg Buttress:
The Wicked E6 6b ***. First continuous ascent by Dave MacLeod, Donald King, Jul 2014.

Cousins' Buttress:
Cousinade 210m VIII,8. Neil Silver, Malcolm Bass, Simon Yearsley. 4 Feb 2015.
Takes the obvious groove on the steep pinnacle on the lower section of Cousins' Buttress, then easier climbing above the saddle. Start as for *Harrison's Climb Direct*.
1. 30m Move right and climb the two short narrow chimneys. Traverse delicately horizontally left past a block to belay in a right-angled corner at the base of the main groove.
2. 25m Climb tenuously up and left to gain a large flake, then trend up and right into the base of the steep groove. Climb the groove with an awkward pull out left at the top to a stance on the edge of the buttress.
3. 30m The steep wide crack above leads to a short awkward wall and then easier climbing in a fine situation to the top of the pinnacle.
4. 35m Move easily along to the saddle, then out left past a large open corner to the foot of the 30m icefall on *Harrison's Climb* where an icy gangway leads out rightwards back onto the buttress.
5 and 6. 90m Climb the icy gangway to a small snowfield then a series of icy corners, grooves and walls to the upper corrie.

Raeburn's Buttress:
Teufel Grooves 120m IX,9. Andy Inglis, Iain Small. 7 Feb 2015.
Varied and interesting climbing up grooves on the right edge of Raeburn's Buttress, with delicate ice climbing and a hard crux.
1. 30m The winter version started via the Great Flake start, climbing ice for 15m

NORDWAND

There is scope for much variation on this part of the face. The original route starts well to the right of the other options. (The original leftwards finish is rarely done.) Noel Williams suggests that three main lines can be identified as follows:

1. NORDWAND (III, Clough & party, 1959) starts on the right-hand side of the face above a 'snow-filled trench on the screes below the face'.

2. NORDWAND DIRECT (IV/V,4) starts much further left at a prominent icefall, and only joins the original route beneath the last steep wall. One of the best routes of its grade on the Ben.

3. NORDWAND SUPERDIRECT (VI,5) starts up a narrow ribbon of ice immediately **right** of Nordwand Direct.
This start was originally called the 'Direct Start to Nordwand' (IV,4 Szuca & party, 1989).
It now has a Superdirect Finish, (VI,5 Barnard & MacLeod, 2015). See p.516. The line shown is the one climbed by Barnard & MacLeod.

Thanks to David Buckett and John MacLeod.
Photo: David Buckett.

until it was possible to traverse delicately left via two corners and a short wall to a spacious ledge below the crux pitch.
2. 30m Start up the corner on the right for 4m until possible to traverse left to above the belay, then go straight up (crux) into and climbing the obvious overhanging corner to its top (semi-hanging belay).
3. 30m Step right and climb the stepped corners, then climb diagonally up left across a slab to the crest of the buttress.
4. 30m Climb the stepped right-facing corners leading onto the crest of the buttress.
Traverse off right into *North Castle Gully* (or continue up *Raeburn's Buttress*).

Castle Ridge, North Face:
Nordwand Superdirect Finish 30m VI,5. Michael Barnard, John MacLeod. 7 Feb 2015.
Climbs the steep wall to the right of the final pitch of Nordwand Direct. The main feature is an icefall which forms down a hanging slab, sometimes with an icicle above. Go up to the icefall, but instead climb steep mixed ground to its left until possible to step right onto its top section. Move up, then take a right-slanting ramp through the upper wall before pulling back left and up to belay. See topo p.515.

Coire Eoghainn:
Sunny Side Up 320m IV,4. Will Rowland, Mark Chambers. Jan 2015.
Start in a bay 100m left from the toe of the buttress. The line climbs an icefall direct.
1. 70m A short ice wall leads to easy snow which is climbed to an ice screw belay left of the main cascade.
2. 40m Follow easy snow to ascend a short steep ice wall. Step left to a good rock belay.
3. 60m A fantastic ice pitch, climbed directly.
4. to 6. 150m of easy snow leads to the plateau.

The German Night Prowler 295m IV,3. Will Rowland, Jakob Rosenhan. Jan 2015.
To the right of the central buttress are three gullies. Each gully has a cascade at the start barring access to easy snow which leads to the summit. This is the furthest right of the three lines.
1. 50m Belay under a black vertical rock wall. Climb the cascade directly.
2. 50m Easy snow leads to a belay before a steepening.
3. 45m Take the left fork of the gully. Climb directly up over an icy step and belay on rock to the left.
4. to 6. 150m Easy snow leads to the summit.

MULLACH NAN COIREAN:
Summit Ridge Central 80m III. Roger Everett, Simon Richardson. 7 Dec 2014.
Just below P917m are three short ridges. Climb the central one in two pitches to the top.

STOB BAN, South Buttress:
Flying Saucer 210m VI,5. Andy Nisbet, Steve Perry. 16 Dec 2014.
An indirect line on the central fault on the front face. (The fault is marked

incorrectly in the Ben Nevis Guide as *North Ridge Route*, although that route is actually further right). Despite icy conditions, a lower barrier wall was insufficiently iced and a line traversing in above it was taken. Start at the base of *South Gully* (as for *Tippy Toe*) and go for 10m to a belay. Continue up (as for *Tippy Toe*) before moving right up a fault to a ledge system which leads right above the barrier wall. Step down and traverse until 10m from the fault line (50m). Gain the fault line, move up and step left for a runner. Climb an icy ramp and over a bulge (bold) before trending right into the main fault line. Go up this to a belay on the left (40m). Continue up and move left to gain the upper crest (50m). Finish up this (60m).

AONACH MOR, Coire an Lochain:
Gonzo 90m IV,4. Andy Nisbet, Jonathan Preston. 23 Dec 2014.
A line of iced grooves right of *The Muppet Show* and left of *Hidden Pinnacle Gully*. The cornice allowed a fairly direct finish.

AONACH MOR, West Face:
Living Dead 500m II/III *. Steve Kennedy. 7 Feb 2015.
The groove line running leftwards up the north (left) side of the middle section of the buttress climbed by *Golden Oldy*. Climb *Downhill Gully* (or the lower section of *Golden Oldy*, then left into the gully) to an icefall which forms at the narrows about one-third of the way up the gully. Climb the prominent groove on the right wall leading diagonally left for two pitches to reach the narrow ridge forming the upper part of *Golden Oldy*. Finish up *Golden Oldy*.

AONACH BEAG, North Face:
Highway Robbery 70m III. Scott Kirkhope, Ken Applegate, Hannah Evans. 19 Jan 2015.
Start 50m down from the col between Aonach Mor and Aonach Beag. Climb an icefall to a snow bay and up to a steep wall. Either head out left to finish up easier ground, joining *Whiteout*, or go right via a shallow gully (more in keeping with the grade).

Time Warp 130m V,5. Roger Webb, Simon Richardson. 14 Mar 2015.
A direct ascent of the chimney avoided by *Blackout*. Start 20m right of the wide entry gully of *Whiteout* below the left side of the mixed wall between *Whiteout* and *Wipeout*.
1. 60m Climb the wall via a series of shallow ramps and steep steps, tending first left, then right, then left again to join the traverse of *Whiteout* in the snow bay below the *Blackout* chimney.
2. 30m Climb the chimney directly for 25m and move up the easier continuation gully to a belay. On this ascent, the chimney was spectacularly choked with ice that created a through route at the steepest section.
3. 50m Continue up easier ground to the top.

King's Ransom, Direct Exit 180m II. Simon Richardson, Roger Webb. 24 Mar 2015.
The prominent shallow couloir between *The White Queen* and *This Sceptred Isle* is the natural continuation to the initial gully of *King's Ransom* (and avoided on the first ascent as it looked too easy). The couloir starts above the initial gully of

King's Ransom (top of pitch 2) and is climbed in four rope lengths. It has probably been climbed before and reduces the overall grade of *King's Ransom* to V,5.

AONACH BEAG, Lower West Face:

Note: Sandy Allan & Andy Nisbet repeated *Prominent Chimney* on 20 Dec 2014 thinking it was new. On the day it was 140m Grade III. The diagram on p261 of the Ben Nevis guide is correct but the description is unhelpful. The following route is an icefall which forms left of its lower section.

Santa 90m V,5. Andy Nisbet, Steve Perry. 7 Feb 2015.
Start about 15m left of *Prominent Chimney* below a right-facing chimney-corner. Gain the base of the chimney (20m), then climb it until a ramp leads out right to below the main icefall. Climb this to easier ground (50m). Finish out right up a curving ramp (20m).

Elf 80m III,4. Sandy Allan, Andy Nisbet. 20 Dec 2014.
Left of *Prominent Chimney* are steep walls. This ice line forms left of these where the angle eases. Two steep sections were avoided (could be climbed with thicker ice), but one bulge had to be climbed.

Dasher 170m III,4. Andy Nisbet, Jonathan Preston. 29 Dec 2014.
A mixed line right of *Prominent Chimney*, escapable. Start at the right edge (lowest point) of the buttress. Climb diagonally left before going up to the crest (45m). Follow the crest to below a summit (45m). Climb a short crack-line to the top and descend to the main ramp (20m). Cross the main ramp (20m) and follow a fault line which diverges rightwards from *Prominent Chimney*. Where this ends, climb a steep wall on the left to the top near *Prominent Chimney* (40m).

Axiom 120m III. Andy Nisbet, Steve Perry. 7 Feb 2015.
The gully between *North Buttress* and *Crevassed Rib* gave a lot of ice on this occasion. This was originally thought to be *Torquing Nonsense* (as in SMCJ 2014), but that route actually started up the gully of *North Buttress* before going straight up. A steep section led to snow bending right to a continuation (going left would have been an escape). The continuation ice led to an easier finish.

Bottleneck Gully, Right Branch 60m VII,7. Steve Perry, Andy Nisbet. 7 Feb 2015.
After gaining the start of the right branch (not included in length), the branch gave steep ice leading to an ice roof, surmounted with difficulty and passing the capping chockstone on the left (30m). Finish rightwards and back left more easily (30m).

STOB A' CHOIRE MHEADHOIN:

Navigator 150m VI,6. Dan Bailey, Andy Nisbet, Steve Perry. 11 Feb 2015.
Good climbing but escapable right into *Goblin Gully*. Start up and right of *Slytherin* towards the end of the buttress. Climb an icy groove, then turfy ground trending slightly right to a steep wall right of *Slytherin*'s icy groove (45m). Pull through the short overhanging wall, then trend rightwards up steep grooves to reach and cross snow and arrive at the base of the next tier (40m). Move right and climb a big icy groove before returning left to a spike (45m). Continue up the right side of the buttress and climb a left-slanting chimney-crack (difficult) to

reach easy ground (20m). Snow for 50m reaches the top (not included in length).

BINNEIN SHUAS, North-West Buttresses:
Bogle Eyed 30m III. Martin Holland, Jim Bayliss. 31 Jan 2015.
Starting from the lowest steep section of the crags containing *Laggan Fantasy*. A left-facing corner just right of a severely undercut wall can contain water ice in quantity. Climb steep ice in the corner and the ice line above. The angle eases and becomes more stepped with height. Above the ice 10m of easy ground leads to a good belay at large blocks.

GLEN COE

BUACHAILLE ETIVE MOR, North Blackmount Buttress:
The following routes are level with the top pitches and on the left of *Saturday Rock* and *The Snake*. They can be accessed by scrambling down the top of the gully between Central Blackmount Buttress and North Blackmount Buttress and then over a large block on a grassy ledge. Topo provided.

Tombstone Crack 20m Severe 4a **. Ewan Lyons. 25 Jul 2014.
Climb the obvious crack on the left of the upper wall starting behind a large block.

Tombstone Wall 30m H.Severe 4b *. Ewan Lyons. 25 Jul 2014.
Start left of the top pitch of *Saturday Rock* from a grassy ledge. Climb the left or right side of the tombstone, then a short corner and wall to a small ledge. Climb the wall above trending left past some mossy holds.

Central Buttress:
Hic 120m VI,7. Michael Barnard, Ron Dempster. 13 Dec 2014.
An attempt at a winter ascent of *Hiccup*. Some superb climbing on the lower cracks.
1. 15m Climb the *Hiccup* crack to a small ledge on the right with spike belay above.
2. 55m Climb cracks just right of the edge to regain the line. Bold slabby ground leads up to the base of a right-slanting ramp going across the north-east face; gain this with difficulty and move across to join *North Face Route* at the base of its upper chimney. Climb the chimney to where it eases off, then move back left along a ledge to a good spike.
3. 50m Continue more easily to the top of the buttress.

Creag a' Bhancair:
The End of Innocence 90m E7 ****. Iain Small, Blair Fyffe. 28 Jun 2014.
This route climbs *Celtic Dawn*, then takes the superb steep grey wall to the left of *Romantic Reality*. Named so as it was climbed 100 years to the day after the Arch Duke Franz Ferdinand was assassinated.
1. 20m 6a Climb *Celtic Dawn* (E5).
2. 35m 6b/c Climb the grey wall above the belay (small wires), trending leftwards to a good jug, good sky-hook on another jug 1m up and left of this jug. Step right and make a dynamic move up to a good hold and move right to a crimpy break

(small cam), then up to a long thin roof Make a strenuous and technical traverse right on undercuts to gain a flake-line. Climb this for a few metres, before more hard moves up and right gain another small roof (more moderate to large cams). Make more hard moves left and up to gain better holds and a slight easing of the angle. Continue up and left to a grassy ledge.
3. 35m 5b Continue up easier ground to the top.

GEARR AONACH, Upper West face:
Twoburkelosis 75m III 4. Dave Burke, Colm Burke. 23 Feb 2015.
Start at the bottom of the buttress just to the left of *Jim's Gully*. Climb over a rocky bulge and up a short snow ramp that steepens quickly. Take the obvious shallow chimney feature close to where the edge of the buttress meets the gully. Good mixed climbing gains a prominent spike (40m). One awkward step following the rib gains a ledge left of the gully exit. Continue on easy ground for 25m to gain the ridge (35m).

STOB COIRE NAN LOCHAIN, Central Buttress:
Tried and Tested 100m VII,7. Andy Nelson, Kenny Grant, Keith Ball. 29 Dec 2014.
The hanging chimney slot and hanging grooves on the wall right of *Satyr*. Start in the corner/bay formed by the *Satyr* wall and the projecting spur of *Raeburn's Ordinary Route*.
1. 30m Climb steep turf up to cracks, and then the squeeze chimney (grunting optional). Belay on the ledge above, positioned to enjoy watching the efforts of your second.
2. 35m Move up to a ledge, then tenuously left into the hanging groove on the front face, which is followed with some stiff pulls to the next large ledge.
3. 35m Climb the balancey wall above the ledge, then scramble more easily to top.

AONACH DUBH, Lower Walls:
Angeline 25m E3 5c **. Gary Latter. 11 Jul 2014.
Good sustained climbing, taking a direct line to the finish of *Lady Jane*. Start at the base of the short easy ramp, just right of *Charlotte Anne*. Climb up then right to a good horizontal slot, place protection in a short diagonal crack above, then move left and up to a good horizontal break. Continue directly up a tiny right-facing groove, then direct, moving right to good ledge. Climb direct from the left end of this to gain the good horizontal break on *Lady Jane*. Finish up this.

STOB COIRE NAM BEITH:
Cartouche 40m IV,4 **. Ken Applegate, Nick Stone. 5 Feb 2015.
This fine sustained ice pitch starts towards the top of North-West Gully, a few metres down and right of where *Central Gully*, *Deep Cut Chimney* and *No.4 Buttress* converge. The pitch takes a direct line up an obvious ice filled groove and finishes on the upper slopes of the mountain, where the angle eases.

STOB COIRE NAM BEITH, Summit Buttresses:
Bodach na Nollaig 90m II. Steve Kennedy. 25 Dec 2014.
Takes a spiralling line on the south-east (left) face of the largest buttress climbed by *Corkscrew*. Start about 30m below and right of the prominent snow gully and

just left of a small projecting ridge. Climb out rightwards by a steep snow ramp to near the top of the ridge, then continue directly, right of a steep wall, to reach the buttress crest (joining *Corkscrew*). Finish by the easy upper slopes.

CHURCH DOOR BUTTRESS:

Wall of the Evening Light 90m E6 **. Iain Small, Blair Fyffe. 10 Jul 2014.
A fine hard route route between *Lost Arrow* and *Kingpin*. Start as for *Kingpin*.
1. 40m 6a Climb *Kingpin* to the groove junction. Climb the left-hand groove and wall above to step right to the belay at the top of the second pitch of *Kingpin*.
2. 50m 6b Climb the groove on the left to step back right to a sloping ledge (possible belay). Ascend a wall to another ledge, then take thin cracks up the centre of the wall to reach the black streak. Climb this boldly to the roof and pull left and through it to gain a diagonal crack in the headwall that leads to a niche. Climb the crack out of this to belay on ledge above.

AN T-SRON, East Face:

New Blues 105m III,4 *. Steve Kennedy, Andy MacDonald. 8 Feb 2015.
The most prominent groove on the upper part of the buttress left of *Sack o' Coal Couloir*. From the foot of *SOCC*, climb the lower easy angled buttress on the left to a snow shelf which leads leftwards to a large block at the start of the groove (55m). Climb the initial groove, move right to avoid a steepening, then back left below a steep wall. Continue up steep mixed ground immediately left of the wall to reach easy ground (50m). Finish by easy scrambling to the summit ridge (not included in length).

Boogie 110m II. Steve Kennedy. 28 Dec 2014.
Left of the buttress containing *New Blues* are two narrow gullies. This route climbs the buttress between the gullies. Start at the foot of the gully at the left corner of the buttress and move up rightwards. A short steepening at about mid-height leads to a narrow slot which in turn leads to easy scrambling.

AONACH EAGACH:

Note: Kevin Woods climbed *Bolly Quaffers Buttress* in May 2015, taking a fairly direct line at scrambling Grade 3. Steep heather breaking out in rock steps, exposed.

CLACH LEATHAD, Summit Cliff:

Note: Routes have been climbed on this face before and not recorded.

Eclipse 140m IV,5. Andy Nisbet, Steve Perry. 22 Mar 2015.
The furthest left and longest of several iced grooves which form on the right side of its summit cliff. The start of the route is tucked in against the left buttress and takes the right branch of two ice lines forming a V (the left peters out). Climb ice through a narrow slot to an overhanging block on the right (30m). Continue up an icy corner to the upper snowfield and blocks after a further 20m (50m). Steep snow to the top (60m).

Springtail 120m IV,4. Susan Jensen, Andy Nisbet, Steve & Katie Perry. 4 Apr 2015.
Some 30m right of *Eclipse* are two parallel ice lines in a slight depression. This

takes the left one. Climb icy and turfy ground slightly leftwards to reach a shallow gully leading straight up to the upper snow (50m). Climb the snow to the top (70m).

Holme Moss 120m IV,4. Andy Nisbet, Steve Perry. 22 Mar 2015.
This takes the right line in the depression. Climb the ice to the upper snowfield (60m). Head slightly right to an iced groove in an isolated buttress. Climb this and steep snow to the top (60m).

Perrylous 110m IV,4. Sandy Allan, Andy Nisbet. 2 Apr 2015.
The most prominent groove is just right of centre. Climb this with two steep sections to reach the well defined groove. Climb this to blocks on the left (50m). Continue right of *Holme Moss* up the isolated buttress and steep snow to the top (60m).

Chairman 110m IV,4. Susan Jensen, Andy Nisbet, Steve & Katie Perry. 4 Apr 2015.
The next ice line to the right. Start 5m right of *Perrylous*. Climb a snow and ice groove to a steepening. Traverse right on a turf ledge (crux) before going up slightly left into the main upper groove. Climb this to the upper section (50m). Finish up the isolated buttress and snow to the top (60m).

Cool for Cats 120m III. Andy Nisbet. 25 Mar 2015.
The rightmost ice line on the face. Start at the bottom right corner of the cliff. Go up to where ramps lead out right and left. Climb the icy left ramp, go back right and climb another icy ramp to reach a snow and ice groove leading to the upper face. Move right and climb snow near the right arete of the face to the summit.

CREACH BHEINN, Zeppelin Face:

The map ref quoted in SMCJ 2008 is corrected to NM 874 585. The Zeppelin Face (SMCJ 2010, p170) contains three well defined lines. *The Rover* (SMCJ 2008, p177) climbs the left-hand line which is essentially a gully. The two lines to the right appear as left-facing corners. *Houses of the Holy* generally follows the middle line (not the rightmost line as previously described). This route climbs the rightmost line (slabby left-facing corner), just left of an easy gully.

Bring it on Home 255m IV,5 *.Steve Kennedy, Andy MacDonald. 4 Mar 2015.
Climb the easy gully for a short distance, then move left onto broken ground aiming for the prominent corner. A snow ramp leads up left into a bay below a steep wall at the base of the corner. Climb the icy corner (thin) and mixed grooves above in one long pitch (crux) trending slightly left near the top. A short pitch leads to the top via a small cornice.

SOUTHERN HIGHLANDS

STOB GHABHAR, North-East Corrie:

Note: Ken Crocket notes that Maclay, Oscar, Rohde and Solly climbed a line at Easter 1903 starting left of *Hircine Rib* but joining it for the final easier section.

Cuithach 105m III,4. Steve Kennedy, Andy MacDonald. 15 Feb 2015.
The prominent open groove left of the main buttress containing *Hircine Rib*. Climb the groove via short ice steps to its conclusion at the foot of a steep rock wall (55m). Move left below the wall and climb steep ice which leads to the upper snow slopes. The cornice can usually be outflanked on the right (50m).
Note: The team wasn't 112 years too late; the route above is different!

Coire Dhomhnaill:
Countdown 200m II/III. Andy Nisbet. 25 Mar 2015.
A gully starting 60m right of and diverging from *The Great Divide*. Mostly snow but with a steepening to enter the main gully (double bergschrund here) and an ice pitch high up. This was thin and fragile but would have been Grade II for much of this snowy season.

BEINN AN DOTHAIDH, Creag Coire an Dothaidh:
Kelvin Grooves 155m III,4. Martin Holland, Andrew Rembrandt, Ged Browne. 24 Jan 2015.
Sections have been climbed before. Start at the lowest rocks 6m right of *Fahrenheit 451*.
1. 35m Climb a steep, right-trending turfy ramp with a short rock wall on the left. Belay at a short wall on the right with capping blocks (first pitch of *Right Guard*).
2. 40m Move left 5m and climb a right-trending groove line. Surmount a short wall to gain a left-trending, partly overhung grassy ramp. Follow this and it's continuation leftwards to a block belay at a snowy gully near *Fahrenheit 451*.
3. 30m Follow the gully easily up and right to a traversing ledge.
4. 50m Step around the nose on the right. Move up to and follow a delicate slabby groove line to below the steep final rock band. Traverse hard right on ledges to gain the final icy groove of *Centigrade* and follow this to the top.

Burnout 175m IV 4. I. Clark, A.McCaig. 24 Feb 2002.
Takes the right edge of the main buttress, traverses round on to the face overlooking the col, finishing up steep icy grooves and walls. A good varied route on steep turf and icy bulges.
1. 35m Start 20m right of *Centigrade* at an icy turf ramp under a short diagonal wall. Climb the ramp, go left round a corner and up ledges to a thread.
2. 35m Continue up steep ice, go right for a few metres, then up and left to a cave with a thread at the back).
3. 40m Climb up bulges to a long airy traverse to reach a large flake.
4. 40m Move right and climb a steep icy groove.
5. 25m Continue to the top.

Quick Fire 65m II. Martin Holland, Graham Crowder. 25 Feb 2015.
Start about 100m north of the Beinn an Dothaidh/Beinn Dorain col just left of a long 5m high vertical wall.
1. 50m Climb the narrowing easy gully line to where it steepens and curves tightly left. Climb through the narrows and then up on good featured ice to belay on a terrace (it is possible to walk off rightwards at this point).
2. 15m Climb the short obvious continuation groove on the left.

CREAG THARSUINN, Upper Buttress:
Arch Chimney 65m V,5. Dafydd Morris, Matt Buchanan. 22 Jan 2015.
By the summer line.

BINNEIN AN FHIDLEIR, Summit Buttress:
Twa Fiddlers 35m V.Diff. Andy Cochrane, Julie Blythe. Aug 2012.
From the base of *Fiddler's Slab*, walk up and left some 100m to the foot of a dark broad slab speckled with quartz, with a lighter broad grey band running up to the left. Start at the left base, where a narrow grassy crack angles in from the right to meet a short broad crack on the left. Angle up and right over the main quartz patch to where the angle eases off. Scramble easily up to a large grassy platform.

BEN LOMOND:
David Webster climbed the three gullies between B and C buttresses in Jan 2015. They are rather dismissed in the last guide but are good lines and definitely not Grade I.

B-C Gully Left-Hand 70m II. Messrs Inglis-Clark & Shannon. 19 Apr 1897.
The leftmost gully, about 50m to the right of *Lomond Corner*. A narrow parallel sided gully (barely 1m wide in places) consistantly steep but never technical.

B-C Gully Central 70m II/III.
A wider parallel sided gully. Follow snow for a pitch to below a short steep mixed or ice step. Pull over this (may be hard) and continue up the broadening gully for another pitch at about Grade II.

B-C Gully Right-Hand 70m III.
The right-hand gully. Follow easy ground into the base of the parallel-sided gully. Ascend a steepening thinly iced slab for about 10m (bold). The line quickly peters out; continue either up the vague continuation gully slightly to the left, or go up a rising snow ramp to the right.

Cave Dance 70m V,6. David Webster, Hugh Macgregor. 5 Feb 2015.
Start up *B-C Gully Left-Hand* for about 20m to belay on good ice on the left. Climb short but steep ice to enter a hanging V-groove and continue up and right to a small cave. Pull steeply over the cave into a flared and overhanging chimney groove (crux). Exit ether right or left, then trend up and left into the obvious continuation gully to its end. A choice of finishes are available above the gully on good turf or neve. The crux is quite serious despite the grade, but the rest of the route is much easier.

BEINN HEASGARNICH, Coire Heasgarnich:
Side Door 90m III,4. George Allan, John Thomas. 7 Feb 2015.
This is the left arm of the V (SMCJ 2009); the right arm is *Gateway Gully*. The crux is the obvious ice bulge through the steepening which leads to easy ground.

The Gatepost 110m II/III. George Allan, Billy Hood. 19 Mar 2015.
With a better start the following should supersede the description given in SMCJ 2009.
The buttress to the right of *Gateway Gully* starting in the second bay to the right

of the gully just beyond the lowest rocks. Climb the obvious corner and take a fairly direct line above.

LOWLAND OUTCROPS

LOCH LOMOND, Ross Point:
Note: Kevin Woods notes that the map reference for Ross Point in Lowland Outcrops is wrong. It should be at NS 372 954.

Muldoon's Crag:
Muldoon's Traverse 60m HVS. George Christie, Ken Johnston. 16 Oct 1976.
This is a crag above Loch Lomond, thought to be at NN 344 075, with a large roof system. Climb an obvious crack to the roof, traverse to the left end of the roof and finish upwards. The roof was large and unprotected but has some pockets and might make a sport route.

GLASGOW AREA, Auchinstarry Quarry:
Defying Gravity 15m E6 6b/c ***. David Macmorris. 16 Jul 2014.
A bold test piece for the elite that dare... Feel your way up the humorous start of *Death is the Hunter*, then continue up the arete of *Nijinski* sticking to the left-hand side of the arete only. Throw yourself for an exciting last dyno (crux), then easy climbing to the top. *Death is the Hunter* nut crack isn't on the route.

Craigmore:
YOLO 12m HVS 5c *. David Macmorris. 16 Jul 2014.
Directly climbing the arete between *Tom and Jerry Wall* and *Rampage*, then finish directly up the face instead of normal top out. *Rampage* gear crack isn't included with the route.

THE BORDERS & DUMFRIES, Swatte Fell, Nether Coomb Craig:
Note: The corrie only gets a mention in the Lowland Outcrops guidebook, but it's a worthwhile venue in the right conditions for a mountaineering day out (lots of Grade I gullies and turfy ridges).

EDINBURGH AREA, Arthur's Seat:
Jagerbomb Hangover 10m E1 5c. Stuart Green. 6 Jul 2014.
Located immediately next to *Fallen Column Climb* on The Long Row. Start in a recess just to the left of *Fallen Column Climb*. Climb the initial bulge with difficulty, then move out right to gain the arete above. Soloed on-sight; easier for the tall.

Craigpark Quarry:
This is the large quarry opposite EICA Ratho which is in the process of being landscaped into a country park. There are several buttresses; South-East facing.
Approach: Park as for Ratho Quarry or just before the bridge over the canal. Head along the southern side of the canal for 150m and turn right to reach the quarry.

Ravens Buttress:
The main wall in the quarry.

Little Miss 8m Severe 4a *. Jamie Sparkes. 5 Apr 2014.
Reminiscent of *Mr Men* at Auchinstarry. Left of the double overhang is a blunt arete on a black wall. Climb directly up this on spaced but good holds. Unprotected until after the crucial mantelshelf but at least the landing is soft.

Stacked Block Route 8m Diff. Jamie Sparkes. 5 Apr 2014.
Between the prow and a double overhang on the left, climb the big stacked boulders to a tricky finish. Well protected.

Bay Area:
The slightly higher, inset bay to the left of the prominent tower; South-East facing.

Circus Trick 10m 6b ***. Jamie Sparkes. 13 Jul 2014.
Contort up the groovy corner at the left side of the bay. If your head ends up by your tail at any point, you're probably at the crux.

The Watchtower:
The most obvious feature of the wall is the prominent smooth tower in the centre which protrudes from the tree-line.

Technical Mister 4m 5c. Jamie Sparkes. 5 Apr 2014.
The short slabby left arete of the tower gives a fun problem to the ledge. Better if the seam is eliminated to give a purer arete experience.

Avenue Wall:
The wall extending rightwards from the watchtower, quite well hidden behind the trees.

Park Life 10m 6b+ ***. Jamie Sparkes. 13 May 2014.
An excellent short, technical and crimpy slab with a perplexing crux.

Pipe Wall:
The rightmost wall and the first encountered on the approach.

Parkin Ride 10m 6b **. Jamie Sparkes. 13 Jul 2014.
A route for northern loafers. Climb the left arete to the big ledge. Shuffle right along it and finish as for the next route.

Cakewalk 10m 6a+ *. Jamie Sparkes. 13 Jul 2014.
Start 2m right of the arete. Grab any two crimps and pull hard enough to bring the stepped ledges into reach. Meander up these to the ledge. Leave the ledge at its right end and make tricky moves to a good flat hold level with the anchors.

The Pie-d Piper 10m 6a *. Jamie Sparkes. 13 Jul 2014.
Gain the ledge using the two boreholes and climb the tricky little flake above.

FAST CASTLE HEAD AREA:
The following two climbs are on a short south facing wall above the pool at the base of the waterfall flowing out of Dowlaw Dean, halfway between The Souter and The Brander.

Waterfall Wall 10m E5 6a. Dominic Jeff, Alasdair Macleod. 9 Jun 2013.
Scramble up the ramp above the pool to wires in good jugs, then climb the wall up and right on crimps to gain a thin seam, which is followed to the top.

Witness the Whiteness 10m E2 5b. Anthony Dodd, Dominic Jeff, Alasdair Macleod. 9 Jun 2013.
Climb the right side of the wall, staying left of the more broken ground on the arete, to gain a crack starting at two-thirds height and leading to the top.

SPORT CLIMBS

A page of climbs, many on Princess Cairn, were accidentally omitted from SMCJ 2014. They can be found in the 2014 New Routes section on the SMC website <http://www.smc.org.uk/Downloads/NewRoutes2014.pdf>.
They are also included here.

Moy Rock:
Eldorado 24m 6a **. Andy Nisbet. 4 Sep 2013.
A route at the far left end of the crag, in the next bay left of *Holly Tree Groove*. Here is a water runnel forming a groove high up and the route climbs the wall to its right to join it at the very top. Start next to a ramp on the right but try not to touch the ramp. Climb the wall to move right under an earthy scoop. Climb a ramp leading right to another scoop where another ramp leads right. Go briefly up the ramp before moving on to the wall. At its top, traverse left into the main groove as high as possible. The lower-off is near the top of the groove.

Kitemark 25m 6c **. Ian Taylor. 2015.
The next line right of *Cloak and Dagger*.

Magnifascent 23m 6a+. Ray Wilby. March 2014.
To the right of *The Fly* and based on *Magnificrack* (original ascentionists agreed with retro-bolting). Clip the first two bolts of *The Fly*, then go up to the layback crack. A good rest at the top of the crack, then climb the wall direct to the lower off. Easier but poorer rock to finish rightwards, then reach back left.

I did it Moy Way 12m 6b+ *. Davy Moy, bolted Andy Wilby. 6 Apr 2013.
The next route right of *Ave it!*. Start from a pedestal, climb the undercut flake-crack and pull over right onto the wall above. Tenuous climbing. Needs traffic to become a classic!

Red Setter 25m 6a *. Andy Nisbet. May 2013.
Start just right of the pedestal of the previous route and climb into a flake system. Near its top move right and climb the wall above. The angle eases to a lower-off at the cliff-top.

Princess Cairn:
A bay with a big holly tree lies 15m to the left of *Moonlighting Meercat*. The following routes are in another bay just to the left.

No More Routes 10m 4+ *. Seb Rider. Jan 2013.
The furthest left route is steep but with good holds. Climb the shallow corner to gain the wall above.

Our Routes 10m 5 **. Seb Rider. Jan 2013.
Climb a flake and wall above.

Moonbow 5+ *. Gregor Callum. Jan 2013.
Climb up the left side of a block to an overhang. Pull over and trend left.

The following routes are in the bay with the big holly tree.

Hogmanay 10m 6a *. Gregor Callum. 1 Jan 2013.
At the right end of the bay. Climb up an open groove using twin cracks. Follow the headwall to a lower-off just to the right.

Get out of my Garden 10m 6b *. Seb Rider. Jan 2013.
The left end of the bay has a blunt arete trending rightwards under the overlap. Pull over this trending right on a slab.

Heatwave 10m 6c **. Seb Rider. 19 Jul 2013.
At the back of the bay left of the holly. Climb up a groove with pockets, pull through a tricky bulge and continue on the slab above.

The following routes are from *Jenny* rightwards.

Ithaca 50m 5 **. Gregor Callum, Seb Rider. Jan 2012.
Continue on from *Jenny* by trending slightly rightwards, then left (30m). The lower-off is above a heather ledge. Two abseils using a 60m rope; three abseils using a 50m rope (there are abseil points).

Creag nan Cadhag:
Fossil Hunters 20m 6a+ *. Paul Tattersall. 2015.
A furthest left route. Starts up a clean wall aiming for a big ledge and steep corner above.

Ronald's Nightmare 20m 7c *. Ian Taylor, Andy Wilby. 2015.
Link *Nuclear Nightmare* into the upper section of *Ronald Raygun*.

Nuclear Cop Out 20m 7b+ *. Andy Wilby. 2015.
From below the final hard moves on *Nuclear Nightmare* follow two bolts leftwards to an independent lower-off.

Thick as Thieves 12m 7b *. Paul Tattersall. 2015.
Start up *Game Over* to the 4th bolt, then head left via some thin and technical moves to finish at the *Nuclear Litemare* lower-off.

Game Over Extension 8a+ ***. Andy Wilby. 2015.
The desperate one bolt extension.

Mhairi Stewart on Coalition Chaos (7a+/7b), Creag nan Cadhag. *Photo: Ian Taylor.*

Coalition Chaos 20m 7a+/7b **. Andy Wilby. 2015.
A right-hand start to *Game Over* giving easier climbing on the lower wall before joining *Game Over* at a jug. You still have the crux of *Game Over* to do!

Goat Crag:
Poster Boy 20m 5 *. Paul Tattersall. 2015.
Interesting new line left of *Teepee*.

A new 3 bolt start left of the original makes *The Noose* and *Snowflake* independent of *Batman and Robin*. No change in grade.

Bamboozle now has an independent start and its own lower-off, so shares no ground with *The Riddler*. New grade is 6c+ **.

Goat in the Woods:
Cote Hanger 15m 7b *. Ian Taylor. Apr 2015.
Start up *Cote d'Or*, then go rightwards through the roof.

Opposite: **St Kilda from Skye**

St. Kilda is seldom seen from Skye, being almost exactly 100 miles distant. This photo was taken from the Inaccessible Pinnacle on Skye on 24/08/2014.

Hirta (left) and Boreray (centre) are visible on the horizon.

Even stacs Lee and an Armin can be picked out either side of Boreray.

MacLeod's Maidens stand out in the 'foreground' on the right.

Photo: Des Rubens.

MISCELLANEOUS NOTES

THE W.H. MURRAY LITERARY PRIZE

As a tribute to the late Bill Murray, whose mountain and environment writings have been an inspiration to many a budding mountaineer, the SMC have set up a modest writing prize, to be run through the pages of the Journal. The basic rules are set out below, and will be reprinted each year. The prize is run with a deadline of 1 May each year.

The Rules:

1. There shall be a competition for the best entry on Scottish Mountaineering published in the *Scottish Mountaineering Club Journal*. The competition shall be called the 'W.H. Murray Literary Prize', hereafter called the 'Prize'.
2. The judging panel shall consist of, in the first instance, the following: The current Editor of the *SMC Journal*; The current President of the SMC; and two or three lay members, who may be drawn from the membership of the SMC. The lay members of the panel will sit for three years after which they will be replaced.
3. If, in the view of the panel, there is in any year no entry suitable for the Prize, then there shall be no award that year.
4. Entries shall be writing on the general theme of 'Scottish Mountaineering', and may be prose articles of up to approximately 3000 words in length, or shorter verse. Entries may be fictional.
5. Panel members may not enter for the competition during the period of their membership.
6. Entries must be of original, previously unpublished material. Entries should be submitted to the Editor of the *SMC Journal* by the end of April for consideration that year. Electronic contributions are preferred and should be submitted via e-mail, although double-spaced typewritten hard copies will also be accepted by post. (See Office Bearers page at end of this Journal for address etc.) Any contributor to the *SMC Journal* is entitled to exclude their material from consideration for the Prize and should so notify the Editor of this wish in advance.
7. The Prize will be a cheque for the amount £250.
8. Contributors may make different submissions in different years.
9. The decision of the panel is final.
10. Any winning entry will be announced in the *SMC Journal*, and will be published in the *SMC Journal* and on the SMC Website. Thereafter, authors retain copyright.

THE WH MURRAY LITERARY PRIZE 2015

THE WINNER OF THIS year's prize is Ian Crofton. His reflective article *The Hills are Alive...* was thought 'a very attractive piece of writing which explores the sense of sound...Special sounds which achieve greater significance in...open space, often reaching deeply into one's psyche and imagination.' All of this, encapsulated in 'limpid, rhythmical prose that at times is almost poetry' was found, despite a little uncertainty of tone in places, quite convincing. There was no uncertainty of tone in the tale which was arguably the runner up. Appearing in all the judges' top threes, MJ Cobb's witty and inventive satire was acidly droll from beginning to end. *The Heights of Allusion* was thought 'a sort of fusing of Creag Dhu patter with James Joyce word-play.' The humour was 'uniformly bleak' and the hard men 'suitably taciturn.' Perhaps the author will develop this 'quirky style' in future work?

Mike Dixon's *A Patchwork of Patey* was thought an 'engaging piece of research' which 'has a heart warming quality indicative of a labour of love.' This piece featured in two of the judges' top threes. Peter Foster, Jimmy Cruickshank and Hamish Johnston all received favourable mention for their studies of Brown, Smith and Heddle respectively. Some liked the crisp objectivity of Foster and Johnston, while others responded more warmly to Cruickshank's obvious emotional involvement with his subject.

Rob Archbold's *One Week in the West* was second on one judge's list. 'It's amazing what adventures can be salvaged from indifferent weather conditions.'

The pieces by cutting-edge climbers Guy Robertson and Julian Lines were remarkable for their content and formed a pleasant contrast between winter and summer, but were felt to be uneven in quality: *Sundance* was 'enjoyed' but the ending was felt 'awkward'; it seemed to imply a continuation. Lines's racy tour of DWS venues would have been improved, one judge thought, if 'the pace had been varied a little'. Perhaps it was a little break-neck? It was interesting that the recent winner of the Boardman-Tasker prize was perhaps experimenting with a different style. But for those of us incapable of following in their footsteps, articles like these contain valuable insights into the mentality required to operate at this level. Nor should it be thought that Andy Nisbet's delightfully unpretentious piece *An Riabhachan* passed unnoticed: a model of economic style.

Overall it was interesting that the experienced writers did best. However, alongside such veterans as Crofton, Jacob, Gribbon and Archbold it was very welcome to see fresh contributors like Ruth Love and Martin Cooper making their Journal debuts. It is very much to be hoped that they will contribute again and that others will come forward to take part in the strange and difficult activity of writing about mountaineering. If it wasn't difficult it wouldn't be worth doing.

Future contributors should note that copy must be received by the end of April.

SCOTTISH WINTER NOTES 2014–15

The 2015 winter was often stormy and started late, but the wet autumn meant that as the mountains cooled down in January, the mid-level gullies and smears began to weep copious amounts of ice providing many opportunities for those poised to take advantage. Despite the copious ice, the technical highlights were mixed routes – Guy Robertson and Greg Boswell's three new Grade Xs and Boswell's new Grade XII in the Northern Corries. Two of these Grade Xs were climbed on sight and are a significant step forward in the development of Scottish winter climbing.

Despite these outstanding successes, opinions are sharply divided as to whether or not it was a good season. Ice conditions may have been excellent, but with few periods of settled weather, there were limited opportunities to take advantage. To the frustration of many climbers, many of the best days occurred mid-week. The statistics bear this out with almost 70% of new routes climbed Monday to Friday – a surprising statistic considering that most climbers operate at weekends. As always flexibility was key, and Andy Nisbet, the grand master of Scottish winter climbing, showed the way by being perfectly in tune with weather patterns and making first ascents of many mid-level ice routes.

Grade X Hat Trick

Greg Boswell and Guy Robertson started their remarkable run of cutting edge routes on 19 January when they made the first ascent of *The Greatest Show on Earth* (X,10) on the north face of Cul Mòr in Coigach. This awe-inspiring route takes the blank wall on the right side of Coire Gorm, which is defended by a large overhang. The wall is vertical above and the line was considered a problem for the next generation. Robertson led the first pitch, a steep icefall leading to a small terrace below the overhang, before handing over to Boswell who then made one of his finest ever leads by pulling through the roof and climbing the poorly protected wall above. This was the first time a new Grade X had been climbed on sight, although Nick Bullock's lead of the crux pitch of *Nevermore* on Lochnagar last season hinted that this breakthrough was not far away.

Four days later, Robertson and Boswell turned their attention to the 100m-high Broad Terrace Wall on Creag an Dubh Loch. The angle tips considerably the wrong side of vertical between the lines of *Sword of Damocles* and *Culloden*, and in summer this section is breached by two mythical climbs – *Flodden* (E6) and *Range War* (E4). *Range War* is the steepest line, but the first pitch is very vegetated and the route has only been climbed a handful of times since its first ascent by Kenny Spence and Duncan McCallum in July 1983.

Boswell had walked into Dubh Loch seven times to attempt the route, but finally on 22 January the stars aligned, and Boswell and Robertson found the cliff white with hoar frost and dripping with icicles and frozen turf. They climbed an alternative first pitch left of the original summer line to the *Grass Balcony*, a welcome ledge in a sea of overhanging rock. Boswell then led the daunting 35m-long overhanging crux pitch (graded 6a in summer), pulling on huge reserves physical and mental strength, leaving Robertson the top pitch of thick bulging ice. The pair gave *Range War* (Winter Variation) the same grade as *The Greatest Show on Earth* at X,10.

Greg Boswell on Range War, X,10 Creag an Dubh Loch.

Photo: Guy Robertson.

Ten days later, Robertson and Boswell teamed up with Uisdean Hawthorn and succeeded on the long sought-after first winter ascent of *The Messiah* on Beinn Bhan. The route was possibly first climbed by Creag Dhu climbers George Shields and Bob Jarvie in summer 1972, but their ascent was not recorded, and the route passed into climbing folklore. The eight-pitch winter route was graded X,10 and completed a remarkable hat trick of three new Grade Xs. 'We didn't intend to go out and climb three new Grade Xs in succession,' Greg explained. 'We've been waiting for these routes for the past few seasons, and with the stormy weather this winter, they all came into perfect condition…all the training and route planning paid off…and to have them be three hard routes is the perfect scenario. Scottish winter at its best!'

Banana Wall

Greg Boswell's final ground-breaking ascent of the season took place on 25 February when he succeeded on the awe-inspiring *Banana Wall* (XII,12) in Coire an Lochain on Cairn Gorm with Masa Sakano. This continuosly

Greg Boswell leads Banana Wall, XII,12 Coire an Lochain.

Photo: Masa Sakano.

sustained route, which takes the overhanging wall between *Fallout Corner* and *Bavarinthia*, is only the second route in Scotland ever to be given a Grade XII rating.

Boswell first tried the route in 2011, but after two failed attempts, he abseiled the line to see if it could be protected. The wall is so undercut that he hung too far out to gain any useful information. With four more years of winter experience under his belt and fresh from his superb trio of new Grade Xs, Boswell felt ready for a return visit. On his first attempt he took a huge ten-metre fall when a placement ripped. After a break he tried again and successfully led the pitch. Sakano followed and they completed the route in the dark whilst battling a rising storm. 'The route is crazy steep but the protection is there if you can hang on long enough to place it,' Boswell explained. 'It is by far the most sustained thing I've done in Scotland.' Boswell considers *Banana Wall* to be M11, which makes it one of the most difficult technical mixed routes ever climbed by placing the gear on the lead.

Early Season

After a very warm November, the winter season finally got underway in the first week of December as westerly winds brought snow to the higher tops. As usual, The Northern Corries were the most popular venue and there were ascents of *The Message*, *Pot of Gold*, *Hidden Chimney* and *Invernookie* in Coire an t-Sneachda, and over in Coire an Lochain, *Savage Slit* and *Ewen Buttress* were also climbed.

The first new route of the season fell to Ally and Gav Swinton on Creagan Cha-no on Cairn Gorm where they made the first ascent of *Punching Numbers* (VI,7), the steep crack-line right of *Mac's Crack*. A couple of days later on Ben Nevis, Will Sim and Andy Inglis set the pace with the second ascent of *Tomahawk Crack* (VIII,9). This excellent route to the right of *Sioux Wall* on Number Three Gully Buttress was first climbed by Greg Boswell and Adam Russell in November 2012.

Ferocious storms the following week relented in mid-December providing a welcome weather window. Martin Moran and Robin Thomas visited Beinn Eighe and made the first winter ascent of *Boggle* (VIII,8) on the Eastern Ramparts 'It was worth the wait and a special thrill to climb a Robin Smith route in winter.' Moran said afterwards. The same day, Guy Robertson and Greg Boswell pulled off the second ascent of *Culloden* (IX.9) on Creag an Dubh Loch's formidable Broad Terrace Wall. This exceptionally steep summer E2 was first climbed in winter by Iain Small, Gordon Lennox and Tony Stone in December 2010. *Culloden* was an inspired route choice as Creag an Dubh Loch is not normally considered an early season venue.

The weather on the run up to Christmas continued stormy and unsettled, but as ever, Andy Nisbet was on hand to visit the right place at the right time. On Stob Ban he made the first ascent of *Flying Saucer* (VI,7) with Steve Perry and on Aonach Mor he added *Gonzo* (IV,4) to the Ribbed Walls with Jonathan Preston.

The weather finally settled down between Christmas and New Year and Uisdean Hawtorn and Murdoch Jamieson nipped in for the second ascent of *Boggle* on Beinn Eighe – an unusually quick repeat of a major route. Three days later, Hawthorn teamed up with Callum Johnson on Ben Nevis to climb *Super G* (VI,6) on the Little Brenva Face. This ephemeral ice route had probably not had a second ascent since it was first climbed by Hannah Burrows-Smith and Dave McGimpsey in March 2002. Also on the Ben, Iain Small and Tony Stone had a productive couple of days making third ascents of *The Brass Monkey* (VII,8) and *The Great Corner* (VIII,8).

Across in Glen Coe, Andy Nelson, Kenny Grant and Keith Ball added an excellent mixed route to Stob Coire nan Lochan. The sustained three-pitch *Tried and Tested* (VII,7) climbs the chimney-corner formed by the spur of Central Buttress and the wall of Satyr and was described as being 'at the sporty end of its grade.' Roger Webb and Simon Richardson took advantage of a short sudden freeze after the New Year thaw to make the first ascent of *Tenterhooks* (VII,8) on Ben Nevis. This steep icy mixed climb on Creag Coire na Ciste between *Central Rib* and *Tinkerbell* brought the first part of the season to a close as more storms rushed in from the Atlantic.

Cold and Snowy

The stormy weather finally settled down in mid-January and a cold and snowy

Murdoch Jamieson and Uisdean Hawthorn on Boggle, VII,8 Beinn Eighe.
Photo: Doug Hawthorn.

spell set in. The snow line was low, which made route choice difficult, but winter climbers are becoming increasingly adept at hunting out the most appropriate venues for the prevailing conditions, and soon a host of excellent routes were being climbed.

Many of the most notable ascents were early repeats, and Erik Baillot and Rob Bryniarski set the ball rolling with the second ascent of *The Sea, The Sea* on Slioch. This legendary Grade VII was first climbed by Roger Webb and Neil Wilson 20 years ago and is the second winter route on Slioch's huge

Andy Inglis on Godzilla, IX,9, Beinn Bhan. *Photo: Iain Small.*

Atlantic Wall to see a repeat. Clearly on a roll, Baillot made the third winter ascent of *Enigma* (VII,7) on Mainreachan Buttress the following weekend, and nearby, Andy Inglis and Will Sim made the second winter ascent of the technical *Pale Rider* (VIII,9) on Beinn Eighe. Further north, Helen Rennard and Simon Yearsley made the third winter ascent of *Castro* (VII,7) on Sgùrr an Fhidhleir and two days later Rennard joined a small group of climbers, who have climbed this magnificent feature more than once in winter, when she made an ascent of the *Nose Direct* (VII,7) with Simon Davidson and Neil Silver.

The relatively low-lying Giant's Wall on Beinn Bhan saw the most activity however, with an early repeat of *The Godfather* (VIII,8) by Neil Adams and Graham McGrath and the second ascent of *Godzilla* (IX,9) by Iain Small, Murdoch Jamieson and Andy Inglis. Small and Jamieson returned a few days later to make the second ascent of *The God Delusion* (IX,9). This Robertson-Benson creation from 2008 is considered one of the most demanding winter routes in the Northern Highlands and was described by Small as 'a masterpiece in route finding.'

Elsewhere in the North-West, Andy Nisbet, Jonathan Preston and Dave McGimpsey added *Jinky* (V,5) to the Western Cliffs of Quinag which are always a good choice when snow levels are low, and James Edwards and Neil Wilson found *Sideshow* (IV,6), a good looking chimney-line in Coire Gorm on Cul Mòr. Over on Mainreachan Buttress, Iain Small and Murdoch Jamieson climbed a spectacular series of bulging ice pitches approximating to the summer route *Private Eye* (VIII,8), and further east, Andy Nisbet and Jonathan Preston added *Twerk* (V,5) to the rarely visited Coire nan Eun in the Fannaichs.

Classic Conditions

In early February the temperature rose, but cold clear nights transformed the snow into névé and the drainage lines filled with ice. On the West Face of Aonach Beag, Andy Nisbet and Steve Perry had a great day climbing *Axiom*

Murdoch Jamieson on The God Delusion, IX,9, Giant's Wall, Beinn Bhan.

Photo: Ian Small.

(III), the central gully on the lower face (a line so obvious that everyone thought it had been done before), *Santa* (V,5) the icy corner left of *Prominent Chimney*, and the steep Right-Hand Branch to *Bottleneck Gully* (VII,7). But Ben Nevis was where the finest conditions were to be found, especially on the mid-height ice routes. The snow was frozen hard and the bright sunny weather made it feel more like spring than early February. For the first time in many years *Gemini* and *The Shield Direct* on Carn Dearg Buttress came into excellent condition and both routes saw dozens of ascents. Nearby, *The Bewildabeast* (VI,6), a Mark Garthwaite-Adam Wainwright route from 1995 saw its first ever repeats with all the parties raving about the quality of the climbing and the sensational positions.On the new route front, Malcolm Bass,

Simon Yearsley and Neil Silver succeeded on a long-standing objective with the first ascent of *Cousinade* (VII,8). This route climbs the front face of Cousin's Buttress using a steep groove spotted by Bass on the second of his previous attempts with Yearsley in 2013. Pride of place went to Andy Inglis and Iain Small for their first winter ascent of *Teufel Grooves* (IX,9) on Raeburn's Buttress. This steep route takes the hanging corner on the right flank of the buttress, but rather than start up the summer HVS which uses the first section of *The Crack*, Small found an independent direct entry. Inglis then made a superb lead of the crux pitch. 'It looked very intimidating from below,' Small explained. 'It was an overhanging corner-crack that had no hooks, just torques, and at the belay Andy's ropes were hanging free in space. Yeah, it was steep!'

As February progressed, the focus increasingly turned to ice and Uisdean Hawthorn climbed an impressive triptych of routes. He started off with the first ascent of *Han Solo* (VIII,7) on Ben Nevis, a thin ice drool hanging above the first pitch of *Storm Trooper* on the left side of Creag Coire na Ciste. 'Uisdean's lead of the smear was impressive,' Guy Robertson commented later. 'The ice was maybe only about three inches thick at best, and a lot thinner in places. All in all it was a pretty cool cerebral experience and I'd have thought one of the harder bits of ice the Ben has to offer.' The next day Hawthorn linked up with Iain Small and Murdoch Jamieson to make an ascent of *The Fly Direct*, the highly prized thin ice gully on Creag Meagaidh's Pinnacle Buttress. Seeing that the neighbouring *Extasy* (a Grade VIII that you can't fall off) was in condition, the trio returned the following day to make the fourth ascent. 'I would have been delighted to climb just one of these routes in a season but to climb them both in two days, after doing a new route on Ben Nevis the day before, left me on a high,' Uisdean said afterwards.

Ice conditions improved further on Ben Nevis and many teams took their fill on rarely formed modern classics such as such as *The Shroud*, *Mega Route X* and *Boomer's Requiem*. Michael Barnard and John MacLeod took advantage of the rarely formed ice to make the first ascent of *Smear Fear* (VI,5), the direct continuation to *Vanishing Gully* and the steep *Superdirect Finish* (VI,5) to Nordwand Direct. More mixed in nature was *Inception* (V,7) a line of grooves and chimneys in the Fawlty Towers area of Secondary Tower Ridge by Steve Holmes and Duncan Curry, and the technical *Red Dragon* (VIII,9) by Dave MacLeod and Helen Rennard that takes the steep crack and wall just left of *The Urchin* on the east side of Tower Ridge. Also on the Ben, seasoned regulars Dave Rudkin and Keith Ball notched up an important repeat with the second winter ascent of *The Crack* (VIII,8) on the front face of Raeburn's Buttress.

Further east, Andy Nisbet, Steve Perry and Dan Bailey added the excellent-looking line of *Navigator* (VI,6) on Stob a' Choire Mheadhoin, a secluded cliff that can only be seen from the West Highland Railway. Nisbet and Perry had an impressive run in the North-West notching up *Barbie* (V,6) on Beinn Liath Mhor (with Sandy Allan), *Batmen* (VI,7) on the Northern Pinnacles face of Mullach nan Rathain on Liathach and the first winter ascent of *Tower Ridge* (V,6) on Ben Hope. The last route was something of a coup being 470m long and snatched in fairy tale conditions of deep rime in advance of a warm front rushing up from the south. Guy Robertson and Uisdean Hawthorn made a successful raid on An Teallach and came away with the first ascent of *Low*

Michael Barnard on Shear Fear (VI,5), Ben Nevis. *Photo: John MacLeod*

Steve Perry on Tower Ridge, V,6 Ben Hope. *Photo: Andy Nisbet.*

Riders (VII,8), a prominent line of corners on the steep lower section of Minor Rib.

In the Cairngorms, Nisbet and Perry continued their good run with first ascents of the icy *Blood Hound* (VI,6) on Lurcher's Crag (again with Sandy Allan) and the steep *Waive Wall* (V,7) in the rarely visited Coire Garbhlach. The most impressive achievement in the Cairngorms however was visiting German climber Ines Papert's ascent of *The Hurting* (XI,11) in Coire an t-Sneachda. This was the fifth overall and first female ascent, but these statistics only tell half the story. The route was climbed on the last day of her visit (after an attempt two days before) during terrible weather with winds gusting over 100mph on the tops. Papert's fall-free ascent of *The Hurting* is almost certainly the finest yet, but remarkably this ten-year old test-piece still awaits an on sight ascent.

Late Season Blues

The weather finally settled down in the middle of March allowing Iain Small to make two excellent additions to Ben Nevis. Starting off with Blair Fyffe, he climbed the *Piece Maker* (VIII,9), a steep mixed line between *Cleft Hanger* and *The Angry Chair* high on the East Flank of Tower Ridge. This high and sheltered part of the mountain retains mixed climbing conditions longer than other venues. Two days later Small teamed up with Uisdean Hawthorn to make the first ascent of *Call Me Ishmael* (VIII,9) on Indicator Wall, an ephemeral and challenging route to the left of *Stormy Petrel*.

Perhaps the most noteworthy late season event however was the development of An Riabhachan by Andy Nisbet who climbed a remarkable 17 new routes in three days. This remote corrie had only been visited a couple of times before by winter climbers and illustrates the remaining potential for exploratory mountaineering potential in the Scottish Highlands. And needless to say Nisbet's visits were perfectly timed, as by the end of March it looked like the spring thaw had well and truly set in.

But it turned out the winter season was far from over as both April and May were unseasonably cold. New routes were added to the high Cairngorms corries until the end of April and thick ice lingered on Ben Nevis. On the third weekend in May, *Green Gully*, *Smith's Route*, *Indicator Wall* and *Hadrian's Wall Direct* all had ascents, an unprecedented level of winter activity for so late in the year. And as I write this at the end of May, snow is forecast on the tops for early June – let's hope the temperatures are helpfully cool for the coming winter season.

Simon Richardson

100 YEARS AGO : THE CLUB IN 1915

I am honoured to have been asked to take on this regular feature, piloted so ably by Robin Campbell over the last ten years or so, although I fear that I will not be able to match his encyclopaedic knowledge of SMC history, his eye for spotting antiquarian inconsistencies or his ability to clarify obscure facts.

Mike Jacob

[Note: the use of *italics* indicates quotation from the *SMC Journal* or other source.]

The 26th AGM and Dinner was held in the North British Hotel, Edinburgh on Friday 4 December 1914 with the President, Dr W. Inglis Clark, in the chair. Club funds were healthy: the main cost to the Club was the publication of the Journal at some 40% of annual expenditure. There was discussion about the practicality of publishing three journals per year during wartime but it was decided to continue as usual. The Committee's report on the attendance of non-members at Club Meets was adopted; this delicately requested members to *consider the Club's convenience* before inviting an over-abundance of guests. Owing to the war the customary afternoon reception was abandoned and the dinner was an informal affair. Thirty-nine members gathered to dine and propose toasts *to absent friends on service* and to sing patriotic anthems *in keeping with the underlying note of national stress.*

Club Meets

The New Year Meet was held at the Loch Awe Hotel from 31 December 1914 to 4 January 1915 with 19 members and guests, some of whom reported *deeply drifted snow, high wind and driving mist* on the hills. The luxurious comforts of this Scottish baronial-style railway hotel, constructed in 1881, no doubt provided adequate compensation. The poor weather continued for the first two days of the New Year and although some members managed to fight their way to the summit of Ben Cruachan *no lengthy mountain expeditions were recorded.* The conditions improved on Sunday and permitted excursions onto the nearby hill-tops and provided views *whose lingering recollection of their beauty forms a rubric in memory's list of days.*

Ex-president Sir Hugh Munro had generously invited the SMC to hold a Meet at his family mansion of Lindertis and so five members (W. Inglis Clark, Ling, Clapperton, Johnston and Young) arrived by train at Kirriemuir on Fri 22 Jan in good weather, to be joined later by Parker from Aberdeen. The following day they were all conveyed up Glen Clova in a Delauney Belleville, a prestigious French automobile akin to a Rolls Royce, and made their way to Winter Corrie of Dreish. They spotted *a sensational gully* (probably Diagonal Gully, Grade III) on the central buttress and Munro promised *a pint of champagne* to the man who could lead it (what a pity it wasn't subsequently named Champagne Gully) but after a tentative probe they turned their attentions to a *long and very steep gully more to the east* (probably Easy Gully, Grade I) and thence to the summit of Dreish. The following day the party made their way up Glen Doll and step-cut up a *broad and prominent gully* in Corrie Fee (probably A Gully, Grade I). As so often happens, the clouds descended and *the hardest part of the day* was finding a safe way down the slopes of hard snow, crampons not then being in common use. There was disagreement in the group and Ling chose his own route down. He wrote (Diary 11) that *coming down I followed the ridge which was pretty hard in parts but much better than the slopes which Parker led the others down. I had to wait an hour for them.* This was because the other men had *incessant step-cutting* down which was *difficult and dangerous*. They should have listened to Ling.

I have described previously the extraordinary search for German spies by several SMC members in 1915 [see 'The Tide Waits For No Man' *SMCJ* 2012]. To summarise: there was a wideheld belief that the enemy had a secret base in the Galloway hills which was supplied by an aeroplane on floats. Raeburn had earlier written to the Committee suggesting that club members were in an ideal position to help *...with a view to locating enemy wireless sending stations or aeroplane depots* and so a group assembled at Glen Trool in March. The military hunt for spies would, of necessity, have been a hush-hush affair and, in any event, the Defence of the Realm Act(1914) forbade the discussion of military matters and imposed strict censorship on the press, which explains why there is no coverage in past SMC Journals. However, as a postscript, I did uncover some further information about the search of the area known as the 'Cradle of Scottish Independence' from where Robert the Bruce fought his guerrilla campaign. Andrew McCormick wrote ['Galloway: The Spell of its Hills & Glens' (Smith & Son, 1932)] that the Culsharg glen, familiar to those who ascend the Merrick by following the Buchan burn from Glen Trool, was recognised as a particularly stormy location where an old shepherd once noticed *the whaups putting their nebs into the ground to avoid being blown away!* Despite this reputation it *once afforded a bield in a snowstorm and saved the lives of a party of the Scottish Mountaineering Society* (sic) *who had intended to spend the night on the Merrick in the fruitless task of endeavouring to find Germans or people signalling to them from the Galloway mountains. One of the party, Mr. Raeburn, Edinburgh, was a member of the Mount Everest Expedition.* It is thus apparent that Raeburn, too, took an active part in the search.

The troops were scattered in the area for several months and McCormick himself witnessed the rope that was set to ensnare any aeroplanes. It was *attached to a spring gun which was to give a signal to the glen folks when the aeroplane struck the cord.* Although the lengthy search did not result in the capture of any spies it did result in the recovery of a valuable hoard of bronze implements and ornaments which can be seen in the National Museum of Scotland, Edinburgh.

After all this unusual excitement there were two Easter Meets in the Highlands. One was held at Kinlochewe at the start of April with, again, 19 members and guests. The first to arrive was Sir Hugh who was forced to return to England the following day due to the ill-health of his son, Thomas Torquil Alfonso, who was being educated at Winchester Colllege. Munro remarked *that it was a long way round from Dorset to Winchester by Kinlochewe.* The weather was dreadful with continual rain at lower levels and a snowline around 2000ft although the afternoons showed some improvement and permitted the ascents of various hills such as Liathach, Slioch and Ben Eighe (which one party crossed unawares until they started to descend towards Ruadh Stac Beag). *Not the least pleasant part of the Meet was spent round the fire each evening, when humorous stories poured forth incessantly, and laughter was loud and continuous.* One has to have a degree of sympathy for any other hotel guests. Letters of good wishes were sent to some members serving in the army but it is not clear why this gesture of goodwill was limited to five. Meanwhile, the Crianlarich Meet experienced similar weather with thunder and lightning thrown into the mix. There were five attendees and Easter Monday saw ascents of Stobinian by one party and Cruach Ardrain by another.

Munro was host again for another Meet at Lindertis over the week-end of 28–31 May attended by Inglis Clark, Ling, Sang, Craig, Galbraith, Marshall, Raeburn, Reid and Rennie. On Saturday, Ling's party attempted a route up the face of Craig Maud but were repulsed and then made for the summit of Mayar. Meanwhile, Raeburn,Galbraith and Reid ascended *the big gully of Mayar* in Coire Fee (B Gully, Grade II, FA) in thin conditions, then descended the nearby buttress in the region of what they called Spout Gully before climbing the east buttress (B Gully Buttress, Grade III, FA). The *courageous leader* [Raeburn, who would be 50yrs old in July] *glissaded down the steep snow slopes...reaching the Lodge comfortably* whilst the others walked up Mayar. On Sunday they all went to Glen Isla by car and split into two parties for ascents of Glas Maol and other hills, including the *steep and ticklish face of Druim Mor* by means of clumps of heather at an angle of 89°. *We tried hard to forget all anxieties and cares during our sojourn at Lindertis but alas! the echoes of war sounded and resounded in our ears…*

As most people are probably aware, nothing now remains of Lindertis House. The formal gounds and policies are neglected and the walled garden is in a state of disrepair, according to a report by the Garden History Society in 2011.

Members' excursions

Clearly, there would be no trips to Alpine regions but, in March/April W.W. Naismith managed to climb the three Pyramids of Gizeh whilst helping to distribute bibles amongst soldiers in Egypt. His account and accompanying photos are interesting: the Great Pyramid (Cheops) *is the one usually climbed...but the tourist route which follows the N.E. angle is now really dangerous for nailed boots, owing to the high polish...no fewer than five soldiers are said to have been killed whilst descending carelessly... The second pyramid (Khafrē) is steeper...in its final 100ft this pyramid is still covered with the original casing of polished limestone slabs and are fitted together so accurately that a penknife cannot be inserted between them.* Naismith was led up by two Arab guides but on a second solo ascent he sensibly used chalk, not to powder his hands but to mark holds which were difficult to see on the tricky descent. There is a co-incidental link between Naismith and polished holds in the following, which describes the activities of W. Ling.

Fortunately, not only did Ling keep a note of his activities but his diaries are, at present, available to be seen at the Alpine Club, London, and I am grateful to Robin Campbell for having made a copy available. Ling was a grain merchant in Carlisle and lived in a substantial house at nearby Wetheral. One might have thought that his outings would have been restricted during wartime but he records no fewer than 16 trips in 1915, including all the SMC official Meets as well as the two Lindertis gatherings and a 2-week trip to Sligachan. The diary entries (Book 12) are too detailed to give anything other than a flavour of a few of them. In May he had an arduous hillwalk with G. Sang starting in Glen Affric and traversing Sgùrr à Bhealaich Dheirg and Sàileag before descending to the road (A87) and walking another 7 miles to Shiel Bridge. Here they *put up at the shepherd's, Macrae, who was mourning a son, sergeant in the Seaforths, just killed.* The War, so distant in every sense, had struck like a snake at this Highland family and many others like them. The following day, in extreme heat, they walked more hard miles and sweated over Sgùrr nan Ceathreamhnan before finally halting at 11 p.m. to bivouac near a convenient boulder. After their sleep they continued to Loch Mullardoch before eventually returning to the Glen Affric hotel. On Skye, on 5 July, he made the first ascent of Central Buttress on Clach Glas with E. Backhouse. The next day they made for the Basteir Tooth and he wrote of Naismith's route *...a crack, which is rather difficult to get started upon, leads up in sensational fashion. The top did need a long reach, otherwise one has to put a great deal of confidence in a sloping foothold which is getting worn very smooth while one reaches for the edge of the top, over which one has to pull oneself.* So, nailed boots were creating rounded holds even then.

In August, with H. Raeburn, he headed for Great Gable, in the Lake District. After prospecting the northern cliffs of Gable Crag they rejected Smuggler's Chimney as *wet and slimy* before climbing to the Westmoreland Cairn *by a steep chimney and face with excellent rock. Then we went down the ordinary Eagle's Nest climb* [Eagle's Nest Ridge via the West Chimney, HD] *lunched and then went up the Abbey Ridge* [presumably, Abbey Buttress, VD, first ascent 1909 by F. Botterill & J. De Vere Hazard]. *This is extremely steep but the rock is fine.* They then went down to Wasdale for tea and met G. Bower. Ling was out climbing again in September, firstly with Mr and Mrs J.H. Bell and then on Pillar with the Bicknell family where they ascended by the Old West Route and descended the Slab & Notch Route.

So, despite the huge social changes that were taking place, for example the necessity for female labour in previously male-dominated workplaces, Ling's diaries suggest that, for those who were able, it was perfectly acceptable to visit the hills for recreational purposes. It was relatively straightforward for civilians to travel by train and there was no food rationing at that stage.

The Journal

The February issue contained just three articles plus the usual proceedings of the Club, Excursions, an obituary of John Muir, Notes etc. and, for the first time, the SMC 'Roll of Honour', a list of members who had enlisted in the armed forces in one capacity or another. The initial roll-call of 29 men (out of a membership of 199) did not include those who had volunteered in various war-related organisations such as the Red Cross although James M. Wordie was included as Geologist with the Shackleton expedition. Reflecting the social status of members in civilian life, the majority qualified for officer ranks ranging from Lieutenant through to Colonel.

Clearly, articles described trips that had taken place the previous year when *the war hung like a dark cloud above us all and prevented full enjoyment* as W. Galbraith wrote when describing 'Some Walks in Skye'. From the top of Ben na Caillich *the view included a flotilla of mine layers and mine sweepers*, replaced by periscopes and conning-towers in more recent times due to naval use of the Inner Sound as a submarine exercise area. Perhaps Skyemen really do possess the second sight, for a native of Torrin describes a route down Blaven as being suitable for a bicycle. Galbraith dismisses this notion but perhaps the islander foresaw the advent of the mountain-bike? A descriptive item by J. Parker about 'The Green Ray' presents eye-witness evidence for one of Nature's rarely-witnessed optical phenomenons now known to be caused by the scattering and refraction of light at the horizon. George Sang wrote about an ascent of Suilven starting from Little Assynt on the A837. He described a climb up Caisteal Liath starting at *an enticing deeply-cleft chimney* a little to the right of Walker & Pilkington's 1895 route. With *no handholds worth speaking of* this sounds like a typical chimney thrutch and then they proceeded by scrambling *backwards and forwards* up a series of loose, heathery ledges until the angle eased and took them to a point above Malcolm's Nose and thence the summit. The complete ridge was traversed before the long slog north back to the road.

The June issue included an article about the Rothiemurchus area and two somewhat academic items about 'Mountains & Art' and 'On Some Old Maps'. There seems to be renewed interest in the various facets of Blaven so the essay by James C. Thomson, in which he describes the first ascent of the North Top's eastern CD Buttress with J.R. Young, may be of historical value to some. The Scottish Ski Club's magazine received a mention largely because of the contributions of several SMC members, the use of skis at that time being more akin to ski-mountaineering than the downhill/uplift version. The 'Roll of Honour' listed promotions, new recruits, injuries and other news, including a letter from Captain Macalister thanking the Club for their good wishes sent from Kinlochewe.

In the Ocober issue, there is more 'On Some Old Maps' and matters liven up when the author, Alfred Harker, has to admit to being completely duped by *an ingenious forgery* and that this fraud (the map reproduced on p.275 of the June issue) *ought to have been within my knowledge*. The section 'Half-Hours in the Club Library' by Thos. Fraser Campbell sounds dry as a bone but is actually a very readable précis of three of our volumes relating to tours of Scotland; viz, John Knox's tour of 1786, J. Lettice's tour of 1792 and Elizabeth's Spence's tour of 1816. It takes up quite a large part of the Journal but is full of pertinent observations and comment. Knox, for example, probably not foreseeing the establishment of the Faslane naval base, recommends the *construction of a royal dockyard and arsenal…from which they could sail at all times and with any wind that blows*. He anticipates our enemies, however, as lying across the Atlantic rather than to our east. Knox covered over 3000 miles in 6 months, predominantly on foot, and was nearly drowned several times as he journeyed to the Islands in open boats. Not bad going at the age of 66. References to the mountains by all three authors are scarce but Lettice, following the writing styles of both Pennant and Dr. Johnson and seemingly adopting their prejudices, describes the scene from the Kings House as *…not the mere negation of beauty but the most positive and even curious ugliness…the carcase of a mountain, peeled, sore and hideously disgustful…* Oh well, it takes all sorts, I suppose. Miss Spence is altogether more genteel although *the earth trembled and the hills shook* for her when she visited Inverness. No, she hadn't been seduced by a native Lothario – it was a mere earthquake.

The Roll of Honour recorded the names of several members who had suffered serious injury and the first death, namely, Major Alexander White who died of wounds received at Gallipoli. Extracts from redacted letters from an unnamed serving officer (almost certainly Charles Inglis Clark) were published under 'Members' War Experiences' and it would seem an appropriate tribute to all those who fought to finish with his words:

…we then zigzagged on foot about a quarter of a mile further, keeping out of sight of the German trenches. We then slunk into a ruined farmhouse and climbed right into the third floor attic, whence we got a splendid view of the German-English lines. …the large holes in the roof made by shells formed excellent view-points. … If the Germans had known there was anyone there it would have

been shelled in a few seconds... By pure accident I saw a puff of smoke in trees about two miles distant... I then drew the attention of the observation officer to it, who became frightfully excited. ... He shouted down the range and position of this newly-discovered battery to the telephone attendant... It turned out that our people had been trying hard for a week to find out the German battery, but without success. By a pure stroke of luck, yours truly was able to be the means of destroying it. ... Splendid!

200 YEARS AGO...

In the late 18th and early 19th century, many English artists toured Scotland and drew Highland landscapes, including mountain views. But these tours were largely confined to Loch Lomondside, the Trossachs, and Perthshire. However, around 1812 William Daniell had the idea of drawing the coasts of Britain. He began in 1813 with Land's End to Holyhead, and in 1814 he proceeded from Holyhead to Portpatrick, sketching objects of interest as he went. Although he described the resulting publications as parts of a 'Voyage Around the Coasts of Britain', it seems that he used boats only occasionally, where parts of the coast were inaccessible by road. It has been described sarcastically as 'Sailing on Horseback'.

The year 1815 was entirely devoted to the Scottish coast. He began his journey in Wigtown in May, and followed the coast round to Dundee in October, including excursions to the Inner and Outer Hebrides, Skye, and the Orkneys, with a week's break in late August at Ardgowan House on the Clyde. Selected sketches were transferred to copper plates and published in the form of hand-coloured aquatints. These are objects of great beauty, and may be conveniently viewed either online at the MOTCO image database <www.motco.com/Series-Daniell-Voyage/> or in the recent edition of the Scottish volumes, *Daniell's Scotland*, published by Birlinn. These are the first drawings of many of our island and coastal mountains.

The original copper plates survive in good condition, and are held by Tate Britain. Uncoloured impressions from these plates have been taken and published online by the Tate. So far as I can tell only one sketchbook from the Scottish 'voyage' survives. This is in the British Museum, and has reference numbers 1867,1012.265-323, one number for each of its 59 pages. I was able to inspect this last year, and was surprised to discover the degree of selection applied by Daniell in choosing sketches for publication. Apart from a few drawings of Ardgowan House, the 59 drawings cover the coast of Skye and the mainland coast between Lochs Hourn and Duich, an area represented only by 20 drawings in the published Voyage. The drawings also included a major surprise.

The First Drawing of the Buachaille?

Page 54 (no. 310) is a very striking, instantly recognizable drawing of the Buachaille, and is inscribed 'King's house – Black mountain – Glencoe', and on the back of the sheet 'Augt.18.1815'. As far as my knowledge goes, this is the first drawing of the Buachaille.

It is remarkable that a drawing of the Buachaille should appear in a sketchbook of the Scottish Coast, but what is more remarkable is the strenuous journey that Daniell must have undertaken to make it. The sketchbook pages are all inscribed with dates by Daniell, so we know from these that on 17 August he was making a drawing of Loch Hourn at Arnisdale. Somehow he 'sailed on horseback' from

'King's house – Black mountain – Glencoe' by William Daniell (1815)
© Courtesy of the Trustees of the British Museum

Loch Hourn to Kings House to make this drawing on the following day. We must suppose that he set off from Arnisdale on the 17th, perhaps staying at Lochhournhead or Tomdoun, and galloped through Lochaber on the 18th, possibly using the old drove road from Inchlaggan to Achnacarry, which cuts the Invergarry corner by 10 miles or so.

It is intriguing that he called the Buachaille 'Black Mountain' (Stob Dubh) whereas the O.S. gave that name to the little Buachaille. I am inclined to think that the O.S. made a mistake, since the neighbouring estate and lodge is of course called Black Mount. It is also interesting that an artist in 1815 should choose much the same composition of bridge, hotel, and mountain as so many photographers do today.

Robin N Campbell

SNOW PATCHES

Members interested in enduring snow patches are directed to *Weather*, the monthly magazine of the Royal Meteorological Society. Recent issues include:

Iain Cameron, Adam Watson & David Duncan '**Six Scottish snow patches survive until winter 2013/2014**', *Weather,* 69/7 (2014), pp190–3. <http://onlinelibrary.wiley.com/doi/10.1002/wea.2286/epdf> retrived 28/08/2015.

Iain Cameron, '**Snow patches in England and Wales during spring 2013**', *Weather*, 68/10 (2013), p255. E-mail contact <iainjcameron@hotmail.com>. <http://onlinelibrary.wiley.com/doi/10.1002/wea.2173/epdf> retrived 28/08/2015.

Adam Watson has also supplied a comprehensive set of references to published work on snow patches: available from Hon Ed on request.

SCOTTISH MOUNTAINEERING TRUST – 2014

Scottish charity number sco 09117

The Trustees met on 11 April and 17 October 2014. During the course of these meetings, support was given to:

J B Irving – Glen Brittle Memorial Hut; A Nisbet – New Routes Editor for Computer; A Ingram – Dundee Mountain Film Festival; A Walker – Students on Ice; Apex 4 – Bolivia; Scottish Mountain Rescue Conference September 2014; Mountain Aid – Mountain Safety Day October 2014; Oban Mountain Rescue Team – Harness/Helmet Project; John Muir Trust – Schiehallion Footpath; Stevenson Adventures – Disadvantaged Young People; Cairngorms Outdoor Access Trust – Upland Path Conference; Jonathan Conville Memorial Trust – Winter Courses 2015; Ladies Scottish Climbing Club – Renovations to Black Rock Cottage.

For the year to the Club AGM in December 2014 the Trustees were AD Nisbet (Chairman) (Ex Officio Immediate Past President of the SMC), R Anderson (Ex Officio Convener of the Publications Sub-Committee), PJ Biggar, WH Duncan, AF Fyffe, CM Jones, JRG Mackenzie (Ex Officio President of the SMC), CR Ravey, DN Williams (Ex Officio Editor of the SMC Journal), and D Whalley. With effect from the Club AGM in December 2014 there were the following changes: WH Duncan and D Whalley have retired from the Trust by rotation. AM James and ER Allan are new Trustees. AD Nisbet has completed his term as Chairman and the Chair has now been taken over by JRG MacKenzie. DN Williams formerly Ex Officio Editor is now Ex Officio President. PJ Biggar is now Ex Officio Editor.

The present Directors of the Publications Company are CR Ravey (Chairman/Secretary since October 2014), K Crocket, BM Whitworth, SL Jenson, and RT Prentice (Publications Manager). CR Ravey (who is both a Director of the Publications Company and a Trustee) provides valuable liaison between the Publications Company and the Trust. RK Bott was a Director and Chairman/Secretary until 30 October 2014 when he retired from the Company.

The following grants were committed by the Trustees during 2014:

J B Irving – Glen Brittle Memorial Hut	Grant £10,000
	Loan £10,000
A Nisbet – New Routes Editor for Computer	£100
A Ingram – Dundee Mountain Film Festival	£100
A Walker – Students on Ice	£250
Apex 4 – Bolivia	£500
Scottish Mountain Rescue Conference – September 2014	£600
Mountain Aid – Mountain Safety Day – October 2014	£250
Oban Mountain Rescue Team – Harness/Helmet Project	£1,500
John Muir Trust Schiehallion Footpath	£3,000
Stevenson Adventures – Disadvantaged Young People	£1,000
Cairngorms Outdoor Access Trust – Upland Path Conference	£500
Jonathan Conville Memorial Trust – Winter Courses 2015	£1,000
Ladies Scottish Climbing Club – Renovations to Black Rock Cottage	
	Grant £10,000
	Loan £10,000

The Trustees record their gratitude to William H Duncan and David Whalley (both of whom have retired by rotation) for their contributions and services to the Trust over the last 4 years. The Trustees are grateful to Andy Nisbet for his contributions as Trustee over the last 4 years and for so ably chairing the Trust Meetings over the last 2 years.

James Hotchkis (Hon Sec SMT)

MUNRO MATTERS

By Dave Broadhead (Clerk of the List)

This report covers 1 January to 31 December 2014. The five columns below give number, name and year of Compleation of Munros, Tops and Furths as appropriate. *SMC member, **LSCC member.

5434	Barbara Farr	2013		
5435	Austin Farr	2013		
5436	Tom Speirs	2013		
5437	Trevor Simpson	2013		
5438	Will Powell	2013		
5439	William Stein	2013		
5440	Nigel Bowler	2013		
5441	Scott McGibbon	2013		
5442	Andrew N. Boggon	1999		
5443	William Bruce	2011		
5444	Valerie Young	2013		
5445	Stewart F. Young	2013		
5446	Jamie Aarons	2013		
5447	Andrew Taylor	2013		
5448	High Monckton	2013		
5449	John M. Walsh	2013		
5450	Caroline Leaver	1997		
5451	John Leaver	1997		
5452	David Harbottle	2014		
5453	Adrian Bornet	2014		
5454	Mark Dawson	2014		
5455	Patrick Montgomery	2014		2014
5456	Patsy Richards	2013		
5457	Eddie Richards	2013		
5458	Trevor Willis	2014		
5459	Neil A. Hawksworth	2014		
5460	Helen Gestwicki	2014		
5461	Gerard Iafrati	2014		2014
5462	John Morgan-Hughes	2007		
5463	Jonathon Morgan-Hughes	2011		
5464	David Stein	2014		
5465	Ewan D. McGregor	2002		
5466	Jennifer M. Johnston	2014		
5467	Richard Johnston	2014		
5468	David Clarke	2014		
5469	Robert J. Hopkins	2014		
5470	Will Copestake	2014		
5471	Stephen Cook	2014		
5472	John R. Swift	2014		
5473	Stephen Fleming	2014		
5474	Elizabeth Willars	2014		
5475	Justin Shiels	2014		
5476	Graham J. Whish	2014		
5477	Ian Macdougall	2014		
5478	Jenny Russell	2014		
5479	Steven O'Keeffe	2014		
5480	Kenny Gaittens	2014		
5481	Roger Rowe	2007		
5482	Janet Drye	2014		
5483	Roger Drye	2014		
5484	Jennifer Mason	2014		1999
5485	Carol Oliver	2014		
5486	Nigel Gee	2014		
5487	John Hall	2014		
5488	Ken Dudley	2014		
5489	Trevor Williamson	2014		
5490	Kev Davison	2014		
5491	Jeffrey Hobbs	2014		
5492	Ian Spalding	2014	2014	2012
5493	Ian Priestley	2014		
5494	Janet Kennedy	2014		
5495	Alan Kennedy	2014		
5496	Suzanne Jamieson	2014		
5497	Neil Macnair	1992		
5498	Tony Coar	2014		
5499	Michael R. Bird	2014		
5500	Philip Dant	2014		
5501	Dawn Robson	2014		
5502	Rob Thomson	2014		
5503	Allan Gilliland	2014		
5504	Bart Teugels	2014		
5505	Allison Robertson	2014		
5506	Alistair Deering	2014		
5507	Diane Langley	2013		
5508	Ian Stephens	2014		
5509	Will Craigie	2014		
5510	Mary White	2014		
5511	Dorothy Fisher	2014		
5512	Mathew Diggle	2014		
5513	Jamie Higton	2014		2010
5514	Donald Graham Sutherland	2014		
5515	James Lynch	2014		
5516	George D. Calder	2014		
5517	Catherine Horn	2014		
5518	Shirley Godfrey	2014		
5519	Susan Geddes	2014		
5520	Harry Archibald	2014		
5521	Robert H. Johnson	2014		
5522	Colin Stuart	2014		
5523	Mark Jardine	2014		
5524	Dougie Bruce	2014		
5525	Henry Marston	2014		
5526	Richard Payne	2014		
5527	Alison P. Brown	2014		
5528	Clare Thawley	2014		
5529	Mark Foster	2014		

5530	Richard Wignall	2014
5531	Rebekah Meeten	2014
5532	John Wheeler	2014
5533	John C. Goodall	2014
5534	Finlay Wild	2013
5535	Jan Beard	2014
5536	Andy Beard	2014
5537	Rorie J.G. Stewart	2014
5538	John Reilly	2014
5539	Robin C. S. Verbeek	2014
5540	Damian Warren	2014
5541	Chris Todd	2014
5542	Rory Matheson	2014
5543	William Grimes	2014
5544	Roger D. Williams	2014
5545	Colin Beggs	2014
5546	John Corden	2014
5547	Michael Anderson	2014
5548	Caroline Fyfe	2014
5549	Richard Wilton	2014
5550	Joy Forbes	2014
5551	Peter Forbes	2014
5552	Karen Forbes	2014
5553	Colin Forbes	2014
5554	Ruth Weedon	2014
5555	Joanne S. Hamilton-Taylor	2014
5556	John Hamilton-Taylor	2014
5557	John Wells	2014
5558	Steve Edwards	2014
5559	Rhona G. Hughes	2014
5560	Akihiko Tamura	2014
5561	Gordon K. Crookshanks	2014
5562	Mike Merchant	2014
5563	Clive Wilson	2007
5564	Viv Forster	2014
5565	Maylene Yeung	2014
5566	Stephen Brady	2014
5567	Scott Robertson	2014
5568	Derek Hepburn	2014
5569	Maureen Paul	2014
5570	Jimmy Paul	2014
5571	Clive Masson	2014
5572	Stephen Ferrie	2014
5573	Hazel Hall	2014
5574	John Hall	2014
5575	Janet Paterson	2014
5576	Chris Leask	2014
5577	Neil A. Milloy	2014
5578	Iain Little	2014
5579	Raymond Bainbridge	2014
5580	Joe Buchanan	2014
5581	Robin Foulkes	2014
5582	Nicholas J. Dorosh	2014
5583	Jonathan Brown	2014
5584	Adam Holloway	2014
5585	Bob Christine	2014
5586	Elizabeth McKinnon	2014
5587	Jackie Carson	2014
5588	Hugh Jones	2014
5589	Peter Lancaster	2014
5590	Judi Syson	2014
5591	Mary Wilson	2014
5592	Liz Munns	2014
5593	Calum Wood	2014
5594	Walter J. MacCulloch	2014
5595	Robert Sivewright	2014
5596	Robin Corlett	2014
5597	Malcolm Sanderson	2014
5598	Ruth Lyon	2014
5599	Robin Wallace	2014
5600	Gordon Dockson	2013
5601	Philip Jackson	2014
5602	Neil McNair Jackson	2014
5603	Linda Cunningham	2014
5604	Alastair Cunningham	2014
5605	Robert Poole	2014
5606	John Danby	2014
5607	Tim Day	2014
5608	Richard Gibbs	2013
5609	Ronald Caunt	2014
5610	Julie Anne Cockcroft	2014
5611	David Cockcroft	2014
5612	Stephen Parkinson	2014
5613	Alastair Ross	2014
5614	John B Smith	2014
5615	Paul Anderson	2013
5616	John R Colquhoun	2014
5617	Ruth Parkinson	2014
5618	Paul Eastwood	2013
5619	Gavin Stark	2014
5620	Andrew Rushworth	2014
5621	Peter McLaren	2014
5622	Peter Colley	2014
5623	Colin Robertson	2014
5624	Simon Randfield	2014
5625	Johnnie Walker	2014
5626	Ian D. Young	2014
5627	Runa McNamara	2014
5628	Alan Hudson	2014
5629	Bob Lane	2014
5630	Carl Richmond	2014
5631	Neil Machray	2014
5632	Lawrence D. Boyd	2014
5633	John Clark	2014
5634	Anita Clarke	2014
5635	Tim Clarke	2014
5636	Douglas S. Murray	2014
5637	Bruce Turner	2014
5638	Martin Southwick	2014
5639	George Bruce	2014
5640	Derek Arnot	2014
5641	Gordon H. Butler	2014
5642	Sally Macintyre	2002
5643	Peter Smith	2014

5644	Helen Rowlands	2014
5645	*Gareth Yardley	2014
5646	Andrew Hall	2014
5647	David G. Boggon	2014
5648	David Perry	2014
5649	Callum Watt	2014
5650	Keith Bird	2014
5651	Andrew McIlhatton	2014
5652	Derek J. McKay	2014
5653	Paula Woolgar	2014
5654	David Adams	2014
5655	Chris Watson	2014
5656	*George W. Wilkinson	2014
5657	Lorna McDougal	2014
5658	Peter Howarth	2014
5659	Isobel Macdonald	2014
5660	Richard Moakes	2014
5661	Gary Edmonds	2014
5662	Louella Edward-Collins	2014
5663	Ruth Anderson	2014
5664	Chris Royle	2014
5665	Simon Royle	2014
5666	John Rosie	2014
5667	Malcolm Charles	2014
5668	Beryl C. Robinson	1993
5669	Tom Hayle	1991 1991
5670	Graham Haley	2014
5671	Malcolm D. Gillies	2014
5672	Katarzyna Duncan	2014
5673	Colin Grub	2014
5674	Paul Johnston	2014
5675	G. Douglas Bonner	2014
5676	Simon A. Morgan	2014
5677	David Caskie	2014
5678	William King	2014
5679	Thomas Walker	2014
5680	Sandy White	2014
5681	Richard Brinley	2014
5682	Nick Bloxham	2014
5683	Clive Eames	2014

Comparing this years data with last year (in brackets): New Munroists 250 (233); males 76% (81%); resident in Scotland 55% (60%); couples 16% (11%); average age 54(54); size of Compleation summit party 10 (12); average Compleation time 23 (25) years; Golden Munroists 10 (7).

As ever I received a large number of very interesting letters. Some readers may be familiar with Radio Scotland's early evening show 'Get It On' whose listeners choose the music following a different theme each day, so I thought it would be fun to suggest suitable songs for Munroists. For example, the first Munroists of 2014 Barbara and Austin Farr (5434 & 5435) may like Birdie Song (The Tweets) as they wrote 'we were delighted to see our first Dotterel and two of his chicks' when they Compleated on Beinn Fhada.

We Are Family (Sister Sledge) would be good for father and son John and Jonathon Morgan-Hughes (5462 & 5463). Rory Matheson (5542) paid tribute to 'my Dad Colin Matheson (4977) who has been my inspiration and companion on just over a quarter of my Munros.' Joy, Peter, Karen and Colin Forbes (5550, 5551, 5552, 5553) are brothers and their respective wives who all Compleated together on A' Mhaighdean. I was particularly pleased to hear from Finlay Wild (5534) after reading his account of his amazing record breaking Cuillin Ridge traverse in last year's SMCJ. By coincidence I bumped into him a few days later on Glasgow's Byres Road, a place seldom frequented by either of us on a Sunday afternoon. He reminded me that he was now the third generation on The List, following in the distinguished steps of his grandfather John Hinde (87) and parents Fiona and Roger Wild (2349 & 2350). When I suggested his song might be Speedy Gonzales (Pat Boone) he looked at me as if I had taken leave of my senses! Appropriately Finlay Compleated on Beinn Fhionnlaidh.

Grandad (Clive Dunn) Tom Spiers (5436) mentioned his grandfather, William Spiers, describing him as 'something of a mountaineering legend'. He was SMC President 1956–8. Joe Buchanan (5580) had an even more tenuous link with the Club, explaining 'I am by nature a quiet and private person who doesn't seek attention, however, my daughter announced to the world on her Facebook page of my achievement and the number of messages of congratulations I received even from people I didn't know was staggering. One of her work colleagues is the stepson of Hugh Munro, the grandson of Sir Hugh Munro and I was pleased to receive a card from Hugh Munro himself and I enclose a copy for your attention.' With a fine black & white photo of Liathach, it reads Congratulations and well done for climbing Grandfather's mountains. Gavin Stark (5619) mentioned that his great-uncle was George Elliot (7) also an SMC member. Apart from Ye Cannae Shove Yer Grannie Af a Bus (traditional) which hardly seems appropriate, I struggled for a song for Isobel Macdonald (5659) who waited for her daughter and 2 grandaughters 'coming home from Australia on holiday, and wanted to do my last one with me along with my son and grandson. We had a great day.'

Memory (from Cats) William Bruce (5443) described his most notable memories as 'meeting a BBC film crew on An Teallach with presenter Nicholas Crane and meeting the future Queen, Camilla on Lochnagar.' This Years Love (David Gray) Andrew Taylor and his partner Jamie Aarons (5446 & 5447) climbed every Munro between 4 January and 14 December 2013 whilst both were in full time employment. Highlights included 'skiing 40 km across 11 Munros from Creag Leacach to Lochnagar.' For further details see <http://munrosinayear.wordpress.com/introduction/>.

Poetry in Motion (Johnny Tillotson) John M. Walsh (5449) summed up his Round in one sentence. 'While the sun rises I will walk on over hill and mountain by path and wild until the sun sets for me in this magnificent land.' As ever, the Compleation poets were busy, including Paul Ashman 'the bard of Penshaw' whose ode for Neil A. Hawksworth (5459) starts thus: 'Schiehallion's the mountain for Neil's last test/a Munro worth this honour one of the best.' Jennifer M. and Richard Johnston (5466 & 5467) were surprised at the summit of Beinn Chabhair by 'our choir of eleven singing a made up Munro bagging song sung to the tune of Abba's 'Money, money, money' plus special T-shirts and the traditional champagne.' Don't Stop Me Now (Queen) Will Copestake (5470) 'started last May 2013 in a sea kayak, kayaked around Scotland and then cycled to and climbed the Munros under my own power across the winter.' Further details of this remarkable unsupported Round can be found on <http://www.ukhillwalking.com/news/item.php?id=68922> or on his website <www.willcopestakemedia.com>. Lovely Rita, Meter Maid (The Beatles) Kenny Gaittens (5480) made an unusual claim that he 'managed to access all Munros avoiding parking charges. This involved organising some different approaches from the main tourist routes.'

My Bonnie Lies Over The Ocean (traditional) Belgian Munroist Teugels Bart (5504) required 20 trips to Scotland for his Round. He sent me a copy of an interview with him (in Flemish) in the magazine 'Op Weg' entitled 'Into the Munro's' (sic). Robin C. S. Verbeek (5539) travelled from the Netherlands for 15 years and plans to keep returning to do the Corbetts. Akihito Tamura (5560) is probably the first Japanese Munroist, though he lives in Livingston. His blog (in Japanese) is at <http://tamura-san03.blogspot.co.uk/> and he reported 'I have never used camping, bothy or YH for Munro bagging. But I've done always by day hiking (longest is 11hr 40min), and by myself alone.'

D-I-V-O-R-C-E (Tammy Wynette) Roger D. Williams (5544) wistfully wrote 'I have no plans to do any more bagging as a divorce would quickly follow if I were even to mention the word Corbett. My wife has managed 150 Munros and

Bovine Munrobaggers on the summit of Stuchd an Lochain (960m), Glen Lyon (July 2015). Photo: John Mackenzie.

considers that a nice round number to finish on.' Where Did You Get That Hat? (Stanley Holloway) Elizabeth McKinnon (5586) prepared for her big day on Beinn Fhada by knitting pom pom hats for all the summit party to wear plus a garland of pom poms for her dog Molly who has only 40 Munros remaining. Heroes (David Bowie) Judi Syson and Mary Wilson (5590 & 5591) sought sponsorship for their Round to raise money for 'Help for Heroes'. Their achievement was all the more impressive as Mary had been diagnosed with Multiple Sclerosis in 2004 and was featured in the Daily Record.

He Ain't Heavy He's My Brother (The Hollies) Philip Jackson (5601) started tackling Munros with his son then in 1990 his big brother Neil McNair Jackson (5602) started joining them. The brothers Compleated together on Ben Hope and Neil explained that 'the SMC Guide has been a terrific resource. It has guided Philip and me in our annual 'where shall we go this year?' discussion for a quarter of a century. It has helped us get up the hills in good order. And it has occasionally taken us to places or in conditions where we said to each other 'if it hadn't been in the Guide I wouldn't've come here – AND I'M NOT COMING BACK!' So do, please, pass on our appreciation for that to the Club.' Chris and Simon Royle (5664 & 5665) had each climbed around 20 Munros before deciding they 'might be the first brothers to have Completed the Munros and been together on every summit' so they repeated these hills during the course of their Round.

Needles and Pins (The Searchers) Robert Poole (5605) highlighted a dilemma faced by many Munroists venturing outside their normal comfort zone. 'For many years Skye appeared a barrier to Compleation, especially the In Pinn. I presume it is considered OK from an ethical perspective to have touched the top of the summit rock and had my head above it rather than standing on it, and being lowered from the top rather than abseiling under my own control (this wasn't the place to learn to abseil!).' Ball of Confusion (The Temptations) While Ben More (Mull) remains the most popular summit earmarked for celebrations, Beinn na Lap has also become a regular choice, leading to some multiple Coincident Compleations. Peter McLaren (5621) reported 'my last Munro on 20 September 2014 coincided with at least 2 others.' One of these, Simon Randfield (5624) wrote 'I believe there were at least 4 other Compleatist celebrations on the hill that day.' This also included Anita and Tim Clarke (5634 & 5635) and their 'summit party of 22 composed a mix of hillwalking and non-hillwalking friends, for 9 of whom it was their first Munro.'

Private Number (Judy Clay & William Bell) Many letters suggest little individual idiosyncrasies. For example Martin Southwick (5638) clearly has a thing for numbers. From his home in Scunthorpe he worked out 'total mileage 1730 miles (2787km), ascent 521,00 feet (159,000m) equating to 6 miles per hill and 1840 feet of ascent per hill. Leaving it a bit late to choose his final Munro he realised 'the number for Sgurr a' Mhaoraich (104) is the same as my house number! To celebrate, my partner bought me a T-shirt with all the mileage/ascent statistics written on it.' You've Got a Friend (Carole King) Richard Brinley (5681), Nick Bloxham (5682) and Clive Eames (5683) Compleated together on Ben Alder and Richard wrote 'as a personal note of interest at nearly 6' 2' and 18 stone I may be one of the larger people to have finished the task! On some of the very remote Munros I have been frequently asked "how did you get here?" revealing their surprise.' A look at the popular on-line photo gallery confirms that Munroists come in all shapes and sizes!

At Last (Etta James) seems appropriate for this year's Golden Munroists who were Hugh Monckton (5448, 56 years), George D. Calder (5516, 51 years), John Corden (5546, 55 years), Hugh Jones (5588, 50 years), Neil McNair Jackson (5602, 54 years), John Danby (5606, 53 years), Ronald Caunt (5609, 50 years), Andrew Rushworth (5620, 51 years), Douglas S. Murray (5636, 58 years) and another SMC member George W. Wilkinson (5656, 54 years).

Never Too Late (Three Days Grace) Andrew N. Boggon (5442) Compleated in 1999, Caroline and John Leaver (5450 & 5451) in 1997 and Neil Macnair way back in 1992. George Bruce (5639) unburdened himself by finally reporting a string of Munro, Corbett and Graham Compleations, starting in 1987. After 37 years with Lochaber Mountain Rescue Team he might have learned to be a bit more prompt in submitting reports! I was of course delighted to hear from all these people as I always assure Munroists that it is never too late to register.

Climb Every Mountain (from Sound of Music) Of more general interest, on 13 October 2014 Rob Woodall (816) became the first person to Compleat the 'ultimate hill bagging list' i.e. the Marilyns (1556 British hills to have at least 150m of descent on all sides) when he climbed Stac Lee and Stac an Armin on the St Kilda archipelago, closely followed by Eddie Dealtry (1452) who became the second. I do not think the Clerk of the Marilyn List will ever be as busy as me, though our member William A. Forbes (4483) is very close.

Don't Stop Me Now (Queen) leads me on to the B side of my report:

AMENDMENTS

The eight columns give number, name and year of each Compleation of Munros, Tops, Furths, Corbetts, Grahams and Donalds.

Num	*Name*	*M*	*T*	*F*	*C*	*G*	*D*
4081	Fiona Reid	2008			2013		
4082	Michael Watson	2008			2013		
4026	David Roeder	2006	2012		2012		
4483	*William A. Forbes	1986	1995	2002	2002	2006	2014
		2009					
3885	David S. Batty	1994	2011	2013	2014		2014
		2011					
23	*Miles Hutchinson	1955	1955	1970	1992	2009	2014
		1992		1998			
		1998					
		2004					
2612	Rick Ansell	2001	1999		2014		1997
892	Jamie F. Stone	1991	2014				
		2014					
3934	Alastair H. Govan	2007	2010	2014			
2342	Anthony P. Weetman	2000		2004	2008		2014
2125	James Henderson	1999			2008	2014	
		2011					
3839	Ray Hunter	2007		2014	2014		
1609	Robert J. Ferguson	1996	1996		2004	2014	
NYC	Carol Pudsey				2014		
409	John Brewster	1985			2014		
		1995					
248	W. Lindsay Wyllie	1981			2014		
		1996					
2658	**Julia Banks	2001	2010		2012		
4213	Trevor Carter	2008	2014				
3468	John Henderson	2005			2010	2014	
2090	John A. Owen	1999		1998	2009	2014	
2774	Howard Jones	2002			2008	2014	
1558	Andy Heald	1996	2007		2011		
		2014					
1225	Jeff J. Burgum	1993	1993	1993			
		2006					
		2014					
3649	Jon Meeten	2006					
		2014					
2268	Susan Henderson	1999	2014	2005	2004	2010	2010
		2014					
2269	George Henderson	1999	2014	2005	2004	2010	2010
		2014					
4006	Chris Pine	2007			2012	2013	2014
358	Michael B. Slater	1984	1987	1987			
		1988		2009			
		1990		2011			
		1993		2013			
		1996		2014			
		1999					

Num	*Name*	*M*	*T*	*F*	*C*	*G*	*D*
358	Michael B. Slater	2003					
		2008					
825	Bernard Smith	1990	2000	1979	2014		
		2009					
641	William A. Nimmo Smith	1989			2014		
		2014					
5140	Peter Bettess	2012		2014			
884	Mark Wrightham	1991					
		2014					
1933	Dave Irons	1998	2005	2005	2010	2013	2014
1248	S. G. Singleton	1993					2007
954	Robert B. Gunn	1991	1991	2000	2014		
1169	Garth B. Fenton	1993	2014	1994	2010		2013
1170	Elaine S. Fenton	1993	2014	1994	2010		
4088	David McSporran	2008			2011	2014	
620	Norrie Muir	1988	2002		1997	2014	
4381	Simon Sawers	2009	2010	2014			
5491	Jeffrey Hobbs	2014					2014
4996	Neil Batley	2012		2014			
3664	David A. Gilchrist	2006			2014		
2432	Brian Kerslake	2000	2006	2009	2014		
3432	Sheila Simpson	2005			2010	2014	
3433	Bill Simpson	2005			2010	2014	
573	Tommy Hepburn	1988	1988				
		2014	2014				
3968	Bob Barlow	2007	2013				2014
3366	Anne Butler	2005			2010		
		2010					
		2011					
		2012					
		2014					
4193	Ron A. Brown	2008	2012		2010	2014	2014
3878	John McKechnie	2007			2014		
1891	Dave Marshall	1993			2014		
		2010					
		2014					
1327	Ian J. Brownell	1994					
		2014					
5288	Jamie Dobson	2013		2014			
3631	Gordon Roberts	2006			2014		
5287	Ian J. Young	2013	2013	2014			
2422	David K. McRonald	2000			2010	2014	
1440	Paul Birrell	1995					
		2014					
827	Pete Craven	1990			2005		
		2014					
798	**Margaret Graham	1990	2013		2004	2014	
		2014					
5351	Chris Warwick	2013			2014	2014	

Num	*Name*	*M*	*T*	*F*	*C*	*G*	*D*
5378	Jim Martin	2013		2014			
3438	Hazel Strachan	2005					2011
		2008					2012
		2010					2012
		2012					
		2013					
		2014					
2162	Wilma J. Forsyth	1999			2008	2014	
2318	Ron Forsyth	2000			2008	2014	
1115	Raymond Shaw	1992			2003		
					2013		
2862	John Edward Casson	2002		2007	2010	2014	
4151	Norman Wares	2008	2010	2011	2014		
4169	Victoria Fuller	2008					
		2014					
4335	Harry Braden	2009	2013				
4804	David Bethune	2011		2014			
4762	Alasdair T.M. Cairns	2011					
		2014					
4949	Duncan Buchanan	2011					
		2014					
3089	Sarah Wingrove	2003					
		2014					
2706	Mark Bull	2002			2014		
2707	Gillian Duncan	2002			2014		
3044	Brian McWilliam	2003			2014		
		2011					
2291	Neil Sandilands	1999	2013	2004	2006	2009	2008
764	Andrew S. Templeton	1990	1991	1999	1992	1997	
		2014			2014		
1911	Martin J. Almond	1997	1997	2014	2012		2013
		2006					
3102	Charles McCartney	1988					
		2003					
		2010					
		2014					
3103	Michael McCartney	2003					
		2010					
		2014					
2003	Bob Macdonald	1998	2006	2006	2006		2014
3497	Richard Knight	2005			2010		2011
		2014					
457	Jim Bloomer	1986		1986	2014		2005
4328	Dorothy Stirling	2009			2010		
		2011					
		2012					
		2014					
62	Hamish M. Brown	1965	1965	1967	1976	2013	1982
		1969		1969			

Num	*Name*	*M*	*T*	*F*	*C*	*G*	*D*
62	Hamish M. Brown	1970		1971			
		1974		1978			
		1975		1979			
		1979		1982			
		1984					

I was particularly pleased to hear from our inspirational member Miles Hutchinson (23) who reported his Donald Compleation on Carrifran Gans which also gave him a 'Full House'. Miles modestly omitted to mention his age but I noticed he joined the SMC in 1955. William A. Forbes (4483) became the third SMC 'Full House' and Miles the fourth. Other 'Full House' reports were Susan and George Henderson (2268 & 2269) who became the first couple and Dave Irons (1933) and Neil Sandilands (2291). While on the subject of Munrosis Proliferens Hamish M. Brown (62) our second SMC 'Full House' notified me of a missing 'Furth' and with seventeen entries on his line ties with Steven Fallon (1045) as the most prolific Compleater, though Steven, with 15 Munro Rounds has a long way to go for 'Full House'. Reporting his fourth Furth Round, Michael B. Slater (358) is well on his way to equalling Hamish's five Furth Rounds and notes that 'Tryfan is more than 70 miles further away from my home in Aboyne than Lugnaquillia!' William A. Nimmo Smith (641) (aka The Rt. Hon. Lord Nimmo Smith) reported a notable second Munro Round, Compleated on Ben Wyvis, which he first climbed 64 years previously, at the age of 7. During this second Round he also achieved a Corbett Round and kept 'records of daily times'. Without driving off the public road but using a mountain bike where practicable his total, walking and biking was 1,715hrs 55min. Total time for Munros 860hrs 20min, for Corbetts 855hrs 35min, giving an average time per Munro of 3hrs 3min and per Corbett 3hrs 52 min. Proliferens is not restricted to males. Reporting her sixth Munro Round after a very snowy winter, Hazel Strachan (3438) reported 'a few challenging days in white out conditions. I walked over a lot of big rounded hills with snow shoes on my feet. Instead of leaving my husband at home most weekends we now have a motorhome to spend time together in. It's certainly made the winter more comfortable.' Harry Braden (4335) went one better and Compleated his Tops without even leaving home 'following the demotion of Knight's Peak, that being my only outstanding Top for several years.'

Reporting a second Corbett Round, Raymond Shaw (1115) mentioned that his dog Grover 'Completed a Corbett Round on 12/08/2003 with me on Clisham' making him the first canine Corbetteer. John Edward Casson (2862) reported his final Graham, Creach Beinn on Mull where he 'shared the hill with a stalker, who shot a stag.' Brothers Charles and Michael McCartney (3102 & 3103) finished 4th and 3rd Munro Rounds respectively on Ben More (Mull). John Brewster (409) and Linsay Wylie (248) arranged a rare Corbett Coincident Compleation on Beinn an Oir which also coincided with the Jura hill race. Sheila and Bill Simpson (3432 & 3433) finished their Graham Round together and noted wistfully 'the weather was wet and windy, which was the same for our last Munro and last Corbett. So much for British summers.' In a similar situation, Howard Jones (2774) observed that 'having done all 3 rounds from my North Wales base I have kept the Scottish economy going in terms of diesel, accommodation and meals out!' Another couple Compleating their Grahams together, Wilma and Ron Forsyth (2162 & 2318) observed 'as many of these hills have no paths, route planning and good navigational skills were essential. We found that information in the book we followed was often out of date, especially as far as bridges and forests were concerned!' Thank goodness then for the excellent new SMC Hillwalkers Guide 'The Grahams & The Donalds' which is sure to increase my workload!

Simon Glover contributed a interesting short piece entitled FINAL FURTHS: AN OVERVIEW in the 2013 *SMCJ* p609–10 and has now published his data online in the form of a blog <http://furthsummits.blogspot.co.uk/>

I am of course always pleased to hear from anyone who would like their achievements added to our six lists. Please write to Dave Broadhead, Cul Mor, Drynie Park North, Muir of Ord, IV6 7RP. For a Munro or Corbett Compleation Certificate, please enclose an A4 sae (with the correct postage please). Check <smc.org.uk> for further details and to view the picture gallery of Munroists and Corbetteers celebrating on their final summit.

Enjoy your hills.

Dave Broadhead
(Clerk of the List)

IN MEMORIAM

ALAN AUBREY THRIPPLETON J. 1967

Robin Campbell writes: Alan Thrippleton was born in Halifax in February 1911, and died in October 2013, in his 103rd year. Alan was a member of long standing, and made an important contribution to the Club's publications. He was joint author, along with Kenneth Andrew, of the first edition of the Southern Uplands district guidebook, published in 1972. However, his principal focus of interest was perhaps the Glasgow JMCS, so it is fitting that we should publish the following tribute to him, given shortly after Alan's death, by Ian Cumming, another stalwart member of the Glasgow Section.

'Most of you will have heard by this time of the passing of our Honorary Member, Alan Thrippleton, my life-long friend and companion of many adventures on the Hill, in kayaks, and in remote camps beneath the stars.

'Alan lived through two World wars and witnessed the evolution of flight from the Bleriot monoplane to the Jumbo Jet and the spacecraft. He was 21 years older than myself, and I had known him for 56 years, as long as I have been a member of the Club. We first met in 1959 when I and my other great friend Bryan Fleming first joined the Glasgow JMCS as 26 year olds. Alan was on the committee at the time; the President was Kenny Bryan, and the Secretary, Chris Ford, whom some of you will remember at the Hut Jubilee celebrations at Elgol. Alan was looked on as something of the Grand Old Man of the Club (he was 48), and with a certain awe for his forthright and uncompromising views

'He first came to live in Scotland in 1948/9 to work at the Rolls-Royce aero-engine plant in Hillington. He was an engineer by profession, and what would now be called a Quality Assurance Inspector – not for Rolls-Royce themselves, but employed as a civil servant by the Government's Air Ministry Inspection Department. Others of my acquaintance at Rolls-Royce, confirm his uncompromising and exacting approach to his calling and to life in general. He remained in this capacity until his retirement in 1977, having moved to the other Rolls-Royce facility at East Kilbride, and having lived in Hamilton for 26 years. Alan and his wife Jean then re-located to Lancaster to be close to their two daughters, Jane and Elizabeth.

'He was a man of wide and varied interests and particularly in everything to do with the Great Outdoors. In his youth, he was a formidable long-distance cyclist, graduating to motorcycles during the 20s and early 30s. Thereafter, he became an enthusiastic and dedicated motorist, and could remember every car he owned over 65 years. Photography was another of his passions, and he excelled at this as in all other things. He was a life-long member of a photographic club, and was frequently called on to judge competitions because of his expertise , experience and reputation.

'Before coming to Glasgow, he had been a member of a caving club in the Manchester area and put up (down) several new routes which still bear his name. On one occasion when he was in his 70s, he took his grandson to one of these caves and got chatting to some young modern potholers about the classic routes. They introduced each other, and on hearing his name, one said, "not the Thrippleton, surely?" Shortly after this, he was introduced and elected to the Derbyshire Pennine Club, a very august and superior body of gentlemen, almost as old as the SMC, and twice as posh, and remained a member for the rest of his life.

'It was Alan who introduced kayaking to the JMCS when I was a very new member, with his accustomed enthusiasm, and we became almost a sub-group within the Club. George Liddle, Eddie Thompson, Bryan Fleming, Gerry McCartney, and several others, now all gone. He was one of our first Munroists at No. 59 on the List (in 1964), and his last major hill-walk was at my own final Munro, Beinn na Lap in 1988 when he was 77. Alan was an early member of the Scottish Sub-Aqua Club, another of his many interests, but fortunately he never introduced this to the JMCS! I am not certain when he joined Glasgow JMCS, but it must have been about 1951, shortly after coming to Scotland. He was Secretary for 4 years from 1964 to 1967, but never aspired to be President.

'His great achievement, however was in the establishment of the Hut at Loch Coruisk, and it was for this that we awarded him the position of Honorary Member after the death of the previous incumbent, Bill (W.H) Murray in 1996. Alan, with his great friend David Witham, an architect, was the driving force behind this enterprise, making many visits to site and negotiating with the landowners and the builder. It can truly be said that it is to Alan and David that we owe this priceless asset. It was with great regret that Alan was unable due to infirmity to attend the Jubilee celebrations at Elgol a year or so ago, but David was there and some of you will remember his speech on that occasion. Alan was the first Custodian of the Hut, and gave assiduous and dedicated service in that capacity for some ten years. It was during this spell that he and several others organized the water supply from the Mad Burn.

'The Glasgow Section Membership List is somewhat misleading in that it shows Alan as having joined in 1996. This is due to the fact that he gave up his original membership on being elected to the SMC. 1996 was the year in which we made him Honorary Member. Very few of you will remember Alan now, but we had the honour of his presence at several dinners in the late 1990s and early 2000s.'

Iain Cumming

ALLAN C PETTIT J. 2003

Allan died on 8 August 2014 exactly three months short of his 70th birthday.

He was born in Forfar and brought up in Brechin. After school at Brechin High he went to study dentistry at Queen's College in Dundee (later, in 1967, it became Dundee University). On graduation he had a couple of Dental Associateships firstly in Glasgow and then in Inverness which is where I first started climbing with him in 1973. He married Val, another keen climber, in November 1972.

At that time the housing market in Inverness was crazy because everyone thought the oil industry would transform the Moray & Cromarty Firths into a new Aberdeen and Allan and Val, unable to find any suitable property, headed back south in 1974. As a freelance journalist/editor Val too was flexible as regards location. This turned out to be a good move as Allan set up his own dental practice in Stirling which became very successful. As I can vouch personally, Allan was an excellent and always up to date dentist. Having been his patient for over 30 years I still remember the first few injections I received from him when I didn't feel that the needle was like a 'lance thrown into the gum', which had often been my former experience. Allan practised intravenous sedation techniques and the Stirling practice grew over the years such that he took on a partner and then opened a second surgery in Bridge of Allan. After a time Allan and his partner split the practice and Allan spent the rest of his professional life in the Bridge of Allan surgery until he retired in February 2008.

Allan started climbing while studying at Dundee and his first climbing partners were fellow students. One of these was Dave Leppard who was doing a PhD and with whom Allan did his early winter climbing and walking. More importantly, although work took him permanently to Switzerland, Dave remained, and still remains, a very close friend of the family.

Allan formed his first regular climbing partnership with another student, Ken Martin, and from about 1967 to 1972 they did a good number of hard routes including an early ascent of Steeple on the Shelter Stone and possible second ascents of Pink Elephant and Rat Race on the Dubh Loch. Another contact that Allan made while at Dundee was Iain Smart who was one of Allan's lecturers in anatomy and with whom he went on two expeditions to Greenland in 1968 and 1969.

In 1968 the central Stauning Alps were then little known but Allan and the group managed ten peaks. In 1969, with Malcolm Slessor too this time, the target was Mount Mikkelsen but the boating trip to the Blosseville Coast with wind and pack ice resulted in the team getting stuck in impenetrable ice floes and a 100 mile walk out through the mountains ensued. All good training for later! As a result of his non-stop activity in climbing and skiing, 'later' for Greenland was not until 1996 when Allan and Gerry Rooney went on a Malcolm Slessor/Bill Wallace organised trip to the Liverpool Coast.

Aside from all this, Dave Leppard and Iain Smart both remember Allan's role as soloist in the Dundee University Operatic Society and his ability to hold a tune. In fact one of Iain's memories of the 1969 Greenland trip is of 'Allan sitting by the shoreline singing to the barren pack ice in his soft tuneful voice'. Allan also sang at various times with the Gaelic and the Stirling University Choirs and he, like Val, had a life-long and passionate interest in music and concert going.

After Allan left Inverness in 1974, he climbed for forty years with a large number of strong climbers and his dedication, application and drive saw a continual improvement in his standard and achievements. His two main partners in this time, Jim Fotheringham and Gerry Rooney, have added their own thoughts on their experiences in separate contributions.

However, in terms of the number of routes climbed throughout the world, it is probably the case that Allan did more, certainly in summer, with Val than with anyone else during the almost 43 years that they were together. The impressive list goes something like this – all over Scotland, North Wales including Anglesey, Pembrokeshire, Devon, Cornwall, Lundy, Lake District, Northumberland at all grades up to E1/2 and overseas they had numerous trips to the French and Swiss Alps, the Dolomites, Norway, Spain, Mallorca, Corsica, Sardinia, Kalymnos (a particular favourite in Allan's last few years), South Africa, North America (including Yosemite and Wind Rivers) and the Bugaboos in Canada (where Allan did the Beckey/Chouinard route on Howser Spire). In addition skiing, on and off-piste and ski touring in Scotland, France and Switzerland, was a major activity with Val and also the children. Allan also managed to get on a sailing/off-piste skiing trip to Arctic Norway.

Throughout his professional career Allan used the flexibility of being a self-employed dentist to balance his working and non-working life so as to maximise the time available for travel, climbing, mountaineering, skiing and ski-touring. Such a choice is, of course, not available to all, but for those who could adopt a similar pattern of life I know of no one else who made use of it so successfully. The arrival of Lewis and Kathryn in the mid-1980s changed this to some extent but these two are clearly chips off the old blocks and both are equally keen on the outdoors (with the addition of surfing). However, when the children were young, Allan, although still a determined climber, mountaineer and skier, was happy just to get outdoors with the family in any way even without climbing.

Following retirement in 2008, Allan continued apace and, like many of us, 'sports climbing' at home and abroad became an important feature of rock climbing. He also discovered bouldering to which he attributed his success in getting his standard up to 6b and 6c.

However, in the spring of 2012 the continuous activity was suddenly interrupted in Sainte Foy when he was skiing slightly off the piste and was swallowed in a sump of snow and buried head first with only his feet and skis visible. He lapsed into unconsciousness and by the time he was extracted he was blue and was only brought back to life as the result of one of the group being an anaesthetist. Good work by the rescue services meant that Allan was safely extracted and he recovered to take up where he had left off but unfortunately this wasn't to be the case. By August he was unwell and what was originally thought to be a kidney problem was diagnosed as lung cancer in late 2012. Although Allan never had a cigarette in his life (possibly the odd cigar), he then learned the uncomfortable fact that around 16% of lung cancers arise in non-smokers.

In early 2013 he was put on a 'wonder' pill (from the US) appropriate to his particular condition and this was thought to postpone the need for conventional chemotherapy by an average of nine months. This was where Allan's grit and determination paid dividends. He tried to carry on, as far as was feasible given the handicaps imposed by his illness, doing as much climbing/skiing as possible. As anyone who climbed with him at that time, even if only indoors, can testify, he was successful in this almost beyond belief. In late August 2013, he, Gerry Rooney and I had a great mountain day on Hell's Lum with Allan leading an E1. By March 2014, three months longer than expected, and although he was still climbing 6b/c on the bolts, the treatment became ineffective and he had to undergo the first session of 'normal' chemo at the start of April.

It shouldn't be a surprise by now to be told that within five days of the end of that session we went to Ratho and made a slightly longer visit a few days after that. By now he was having to climb with a pain pump regulating the release into him of whatever drug it was. This continued so well that after a fortnight we were back at Kirrie Hill and did five routes.

So it carried on and he achieved his objective and got back to what is now known as 'trad' climbing in early July when he and I had a great wee day on Polney where he led Ivy Corner and The Chute – not bad for someone who had just over a month to live. He surpassed this the following week when he and Gerry went to Skye and Allan led Crembo Cracks.

However that was to be it for climbing and thereafter he bore his remaining few painful weeks in hospital and finally at home with his usual stoicism.

In a nutshell, Allan was the most widely travelled, enthusiastic, dedicated and prolific climber I have known. However, his other interests, including skiing, reading and music meant that he was by no means a one dimensional individual. As a dentist, I know that he was adored by his patients. In the climbing world, apart from the respect for his ability and achievements, he was also a popular and well liked guy – something not always easy to achieve in our world!

All his many friends in the Club extend their sympathies to Allan's wife, Val, and to his two children, Lewis and Kathryn.

Dave Jenkins

Gerry Rooney writes: the somewhat disparate group of climbers of the Starav MC met on a Tuesday night in the Doublet pub in Glasgow's west end. After joining the club in 1976, that was where I first met Allan. As we both had independent climbing histories and partners, our initial contact was fleeting. However, his passion for the mountains, as testified by not only the range of routes done in the UK but also by his impressive Alpine catalogue, was obvious. In the early eighties, possibly because it suited both our lifestyles at the time, we started to climb together on a regular basis. He was the better climber being more focused and having more drive. However, we shared the same outlook and ambitions. Never looking for the extreme but always for some new challenge, something different and exploratory that offered an element of adventure. The result was not only trips to numerous places in the UK but also regular sorties to Les Ecrins, forays into the Alps at Chamonix and routes in the high passes of Switzerland as well as the crags of Austria and Italy. Even after 30 years, his unabated enthusiasm helped generate future plans and speculation about the possibility of some unresolved ambitions such as the Nose of El Cap in Yosemite, Lotus Flower Tower in NW Canada and returning to tackle routes in the Dolomites.

Over the years some great climbs and some scary moments were experienced on the rock and ice of the Scottish hills. We had our statutory share of blundering about in zero visibility, battling our way through a 'hoolie', navigating in a whiteout and descending in the dark. One episode in Dubh Loch remained imprinted on our minds. Allan tenuously belayed to a small nut and No.1 Friend placed more in good faith than anything else and I, precariously teetering 100 feet out, on minute holds in a cramped position with a nut extractor caught in my sock preventing any upward movement. There was also the occasion in Pabay when, after a 200ft misjudged abseil, he ended up 10ft out from the rock and 15ft above the sea. A potentially serious situation was eventually resolved by him performing an impressive piece of lassoing. However, such incidents were few, and his judgement in any climbing situation was always sound and reliable. His enthusiasm and motivation remained undaunted and infectious throughout the years we climbed together.

Memorable moments were not exclusive to actual climbing. Great nights were had in the Starav hut in Glencoe. A blazing stove, good company and endless climbing stories that were not immune to a degree of embellishment. Relaxing after a day's climbing in the NW of Scotland with the occasional Toscano cigar and a dram and camping in the ancient corrie of Beinn Eighe hold an enduring significance as well as memorable unexpected moments like watching the Basking sharks feed off the cliffs at Pabay or, by sheer chance, seeing a Minke whale suddenly breech off the beach at Mingulay. Allan's Angus origins even intruded into our climbing vocabulary with the likes of 'degging it down' meaning heavy rain therefore no climbing or if I had gone off-route on a pitch, a dry and somewhat sardonic 'you've gang up the wrang dreel, loon' would waft up from the belay stance.

Ski touring at home and abroad also featured with trips involving the likes of intimidating couloirs in Les Ecrins, the north face of Mt Tacul and skiing down from the Vallot Hut on Mt Blanc to the Midi halfway station. A traverse of the mountains on the Liverpool Coast of Greenland with only a photograph of the area taken at 30 thousand feet as a guide provided an indelible memory. We arrived at the Inuit settlement of Ittoqqortoormiit (Scorsbysund) where we were taken in by the resident doctor. Having stayed a couple of nights we hired local Inuit hunters to take us and another companion by dog-sled back to the Constable Point landing strip where we joined the rest of our party for the flight back to Iceland.

Allan was not only a climbing partner but also a companion and friend. The trust and dependency that developed in our climbing partnership extended into other aspects of our lives. It was a friendship that was deeply valued. When I was seriously injured by rockfall, he was not only supportive in my recovery but showed great patience in my slow integration back into skiing and regular climbing. Possibly something that only those who are passionate about the mountains can fully appreciate. He was an easy companion who had a wide range of interests ranging from environmental issues and Scottish politics to literature, art and music. Strong opinions were often openly expressed but were never acrimonious. Although I never did share Allan's love of classical music and opera (he was a fine singer himself), he could be converted to Springsteen, Radiohead and the Dixie Chicks while sitting in the car on our sojourns North and South.

Indoor climbing walls became a place not only to train regularly but also to meet up with Dave, Colin, Cam, Geoff and others which, among other things, provided the opportunity for a bit of ribald banter with me being targeted as the only non-member of the SMC. After the diagnosis of cancer, Allan was adamant that this prolonged his climbing and was crucial in maintaining the resilience needed to deal positively with his gradual deterioration.

Despite many fine bolt-climbing trips to various parts of Europe, there was a particular affinity with traditional climbing in the NW of Scotland. It was on such a trip that he informed me of his condition and despite his considerable discomfort, was where we did our last climb. A multi-pitch HVS route in Skye ending on the Cioch. Scotland was at its best. Magnificent mountains, traditional climbing on warm rock, no midgies and beautiful weather. Somehow it felt in keeping with his love of climbing.

As friends we had spoken of many things and knew each other's strengths and weaknesses. I remember one conversation when we spoke of death and speculated what others might say of us. We laughed at the possibility of 'I'll never forget what's his name'. If he could read this now he would be laughing and probably tell me to get a life. But I could assure him that neither he nor his name will be forgotten.

Geoff Cohen writes: Although I had known Allan a little for many years it was only in the last few years that I got to know him much better. The more time I spent with him the more I liked him. Together with his very old pal Gerry Rooney and pals of mine such as Des Rubens and Gordon Macnair we had happy weeks in North Wales, Mingulay and the French Ecrins, plus lots of chatty afternoons at Ratho. Allan was one of those people who was always happy to talk about climbing, and could tell a good story really well. His tales of expeditioning with Iain Smart and Malcolm Slesser were always riveting. But much more than that his wide interests made him a great companion whether talking about birds, music, cooking, dentistry or myriad other subjects. I found him such a warm personality that I really enjoyed visiting him in hospital, and perhaps got even more out of it than he did. He was able to talk with great frankness about his illness and faced it with courage but also indomitable optimism. Until right near the end he continued to talk about climbs he hoped to do in the future.

Allan was an excellent climber in the E2/E3 grades. Even when he was visibly wasting and had lost so much muscle he could still climb 6b/c indoors and had no trouble with classics like Prophecy of Drowning on Pabbay. He was also a very experienced skier – and though not a skier myself I enjoyed listening to his description of his Alpine touring and off-piste escapades. His amazing survival after being buried headfirst in deep cold powder to such an extent that his heart stopped was a tale that bears many retellings. It was such an irony of fate that but a few months later he was diagnosed with terminal cancer. Thanks to the 'miracles' of modern medicine he was put on a 'wonder drug' that gave him another year of relatively trouble free life. He used it to the full, packing in as many trips as he possibly could to his favourite haunts with family and friends. But the experts had warned him that the treatment would only work for a limited time and after about 14 months his illness began to trouble him much more. He continued fighting it to the end. Like many of his friends I really miss him, and like to think that, as he said to me on his deathbed, we will meet up again 'in the great campsite in the sky'.

Jim Fotheringham writes: I first met Allan and his wife, Val, in 1974 in the Wagnerian setting of a forested campsite in the Engadine valley with thunder rolling around the cliffs, lightning illuminating the summits and torrential rain, as I struggled to erect my homemade tent.

I was an impoverished dental student – and climber. Allan had just started his own practice. He gave me encouragement to continue when I was seriously questioning whether dentistry was my future.

We became firm friends and Allan became a mentor not only as a dentist but also as a proponent of that most arcane branch of mountaineering – Scottish winter climbing!

My first route with Allan was the Smith-Holt route on Orion face. I hitchhiked from Birmingham and was a day late back for clinic for that one. Many routes followed over the years – Point Five, Orion Direct, Hadrian's Wall, Minus 2, Eagle Ridge, Indicator Wall – to name but some. However, it's not the succession of IVs and Vs that I remember most. It was the steady diet of corniced, stormy finishes, descents in the dark, navigating off the summit of the Ben in howling winds, frost burn whilst struggling across The Cairngorm Plateau – all the while gaining knowledge and confidence from Allan in this harshest of mountain environments.

We, also, started to do ski tours – on primitive Langlauf gear – often done in conditions too bad for climbing. One notable trip involved skiing in to Beinn a' Bhuird and camping on The Col where Allan's new tent was obliterated by the storm and we almost lost our boots in the chaos. (We did Mitre Ridge on another trip!)

Soon after meeting Allan and Val I had moved to Carlisle and so Allan and I were regularly climbing together. Our ambitions were mutual and, over the years, we managed some prestigious ascents for the time – Unicorn, Kingpin, Yo-Yo, and Shibboleth in Glen Coe. (On the latter, we even gave a well-known Lake District pair a top rope – at their request!) A frosty Easter day on Arran froze up the usually wet cracks to give us the second free ascent of Brachistochrone. Allan may have been my climbing mentor but I was teaching him to jam!

Bank holidays and long weekends would see Allan coming south of the border. Our 'tick list' included some great days on Gogarth. I remember doing The Moon one sunny morning and The Syringe in the afternoon (a most fitting name for a couple of dentists) and a testing ascent of T-Rex.

Since that first fateful meeting, Allan and I regularly re-visited the Alps. The Dru became our 'bête noire' with 'almost' ascents of both The American Direct and The North Face. Both involved stormy bivouacs below the summit and abseil descents in the rain.

More dramatically successful were ascents of The West Face of the Petit Jorasses, The Gervasutti Pillar and The Innominata Ridge on Mont Blanc. The latter I still consider to be one of the finest multi-day experiences in The Alps.

I probably bivouaced more with Allan than with any other climber. I hasten to add that this was not because of slowness – Allan was one of the fastest climbers I know on mixed ground. Some were planned – as when we did an early (first) British ascent of the right variant on Les Droites N. E. Pillar Direct. That was a full day of TD^{-} rock climbing followed by a day of mixed climbing. I well remember sitting at Montenvers after those two extreme days and sipping beer as the sky darkened, the thunder rolled and the raindrops started. This was one of the great Alpine experiences!

Some bivouacs were unplanned – as on an early (first?) British ascent of The Gogna Route on the S. Face of The Marmolada. This was memorable because it was the only time I have ever spent the night hanging in a harness standing on the belay to finish the last few grade V pitches in the dawn. We then had to traverse the summits of The Marmolada on ropes buried in the ice before the long descent.

My first non-Alpine big mountain trip was with Allan to Mt Kenya where we did an early ascent of The Diamond Couloir, followed a day later by the second ascent of The Scott-Braithwaite route on the S. Pillar of Nelion. This was a wonderful experience on an extraordinary mountain.

I look back on those days with Allan as the ultimate adventures! Whether in desperate conditions in his native mountains or in the exotic grandeur of The Alps – we were climbing major routes with minimal information. In the days we climbed together, the gear was poor or non-existent in winter, and Alpine guidebooks were often misleading or erroneous. Complete trust in your partner was the order of the day. My trust in Allan was total. His judgement to go on or go down was always sound. He was stoic when the going was tough, cheerful and even ambitious when the sun was out! They were great days with a great companion. I always thought we'd climb some more and I shall miss that. While I have some great memories, I shall miss Allan!

A WILLIAM (BILL) LAUGHLAND J. 1950

Bill Laughland joined the Club in 1950 having been proposed by Ross Higgins and Willie Speirs and many of his trips were on outings with the Glasgow Section of the JMCS with Ross as his usual companion. He also climbed with Herbert Turnbull, Ian Charleson, Bill Watson and Russell Marshall. In the years following the war, it is unsurprising that most of his expeditions were close to his home and he traversed most of the hills and ridges in Arrochar, Arran and Glen Coe many times.

He also delighted in extended tours in the North-West with one particular expedition in mist and rain commencing by Loch Stack then by Kylestrome, Lochinver, Ullapool, Dundonnell, Gairloch, Torridon, Achnashellach, Glen Shiel, Kinlochhourn and then by Loch Arkaig to Fort William. He made occasional rock climbing visits to the Lake District and visited the Wicklow Hills in Ireland.

In professional life he was a Fellow of the Royal College of Surgeons specialising in obstetrics. In his early years he taught in Liverpool finally holding a consultant's post in Glasgow. He was a big fellow with big hands but a smooth delicate surgeon. It was a pleasure for juniors to see him work.

Bill enjoyed country life and had houses in Glasgow, on Loch Fyne side and in Skye. He had a great love of dogs, especially German Shepherds. They were all called Jade. He also had great fondness for Turkish cigarettes, Daimler cars, Scottish art and malt whisky. He died in Glasgow on 15 November 2014.

JRRF

Anne Laughland writes: Bill got great pleasure and enjoyment from climbing and was proud and pleased to be a member of the SMC. I am very grateful that you continue to send me a copy of the Journal: Bill enjoyed it so much. He had a deep and abiding love of the hills.

BILL M.M. WALLACE J. 1961

My father Bill Wallace died in February 2014 and was buried at Sannox on Arran, in sight of Cioch na h-Oighe and some of his favourite climbs. I was asked to stitch together a bit of history in respect of my father's climbing and hill walking exploits over the years. He will always be best remembered for his extensive knowledge of the Arran hills, but he did visit many other places.

As far as I recall, his first taste of hills was on Arran as a youngster on family holidays in the mid-1930s. The family also visited Tiree three times in 1937–40, so it's perhaps lucky that he also visited Arran. In his late teens, Bill started going by bicycle to the hills north of Glasgow, Arrochar and around Crianlarich. He would climb all day and then cycle home. He was also playing Rugby and Tennis at that time so fitness was not a problem! In 1943 he was called up, and was away for almost three years. On his return, he started studying Medicine at Glasgow University and restarted his rugby, tennis and hill walking. His wife Anne, whom he married in 1951, was a talented tennis player and a very sympathetic non-climber, so their sporting passions did not clash. He lived and worked in Dumbarton and Glasgow until 1956 when he moved to Kilmarnock and began a career in Pathology. I don't have any climbing logs from those early '50s, but I am fairly sure he was still out on the hills.

For the next 31 years, he climbed or walked on average 40–50 days every year, about 75% of the time on Arran, often finding new routes on the Arran granite. He also managed over 20 trips to Skye, of roughly 3 to 4 days each as well as regular visits to Glen Coe and Nevis, punctuated with occasional trips to the

Lakes, North Wales, Assynt, Arrochar, Black Mount, Monte Rotondo in Corsica, Dachstein and Teide in Tenerife. For local entertainment he often took me or my brother to Loudoun Hill after he had finished work for an evening climb.

Bill was a man of a generous nature and consequently made a lot of friends on the hills. Many of his days out are marked with well kent Scottish climbers. He climbed with Willie Nicol, George Gilbert, Hugh Stirling, Grace Hamilton, Jim Johnston, Ken Andrew, Ben Humble, Dick Sim, Jim Simpson, Sandy Cousins, Andrew Maxfield, John Harrison, Jim Armour, Cliff Heath, Alleyne Dinwoodie and many others whose names I failed to decode from his extensive log book! While I was still at school in 1968–69 he embarked on compiling the rock climbing guide to Arran, incorporating lots of new routes established in the 1950s and '60s. I well recall the house littered with photos, maps, drawings and letters from all over the UK. His wife Anne helped proof read the guide, and translated his sometimes doubtful left-handed handwriting! The guide was well received in 1970 and a revision issued in '79. It has been re-done since that date.

He was never a climbing 'tiger', preferring to find a challenging natural route instead of something requiring too much equipment. On one snowy winter outing in February 1983 from North Glen Sannox to Cir Mhor via the Castles on Arran, Bill and companion had to cut steps for the upper 3–400ft. As it was pretty iced over at the top as well they were obliged to don crampons, but only one each! They managed OK and came down safely. I don't know who was carrying the crampons!

He often said that it was sad that the lack of extreme routes on Arran made it less attractive to modern climbers. That said, there is still a lot of enjoyment to be had on Arran granite.

On retiring to Arran, he continued to tramp all over the place, climbing less daringly, but always on the lookout for new lines. If the cloud was down too low, the solution was to go bouldering and there are lots of interesting boulders round the coast of Arran.

His last ten years, after his wife died, were mostly on his own, still walking until his knees eventually limited his outings. He was quite sanguine about the knees. 'After what I've done to them, they don't owe me anything!'

His love of the hills was sustained for 70 years, a perfect use of one's three score years and ten.

Graeme Wallace

BILL SKIDMORE J. 1969

Bill Skidmore was a man whose genial nature won him many friends both within the climbing community and outside it. As a climber he lived through a period of exploration and change in Scottish mountaineering and made important contributions to the development of climbing in the south-west of Scotland.

Bill was born in 1937 in Gourock and grew up there with the Loch Eck and Luss hills as a skyline across the Firth. These hills were his first introduction to the freedom of the uplands; despite the transport problems getting there in those days when car ownership was a rarity and travelling to them involved ferries and buses. On leaving school he joined the drawing office at Scott's shipyard where

he met a number of other young men interested in climbing and joined the Greenock Mountaineering Club. His early development as a climber was interrupted by National Service and he spent two years 'avoiding the last three Communist guerillas in Malaya'.

It was on his return that a group of like-minded young men from the three towns and from further down the Firth started to form. Bill's climbing ability and natural charm made him the central figure in what became known as the Greenock Team (inaccurate label, but convenient). In his later climbing career he also climbed with a number of others, notably John Gillespie and Graham Little.

He was not only a naturally good climber (his height was occasionally useful), he was careful and safe. These were desirable qualities in those days of primitive equipment. Most of our early climbing was with tricouni-nailed or Vibram soled boots with Woolworths' sandshoes reserved for the mica schist wrinkles of Arrochar. Laid nylon ropes were rigid and gear for runners was nigh non-existent - falling off was definitely not on the agenda. In later years Bill's runner placements became legendary; when he put them in they stayed in. As his frequent second I had many struggles to recover the gear and several times had to accept a swing on the rope as both hands and a hammer had to be employed (there's a minor variation on Armadillo resulting from one of these episodes).

His generation saw the development of climbing equipment towards the sophisticated gear of to-day. We progressed from the carefully selected pebbles in the pocket to the home-made chocks fabricated from aluminium plate and rod (shipyards have their uses) to the era of chocks and cams. Bill was a natural fabricator and made or adapted much of his climbing and camping equipment. There was the piton carrier made from kilt pins, the Prussicking devices made from aluminium plate, the Friend retriever fabricated from a short length of aluminium tubing and a bent bicycle spoke, the strap-on tricouni-nailed plates for mixed climbing, the drilled-out camping cutlery and much else besides. The doss on the Brack was fitted with a stove and a curtain of draughtsman's linen. Daedalus would have been proud of him. (He was also the only person I know to have incorporated a sheath into his climbing harness to take a small knife.)

In the early sixties cars were not easily available to young working men and the motorbike was the cheaper form of transport and for a few years we biked and camped both winter and summer. There was the weekend on Ben Nevis when it was so cold that eggs froze; the time when the tail-end of a hurricane buckled my A-poles in Glencoe and we decamped to Oban and the Bridgend Bar where we marvelled at the potency of the beer until we realised that, yes indeed, there were twin sisters behind the bar. Weekends when we lay in the tents until it was time for the Clachaig as the rain kept coming down and (of course) the many nights of torment by midges. But we got sufficient climbing in to gradually increase our standards and attain some degree of acceptance by the climbing community.

Although it was a delight to roar across Rannoch Moor summit on a fine June evening and see the summit of the Buachaille pink in the evening sun, winter motorbiking was only for the dedicated. Comfort levels were low and kneecaps frozen on the Friday night only thawed sometime on the Monday. But Bill, as usual, showed individuality. He obtained a sidecar which had been used by the Greenock Parks Department and coupled it to a single-cylinder 650cc Panther. This green coffin required the ballast of a small anvil to keep it stable when not fully laden for climbing trips. When the Panther died the coffin passed to another member of the team until it was separated from his motorbike by a sheep. (The wheel ended up in the prototype MacInnes wheeled stretcher.) This period is elegantly described in Jim Crawford's article in the 1989 Journal.

Bill was always looking for new routes. His early explorations were on Arran where the Greenock Team put up some landmark routes like The Blinder and the Rake on the Meadow Face, West Flank on Chir Mhor and Armadillo on Cioch na h-Oighe.

There were other good rock routes too, as the First Ascent list in the Guide will show. The first winter ascent of Nuis Chimney with Jim Crawford was another notable coup for its time. Remember, single axes and clumsy crampons were the norm. At Arrochar there were the excellent quartet of rock routes on Creag Tharsuinn and also Mammoth and Mainline on the Brack. The Brack routes involved the use of pitons (not unusual in those times) and we also had a brief fling with pure aid climbing in the ascent of Sideline on the Brack. This was an ideal autumn ploy as it overhung so much that the rock was always dry. As far as I know a free ascent awaits. Another Brack landmark was the winter ascent of Great Central Groove.

By the late sixties marriage had hit the team but two-man tents were replaced by bigger models and family camping weekends in Glen Etive and holidays in Glen Sannox were common. A fair amount of rock-climbing also occurred on these trips (notably the first ascent of Armadillo).

In the mid-eighties life changed for Bill. Scott's shipyard closed and his marriage ended. He also had a serious heart attack which was an indication of health problems to come. A new attachment took him to Kintyre where he found another job as a draughtsman with Argyll County Council. Despite his heart attack and the effects of the associated medication he never lost interest in climbing and when he discovered the delectable crags at the Mull of Kintyre he quickly rounded up Graham Little and became involved in their development; taking part in a number of first ascents.

Later he and Mary moved to Lochcarron where he again found himself among the hills. He did some climbing but the aftermath of his heart attack and circulatory problems associated with diabetes limited his activities (Bill was honest enough to declare that they were the price he paid for thirty years of smoking). But he took on the Custodianship of that awkward hut Ling in 2001 and ran it until 2008. It was soon spruced up and adorned with notices and checklists in his neat script.

His other services to the Club included joint authorship of the Arran Climbers' Guide (1979 Edition), Committee membership (1974–77), Vice-Presidency (1978–79) and President (1979–80). His brief tenure in the latter two offices is explained by the fact that he took over the Presidency on the death of Bob Elton halfway through his term. Bill was always diffident about his time as President but he did have a lasting effect on the AGMs. Previously they had tended towards performance art with motions and counter motions flying about accompanied by that mythical beast 'the direct negative'. With his trade union experience and a small volume entitled The Little Guide to Chairmanship, Bill changed the AGMs from a bourgeois rammy to smoothly operating business meetings. Previously, it had sometimes been a desperate rush to get to the bar between AGM and Dinner; so remember him for that as you sup your pre-dinner pint. An Honorary Vice-Presidency in 2012 recognised his contribution to the Club.

Circulatory problems associated with diabetes blighted his last years. Despite fitting of stents in his legs he had to have the toes on one foot amputated. Breathing difficulties were only partially alleviated by the fitting of a heart pacemaker last year. He died on the 21 December 2014. Even during his period of health problems he was always outwardly cheerful and many will remember Bill as a jovial giant. A man of many friends and many abilities.

Bob Richardson

Graham Little writes: it was a Stanley and Livingstone moment when we first met in Glen Sannox in April 1979 and the start of a long friendship. We made the first ascent of Black Cave Pillar a month later, you shared some mountain secrets with me and then off we went to Sudan on a mission impossible – playing at being secret agents.

No list of climbs could possibly convey the fun we had together: bending ethics on Arran, as kids in a sweetie shop at the Mull of Kintyre and searching out remote coves on Colonsay. You always were an innovator – designing, making, adapting, reusing – there are several well-known routes where the bolt belays originated from a Clydeside shipyard!

I still have the postcard that you sent me after I returned from a Himalayan trip: a picture of the low hill near your house at Clachan in Kintyre with a carefully added capping of Tipp-Ex and reference to Himalaya peaks being nothing in comparison to the eternal snows of Dun Skeig!

In later years, after you'd moved up to Lochcarron, I saw less of you but still looked forward to Christmas communications and the occasional meetings at garden parties in Inverness.

Even as your health began to fail you were never sorry for yourself, always finding reasons to enjoy life rather than gripe about the hand it had dealt you. Just a couple of days before you died I read the note on your 2014 Christmas card. It was as quirky and entertaining as ever. Commenting on my 2014 newsletter, you wrote:

'My life is much more interesting – had a "pacemaker" fitted last week (good name for a route) – I call it my I.E.D. Seems OK. Somebody sent me a free copy of the Inner Hebrides/Arran rock guide. If you instigated that, many thanks. Some book; changed days; makes me feel right "out of the loop" (another good route name).'

On your 2012 Christmas card these lines were penned; you suggested that they were a fitting ode to climbers:

They cannot scare me with their empty spaces
Between stars – on stars where no human race is.
I have it in me so much nearer home
To scare myself with my own desert places.
(From 'Desert Places' by Robert Frost)

So Bill ('Dad's big friend' as my young son used to call you) thanks for all the adventures, the laughs, the campfires, the whiskies, the words of wisdom, and, of course, the new routes.

ROBERT (BOB) HILLCOAT J. 1961

It's been a tough last few years losing some of our older members, guys who have been around for a long time. Malcolm Slesser, Bill Wallace, Gerry Peet, Donald Bennett, Bill Skidmore, Charlie Rose and Derek Fabian. So it is with personal sadness that we record the passing of Bob Hillcoat. I expect many of the younger members will not know of Bob, but to those of a certain age, he is well known for his contribution to the club and to mountaineering in general.

Bob was born in the town of Renfrew in 1928 and was just short of his 87th birthday. I got to know Bob, as did a lot of Boy Scouts in the Renfrew area, through his help in introducing us to the local hills around Loch Lomond and

Arrochar. He took a group of us up Ben Lomond on a midnight hike in 1960 to see the sunrise, unfortunately it was cloudy so on that occasion we missed the great view down to Ailsa Craig. However, climbing the Cobbler was a more exciting adventure; here was a hill with lots of crags and a superb summit. Bob himself was a keen Boy Scout and in his younger days attained the top honour of King's Scout and represented Renfrewshire at Windsor Castle in 1946. So there was always an affinity with the Scout movement.

After his school days, he chose to be an accountant, but had to complete his national service first and was mainly based with the army at Fort George and latterly in Trieste in North Italy. These two areas must have given him a taste for the Highlands and the Alps. However his accountancy was to stand him in good stead as our treasurer in the SMC.

In the 1950s and '60s he was employed by the National Trust for Scotland in Edinburgh where he worked with the eminent ornithologist George Waterston and made expeditions to St.Kilda and Fair Isle to study the sustainability of the crofting industry and of course it was an opportunity to enjoy the local wildlife. After one of his expeditions he was described in the Glasgow Herald as "Sir Robert Hillcoat" a befitting, if un-bestowed title. He was invited to many garden parties at the Palace of Holyrood.

Bob joined the SMC in 1961 and was honorary treasurer from 1979 to 1989. It was during his time as treasurer that we met up again when I became custodian of Lagangarbh Cottage. Each month I would go along to Bob's house in Renfrew and give him the details of the takings. He was very generous in loaning me some of his mountaineering books including Heinrich Harrer's 'White Spider' which captivated me and gave me a hope that one day I might climb the north face, which unfortunately was not to be. However Bob told me of his ascent of the Matterhorn via the Hörnli Ridge which again I longed to climb and his enthusiasm saw a few of us climb the mountain via the Italian Ridge in 1989.

Bob was a great climber, skier and golfer. His father was captain of Renfrew Golf Club in 1927 and obviously passed on his talent for the game. Bob loved the outdoors with a passion and it was with great delight that he moved to Aviemore for the last part of his life and was regularly skiing up to the age of 85. His last few years must have been dreadful for a man who loved the hills. A terrible stoke immobilised him and kept him lying in a bed for four years in a local hospital and the Southside Nursing Home. The staff there was fantastic and he was always pleased to see any friends that could make it in for a visit. He could still chat about adventures and recognised people on the photos in his room. Bob was particularly fond of dogs and loved it when I brought in my daughter's Spaniel 'Meg' in to see him. I think it reminded him of his own favourite dog Dougal. And so it is another farewell to a great servant of the club and lover of the outdoor life.

Curly Ross

CHARLES STUART ROSE J. 1952

Charlie Rose was one of the first people I met on joining the EUMC, way back about 1947 and he is about the last survivor of my generation. He did all the student things – climbed on Salisbury Crags on Sunday mornings, got ritually chased by the park-keepers. One Sunday we all got trapped and had to give our names; it was quite a haul for the keepers; they got the names of half a dozen Professors from various faculties.

Charlie was a good all round mountaineer with an amazing physique. He took part in the ritual ascent of the castle rock on Charities Day and in the ascent of the Scott Monument when a large flag was furled from the topmost pinnacle. The offending flag was removed by council workers before 9 a.m. the next morning. It involved the erection of scaffolding and was a creditable, indeed superior effort on their part.

After graduating from the Art College he went to seek his fortune in London, working for Unilever as an Art Buyer. More importantly he forged a parallel career in the Teritorial Army becoming a Captain in the parachute regiment. He very casually mentioned some of his weekend exploits. One I remember was a night drop in Denmark with a heavy kitbag of equipment dangling on a rope from his harness; the kitbag hit the ground first and slowed up the descent. He was back at his desk on the Monday morning.

In 1958 he was a member of the Scottish East Greenland Expedition and made some first ascents in the Stauning Alps including the crossing of the Col Major. He subsequently made two climbing trips to Nepal.

He returned to Scotland in1966 to a house with a view in Alligin where he and Priscilla raised a family. He did various jobs there and at one stage worked on a local fish farm, owned ironically by Unilever. He and Priscilla became dedicated members of the local community. He kept up his climbing in Scotland and for a time was leader of the local Mountain Rescue Team. He had his small boat on the beach below his house; the dream that so many have but seldom achieve.

His house in Alligin was always welcoming and conversations with Charlie

were always wide-ranging and not short of opinions. Few of his friends in the Club are left to mourn his passing.

Iain Smart

Peter Biggar writes: as long as people keep climbing at Diabaig Charlie Rose's name will live on because, most unusually nowadays, an area of cliff, Charlie's Dome, and a climb on the Main Wall, Charlie's Tower (60m HS 4b) are named after him. The latter route and Gamhnachain's Crack (75m HVS) on the Main Cliff were climbed with the redoubtable Allan Austin and R Valentine in 1976. The 1970s were a good time for Charlie in climbing terms for in '71 and '72 he discovered the climbing potential of Coire Rudha-Staca on Beinn Eighe and pioneered five routes including Thin Man's Ridge (HS), the delightfully named

Independent Pineapple (S) and Spog aig Giomach (S). His companions were Ronald Turnbull and David Howard. Midge Ridge (V Diff) was climbed with S Peterson.

Charlie was a good friend of the late Dick Balharry and both of them delighted in telling the tale of how they dragged the elderly Lord Howick Head of the Nature Conservancy up the Cioch in Applecross. This gentleman suffered from some complaint which meant he had to have frequent rests and they didn't get back to Kinlochewe Hotel until very late: whereupon his lordship woke everyone up to applaud his achievement.

Charlie was our neighbour and friend in Torridon for some 35 years. Always a fascinating conversationalist, he spoke the purest English of anyone I can remember and never changed the way he spoke. He liked his hot drinks hot and his cold drinks cold. You never came to Heathercliff without receiving warm hospitality. Charlie Rose was a real gentleman.

COLIN D GRANT J. 1973

Colin had been a member of the SMC from 1973 and served as vice president from 1991 to 1993. He died in his sleep on 3 September 2014. He was a distinguished academic and committed educationalist. His achievements in that regard are well reflected in the fact that his untimely passing has been the subject of obituaries in a number of academic journals as well as the pages of the Herald and the Scotsman. However, this obituary will focus on the other great passion of Colin's life– mountains and climbing and his time spent with those who shared those experiences with him.

Colin's lifelong engagement with hills and climbing began with his parents and his sister Fiona in walking and skiing both at home in Scotland and in the Alps. Boarding school in Scotland continued the experiences but the greater degree of formality accompanying that perhaps explained a predisposition towards a slightly more earthy relationship with the Bens and Glens. This first became manifest in his taking up residence in Altnafeadh in the mid-1960s with the likes of Malky Macrae and Big Bob Jarvie. It was not long however before elements of the Rannoch doss from further down the Glen gravitated towards Altnafeadh. There they were busy working their way through the graded lists of the Glencoe guide when they were joined by the 'Dumbarton Boys' including Ian Fulton, John Jackson and Ian Nicolson. This served to drive standards up and in due course led to a return to the Rannoch Doss with by now a very strong team of regulars including amongst others Ian Fulton, Colin Stead, Ken Crocket, John Hutchinson, Stuart Smith and Morton Shaw. All of this is derived from one of the many records I have been given access to by Colin's family from 'the campaign room' at home. There, in a typically organised Colin fashion, the hills, the climbs, the dramatis personae are all faithfully documented. Indeed, in tabulated fashion one might find the lists of climbing friends over the decades classified variously as Strathclyde University, Old Rannoch, New Rannoch and Family / Friends! The keen eyed observer will have noted that even at that early stage there was a considerable overlap between the ranks of the Rannoch and the future membership of the SMC and indeed came to include a number of future Presidents, Vice

Presidents and Committee members.

The 'Old Rannoch'were Colin's climbing associates during the 1970s when they climbed extensively across Scotland and, where resources permitted, the Alps. The home rock climbing grounds of Glen Coe, the Etive slabs, Ben Nevis and the Cobbler were no less frequented than the more remote venues such as Carnmore, the Cairngorms, the far North west and even a trip to Sron Ulladale. It was during the winter months however that the group, including Colin, opened up new winter climbing areas. Accompanied by Colin Stead he did the first ascents of Slow March and Far West Buttress on Beinn An Dothaid. He did the first winter route on Creag An Socach, climbing Second Coming along with Ian Fulton, the same pairing also producing Central Grooves on Ben Cruachan. Once again with Colin Stead he opened up the account of new routes on Meall Buidhe with their ascent of The Circus and similarly with their ascent of BO Buttress in Coire an Dothaid. On the Ben in the early 1980s he added Slab Rib Variation again with Colin Stead. In the late '80s he teamed up with Roger Everett to climb Turf Walk on Aonach Mor in the early development of that venue. As the 1970s pushed into the '80s the ranks of the Old Rannoch began to be beset by pressure from climbers emerging from the university clubs of both Strathclyde and Glasgow Universities. With two of their number, Chris Rice and Roger Webb, he added Nightshift on Ben Alder in the late '80s. The Wednesday club night at the Stirling Castle became a very busy fixture with arrangements being made at furious pace as multiple deals and side deals were made for climbing destinations, route preferences, climbing partners and, crucially, car spaces. It did not pay to tune out of any conversations once you thought an arrangement had been made! This was not really Colin's type of arrangement. As well as being well organised Colin was incredibly loyal and completely committed. An arrangement once made was there to be honoured. In due course we each recognised the possibility of the mutual advantage to be had in being free of the Wednesday night arrangement frenzy and became the climbing partners we were for the decades to follow.

It was during the years of the '90s however and into the new millennium that Colin brought his formidable organisational abilities to bear and began to marshal the unruly masses of the Rannoch into something resembling a club with annual dinners, autumn bothy meets and, crucially, Hot Rock trips to the bolt clipping flesh pots of Spain, France, Italy and even the USA. In latter years there were also "Hot Ice Trips" to a variety of venues in Europe. The large number of such trips which Colin arranged and took part in amply demonstrated not only his ability to move with the times but his positive enthusiasm in doing so. It is to be remembered that he was one who grew up in the era of step cutting in the 1960s and who in his sixties eagerly adopted the use of leashless ice axes. An abiding memory will be of Colin at Glasgow Airport counting the Rannoch in, resplendent in North Face cap, blue neckerchief, Teva Sports sandals (with socks, of course!) brandishing the blue document wallet which contained, for many of us, the key to getting on the plane, into a hire car at the far end, a space in a self-catering shed and finally the beta for the routes! It was not for nothing that he came to be known, only slightly tongue in cheek, as the Papa del Rannoch.

All that was just a means to an end; it was all about the climbing and the hills. It was here that his commitment came to the fore. A route once embarked upon was not to be backed off from lightly. On more than one occasion climbing partners encountered the full 'deaf ear treatment'. However, he was the consummate climbing and walking partner – safe, steady, sorted. In winter quite how he managed to keep track of the two axe loops, cows' tails attached to the axes and cords attaching mitts to wrists was quite beyond me. Oft times he would gaze in despair at the colourful, robust but ultimately unhelpful plaited hawser which I conspired to create in the course of the route. His climbing, especially in winter, was deceptive in appearance. The steady progress often made it look like the climbing was okay but on closer acquaintance it quickly became obvious that it was anything but.

His navigation skills on the hills were second to none. Ah, the joy we had when he managed to best the honours graduate in topographical sciences (who shall remain nameless, but who now specialises in remote crags in winter…) on a clag ridden Ben Alder on one of the Autumn bothy trips. Put him behind the wheel of a car in a foreign country right enough and things could go badly awry. T junctions and roundabouts – left or right, clockwise or anti clockwise – they all presented major challenges. Colin gradually began to address this by reference to something approaching a Buddhist mantra; once behind the wheel one might hear the gentle incantation 'Drive on the Right, Drive on the Right'. The only spinning wheels to accompany it however were those of the rival teams seeking out pole position to get to the crag first.

Outwardly Colin could give the impression of being stern and frankly a bit forbidding. A number of his former students whom we encountered, out of university, in a climbing context gave every appearance of rabbits caught in the headlights. At SMC AGMs I at least got the impression of a frisson of anxiety running through the meeting as the Professorial hand shot into the air at a crucial moment. In reality he was a kind, compassionate and understanding friend. That is not to say that he would suffer fools gladly. You patronised at your peril. So it was that when a hapless student happy with the day's cragging but trespassing into condescension sought to assure Colin back in the Ling Hut that 'Diabeg Pillar is really very good, you ought to do it'. Well, the air set to crackling, metal began to hum, 'I've done it five times' which was of course true.

The Scottish hills of course also bore witness to his commitment to the outdoors and, in a trait not normally associated with hill walking, his competitiveness. He was on his third round of Munros and snapping at the heels of a number of the Rannoch who were dipping for the line to compete their second, and in some instances, their first round. And woe to the thoughtless padder who had to stop mid ascent on a hill outing to put on or take off gear as the peloton, with Colin in the vanguard, swept majestically past.

Of course competitiveness loomed large in Colin's approach to other things outside walking and climbing whether it be squash, tennis or golf. Indeed, on one of the Majorca trips the morning's cragging at the Boquer valley was foregone just to impress upon the upstarts his supremacy at table tennis. The things he did, he did really, really well.

He was a committed member of the SMC as was evident from his work during the period of Vice Presidency. He cared passionately about the hills, Scottish Climbing and the club. It was rare for him not to attend the SMC Dinner, he valued the opportunity to catch up with old friends, pick up on what had been happening and offer his view on the proceedings of the club. The venue for his last Munro second time around was Lagangarbh. The hut was packed to capacity with SMC members, including Morton Shaw, who was sharing his last Munro first time around with Colin (on his second round), both compleating on Stob Na Broige of Buachaille Etive Mor. His favourite club venue however was Ling Hut, revelling in the location and the atmosphere lent to the hut by the comradely gaze of Ling and Glover in the photograph celebrating their great partnership on the hills of yesteryear.

The last mountain route with Colin was at a Rannoch weekend he had organised in Arran. Mosque on A' Chir, with Colin's lifelong friend Morton Shaw (who had done the first ascent with Ian Fulton) accompanying us to photograph proceedings and offer route finding advice – albeit he had last been there some 48 years before. Others did ascents of South Ridge Direct, some went running, others kayaking, all to return to Colin's house at Blackwaterfoot for a 'Rannoch curry'. All of which was co-ordinated by Colin. He was a vital force for the good.

So it was that last November Rannoch Old and New set out from Lagangarbh by various routes, including obscure link ups between North Buttress, Easy Gully, Curved Ridge and D Gully Buttress, whereby a subdued team eventually assembled on the summit of the Buachaille Etive Mor. On that glorious morning Altnafeadh lay below, Rannoch Moor stretched out to the East and the Ben humpbacked the horizon to the North. There, under the watchful eye of the Raven, Colin was committed to the hill one last time.

The loss is profound, the memories endure, we will speak of him often.

Finally, our thoughts go out to Colin's wife Maida, his two boys John and David and his sister Fiona.

John Dunn

DEREK J FABIAN J. 1966

He knows not where he's going
For the ocean will decide –
It's not the DESTINATION…
…It's the glory of THE RIDE

A quirky card sits on my shelf showing a plump Zen Dog, the sun is high in the heavens and he is wearing sunglasses, reclining in a floating bathtub, and meditating…This portrayal conjures up an image that doesn't quite fit the personality of Derek Fabian at all. His qualities were the exact opposite. This was the man of action, always with some fresh scheme to fulfil, and often with as much help from others as he could enlist.

It is the last phrase of the doggerel that rings true because it portrays what it was like to get involved in one of his plans. In later life he cut a slight grizzled figure, after a long lifetime driven by too much motivation and activity which had kept him sparse and on the go. Nor did he hide away behind dark glasses because this would have masked any open cajoling invitation to assist and embark on yet another of his way-out projects. His mind worked to plan many a destination, then to pursue it with enthusiasm, and without any doubt on his part that the outcome would be as he had prophesied. It was ever fruitful to join in his next adventure but always to keep a cautious weather eye on what could happen if things went askew.

I've heard it said that Derek functioned and succeeded because he was gifted with 'improbability drive'. Yes, he had the drive, and as for improbability there are few who could think up some unlikely project and embark on it without second thoughts of its feasibility and ultimate completion.

For example, years ago in 1962 we had a protracted discussion when he representing the Royal College of Science and Technology and I flying the St Andrews' flag pushed forward our respective choice of expedition. He argued for a return to the Andes where he had worked as a metallurgist for a mining company in central Peru and where he tagged on to the Edinburgh Andean Expedition 1958 to join Bill Wallace, Hugh Simpson and Myrtle Emslie on their successful ascents[1] of the Nevados San Juan and Chinchey (6223m). I was pushing for Greenland, visited by St Andrews in 1961. In the end Greenland won the day. However a big snag developed: at New Year while descending to Torridon village in the dusk from Liathach his wife Janet slipped and fractured her leg. In the aftermath it seemed unfair to his wife and children to vanish abroad for months and Derek withdrew, but as the summer approached he changed his mind. There was now no vacancy in the expedition party so he conceived one of his improbable ventures. He would follow on later after we had gone, board any boat going up the coast, hire a dog team, travel a hundred miles through peak-studded icefields to join an expedition which itself was playing it by ear and hadn't a clue where it would be when he, if ever, joined it. Luckily he realised the improbability of his plan and probably thought up an alternative challenging scheme. Nevertheless if he had embarked on this impossible task he could well have turned up at some lonely campsite at dinner time and wondered why we were so amazed at his crazy journey.

It was in a similar vein in 1985 on his way to a scientific conference in Japan

[1] '6000 metres', *SMCJ*, 40/199 (2008), 78–86.

that he diverted and journeyed over the Indian sub-continent for a five day participation with Graham Little and his companions who were exploring and climbing in the Parbati valley in the far Himachel Pradesh. After a bit of upping and downing to claim a hill he trekked out to Kullu, narrowly avoided being arrested, and continued on his way. This time he got to his destination, plus…

It all began in the early fifties when some outdoor activities were fitted in with getting a couple of degrees in Chemistry in London University. Those were the days when one constructed rather than bought ready-made scientific equipment so he capitalised on a new skill to write a reputable textbook on the art of glassblowing. For someone always wanting to travel from here to there and back again a beat-up old London taxi fitted the bill. There were sandstone bulges to climb at Harrison Rocks, sallies to North Wales, and summer alpine excursions.

When the time came to start to earn his living he and Janet travelled to Vancouver in 1954 to a post-doctorate post at the University of British Columbia. It was there at chaotic Scottish country dance sessions followed by home-brew rehydration sessions that Derek and I met, and thereafter our paths crossed on mountaineering escapades. We shared outings with the Canadian Alpine Club up tree-infested valleys clad with virgin forest reaching up higher than any Munro, and when every weekend trip could turn into an unpredictable alpine endurance exercise.

In 1957 he landed the industrial job with the Cerro la Pasco Corporation in La Oroya in Peru and as a farewell big deal he was one of six climbers bound for an attempt on the Nooksack tower across the border in Washington State. This tower was a semi-isolated rock monolith gained by a 200m hard névé couloir followed by 400m of Grade 4 rock, both solid bedrock and shattered blocks, attached to the northeast ridge of Mount Shuksan (2783m).

Every weekend in British Columbia was a struggle of indeterminate duration along river courses and up through fallen logs, spiky Devils Club undergrowth, pushing against flattened branches of Slide Alder. It was a finale for Derek to remember before he thought about going up any bare Andean slopes.

We were two teams: we were the B Team; myself with a good broad Ulster accent, Brendan Moss with his quirky Dublin brogue, and Derek the quiet spoken Englishman who was about to acquire a fearsome melange of accents. We toiled up for five hours until we got the first flat space to pitch a tent. Dinner was cooked on a dry rotten cedar wood fire, and to bed after climbing talk at 11 p.m.

Stars were still shining when we left for the couloir. Our proposed route under a glacier snout was rejected when serac blocks rumbled down and swept the slabs. The other, faster team was granted the privilege of step cutting and gaining the broken ridge. They were returning when we reached the top after seven hours; our verdict 'one great manure heap'. Derek blethered away unaware that he was speaking in a newly acquired Irish accent; Brendan and I kept quiet and passed no remark on this interesting metamorphosis. Darkness overtook us before we reached camp at midnight. The others had gone home. We were back in Vancouver at the time it was normal to knock off work. Too bad, but this was nothing to Janet's amazement and rejection of her strange polyglot man, the husband whom she had given up for lost but who returned bewitched by leprechauns and speaking in strange tongues. Luckily it wasn't a permanent affliction.

That wasn't the end of his brushes with the enormous expanse of the untrammelled mountains stretching up the western coast of Canada and in 1964 he got to organise a project[2] whose main destination was a Mount Burkett (2990m) on the Stikine ice field. To help get there they pulled off a film advertising stunt

[2] 'The Scottish-Canadian Coast Range Expedition, 1965: (1) General Account' by Derek Fabian, and '(2) The Ascent of Mount Burkett in 500 Words' by 'the indefatigable and indefinable' Eddie Thompson. *SMCJ*, 28/157 (1966), 186–90.

by persuading the Rootes motor group to provide a small convoy to drive a bunch of bearded mountaineers from Toronto to Alaska where they hired a helicopter to fly in the six-man part, and in a month of alpine sun got up several peaks with Burkett in their bag.

In the Sixties we, and other returned emigrants, were in Scotland and met for family get-togethers, climbing on Ben A'an, and in Torridon and Glen Coe. Once when we camped in Glen Etive we found that the Forestry Commission were looking for tenants for Inbhir-Fhaolain cottage that was later to become the hut for the Grampian Club. It was hard to curb his enthusiastic advocacy of getting this property as a holiday cottage but fortunately we were rejected for more reliable occupiers. Of course, Derek would have relished the chance to turn it all upside down and create something unusual. This was consistent with a natural talent to design and plan, acquire materials, and with some help from 'volunteer' labour backing up genuine tradesmen but nearly on his own, he constructed a trio of architecturally interesting wooden houses culminating with a highly original home on an open hillside with cliffs behind and the river Clyde below.

On the western seaboard he placed a cosy 'boathouse' with all mod cons including a trickling water supply from a bog and a septic tank buried under seaweed and stones just above the shoreline. However the genuine boat shed was a Heath-Robinson construction plonked against a cliff up a hidden right-angled creek with barely adequate water depth to extract his boat at the spring tide. It may sound frustrating but before the access channel was scooped out it was not unusual for his yacht to be marooned until the next monthly spring tide allowed her to be extracted to her mooring at the summer anchorage. Once Norman Tennant and I watched the water level creeping to within millimetres of the point of flotation and then sinking imperceptibly down again. Was the thwarted Skipper downhearted? Not at all: there was always more tinkering and alterations to be done, and they were always easier to do under the boathouse roof than out in the bay.

It was here that his real love lay in the challenges awaiting his succession of vintage aesthetically pleasing wooden craft, all with the name Malin in one form or other, that he sailed for nearly four decades on and beyond the seaways of the west coast. This messing about with boats never would stop until the wrenching conclusion came when he was no longer was able to do all the demanding things that sailing and maintaining a boat and 'boathouse' demanded. One of his last tasks was to help replace the 'boathouse' roof with long-lasting metal sheets in a tasteful green tone blending with the natural hillside colours.

When the club decided to update the District Guidebook to the Islands of Scotland he was an automatic choice to share in its authorship, and he was to cover the Small Isles and the Long Isle, Orkney and Shetland, and even the offshore and outlying northern islands. He had the wherewithal and found the time to pursue this most desirable aim. It was published in 1988 and when a second edition was inevitable he seized on his wish to replace his B&W photo of a distant tiny figure on the top of Ainshval in the Rum Cuillin with an identical colour photo. When Mistress Malin anchored again in Loch Scresort it was close to where she had anchored with the Bennets and Robin Chalmers in the SMC Centennial Yachting Meet, but this time alone in quietness and free from the varied flotilla cramming the loch in 1997. The Skipper and Mark Hutcheon, the essential genius who ensured that all the electrical and electronic bits and pieces worked, set off late to the summit of Trollval. There the requisite standing figure was aligned on Ainshval and Derek shot a plurality of photos. On board I made the meal, ate and waited as the summer dusk deepened then went to bed. They came phutting out in the dinghy in the dimmest hours of night and overcome with the day's effort went straight to their bunks too tired to eat their dinner. Project and mission accomplished.

Many the voyages he and his crew, often including SMC members, made around the delectable islands of the west, and not to forsake his mountain attachments the Skipper would try to get in a Tilman-like ascent of a nearby hill close to any anchorage. He and his cook, galley-slave and deck-hand Ewa Maydell-Fabian managed several successful trips, not to dwell on aborted efforts, to land on that ultimate thule of St Kilda[3]. This voyage firstly took Malin with Norman Tennant in 1982, next Malindara with Allan McNicol and Robin Chalmers in 1992, and finally Mistress Malin with myself and Mark Hutcheon in 2003. In 1996 they circumnavigated Ireland clockwise with Drew Somerville and Robin Chalmers[4], and as a grand far-flung finale in 2002 penetrated the labyrinth passages of the Faroe islands[5] having already reached beyond the Arctic Circle to the Lofoten islands[6] in 1998. These trips were piling up well-earned sailing awards from the Clyde Cruising Club; there was no stopping the rampant Skipper. There was drama too when Douglas Scott had a mild stroke and had to be helicoptered off the moving yacht with chaos flying all around as insecure fitments took off in the sweeping downdraft[7]. Graham Little, as a co-author of the Islands guide, was once inveigled into accompanying the Skipper on a fact-finding voyage 'just sailing into the nearest bay, take a leisurely stroll to the crag, do a route or two, then wander down, with the sinking sun, to bottles of wine and real food. It all sounded too good to be true!' Of course, it never worked out like that. Up there on the northwest flank of Orval in Rum was its unclimbed notorious desperately loose 30m metamorphosed basalt pinnacle on which any serious rock enthusiast can test his mettle, there were shearing holds and spilling runners for a 10m fall, and it was a battered carcase, racked with pain, that hauled itself on to the minute summit. Two slings cut to be elongated and tied together gave a fraught abseil to terra firma where his belayer offered well-earned congratulations[8]. Was this the glory of a ride?

Always Derek had an academic career to pursue at Strathclyde University and during his thirty four years of tenure it eventually took him to the pinnacle of his profession. However, always on the lookout for fresh vistas he managed bouts of study leave taking him variously to the Eidgenossische Technische Hochschule in Zurich, the Universitat in Karlsruhe, Simon Fraser University in Vancouver, and even locally to Stirling University.

In 1994 having fitted in another research visit to the University of Auckland in

---

[3] 'St Kilda in Mistress Malin', *Clyde Cruising Club Journal*, 2004, 19–21.

[4] 'Rounding Ireland in Mistress Malin 1995', *SMCJ*, 36/187 (1996), 183–92, and *CCCJ* 1995.

[5] 'Faroe Islands voyage', *CCCJ* 2002.

[6] 'A Long Way by Sea to Climb a Mountain: The Talisker Islands', *SMCJ*, 37/190 (1999), 225–8, and *CCCJ* 1999.

[7] 'Derek Fabian reports on a Helicopter Lift-off', *SMCJ*, 36/187 (1996), 116–17, and *CCCJ* 1996.

[8] Graham Little, 'Close to the Wind', *SMCJ*, 33/176 (1985), 164–7.

New Zealand he and Ewa bought an ancient decrepit camper van and explored all over South Island before returning home and leaving the van behind. Next year they went back again, stuck the van together with sufficient fibreglass matting 'to get warranted and registered,' and Derek with climbing partner Ron Hockey set off toiling circuitously over river, valley, hill and glacier towards the antipodean Matterhorn. Up the spectacular crest they went, with rope on and rope off, reaching the summit of its beautiful white glistening pyramid together. The day was still and cloudless, and they had it to themselves[9]. This was Mount Aspiring (3030m) and it sounds just right for his last big mountain summit.

Yes, mountains to him should always be within reach, with skiing in season and sailing waters nearby, and placed conveniently to satisfy his desire to delve into the choice corners of the wide world. We know not where he's gone, but we know the glory of his ride…

In February 2015 this restless irrepressible octogenarian driven by some improbable dark energy allowed his Skyrover Defender to take him away, to another project in the far beyond…

Phil Gribbon

DICK BALHARRY J. 2010

When Dick Balharry arrived in the Cairngorms in 1974 we knew that mountains were going to move. He was already a legend from his work at Britain's first National Nature Reserve at Beinn Eighe, in Wester Ross. A BBC documentary about life in the Nature Conservancy at Beinn Eighe had just been broadcast. We called it 'How the West was won' in recognition of the action packed existence of Dick and his colleagues. Fighting forest and moorland fires, climbing the hills on mountain rescues, safeguarding eagle nests, regenerating native pinewoods, culling red deer herds and building trails, camp sites and car parks seemed to fill every day.

This action packed life was, however, complemented by much debate and discussion about the inter relationships between people, wildlife and the use of land and sea. As his career developed Dick built a reputation across the UK and beyond as one of Scotland's finest naturalists and advocates for the conservation of nature and wild places. There was never a dull moment with this friend and colleague of 40 years.

Dick worked until his final days. In early 2015, at his house in Newtonmore, looking out over the splendid garden that he and Adeline had developed over nearly 20 years, he explained that his time was up, how a minor indigestion complaint before Christmas had become a diagnosis of oesophageal cancer, with all its brutal consequences. He reflected on a full and rewarding life, so many fascinating experiences and so much shared with family, friends and colleagues. But that was enough looking back, he insisted – now we had to discuss the issues of the day as Dick prepared a final contribution – his vision for land use in Scotland. It was poignant that he died on 22 April, recognized worldwide as 'Earth Day'. A few days before, in Glen Feshie, the Royal Scottish Geographical Society awarded the Sir Patrick Geddes medal to Dick, an award that he shared with

[9] 'Aspiring to Summits in New Zealand', *SMCJ*, 36/188 (1997), 441–4.

Adeline. Dick's paper for that occasion, his land use vision, explores the relationship between nature and human activity in the Highlands and Islands and the challenges to be overcome in making that relationship more harmonious <www.rsgs.org>.

Dick's first exposure to the natural world and his fascination with it came as a boy living in a small village on the outskirts of Dundee where 'I was given total freedom to explore the woods, marshes and fields and these became my natural habitat' (RSGS paper). No wonder that a strand that ran through Dick's life was a deep desire to expose others to the wonders of nature, from their earliest days, and build an appreciation of the significance and interconnected character of the natural world. No wonder that Dick was an absolute defender of the freedom to explore and a key player in securing Scotland's right to roam and other elements of land reform.

Dick engaged a wide audience, out in the field and beyond – a captivating speaker at meetings and conferences, a well respected writer and broadcaster. But he avoided creating any impression of self importance – once I described him as a 'wildlife expert' but was told to correct this to simple 'naturalist' – Dick was wary of anyone calling themselves an expert!

His skills and contribution to Scottish life was reflected in the award of an MBE for services to nature conservation in 1996, honorary doctorates from the Universities of Aberdeen (1995) and Abertay (2010) and the RSGS award. He much appreciated his honorary membership of the Scottish Mountaineering Club, a fitting tribute to a lifetime spent in the hills and one which had such significance for safeguarding the wildness and beauty of Scotland. And it was in journeys through wild places that Dick was at his most effective, influencing his companions through acute observation backed up by debate and discussion. A day spent leading the then chairman of the Nature Conservancy, an elderly Lord Howick, up the Cioch Nose in Applecross, was no doubt a memorable experience for all concerned. But once again it enabled Dick to establish the priorities for Scottish conservation in the mind of a powerful figure from south of the border.

Dick had one of the shortest careers in the industrial world. After a year's training in an engineering college in Dundee he turned up for work at a local factory. He left within the hour convinced that an environment dominated by noise, the smell of hot oil and cigarettes, was alien to his own interests. For Dick the future lay in the great outdoors, beginning with gamekeeping near Tighnabruaich and stalking in Glen Lyon. But for most of his career Dick worked for governmental organisations, first with the Red Deer Commission and then with the Nature Conservancy, starting at Beinn Eighe in 1962, aged 24, eventually with successor organizations in Aviemore and Aberdeen, finishing his career in 1997 as an Area Manager with Scottish Natural Heritage. This, however, was just one rung on the long environmental ladder which Dick climbed through his life. After SNH came a stint as a board member of the Scottish Environment Protection Agency as well as various roles in voluntary organisations – Chair of the John Muir Trust, Acting Chair of the National Trust for Scotland, President of Ramblers Scotland, Patron of the Whale and Dolphin Society, Chair of the Cairngorms Access Forum – all these different roles, combined with his skills as a communicator through writing, photography and broadcasting, made Dick one of the best known figures in the Scottish conservation world, but also with a reputation extending much further afield. That started back in 1969 when he secured a place on the International Seminar on National Parks and Equivalent Reserves, a course run in various protected areas in North America. To fund his attendance Dick's expensive and much cherished photographic equipment was about to be sold until, at the 11th hour, the Nature Conservancy agreed to meet the costs. It was money well spent, despite official policy being to support staff of more senior position for such ventures – Dick built up an impressive range of contacts in nature protection worldwide and became a strong advocate for the establishment of a national park system in Scotland, eventually secured by the passage of the National Parks (Scotland) Act 2000.

Central to Dick's personality was an ability to form warm and personal relationships with people in all walks of life. Everyone had time for Dick, be they royalty, politicians, officials, landowners, stalkers, farmers, crofters and anyone out and about in the hills. A day out with Dick was a stop/start affair – few people walked past him without getting a cheery greeting, usually followed by some discussion about what they were up to and what was happening in the surrounding land.

Three issues were of the greatest significance in Dick's engagement with the natural world. During the 1960s scientists became increasingly concerned about the long term impact of persistent insecticides on the environment, with implications for human health. A focus for investigation was the poor breeding success of birds of prey such as the golden eagle and peregrine falcon. Dick played a key role in field investigations of these species in the West Highlands, helping to demonstrate the insidious spread and impact of these chemicals as they accumulated in food chains, even in the most unpolluted areas of the UK. The consequence was world wide prohibitions on the use of such chemicals in agricultural operations and a much greater sensitivity to the environmental impact of intensive land uses.

Deer and trees were central to Dick's life. From his earliest days as stalker and gamekeeper through to his final weeks he questioned the relationship between land, landowners and the public interest. Nobody could better him in debate about Scotland's ancient forests and their relationship to the herds of red deer which, in far too many places, roam in vast herds nibbling away at any seedlings or saplings that poke above the heather. Dick's practical knowledge of deer management, combined with a deep familiarity of the condition of our native pinewoods, from Sheildaig and Beinn Eighe in the west to Balmoral and Glen Tanar in the east, made him a key spokesperson on land reform. Repeatedly he challenged those who insisted on out of date approaches to deer management, demanding that those who derived much pleasure from "recreational killing" should face the consequences of their association with degraded landscapes and management practices that left vast areas of native woodland overgrazed and slowly declining through lack of natural regeneration. Over the years Dick became an ever stronger advocate for the better control of red deer populations, enabling woodlands to regenerate and to avoid planting, fencing, fertilizing or other intensive techniques in and around our ancient woodlands. By contrast, on hills where all woodland had disappeared long ago and there was no prospect of natural recovery, he would support native woodland planting as part of biodiversity restoration programmes.

The purchase of Creag Meagaidh National Nature Reserve in 1985 by the Nature Conservancy Council provided the opportunity for Dick to demonstrate what needed to be done. A sustained programme of deer reduction in the early years ensured that, within 10 years, prolific regeneration of new woodland over large areas of the reserve had been secured from the degraded birch woodland that had been left from previous private ownership. But it required a person of Dick's determination and knowledge to resist the pressure from surrounding landowners who objected to this modern approach to land use – no doubt the squealing and complaining continued in the tearooms and bars of the House of Lords, where too many decisions on Scotland's land are still made.

The Creag Meagaidh experience, combined with years of effort to secure better conservation of native pinewoods in the Cairngorms, stood Dick in very good stead when others sought his advice. While many of Scotland's traditional landowners took the advice and did nothing to change their approach two individuals from further afield took action. Lisbet Rausing from Sweden, owner of Corrour Estate and Anders Povlsen from Denmark, owner of Glenfeshie Estate, worked with Dick to bring about fundamental changes in deer management to reduce grazing pressures over all their land. It was a fitting tribute to all this effort and aspiration that Dick's last journey into the outdoors was to Glen Feshie to receive the RSGS medal, in a landscape dominated by one of the Cairngorms' ancient pinewoods, surrounded by prolific natural regeneration. May others walk the same way and learn what is needed for the future. For Dick the path through Glen Feshie was clear – a route towards a new vision for the hills which encompassed the public interest alongside the empowerment of the landowner to manage with confidence and transparency.

For the rest, for those immersed in the concept of the traditional sporting estate, Dick had some straightforward words – 'they embody the selfish greed of a Victorian era, outdated and ludicrous' (RSGS paper). And, when his advice to the RSPB on the management of their Abernethy Reserve in the Cairngorms was ignored, he did not hesitate in describing such planting proposals as "ecological vandalism and a complete waste of money" (Scotsman 4 March 2015). He lamented the drift of some conservation organisations from guardians to gardeners.

Finally, in his last years, the big issue that engaged Dick was the debate over climate change. Increasingly he related his vision for the hills to the need to manage vegetation and watercourses in ways which enhance the capture of carbon, reduced the expenditure of fossil fuels and provided downstream benefits. Restoring the natural resilience of land and sea became a central theme to much of his thinking, a core part of his writing and debating. He modified his personal transport modes and spent much time and effort on solar and biomass installations in his Newtonmore home. Whether on the hill or beside the wood burning stove Dick led by example, challenging us all to think about our own lifestyles, never forgetting the man who led the way.

Dave Morris

JAMES RAINY-BROWN J. 1973

Mountaineering and mountains were an important part of James Rainy-Brown's life. Introduced to them by his father (an SMC member) he always felt at home just being in the mountains, and walked them extensively. As a pupil at Merchiston Castle School and a student at Edinburgh University, he was primarily interested in rugby and athletics. After graduating, he returned to the school as a teacher and continued these interests, mainly as a coach, injury limiting his own participation. He increasingly developed his interests in mountaineering and the mountains.

In 1963 he founded the school's first mountaineering club, which provided an important introduction to the mountains for generations of pupils thereafter. In the early days, the attitude to supervision of such an activity was very different from the expectations of today. The emphasis was on self reliance coupled with enjoyment. On a half term trip to Glen Coe, James bid two of his keener pupils farewell in the morning as they headed for North buttress on the Buchaille. After one severe and three VSs, two tired 16-year-olds returned to camp in Glen Etive for a debrief with James, followed by a trip to the Kings House.

In addition to taking on the leadership role, he also continued as an active mountaineer himself, always in Scotland, usually on long walking expeditions whilst introducing young pupils to the sport. Although not a technical climber, he made great efforts to encourage young pupils to rock climb and supported their progression. He was also an accomplished painter of mountain scenery and had an extensive knowledge of flora and fauna.

Teachers who create opportunities for pupils and inspire their interest can be hugely influential to younger generations. This was very much the approach that James adopted towards promoting mountaineering. As a consequence many pupils are extremely grateful for having been introduced to a sport that has remained with them for a lifetime.

Mike Watson

MICHAEL JOHN O'HARA J. 1973

In 1954–5 Mike O'Hara was in his third and final year as an undergraduate at Cambridge University. I was then in my first year, and one of the first things I did was to join the Cambridge University Mountaineering Club. The club was highly active both at meetings and meets, as I quickly found out. The President of the 1954–5 year was Eric Langmuir, the secretary Bob Downes, the Assistant Secretary (meets) Mike O'Hara and the editor of that year's annual journal Cambridge Mountaineering was John Peacock. Three others were on the committee but these four were especially active climbers with each other in various combinations. Eric's presidency ended in summer 1955 and Bob Downes took over. However he moved at the beginning of 1956 to work with White Hall, Derbyshire, and thus Mike became president of the mountaineering club in the first half of 1956. He stayed in Cambridge as a research student in geology from 1955–8. Meanwhile several further potential climbers, including myself, got to know Mike and climbed with him. His excellent articles about his climbs were published in the Cambridge Mountaineering Journal 1954–8 and in the Climbers Club Journal 1958.

Mike O'Hara outside the Torino Hut.

The Cambridge Mountaineering 1954 journal contained Mike's article Otherwise Uneventful which was conceived during the summer 1953 after his first year in Cambridge. The summer was primarily a geology expedition to Spitsbergen but they had a couple of weeks of substantially warm weather even in Arctic Norway (70° north). Mike and a few friends climbed two hills near Tromsø. They are at heights of about 3500 feet each, with some sections of rock climbing and then excellent ridges to the respective summits. When I bought the journal in 1954 I read most of it including this article before I actually met Mike. Now I have read the article again. From the two relatively modest mountains, the then young Mike had written a wonderful article. I can hardly imagine that his writing and of course the climbs were from more than 60 years ago.

The following journal, 1955, contained Mike's article on The Trilleachan Slabs in June 1954. Two first ascents were led by Eric Langmuir, with Mike, Tony Mallinson and Miss J.M. Tester on the first of the two, namely Sickle (13 June 1954). The next day Spartan Slab was first climbed by the three men. Both climbs are VS; Spartan Slab was recorded as much the better of the two. Almost three years then elapsed until further excellent new routes were done on Trilleachan Slabs from April 1957 onwards, mainly by the Creag Dubh Club. Meanwhile, Eric also wrote an article in the 1955 journal, Nothing Venture, in which he, Mike O'Hara (though no last names in that article), John (surely Peacock) and Arthur (presumably Muirhead) did the second and third ascents of Minus Two Buttress, Left Hand Route, on Ben Nevis one day in late summer. Mike led much of that climb.

In the 1956 journal Mike wrote an article of two parts called Night and Day. The respective events were some months apart, in which the 'Day' was in perfect but short sunlight in January. This was his only writing of a winter ascent in the 1950s. There were Mike and four others in the group and these were noted only by their first names in the article (like the three with Eric in the 1955 article). The path was icy even on some early sections up from Glen Nevis while it was still dark. Their actual climb was not decided in advance. From the article it appeared that they did not have crampons on the climb. Crampons were not universally used in Scottish winter in the mid-1950s. Nevertheless the group's progress was good, and when it became too steep for kicking they cut steps with one axe each. Mike led up Observatory Gully and into Gardyloo Gully. There was a pitch of ice, then more snow, a partial gap in the cornice and then wonderful bright sun. Mike had led the first rope of two and the other three were on the second rope. From the summit there was a long descent with more ice on the path. It was dark again by Fort William. They had a great dinner and next day were on the journey south.

The Climbing Notes of the 1956 journal contained many events from summer 1955 including Ben Nevis, with the first ascent by Bob Downes and Mike and Eric of the North Eastern Grooves, the second ascents by Bob and Mike on Gardyloo Buttress and by Eric, Bob and Mike on Minus Two Buttress, Right Hand Route, and an early ascent by them on Route II Carn Dearg Buttress.

Also in the 1956 journal there were two articles by other authors about climbs with Mike. One of the articles was by John Peacock who with others had been on an Alpine meet in La Berarde in the French Alps in July 1955. Mike and John with two others climbed the North East Pillar (of Les Bans) under much snow on the upper part. Moreover, as described in the Climbing Notes, Mike with a sizeable party did La Meije Traverse, magnificent, and Mike with John Peacock and Roger Smart did Pic Coolidge by the South West Ridge, probably the second ascent, and said it ought to be the last due to loose rock.

In north-west Scotland in late August 1955 Mike and R.E. (Bob) Kendell joined together for the remote area between Shenavall and Carnmore. The weather had previously been mixed but now became excellent and they did several fine first ascents on the Maiden Buttress and Na Bearta Buttress. Bob's article was in the 1956 Journal and entitled Torridonian, but actually this is a generic area including An Teallach and some other mountains. Their actual climbs were done on Lewisian Gneiss. This is the oldest rock type, which is mainly in the basement of the north-west, but has impressive rises with rock routes especially within Carnmore .

The 1957 journal with 1956 articles and Climbing Notes has Mike's excellent article Carnmore. Mike with Marjorie Langmuir and George Fraser with Peter Steele converged on the prime Carnmore area during the last few days in March. Most notably the first ascent was made of the original Fionn Buttress by Mike and George, and was described vividly in the article. Several other first ascents were done by various combinations of twos. The article ended with the evenings of meals, chatting at ease and gazing outdoors towards the deepening twilight.

In June 1956 Bob Downes and Mike O'Hara went on the Ben again as noted in the Climbing Notes 1957. With M.C. Prestige they did the first ascent of Minus One Buttress, a more direct and finer route than North Eastern Grooves. Two days later (13 June) Bob and Mike did the second ascent of Sassenach which at the time 'seemed a terrific climb and a long day – perhaps the greatest mountaineering route in Britain'. Above the crux there was notably loose rock and a spell of bad weather on the Great Chimney, and the total climb took 11 hours.

Later in June Mike and others returned to Carnmore. He and Bob Kendell did the fine Red Scar Entry, and Mike also led or followed some of the other first ascents.

Then in July Mike and George Fraser with Peter and Bob went to the Alps, with the notable ascent by George and Mike of Between Showers, a considerable understatement regarding the Piz Gemelli NNW ridge, in bad weather on the second day on the upper part of the mountain. A few days later they were near Courmayeur and met Bill Turrall and myself. Fraser was the spearhead and was keen for Route Major. After taking a cable to Torino we six set off towards Mont Blanc as darkness approached. From the Fourche Refuge we heard a huge avalanche on the Brenva Face. George with Peter and Bill Turrall considered the Old Brenva would still be okay, which it was given their speed. Meanwhile Bob Kendell became temporarily unwell so the three of us turned back to Torino. See the photo of Mike. It was Mike's last Alpine climb that season. George and the others did some excellent Pyrenees climbs. I compromised with an Arolla climb before returning to Britain.

In 1958 Mike with George jointly wrote an article in the Climbers Club Journal. This was the front article and was called Highland Dragon. At the end of the article was noted 'We named the climb Dragon, partly because it was fierce and partly because it was George who won the victory'. The climb was on 22 April 1957. Mike with various companions had done several earlier first ascents on Carnmore Crag and elsewhere within the Carnmore area. One of these in early April 1957 was originally Fionn Castle, to the left of the 1956 Fionn Buttress. However it became clear that the finest ascent was up the lower left of Fionn Castle, then across right, in balance but on great exposure, to join and finish up the original Fionn Buttress. This combination, now simply called Fionn Buttress, has become the chosen route from then onwards.

In May Mike and I in Cambridge had plans, or more accurately Mike had plans and I listened and joined enthusiastically. Thus in June 1957 Mike, David Fagan and myself went up to Ben Nevis again, for three days, in the fourth successive June visit by Mike. In the meantime Centurion had been climbed in August 1956 by Whillans and Downes. Mike was now extremely keen to do the second ascent. The weather was good and we did a day 'training' on the second ascent of Minus One Buttress then a rapid ascent of Minus Two Left Hand. Next morning Mike and I set for Centurion. David with two others did Route II quite quickly and Dave joined us on Centurion before we had got beyond reach with the rope. Mike lead excellently throughout up to the Route II traverse but none of us could climb the second crux above, so we traversed right to finish via Route II. Although we did not complete via Centurion's top section, it was still not bad for June 1957. I accordingly wrote an article in the Climbers Club Journal 1958, namely Shirtsleeves on Ben Nevis.

The three of us then travelled to Kernsary and walked into Carnmore, and were soon joined by Nigel Peacock and Richard Hargreaves. In various combinations we did first and second ascents, notably the second of the Fionn Buttress (the combination as above) and the second of Dragon by myself and David Fagan. On the latter Mike and Richard watched from right of the top of the Carnmore Corner calling encouragement to us and photographing.

Although Mike did not write an article for the Cambridge Mountaineering 1958 journal he did write therein an Interim Guide of climbing in the Carnmore area. This extended broadly in the Guide. It included Beinn Lair and other north eastern mountains above Loch Maree as well as the more immediate Fionn Loch and related crags, and amounted to 36 pages in all. Mike with various companions did first ascents of about 40 rock climbs from 1955 to 1957. Almost all of these are still present in modern guides i.e. Northern Highlands Rock and Ice Climbs volume 1, 1993, and its successor Northern Highlands Central. The only exception was a minor one near the summit of A' Mhaighdean, which was noted to be very similar to if not identical with an earlier climb Triple Crags Route by A.J. Bennet and party in 1951. Impressively some of Mike's first ascents are contained in the selective volume Scottish Rock Climbs (SMT 2005) including Fionn Buttress and Dragon.

In July 1957 Mike with George Fraser and Marjorie Langmuir did a short visit to the Pyrenees, with three climbs among Gavarnie and the Pic du Midi, as recorded in the relevant part of the Climbing Notes in Cambridge Mountaineering 1958.

In April 1958 Mike was at Carnmore Barn and Crag again with several friends including Ted Wrangham and Roger Chorley. Wrangham and a companion did the third ascent of Dragon. Chorley had had poliomyelitis the previous summer but was tough and fit enough with a stick and rucksack to do the considerable walk into Carnmore.

When Mike was in the far north-west but not climbing he was doing practical geology research on ancient rocks, especially at and near Scourie with its Lewisian Greiss. As noted, Carnmore Crag is the most impressive rock cliff of Lewisian Greiss, which is elsewhere mainly a basement region of this most ancient of rocks.

1958 was Mike's third year as a research student, and he soon started to write up his PhD. If this was to be successful, it meant giving up climbing if only temporarily. Also Mike had learnt about two climbers in particular who had been very close to him but who had died on different great mountains: Bob Downes from pneumonia high on Masherbrum in 1957 where Don Whillans initiated and others helped the descent of his body to Skardu; and George Fraser, who with Mike Harris in 1959 disappeared near the summit of Ama Dablam. Mike O'Hara in due course became a lecturer and upwards at the University of Edinburgh and became a Fellow of the Royal Society of Edinburgh in 1969, by which time he was married with children.

I had had a few intermediate climbing visits to Carnmore, of which one was with Paddy Buckley and some of his family. Paddy then met with Mike to visit Carnmore . He did this starting in late spring 1972, as Paddy describes below, and Mike became a member of the SMC in 1973. Eventually Mike moved to a professorship at Aberystwyth, and in due course became a Fellow of the Royal Society (London) and remained as a geological scientist throughout his life. Both Paddy and I remained in touch with him for many years. In 1991 Sybil and I went running and walking in Central Wales one weekend and had a wonderful Saturday evening with Mike and Sue and their children at their home in a village near Aberystwyth. Over the years Mike remained close to Eric until Eric's passing away in 2005, and both Mallinson and Mike wrote his detailed In Memoriam in the SMC Journal 2006.

Mike opened up many new climbs during the time I knew him well and reports of these in journals and subsequent books will remain a lasting testament to his achievements.

B.E.H. (Ted) Maden

Paddy Buckley writes: my own love affair with Carnmore was kindled by the leading article in the *Climbers' Club Journal* for 1958, called Highland Dragon. It began: 'Carnmore is the most wonderful place in all Britain; remote, vast and beautiful in a fashion not found elsewhere in the Highlands.' O'Hara's lyrical introduction had me hooked straightaway, but the accompanying photograph blew my mind. It showed one man seemingly alone on a huge sunlit wall, below an overhanging roof, with the slack rope hanging vertically below for a good fifty feet. That man was Ted Maden, who with David Fagan made the second ascent of Dragon in June 1957. Ted had wanted to belay further on, but Mike, who was taking that photograph from the Heather Bay, insisted that he should use the cat's cradle stance which had proved so worrisome on the original ascent.

My first contact with Mike was on the steps of the Royal Society building in London, where he was due to give a lecture. He had not been back to Carnmore since graduating from Cambridge University. We arranged to meet again at Carnmore in June 1972. I came in from Kernsary with a few climbing friends from Ipswich; Mike walked in from Dundonnell with Sue Howell, later his wife. The barn that night was a very convivial place; the O'Hara exuberance adding to the glow of the fire. He was a brilliant raconteur, and he was in his natural element, among climbers in wild places.

Next year he was fit enough to tackle Dragon for the second time. There were three of us on the rope. Mike in the middle led up the first slab pitch. I led the wall pitch as far as the yellow groove, and brought up Mick Goad to lead through across the scary hand traverse. When Mike reached me, I noticed that he had attached jumar clips to his rope, prepared for the seriousness (and memories) of the crux. Mick Goad anxiously checked all his belays, but with a tight rope in front and a slack rope behind, O'Hara made the crossing safely.

The last time we were together at Carnmore was at Easter 1975. An unseasonal blizzard had pinned us to the barn. When it was over we walked up the track towards Sheneval. We came across a young deer calf floundering in the deep snow. Mike dragged it behind a boulder out of the fierce wind. On our return the calf had not survived. Mike picked it up and draped it over his shoulders, lugging it down to a spot just outside the barn, where he gralloched it with a Swiss army knife. Sue looked on with a vegetarian's distaste, but later at supper, enjoyed her first taste of fried deer kidneys and heart.

Mike's last visit to Carnmore was in 1999 when he walked in with Eric Langmuir. They were carrying the ashes of Eric's sister, Marjorie Langmuir, who had been with Mike during all his early explorations of the area in the mid 1950s. Marjorie never married. She became a doctor in Aviemore, until her death in 1998.

Mike and Ted Maden were willing to sponsor my application to join the SMC and duly introduced me to winter routes on the Ben and in Glencoe. Camping in snow by the side of the Allt a' Mhuilinn, Mike brought out his pocket chess set to while away the waiting hours. He check-mated me, twice, but then the sun broke through. As an introduction to the Ben in winter, Mike showed me the delights of Tower Ridge. Later on he took me to some of his earlier climbs: the NE face of Ben Nevis, the midge infested Trilleachan slabs in Glen Etive, and the airy rampart of Stac Pollaidh. I led him up Mur y Niwl in Snowdonia on a cloudless New Year's Day.

In 1976 I had been made redundant, and with my wife's encouragement, applied to join Douglas Anderson's Scottish Expedition to Tierra del Fuego. Before we could set off though, we had to build the boat; constructed from reinforced ferro cement. It became a 60 foot, 40 tons ketch called Eloisa. Mike and Sue offered me lodgings in their house at Loanhead, and each day I cycled through the city to work on the boat in a small yard near Granton. Mike was a kind and generous host and I treasure the months I was his guest.

Others will write of his achievements as a geologist. He certainly made me more knowledgeable about the rocks we encountered on our climbs. While he was still Professor of Geology at Edinburgh, he showed me slices of rocks taken from the moon. Around this time he was considered as a maverick by the US scientists for his theories on lunar geology. He told me that, in time, he would be proved right. Eventually he was.

We lost touch. A few years ago I learned that he had developed Parkinson's disease. More recently I rang Mike to ask him to write my obituary for the SMC Journal. He replied that he would write mine if I would write his. So here is my farewell to a dear friend. We had some great times together. Rest in peace.

JAMES MICHAEL TAYLOR J. 1954

Mike Taylor was brought up in the North-east fishing town of Peterhead where he attended the local Academy. In his teens he joined an adventurous scout troop and this helped foster a keen interest in the outdoors. After leaving school he went to Aberdeen University to study medicine. One Friday evening in October 1949, on the bus going home, he met a fellow first-year medical student and discovered they had a mutual interest in climbing. His new found friend was Tom Patey who lived in the small town of Ellon, half-way between Aberdeen and Peterhead. Between them they bought a hemp rope and together with Charlie Morrison, Patey's school friend, they started exploring the 12 miles of coastline between Collieston and Peterhead. From 1949 to 1952 they pioneered more than 50 climbs, mainly on the pink granite at Longhaven where the old quarry workings combined with the natural sea cliffs provided a miniature mountaineering arena with ridges, towers, steep walls and slabs. Their initial intention had been to gain sufficient climbing experience to be able to ascend any peak in Scotland, yet despite this modest aim they produced many classic climbs like Alligator Crawl, The Great Diedre and Tarzan Wall, all climbed in nailed boots.

By 1952 Mike and Tom were prepared to attempt more ambitious climbs on the sea cliffs. At Cove, just south of Aberdeen, they teamed up with Bill Brooker to investigate The Spigolo, a great 180ft. vertical blade of rock at the entrance to a deep inlet. The first 100ft. of rock was described as not above reproach but beyond this it became indescribably bad. Part of an overhang crumbled away under the leader leaving him hanging by his hands. As soon as a piton could be inserted, the last man climbed all the way round and lowered a rope for the other two to complete the last 80ft. (Now graded E2).

Mike was a major player in the development of winter climbing in the early 1950s. His first new route in the mountains was Scarface on Lochnagar, climbed with Patey and Goggs Leslie on a cold December day in 1951. The cliff was snow-free at the time so the ascent was deemed a rock climb. The next month he was back on Lochnagar to climb an icy Gargoyle Chimney with Brooker and over the following few winters he was involved in the first winter ascents of The Stack on Lochnagar (with Leslie and Leslie Fallowfield), Scorpion on Carn Etchachan (with Patey, Ken Grassick and Graeme Nicol), North West Gully on Creag an Dubh-loch (with Patey, Brooker and Johnny Morgan), Eagle Ridge on Lochnagar (with Patey and Brooker) and Eagle Buttress (with Brooker).

On The Stack he led the whole route. It was a real tour-de-force for the time

with all the rock coated in deep wind blown snow. At the exposed left traverse he solved a hard move by inserting the pick of his Grivel axe into a crack. 'Because of the beautiful thinness of the pick, I used it torquing horizontally on the key passage.' He had found his cherished axe on the Innominata Ridge of Mont Blanc at the site of the Bivouac Eccles. The shelter had been destroyed by stone-fall a few days before, killing the two occupants. His mother hated him using this axe of 'woeful provenance' and offered to buy a replacement – naturally at that age, the offer was spurned. Mike and Tom used their axes without the wrist sling. 'At difficulties we put the axe down behind the straps of the sack or just stuck the pick in a convenient bit of snow and climbed with free hands.'

After Eagle Buttress he made three further new winter routes, the crest route on Raeburn's Buttress (Ben Nevis, 1959) with Brooker, Inverlael Gully (Beinn Dearg, 1963) with Nicol and Patey, and False Gully (Creag an Dubh-loch, 1964) with Grassick and Bill James. The latter (led by Grassick) he found very hard and later said he couldn't understand why Kenny had given it such a soft rating of Grade IV.

Away from the coast Mike made some 20 new rock climbs mostly in the Cairngorms, but also at Applecross where in 1952/53 he and other Aberdonians explored the north buttresses of Sgùrr a' Chaorachain (North Wall Route and

Jupiter) and Meall Gorm (Cobalt Buttress). Some of his best known climbs in the Cairngorms are Parallel Gully B, The Clam and Route 2 on Lochnagar; The Black Tower in Coire Sputan Dearg, Sticil Face on the Shelter Stone Crag and Squareface on Beinn a' Bhuird. His last new rock climb was the Wee Devil on Hell's Lum Crag, climbed with Patey in 1961.

Mike had three short alpine trips in consecutive years. In July 1951 he and Patey visited Arolla and Zermatt climbing some of the higher peaks including the Zinal Rothorn and the Matterhorn. The following year they were part of the Aberdeen contingent based in Chamonix. Here they made a number of ascents on the Aiguilles before crossing to Courmayeur to traverse Mont Blanc via the Innominata Ridge (where he found the axe). In 1953 he returned to Chamonix for sterner challenges finding success with the Ryan-Lochmatter route on the Blaitière, the République Arête on the Charmoz and the Arête Sans Nom on the Aiguille Verte.

He joined the Club in 1954, the same year that work commenced on a climber's guide to the Cairngorms. Initially, he assisted during the exploratory stages but thought it unrealistic in his final year of medicine to attempt any more than that. Patey and Mac Smith carried out the bulk of the work, with Smith left to edit and write it all up in his two-volume guide published by the Club in 1961/62. In 1955 Mike graduated, then spent a year in English hospitals before serving for two years in the R.A.M.C. in Germany. He then did 18-months' training in Aberdeen before joining the Peterhead Group Medical Practice, where marriage, three children and an interesting job pushed climbing further into the background. He served on the Club committee from 1967–70.

In the early 1960s Mike was involved in a sobering accident with Sidney Wilkinson while attempting a winter ascent of his own route, Scarface on Lochnagar. This experience had a lasting effect and henceforth he concentrated his winter activities on ski mountaineering. In the winter of 1978 he completed the first crossing of the Scottish Haute Route from Crathie to Fort William with his good friend David Grieve.

I first met Mike in February 1974. It was late afternoon at Allt-na-giubhsaich. He and Derek Pyper had just completed a ski tour over Lochnagar and Rob Archbold and I were relaxing with a mug of tea having climbed Eagle Ridge. I distinctly remember how enthusiastic and full of praise he was about our climb yet he never once mentioned he had been on the first winter ascent 21 years previously. For many years he was a stalwart on the Aberdeen table at the Dinner and after these annual events moved to the Highlands, he often provided a warm welcome at his house in Aviemore. In the early 1990s he enjoyed a taste of some old pleasures with younger climbers Niall Ritchie and Jaz Hepburn. On one occasion, prior to the 1992 Dinner in Kingussie, he accompanied a few of us on an ascent of The Honeypot in Coire an t-Sneachda. Now in his sixties and not having done any winter climbing for years he was completely unfazed by the climb. Afterwards he said: 'Ski mountaineering is great – and as hard as you like – but it is not quite the same!'

Around the time of the Millennium, his gatherings at Aviemore on the Friday evening before the SMC Dinner became a regular occurrence, these latterly being referred to as the 'pre dinner dinner'.

In 2007 Mike suffered a terrible blow with the death of his wife Dot (Dorothy Murison). He sold his house in Peterhead and moved to Yorkshire to be close to his son, Colin and his family. He kept the house in Aviemore and spent a lot of time there with family and friends. There were a number of very enjoyable evenings, looking at slides, reminiscing and supping the amber nectar. In May last year he became very ill and entered hospital in Yorkshire. He wrote to me at the time: 'I have cancer in my spine for which I embark on radio and chemo therapy – ouch! If it works I hope we can have a wee meet of the distilled Aberdeen SMC coterie towards the end of the year. I would enjoy that.'

He died peacefully in Easingwood, North Yorkshire on 7 November 2014, aged 84.

Mike was a proud, modest Buchan loon who had 60 happy years with the Club. In his younger days he was an outstanding mountaineer but work and family became more important. He said a retirement accolade from his 10 young partners that he had run the 'busiest and happiest' practice in Scotland meant more than any small print in a guide book.

He is survived by his three sons, Neil, Colin and Graham to whom we extend our sympathies.

Greg Strange

Derek Pyper writes: my first encounter with Mike Taylor was in 1962 when I had just joined the Club. The friendly voice at the other end of the phone line was Mike asking if I would care to accompany him to the Club Dinner in Edinburgh.

I had never met Mike but I certainly knew of his exploits with Patey, Brooker, Nicol and Grassick – hallowed names to young climbers in the North-east. So, with great alacrity, I accepted his kind offer and have never regretted it.

Most of Mike's best climbing was done in the 1950s, but in the 1960s, although still climbing he became increasingly interested in skiing– particularly ski-mountaineering. We had both pottered around on Norwegian light skis, touring in lower Deeside and over some of the Glen Shee hills, but he had spent many days under the tutelage of Adam Watson and David Grieve and became proficient on all sorts of terrain. I, on the other hand, looked on skis just as a means to reach the more remote winter climbs in the Cairngorms.

It was meeting, at Club Dinners, people like Bill McKenzie, Malcolm Slesser and Alan McNicol, who told us both, that in order to get the most pleasure out of skiing in the mountains, it was essential to learn to ski. Up until then we had both studiously avoided ski areas with their 'crammage of humanity'.

We were also advised to buy Alpine skis and bindings which were suitable, for the piste and hill. Tales of skiing from hut to hut in the high Alps and whizzing down long, pristine slopes convinced us that this was the way forward. So, at Mike's insistence, we often headed for Glen Shee and practised, up and down all day without a stop – it was often like that with Mike. Getting your money's worth was the order of the day. Long ago you could do that at Glen Shee!

His mountaineering ability, added to this new-found skill, made him a formidable ski-tourer. Long touring days ensued all over Scotland, particularly in the Cairngorms, where his knack of working out great traverses employing the use of two cars was something we all benefited from.

He was very proud of the multi-day Scottish Haute Route which he completed with David Grieve in 1978, but it was the Alpine ski-touring that he really enjoyed. He felt it was an extension of his Alpine mountaineering in the 1950s when he climbed some of the classic routes in Chamonix, which gave him an appetite for the high-mountain environment.

Many of Mike's Alpine trips combined piste skiing with his wife, Dorothy, and touring with Club members. A trip to the Silvretta region of Austria accounted for the ascents of the Piz Tasna, Gems Spitze, Jam Spitze, Gross Piz Buin and the Silvrettahorn – crossing numerous cols on the way.

A visit to Norway with David Grieve gave him the opportunity to ski over some of the high peaks of the Jotenheim, but, his heart was in the Alps. So it was with an Aberdeen/Glasgow party he skied the classic Haute Route from Chamonix to Zermatt climbing on route the Aiguille du Tour, Rosablanche and the Pigne d'Arolla.

Then a few years later, with roughly the same party, he made a traverse of the Vanoise from Pralognan to Val d'Isère climbing Mont Pelve, Pointe du Dard, Pointe de la Réchasse, Sommet de Bellecôte and the Pointe de la Vallaisonnay.

Expeditions farther afield found him on Mount Kenya, Mera Peak in Nepal and ski-touring in Svalbard, Spitzbergen.

Mike was always studying maps and guide-books for different ways to enjoy being in the hills. One night, in Aviemore, Naill Ritchie, Jas Hepburn and myself were enjoying his generous hospitality when he hit us with a scheme – the Tour de Cairngorms on mountain bikes. He craftily caught us at a weak moment.

This involved starting from the house and heading for Bynack Stables, over the Larig an Laoigh, down Glen Derry to the Linn of Dee, up Glen Dee, through Glen Feshie and back to Aviemore. We took 12 hours and we all agreed it was one of the best days in the Cairngorms we had enjoyed. All the glorious aspects in one fell swoop. Nowadays, our mode of transport would probably incur the wrath of Cairngorm purists (quite rightly so), but we were a lot younger and it seemed like a good idea at the time.

Mike completed the Munros in 1984 with a ski tour over Càrn Gorm accompanied by about dozen friends who joined him for a celebration party in Speyside. It was appropriate that his final Munro was done on ski for it was always his intention to ski as many of them as possible.

I've always thought that the Club really missed out with his lack of Journal contributions, but he did write the occasional book review, and to get an inkling of his sense of humour, read his take on 'Ski Mountaineering in Scotland', *SMCJ*, 34/179 (1988), 179.

Mike will be well remembered for his easy-going friendliness, enthusiasm and for always being first up in the morning and rarin' to go – no matter what the weather.

Graeme Nicol writes: I first met Mike Taylor, albeit unknowingly when I watched an Aberdeen University Lairig Club party climbing the original route on the Black Spout Pinnacle in June 1952. The leader climbed very neatly and elegantly and I later learned his identity. I was not at that time aware that by the year's end I would climb with Mike on the first ascent of Scorpion on Carn Etchachan, and on a very stormy ascent of Tower Ridge on Nevis. We were two ropes of two: myself and Tom Patey, Mike and Bill Brooker. Bill and Mike spoke to each other throughout as they imagined an Alpine Club duo would have done in Victorian times.

Much of my most enjoyable climbing with Mike was on the sea cliffs near Peterhead. A day's climbing would be followed by a visit to the Blue Toon where Mike's parents were extremely hospitable and in later years Mike entertained in his own home.

PETER BILSBOROUGH J. 1982

Peter Bilsborough died on 15 January 2015, aged 63, after a short illness from cancer. He was born in Warrington but took up a PE post at Daniel Stewart's College in Edinburgh in 1975. From there he moved to the still relatively new Stirling University in1978, where he would remain for the next 36 years. Over that time he witnessed and influenced major developments in sport at the University. By the time he was appointed Director of Sports Development in 2001, he had helped in establishing the National Tennis Centre, the Women's National Football Academy and the National Swimming Academy on campus. Partly in recognition of his commitment to the latter he was invited to write the centenary history of Scottish swimming. He established a sound working relationship with the Scottish Institute of Sport and the Commonwealth Games Council for Scotland, both of which were housed on the University campus. It came as no surprise when Stirling was chosen by the Scottish Government to be Scotland's University for Sporting Excellence, in 2008. Simultaneously, the Scottish Funding Council awarded £500,000 to Stirling for an expansion of its sports scholarships scheme. Peter was the administrator of the resulting Winning Students' scheme which is open to talented sportsmen and women at Scottish universities and colleges. A growing number of students have been successful at Commonwealth, European and Olympic level. He taught courses in the Department of Sports Studies which was established in 1999.

Peter's professional interests were not limited to sport at the University. He played a very active role in Stirling District Sports Council from its inception in 1981 and helped to develop the most extensive community access arrangements of any Scottish university. He was a prominent member of the Scottish Physical Education Association, including the role of editor of its journal for twelve years.

Peter was an enthusiastic climber in summer and winter but the time he could commit was constrained by his teaching and administrative duties at the University and elsewhere. He and his family were passionate cyclists, and they spent holidays cycling throughout France and Spain.

A close colleague Raleigh Gowrie, paid tribute to him – 'His love of sport was contagious, from supporting the University football club to mountaineering, rock-climbing and cycling. I feel very lucky to have worked alongside such a warm and caring man.'

He is survived by his wife Ellen, and children Ruth, Easton, and Amy.

Ian Thomson

Neil Morrison writes: Pete Bilsborough was someone who put everything into whatever he did. He joined the University of Stirling as its first Graduate Assistant in the Sport and Physical Recreation Service and was a key player in building it into the renowned School of Sport it is now, holding a number of posts until becoming Director of Sports Development and School Manager in the School of Sport. Posts like this can sound like huge administrative posts and I am sure that aspect was never far away however Pete was a leader who lead by his actions whether coaching, organising or participating (with his runs up Dumyat from the University Campus being at the extreme end of that). In addition to leading the School of Sport Pete was a key player in Scottish Swimming from the grass roots level of coach right up to Board member. Pete was also a husband to Ellen and a father to Ruth, Easton and Amy.

The Pete I knew was in the very first years of his time at Stirling University when he became a central member of the Stirling posse of the late 1970s and early '80s. He had moved from Edinburgh and quickly hooked up with the motley crew that included Ian Duckworth, Geordie Skelton, Rhod Stewart, Bob Duncan and others. It struck me from early on that while the rest of us used to get the runaround and wind ups from Duckworth all the time Pete didn't and I can only assume that it was due to his calm but firm nature and his own very sharp wit. I also suspect, but cannot confirm, that he had put it to Ian that despite his diminutive height he was not a man to trifle with. Pete would bide his time and then unleash his wicked sense of humour. In the days when, as grown men, we would stop off in Berwick at the joke shop on our way to Northumberland Pete was not averse to buying products to use on the occupants of the other car, or even better, Edinburghers. Itching powder in the socks was a favourite.

On the rock Pete was a fantastic technician and watching him climb was a pleasure. His gear was racked meticulously and his progress never seemed rushed or flustered even when fighting some hideous crack on some Northumberland moor. During the early 1980s we travelled far and wide in both summer and winter and climbing with Pete was a key part of my apprenticeship as the coaching and teaching skills he was already using in his job naturally came out on the crags and in the mountains. They perfectly complimented the wilder approaches of others. Sometimes people can be compared to the cars they drive and Pete was a Saab driver in the days when they were very solid, durable and a little bit different – though not extravagant. Towards the mid 1980s Pete met Ellen, a local primary teacher, and his time became more focussed on their relationship and his work and we saw less of him though we too grew up and moved on or away.

Pete was a great guy and friend and many memories stand out for me, Blue Riband in Glen Coe, The Moon at Gogarth and the run in Pete and Ian had with the gun wielding farmer at Longhaven. They were special times and Pete was a special guy. Our thoughts are with his wife Ellen and three children, Ruth, Easton and Amy, at this time.

SAMUEL LAIRD GALBRAITH J. 1975

I met Sam through the GUM Club, and right away enjoyed his sharp intellect; he could give as good as he got, with embellishments. Sam was born in Clitheroe, Lancashire on 18 October, 1945. The family later moved to Greenock when he was a child, and Sam considered himself Scottish thereafter. His professions in medicine and politics have been well covered elsewhere, and here we concentrate on his mountaineering. As anyone who has ever climbed with medics would agree, their busily constrained life style usually includes last minute, late night plans, often following a hard day at the medical front. I proposed Sam for the club but did little climbing with him, usually meeting him in a Byres Road pub;

accordingly the accounts here have been garnered from his earlier climbing partners Ewan Macdonald and Andrew Bradley, and of course his wife Nicola, for whom many thanks. Sadly, Sandy Reid, a third climbing partner, long friend and SMC member, died suddenly in February 2013, with Sam writing his obituary for that year's journal.

Other than an early ascent of Ben Nevis in 1955 aged nine, his mountain activities began in the mid-1960s, initially with the popular big Munros east and west, winter or summer. This climaxed in September 1974, when he made a traverse of the Cuillin Ridge in poor conditions, with constant rain from Banachdich on, leading most of the way. Winter hills included, often with Ewan, Liathach, Tower Ridge and the Aonach Eagach. Rock and ice took off in 1967, initially climbing with Ewan Macdonald. In these far-off days, until Spike and Sudsy opened Nevisport in Fort William, gear was sparse. During their holidays, Sam and Ewan were both medical students at the Belford Hospital in Fort William. This obviously provided them with endless opportunities for rock climbing on Polldubh and Garbh Bheinn initially, while the frequent arrival of injured climbers at A&E was not discouraging, as Sam had been scrambling for some time, and Ewan had climbed the Douglas Boulder aged 13, thanks to Dr John Berkeley, who was the CIC Custodian from 1955–67.

Like many a young climber, the pair had very little gear but lots of brass neck, so winter climbing on Nevis was soon taken up. The first real outing was the easy, Grade 1 Red Gully. They were accompanied by a very nice Indian medical resident, who was keen to join them. Sam of course reassured him that it would be no bother at all. Sam had sourced for Ewan an ancient, broken ice axe which had a hugely impressive pick. This was useful for embedding in turf but not much else, and Ewan had it reshafted. Sam was proud of his slightly more modern, long metal axe. Bendy boots of course were then the norm, sourced in ex-Army and Navy stores but at least they had the essential Commando soles. Until then, they had been climbing in old, second-hand and poorly fitting hobnailers.

Ewan had woolly jumpers, but Sam was better dressed with an old, scruffy Harris tweed jacket. This he wore for years on all formal occasions, climbing, parties, the pub, bed, though Ewan thinks that he did remove it when he entered the operating theatre.

The Red Gully expedition set off on a warm spring day. Their Indian colleague was wearing his suit, overcoat and shoes, but he was kept in the middle. The route was completed by pulling him up with the usual body and ice axe belays in soft snow, and to eventually emerge into a brilliantly warm sunset was a magic moment for all three.

Following this triumph (to call it an ice breaker would not be accurate given the conditions on the day), Sam and Ewan decided to attempt Gardyloo Gully, using the same gear but without their colleague. Ewan had an old PVC fishing jacket and jeans, but Sam had his faithful tweed jacket and also a cagoule, as by now he was winning all the student prizes and had more money for such luxuries.

Sam was also able to afford an ice dagger, which enjoyed a brief and exciting following by the few. It was bought with a discount from Nevisport, who by then had their first shop at the top of the Pier Brae. Ewan was unable to buy one, and made good instead with one of his mother's better kitchen knives. From who knows where Sam obtained an old hemp rope with a dubious past and terminal exhaustion, and the intrepid pair launched themselves onto an unsuspecting Ben Nevis. The long approach to Gardyloo Gully finally found them on the final pitch, and Sam began to cut steps up this through the spindrift. Communication was rapidly extinguished until the rope ran tight and Ewan followed, useless ice dagger put away and kitchen knife stowed between his teeth. Existing steps helped ensure the pair's survival from this baptism and a triumphant and relieved exit before surprised walkers on the summit.

Bachelor medics being what they are, on another occasion a ceilidh in Arisaig with much liquid refreshment led to a 3 a.m. arrival in the Fort via some graceful 360° spins on an icy road. Undaunted, the hungover duo had decided to attack the long-suffering Ben again; soft, slushy snow and impaired well-being delaying a finish to their gully until a dusk arrival at the summit secured a fittingly atmospheric finish. Then followed a comedic realisation that neither had packed a compass. A careful roped descent aiming for the Red Burn saw them reach Steall at about 10 p.m., with the car at the golf course. By this time the rescue had been notified, but assuming that the doughty pair were 'experienced and well-equipped,' it was decided to wait it out. Their eventual return to Ewan's mother's kitchen saw a big dram and food, served under a huge cloud of embarrassment.

Like many a GUM club member, Sam eventually segued into the SMC and began attending the CIC Meets on Nevis. These were classic times, spoiled only by bad weather and the occasional lack of a hut key. Such as the time when hearing that Ken Crocket had a key and was due on the meet, Sam, Ewan and Sandy Reid took to the furrowed bogs starting at the golf course at about 10 p.m. as usual. The hut was forlornly empty and locked however, so Sam and Sandy bivvied in the snow while Ewan, who had only a survival bag, perched upright in the old radio hut. Older members will recall this as the one which mysteriously appeared one day, bricked onto the gable end. Crocket meanwhile (who himself has spent some happy hours in the same upright condition), turned up the next morning, having spent the night more comfortably elsewhere. When they met, and with the weather continuing grim, the bivouackers had had enough and went down.

Between 1979 and 1983, Sam and Andrew enjoyed a stream of classic rock climbs round Scotland, including Swastika on the Trilleachan Slabs in August 1979, and South Ridge Direct on Cir Mhor in superb September weather the same year. As an unprotected second on the traverse of 'The Moustache' of Swastika, Sam was mightily relieved to gain the belay, though the climbing was well within his ability. Hammer was also climbed.

Sam introduced Andrew to ice climbing, who found that since the skills needed were similar to rock climbing, he was able to help Sam complete some of the winter classics that he thought were beyond him and Sandy. The highlight was probably an ascent of Point Five Gully, in late April and probably in 1981 or '82. The two climbed this from the CIC Hut and were first on the route, finishing in the midday sun. Sam was ecstatic, it had been a route he had long aspired to, and he was very proud of having climbed it. There were also trips to the Alps and a Himalayan visit in 1985, not forgetting skiing and running.

As we know, Sam had a strong social conscience, and so with the view that he could help more, in 1987 he was elected Labour MP (Westminster) for Strathkelvin and Bearsden. He married Nicola the same year. Then a carefully planned ambush of the chair of the Scottish Sports Council by Hamish McInnes, Eric Langmuir, Sam Galbraith and Michael Forsyth led to funding being made available for the Scottish Avalanche Information Service. Two years later, he was diagnosed with fibrosing alveolitis, a rare genetic condition from which an elder sister had died. In 1990, with days to live, he received a lung transplant at the

Freeman Hospital, Newcastle. Continuing in politics after recovery, his main political chance came after ten years in opposition with promotion in 1997 to health and sports minister in the Scottish Office under Donald Dewar. This was followed in 1999 with a position in the first Scottish Cabinet as Education Minister, and latterly in 2000 as Environment, Sports and Culture Minister.

Sam retired from frontline politics in 2001 to concentrate on his family and his health. At that point the chairman of the British Medical Association's Scottish council said his greatest contribution as a minister had been to gain political acceptance of the links between poverty and bad health, hitherto resisted by governments. In 2006–14 he was Chairman of the Scottish Maritime Museum, on the Clyde. A modest family yacht provided real-life knowledge of the sea.

It may well be that mountaineering, with its numerous challenges, provided extra courage and will to live for Sam. As an early lung transplant patient, he was given a 50% chance of five years to live; he survived almost five times that, dying with an infection at Glasgow's Western Infirmary on the 18 August 2014. Sam is survived by his wife Nicola Tennant and three daughters, Mhairi, Heather and Fiona.

Ken Crocket

Alfie Ingram writes: Samuel Laird (Sam) Galbraith was one of that small group of remarkable people who combined outstanding careers in medicine with a passion for the hills. Although born in Clitheroe, Lancashire (18 October 1945) Sam was brought up in Scotland after his family moved to Greenock, his early education being at Greenock High before moving on to Glasgow University where initially he studied religion, which was quickly dropped in favour of medicine, obtaining an honours degree in that subject in 1968. Other achievements quickly followed becoming a Fellow of the Royal College of Surgeons in 1975, a consultant in 1977 aged only 32, proving to be a neurosurgeon of outstanding ability. Despite being a brilliant neurosurgeon Sam turned to politics, through which he believed, he could help more people than he ever would as a surgeon, and in 1987 he was elected Labour MP (Westminster) for Strathkelvin and Bearsden. After ten years in opposition he had his reward in 1997 when he became health minister in the Scottish Office under Donald Dewar, where Sam showed he was the ideal man to affirm basic principles and restore morale in the NHS through investment in hospitals and frontline services. In 1999 Sam became a founding member of the new Scottish parliament, in which he was given the position of Education Minister in the first Cabinet. A notably feisty parliamentarian it was not unknown for him to use colourful language on occasion. In the midst of all this activity, at the age of 44, he was diagnosed with fibrosing alveolitis (a hardening of the lungs), and with days to live received a lung transplant at the Freeman Hospital, Newcastle, after which, with typical Galbraith fortitude, Sam defied all the odds to become later recognised as the world's longest surviving lung transplant patient.

However, the challenge to health of pursuing a highly active political career was to became too great, and in March of 2001 Sam left politics, to return to Glasgow University this time in a teaching capacity. The University subsequently recognised his achievements by awarding him an honorary Doctorate. In addition to his teaching commitments Sam became Chair of the Scottish Maritime Museum in 2006, a position he held with distinction until 2014.

It would seem that all of the above would leave little time for other interests or activities, but Sam was an avid mountaineer developing his passion for the hills from an early age through the Scouting movement. Sam's most active climbing period was in the late 1960s early 1970s – the so called second 'Golden Age of Scottish Climbing Exploration' – and although he summited many of Scotland's mountains he is not recorded as a Munro 'compleater' probably because he had a penchant for tackling 'pushing to the limit' climbing routes mostly as lead or solo, notably with scant regard for the worst conditions (both summer and winter) that Scotland could muster. Initially a member of the Glasgow University Mountaineering Club (GUMC) Sam became a member of the Scottish Mountaineering Club (SMC) in 1975, and continued to enhance his expertise and experience through expeditions to both the Alps and Himalayas.

However, the time constraints of his medical and subsequent political professions, but in particular his health difficulties greatly limited Sam's opportunities to venture into the hills. Sam had no direct involvement at any time with mountain rescue, but in his role as health minister he looked favourably on the service. Although much of his neurosurgical work was carried out in the Glasgow Southern General, as a young surgeon Sam opted initially to work in Fort William to be closer to the hills. In later life he said he did not miss politics at all, but still looked with longing at the hills he could no longer climb.

PROCEEDINGS OF THE CLUB

At the Committee Meeting of October 2014, the following mountaineers were admitted to membership of the Club. We welcome:

SARAH H ATKINSON (50), Book-keeper, Farr, Inverness.
ALISTAIR W M BARNARD (46), ROV Pilot Technician, Nairn, Morayshire.
ROBERT WATT (47), Business Manager, Errol, Perthshire.

And at the Meeting of April 2015:

HUGH F BARRON (55), Chartered Geologist, Edinburgh.
ADRIAN CROFTON (44), Doctor of Medicine, Aberdeen.
UISDEAN HAWTHORN (24), Joiner, Glenelg, Inverness-shire.
FIONA MURRAY (49), Civil Servant, Aviemore.
M IAIN THOW (56), Walking Guide, Castleton Hope Valley, Derbyshire.

The One-Hundred-and-Twenty-Sixth AGM and Dinner
6 December 2014

2014 found the Club back in Fort William for the 126th AGM. The weather on Saturday was appalling and this helped swell the numbers at the afternoon talks. First up was a film from Andy Tibbs guiding us through the development and training Davie Moy needed to undertake to create a committing and technical traverse route at Inverness outcrop, Ashie Fort, (2 feet off the ground). This was followed with slides and some video at somewhat higher altitudes of climbs and adventures in the Indian Himalaya by an SMC team including Steve Kennedy and Des Rubens.

The AGM followed and was typically business like. To move with the times the club does expect to make more use of Facebook although it was recognised that many members may need training. The SMC Journal had just been distributed but the additional cost of using Cordee to undertake this exercise has meant that it is possible that a team from the club will undertake this task in future.

The Archivist reported that he was pleased to find an early visitors book for Ossian's Cave dating from the 1930s.

One issue that did generate concern and discussion amongst members was how accountable the Trust was to the club. Legally the Trust must report to the Charities Commission but the feeling within the club was that we should, at least, be able to comment on how the Trust conducts its business.

The AGM closed with the Secretary announcing that it is hoped that the next Dinner and AGM will be in Carrbridge.

The Dinner progressed well. The food was fine, the wine flowed and the only problem was that the Guest Speaker, Stephen Venables, was unable to attend. Due to his late call off, no alternative speaker was asked, although John Fowler did bring out a 125th Club Anniversary Quiz, the Club Song had more verses and a rendition of Dark Lochagar and two more songs were added by Curly Ross. So none of us should feel short changed.

The Dinner ended with the outgoing President, John Mackenzie, handing over the presidential memorabilia to new President, Noel Williams.

Fort William provided more wet weather on Sunday and those who wished joined the President's walk in Glen Nevis for a guided geology tour. This had one of the largest turnouts for a President's walk that I can remember. Once the tutorial was over, the class retired to the hotel for final coffee and drinks before we dispersed for our respective journeys home.

Chris Huntley

Lakes Meet, Robertson Lamb Hut, Langdale
5–7 September 2014

The Lake District Meet is now a regular and popular event in the Club's calendar and 12 Members and 6 guests once again gathered in the Wayfarers Club's excellent Robertson Lamb Hut in Greater Langdale. The fine weather that had characterised the late summer of 2014 persisted over the weekend and attendees enjoyed blue skies and wall to wall sunshine. As a consequence, the fells and crags saw a great deal of activity. The full gamut of climbing difficulty was tackled from Diff to E1 and climbs completed over the weekend included:- Bracket & Slab, The Purple Edge, Asterisk, Whit's End (Gimmer Crag); Holly Tree Crack, Flarepath (Helm Crag, Grasmere); Capella, Venus (Pavey); Direct Route (Castle Rock); Slip Knot (White Ghyll); Baskerville, Mamba, Ophidia (East Raven); Ewelogy, Me, Sheepish, Shaun (Birk Knott Crag); West Buttress, Route 2 (Tarn Crag). One Member remarked that it was the best weekend of trad climbing he had had for many a year. Others at various times stravaiged over Pike of Blisco, Cold Pike, Crinkle Crags, Bowfell and Side Pike. As ever, the highlight of the weekend was the multi-course dinner, complete with fine wines and whisky, provided by Dick Allen and prepared by Dick and his able assistants. It is a measure of Dick's largess that several of the more elderly attendees were obliged to demand a small portion of the main course rather than the yard and a half of Cumberland sausage that is Dick's usual per person unit. The Lakes Meet is always an enjoyable and convivial affair and that, in no small measure, is down to Dick Allen's efficient organisation and quiet good humour. His efforts were much appreciated by all present.

Members present: Hamish Brown, Andy James, Robin Campbell, Jane Murdoch, Stuart Murdoch, Colin Simpson, Simon Fraser, John Wood, Gordon MacNair, Jim Beaton, Dick Allen, David Stone.

Guests: Pete Bettess, Ian Gray, Max Biden, Bernard Newman, Jan Newman, Maureen Suess.

David Stone

Lake District Meet – September 2014

Back row (L. to R.): Hamish Brown, Pete Bettess (guest), Andy James, Ian Gray (guest), Robin Campbell, Max Biden (guest), Jane Murdoch, Bernard Newman (guest), Jan Newman (guest), Stuart Murdoch, Colin Simpson.

Front row (L. to R.): Simon Fraser, John Wood, Maureen Suess (guest), Gordon MacNair, Jim Beaton, Dick Allen, David Stone. *Photo. David Stone.*

The Past Presidents' Lunch, Huntingtower Hotel, Perth, November 2014. Photo:JRRF.

Ski Mountaineering meet, Strawberry Cottage 20–21 February 2015

For the ski mountaineering meet 2015 we used the An Teallach Mountaineering Club Hut; Strawberry Cottage, near Athnamulloch in Glen Affric. Grid Ref: NH132207. Altitude 250m.

Access to the hut involves five miles of rough track which is motorable with care for cars, although 4x4s fare better. Snow chains were not required despite the complete snow cover. An access restriction on the number of cars allowed, meant that three athletic members had to use a good headtorch plus mountain bikes.

The earliest activity which could be linked with the meet was on Thursday 19 February. Chris Ravey and Chris Dickinson skied up the Corbett Meall Dubh (783m), an obvious choice for a foul weather day as it can be seen (cloud permitting) from Chris Dickinson's hot tub! They walked up into Coire Eoin and put skis on at around 530m. Skiing up into whiteout conditions and 60mph winds they achieved the summit, and by the time they got down the snow level had dropped down to about 480m. Thereafter, they beat a hasty retreat to the hot tub!

The evening of Thursday 19 February the advance guard of Chris R and Colwyn arrived at the car park GR NH201233, at the east end of Loch Affric at 2100hours. They transferred to a single car finally arriving at the hut by 2230hours. The hut facilities include lighting by solar power, a petrol-driven electric generator; cooking by gas; wood-burning stove with logs supplied. At this time of year the flush WC was not working, so water required to be carried in a bucket from the river 100 metres away. Any call of nature had to be carefully anticipated.

Next morning a leisurely start and high snow line saw them walk south up Gleann na Ciche as a magnificent Golden Eagle quartered the sky. At the end of the plantation they headed directly for the sporting ridge on the south side of the glen. Traversing Sail Chaorain (1002m) to finally arrive on the very windy and snowy summit of Sgùrr nan Conbhairean (1110m GR; NH129139). They did regret not having taken their skis with them, but enjoyed a gentle rolling descent in soft snow back to the floor of the glen and a reasonable, if wet walk finally arriving at the hut by 15:30. They stoked the stove to ensure the hut was suitably warm by the time the others arrived on the Friday night. Brian was first to arrive after cycling along the snowy track by moonlight, porterage of his gear having been negotiated in advance in Colwyn's 4x4 vehicle.

Navigation was an issue that night, but only to find the hut! As Bob cycled out of the car park he was casually asked, 'do you know the right route?' He replied, 'No, but Dave does,' before cycling off in the wrong direction, leaving an exasperated Dave to first shout, then cycle in pursuit.

Saturday 21 February: despite the low cloud and strong winds, Bob and Dave walked up the established footpath to the summit of Càrn Eighe. The north ridge out to Beinn Fionnlaidh was a temptation but time limited their ambition and they returned back along the ridge to Mam Sodhail and directly down the ridge to the path behind the hut. They recognised the ski tracks left by Moira, Adrian and Colwyn on their visit to Creag Coire nan Each (1055m) earlier in the day, where they had found enough snow for a reasonable ski descent despite being blasted by the strong winds.

John, Mandy, Stan and Des walked from the cottage NE to the bridge over the Allt Coire Leachavie. They then took the stalkers' path which rises under An Tudair Beag into the mouth of the hanging valley of Coire Coulavie. Able to put on skis just above the start of the stalkers' path at the entrance to the corrie, the snow was a little wet; they discussed options in light of wind, terrain and snow conditions. Continuing up the corrie for about a kilometre, they then headed for a poorly defined shoulder which drops eastwards from near point 1056m on the OS map, the Munro top Creag a' Chaoruinn. In improving weather, they reached an altitude of about 920 metres where they encountered the final steep summit slopes. Unfortunately, these slopes were loaded with windslab and little choice was presented other than retreat. They enjoyed skiing a fine line back to the floor of the corrie avoiding avalanche prone slopes. The snow proved to be rather heavy, so the skiing wasn't as effortless as had been hoped for – a common disappointment. However, all agreed they had enjoyed a fine mountaineering day out.

After a leisurely start, Chris Ravey headed straight up onto the east ridge of a small knoll called Creag a' Chaorainn, immediately north west of Strawberry Cottage. With skis on at 450m he linked snow patches onto the ridge and followed it up to around 900m. Observing great snow in the upper part of Spùtan a' Ghobhair he followed this snow filled watercourse all the way down to 400m, making a circumnavigation of Creag a' Chaorainn and Creag a' Bhalgain with good skiing and a Golden Eagle overhead for good measure.

Brian and Amy eschewed skiing on the Saturday morning and set off on foot for Coire Ghaideail on An Socach to investigate the east-facing part of the corrie lying north of the lochan. This foray was prompted by dialogue on social media between Andy Nisbet and earlier visitors to Strawberry Cottage in November 2014 when a grade II route was reported in the coire. The low cloud and snow obscured the geography of the coire during the approach but on reaching the lochan it became apparent there might be a number of short (1 pitch) routes on the lower crags. However, the cloud cleared and a buttress high up to the right leading onto the south ridge just south of the summit of An Socach offered a more tempting and worthwhile objective. On closer inspection, the buttress was found to be more broken but provided three short pitches (120m, Grade III), albeit with difficulties mainly confined to the lower section. A short chimney and icy groove provided the main interest of the route before a snow crest was reached, this being followed by steep snow leading to the south ridge at 850m. After a visit to the summit cairn of An Socach, Brian and Amy descended into the coire by steep snow south of their line of ascent to inspect the lower crags, closer to the lochan in the coire floor. Satisfied that they had made the optimum choice, they named the route Summit Buttress and then returned to the hut in the pleasant late afternoon sunshine.

Come dine with me on Saturday evening was spent with each team claiming that they, and only they, had enjoyed the best weather, snow, views and experience of the day in a competitive but genial and convivial evening.

Sunday 22 February: the forecast and experience of worsening weather meant that, helped by the fresh westerly wind everyone fled from the glen. Brian, Bob and Dave cycled out behind the cars with Brian reaching the car park shortly after the cars having been able to freewheel faster by bike on the snowy downhill sections! They then enjoyed morning coffee in the Tomich Hotel, before heading for home! Another successful Scottish Mountaineering Club Ski Mountaineering meet, and for once they didn't end up skiing at the pass of Drumochter yet again!

Members present: Colwyn Jones (convenor), Chris Dickinson, Adrian Hart, Stan Pearson, John Peden, Chris Ravey, Bob Reid, Des Rubens, Brian Shackleton.

Guests: Moira Baptie, Amy Goodill, Dave Howard, Mandy Peden.

Colwyn Jones

Easter Meet, Inchnadamph Hotel, Lochinver
9–12 April 2015

Members and guests returned to this well-known hotel with the surrounding hills still topped with snow and looking magnificent in the clear sunlight. A fine forecast augured well for the Meet: three days filled with a variety of pursuits which included climbing, scrambling and walking. Most of the north-west summits were re-visited including Stac Pollaidh, Suilven, An Teallach, Quinag, Meall Coire an Lochain, Meallan Liath Bheag, Cul Mòr, Arkle, Cranstackie, Beinn Spionnaidh, Ben Mor Coigach, Ben Hope, Ben Stack, An Socach, Càrn Gobhar (Mullardoch), and Beinn Dearg (Atholl), many enlivened by winter conditions on northern slopes.

Climbs were made at Strone Crag, the Rock Garden and the inevitable Crag X, all very pleasant when out of the wind. Friday night's entertainment was provided by the President, Noel Williams, who gave an excellent presentation which starred a unique fossil, found by our member Dick Allen, when he was a boy. The research

Easter Meet 2015 – Inchnadamph

Standing (L to R): John Wood, Pippa Cocker, Mike Cocker, Bill McKerrow, John Fowler, Gordon Macnair, Dave Broadhead, John Hay, Phil Gribbon, Peter Biggar, Roger Robb, Simon Fraser, Peter Macdonald, Mike Watson, Raymond Simpson, John Mackenzie, Eve Mackenzie (guest), Colin Stead, Helen Forde, Cam Forrest, Cath Fryett (guest), Calum Anton (guest). Front row (L to R): Robin Chalmers, Geoff Cohen, Paul Brian, Noel Williams (President), Iain Smart (Hon President), Andy James, Lucy (guest), John Temple, Bob Aitken. Photo. David Stone.

behind this fascinating story was both engrossing and geologically instructive. Most of the company even after their day's exertions, fuelled by fresh air, food and drink, managed to stay awake.

On Saturday, lower temperatures and intermittent snow showers and sun saw more ascents, many members armed with ice-axes. The evening found the Club and guests sitting down to an excellent three course meal, the customary and long-lasting 'Malcolm Slesser' whisky flowing. John Hay presented John Fowler with a set of crystal whisky glasses in a stag-horn decorated holder as a 'thank you' for organising the Easter meets and to celebrate his twenty-five years as Honorary Secretary – Cheers!

Sunday dawned raw and windy as all set off homeward.

Present in the hotel were R Aitken, PV Brian, RDM Chalmers, MT Cocker, Pippa M Cocker, G Cohen, Helen GS Forde, C Forrest, JRR Fowler, S Fraser, JYL Hay, AM James, PF Macdonald, JRG Mackenzie, WS McKerrow, G Macnair, RJC Robb, GR Simpson, AC Stead, IHM Smart, D Stone, DN Williams (President), ML Watson and JA Wood.

Present at the Naismith Hut in Elphin were PJ Biggar, DJ Broadhead, PWF Gribbon, BG Hard and DJ Temple.

Our guests were C Anton, Cath Fryett and Eve Mackenzie.

Helen G S Forde

Skye Meet, Allt Dearg Cottage, Sligachan
9–16 May 2015

Apart from a couple of days the weather was generally very poor, but people were out most days. Dave Broadhead did Creag Mhòr, a Mailyn above Strome Ferry, on the way to Skye. Tom Prentice did A' Chralaig and Mullach Fraoch-choire in Glen Shiel on his way too. Noel Williams went down High Pasture Cave near Torrin with a group from the Lochaber History Society.

Sunday was grim, but Dave and Tom did Ben Lee above Sligachan. Monday was not much better, though Dave and Tom again braved the weather and bagged Beinn na Seamraig, another Marilyn, above the Kylerhea Road. John Temple, Cath Fryett and Noel visited the Old Man of Storr. Cath and Noel battled their way to the summit of The Storr in ferocious wind. They had enough trouble keeping their feet and so abandoned the idea of looking for a possible Colby Camp.

Tuesday was also unpleasant, though Dave and Tom bagged Arnaval above Gleann Oraid, and then from Talisker Bay bagged Biod Ruadh and returned via Sleadale Broch.

The weather improved on Wednesday, especially later on. John, Cath and Noel visited Raasay for the day and went in search of the amazing fissues[1] on the eastern side of the island. On the way they found a small crag on a desolate stretch of moorland packed with impressive fossils (Pecten). They also bagged Dun Caan before returning to Churchton Bay. Dave and Tom did the Coire Lagan Round integral. Raymond and Linda Simpson were also in the Cuillin and did Sgùrr a'

[1] Jim Salvona, *A Guide to the Awe-inspiring Raasay Fissures*, 2008.

Skye Spring Meet *L to R: Peter Wilson, Raymond & Linda Simpson, Alan Smith, Paul Brian, Robin Campbell and Peter Macdonald. Photo: Tom Prentice.*

Bhasteir and Sgùrr an Fhionn Choire. Peter Macdonald did Glas Bheinn Mhòr above Luib. Peter Wilson and Alan Smith did six routes at Moy on their way to Skye.

Thursday was the best day of the week and people took full adavantage. Dave and Tom did the Round of Coire a' Ghreadaidh. Raymond and Linda did the ridge from Sgùrr Dubh to Sgùrr Sgùmain and descended the stone shoot. Peter, Paul Brian and Robin Campbell only had a half-day outing (12hrs!). They crossed from Harta Corrie to Glen Brittle via Druim nan Ràmh and Coire a' Tairneilear. Alan and Peter did Snarg on Marsco.

Present: Paul Brian, Dave Broadhead, Robin Campbell, Cath Fryett (Guest), Peter Macdonald, Tom Prentice, Raymond Simpson, Linda Simpson (Guest), Alan Smith, John Temple, Noel Williams and Peter Wilson.

JMCS REPORTS

Edinburgh Section: May 2015: a funny time of the climbing year. Lots of climbable ice still lingers high on Ben Nevis but few people, if any, can shake off the seasonal impulse that one should be rock climbing now, even at the risk of fumbling with freezing fingers in the continuing low temperatures. Taking the opportunity of this seasonal interregnum to look back over the year of the Club, the winter season that has just ended afforded many opportunities for getting on the classic routes that formed so often in one's youth – the Curtain on the Ben, Deep Cut Chimney in Glen Coe, for example – but which seem only sporadically to appear in the UKC log books nowadays. Our annual winter trip to the CIC Hut was blessed with fine weather and good conditions; there is not a lot that beats a sunny late afternoon view from the summit of the Ben, with the complacent satisfaction of a route done and the prospect of a crisp walk back down Coire Leis for good company over a dram in the hut. Our summer meets took place in the usual mix of good and bad weather, not unusually on the same day; for instance in Glen Coe in June when those of us on the Etive Slabs basked in the sun while the unfortunates on the Rannoch wall endured intermittent blatters of rain and hail.

Lots of members have had climbing holidays abroad, in the Alps, at sun rock locations and further afield, including two separate trips to Denali. A specifically JMCS party had a week in Chamonix in July. These excursions do not necessarily encounter more settled weather than we find in Scotland, nor is the environment necessarily free of insect bother (mosquitoes rather than midges), but foreign trips do produce a fine varied crop of photos for the annual slide/digital image night. And it is not all climbing; this year we had everything from ski touring in Austria to mountain biking in California, with a bit of Scottish west coast kayaking thrown in.

Our annual dinner at the Kings House in November 2014 was enlivened by a thought provoking after dinner speech from our guest Robin Campbell. His thesis was that there is something of the social outcast – deviant, even – in every mountaineer. I don't think all of us were ready to accept that we lived at least partly beyond the pale, but Robin certainly stirred us up with his typically learned and eloquent speech. Our other guest for the evening was David Hughes, of the London JMCS, who was with Robin Smith on the first ascent of Yo-Yo all those years ago. It cannot be often nowadays that a club is privileged to have two of the great Smith's rope mates – Campbell and Hughes – as its guests and we were delighted that both of them had made the journey north to be with us.

If you are interested in joining the Edinburgh JMCS, we always welcome new faces. Please come along to our Monday or Wednesday night activities and meet and climb with some of the existing members. We go to Ratho on winter Wednesdays and Alien Rock on winter Mondays. During the summer we will be inside or out, depending on the weather; you can see where we are going by looking at our website which also lists our forthcoming weekend meets. Just Google 'Edinburgh JMCS'. It is probably best to contact Nils Krichel, the Membership Secretary, beforehand to make sure there has been no last minute change of venue.

Our huts are available for booking by kindred Clubs; please contact the Custodians whose names are shown below. We have the Cabin in Balgowan, between Laggan and Newtonmore, and the Smiddy at Dundonnell in the North West.

The present committee includes: Honorary President: John Fowler. President: Terry Lansdown. Vice President and Smiddy Custodian: Helen Forde (30 Reid Terrace, Edinburgh EH3 5JH, 0131 332 0071). Secretary: David Small (5 Afton Place, Edinburgh, EH5 3RB, <secretary@edinburghjmcs.org.uk>). Treasurer: Bryan Rynne. The Cabin Custodian: Ali Borthwick (01383 732 232, before 9 p.m. please). Membership Secretary; Nils Krichel <nils.krichel@gmail.com>.

David Small

Glasgow Section: despite the weather the Section had another very successful and busy year. The President is Philip Smith. Secretary, Charles Craig. Treasurer, Justine Carter. Meets secretary, Iain Sneddon. New members secretaries, Mark Gorin and Simon Taylor. Club membership currently stands at 92 members, consisting of 51 ordinary members and 41 life members. Three new members joined in 2014 and your humble author was elevated to life membership in 2014. The Section now has a Facebook page and everyone is invited to log on and if you choose join!

The New Members Secretary role is split between Mark Gorin and Simon Taylor. You should contact them if you want to go on a meet or find out more about the club <newmembers@glasgowjmcs.org.uk>. New members are welcome to come along to any of the club meets.

Reflecting the enthusiasm within the club, throughout 2014 there were 23 official weekend meets including the annual work meet to the fine club hut at Coruisk on the late May bank holiday where general maintenance and tree planting were undertaken and electric lighting was successfully installed. Coruisk provides simple, cheap and ferry accessible accommodation; see the website for details <http://www.glasgowjmcs.org.uk/coruisk.php> or to book the hut e-mail Coruisk Hut Bookings: Iain Sneddon <coruisk@glasgowjmcs.org.uk>.

Throughout the year JMCS meets were held across Scotland, the Lake District and in all 5 of the SMC huts. The indoor wall of the Glasgow Climbing Centre hosts an indoor Thursday night meet every fortnight, with cappuccinos available in the Balcony Café. Midweek meets are held to local rock climbing venues over the summer; see the website for details.

The annual general meeting and club dinner, where we had 25 diners, were again convened at the Kings House Hotel in Glen Coe on Saturday the 29th November 2014. The week before the AGM the president, Phil Smith, held his presidential bothy meet in the fine Resourie bothy in Ardnamurchan.

The substantial snow was a problem for many Scottish winter routes but two members succeeded on a wet winter traverse of the Skye Ridge with a wet overnight camp near Con's Cleft. Other routes included Poachers Fall, Salmon Leap and Sickle. The Easter trip staying in the Naismith Hut in Elphin, was very well attended with a memorable club traverse of Foinaven in clear, cold and brilliant weather.

A grand total of nine members were present at the traditional midsummer evening meet on the Cobbler. They climbed various classic rock routes in extraordinarily good weather before rising early to get to work the next day. The summer provided some good mountain route conditions with an ascent of The Steeple in September.

Overseas trips by members started early with off piste skiing in Chamonix, where conditions were better than expected in early January (22–26). February saw an ice climbing trip to Rjuken in Norway. The winter was continued with 5 members initiating a cross-country skiing meet to Levi in Finland (67° north and −20°C at night). Members summited on Levi 530m, Kätkätunturi 505m and Pyhätunturi 450m, enjoying excellent cross-country skiing, chilly conditions, reindeer, occasional rest, huts/reindeer skins and sausages, not to mention saunas and rolling naked in the snow etc… Later the Lyngen Alps saw a group ski mountaineering, ice climbing, mountaineering and perhaps the first ascent of a ridge in a little travelled part of the Lyngen alps.

The winter was completed with an April ski touring visit to the German speaking area of Alto Adige in Italy. Peaks included Schneefernerkopf (2875m), Gran Zebru or Konigspitze (3859m), Schwarzkogel (3016m) and Westliche Karwendelspitze (2385m).

During the summer the Ecrin Alps in July had a club group climbing and mountaineering with some success and Kullaberg in southern Sweden was explored confirming the potential for traditional sea cliff climbing. Contrary to the name, The Baltic was warm enough for swimming. The Valais Alps were visited in August and this included an ascent of the South ridge of the Lagginhorn. In October the President and Treasurer visited Sikkim, to trek to this remote area and scouted Kanchenjunga, also narrowly avoiding the tragic Annapurna storm. The end of the year saw a sport climbing trip to Costa Blanca.

Colwyn Jones

Lochaber Section: We had a busy programme of events over the year starting with a slide show from one of the members taking a look back at club outings, both at home and abroad since the 1970s, which was the spring board for many discussions over the evening. We continued the winter slide show series on a trip to Greenland with the breathtaking scenery and tales of some gripping ascents of impressive looking mountains, as well as an exciting dinghy trip up a fjord to access the expedition site.

Our weekend meets started with a trip to The Smiddy at Dundonnell where the snow line was well down even the smallest of hills in February, to being non-existent on all but the very highest of hills in March in the Northern Cairngorms. April saw a trip to Glen Clova which was very wet and cold followed by some nice summer weather in the southern Cairngorms near Braemar in June. In terms of weather and mountain scenery, Skye always trumps everywhere else. On an ascent of Pinnacle Ridge on Sgùrr nan Gillean during August, we left the car wearing T-shirts and sunglasses. Approaching the start of the ridge we had donned jackets to keep out the wind chill and by the top of the second pinnacle it was raining steadily and by Knight's Peak we had sleet and I am sure there was even some light flurries of snow by the time we reached the top. Scottish mountaineering at its best. During a meet to Elphin all present took advantage of some reasonable weather, including a traverse of Suilven with the top staying in the cloud until we had descended.

Steall Hut is proving popular as ever with individuals and groups taking advantage of the location in the middle of some very popular mountain terrain.

Kenny Fogo on the 'all weather' ascent of Pinnacle Ridge, Skye. *Photo: Iain MacLeod*

Having carried out a lot of work to the hut over the previous 12 months a meet was held for club members at the hut in July. During the weekend some maintenance was also carried out including decoration of the kitchen area. On a hot summer evening there cannot be many places that rival this location for quenching the thirst after a good day on the hill. Further information and contact details for Steall Hut can be found at <www.steallhut.co.uk>.

2014 was brought to a close for the club with our dinner weekend which was held in the Kinlochewe Hotel and again followed on after the club AGM. Many issues were discussed including increased costs for Steall Hut and membership numbers and fees. These are perennial issues that are brought up on a regular basis, but the meeting felt there was optimism on these topics with the club continuing to remain sure footed. After many years service to the club as treasurer, George Bruce decided it was time for the younger members to take over. The meeting unanimously accepted Ken Scoular as the new Treasurer, as he would have more time to carry out his duties seeing as he was due to retire. On behalf of the club I would like to thank George for his efforts in looking after the cash.

President: Phil Stevenson; Secretary: lain MacLeod, <ia.macleod@btinternet.com>; Treasurer: Ken Scoular; Hut bookings: Ewen Kay; Hut Custodian: John Matheson.

lain MacLeod

London Section: the highlight of the year was the Section dinner in November, hosted at the Ogwen Bank Caravan Park and Country Club, just outside Bethesda in North Wales. The dinner celebrated the 75th Anniversary of the founding of the London Association, the predecessor of the JMCS London Section, and the 50th Anniversary of the purchase of our club hut 'Glanafon'. We were delighted that Noel Williams from the SMC and Simon Fraser from the Lochaber Section could join us. It was also special that of the small group who instigated the purchase of Glanafon, Peter Whitechurch and Hugh Jordan were present as well as former members from across the years, with representatives from each generation that has climbed with the Section and enjoyed using the hut. Andy Hughes provided a musical accompaniment to songs sung back in the sixties. All in all it was a delightful evening of reminisces and re-kindling old friendships.

During the remainder of the year the best attended meets continued to be our winter and summer forays north of the border to Elphin in February and Coruisk in June although the weather was a little unkind on both occasions. David Hughes's catering for the winter meet was of the customary high standard, replenishing bodies made weary by snow and high winds. While the June meet witnessed a couple of unsuccessful attempts on the main ridge traverse a weather window did permit ascents of the Dubhs ridge.

Members were also active sailing in the Hebrides and climbing in the Austrian Alps. There was good rock climbing on meets at Pembroke in May, in Langdale at Easter, the Peak District in May and from our home base in Bethesda. Throughout the year, the active membership enjoyed long days in the hills.

At the end of 2014 membership stood at 42 with five additional life members.

Officers for 2015: President: John Howes; Secretary: John Firmin (telephone 0208 291 2141); Treasurer: David Hughes; Glanafon Hut Bookings: Rod Kleckham (telephone 01252 721049).

John Firmin

Perth Section: the Perth Section's membership remains healthy at 78 and new members continue to join regularly. A full and varied calendar was on offer this year with 21 scheduled meets including day and weekend meets, giving members a diverse choice of mountaineering pursuits including rock and ice climbing, skiing, Munro and Corbett ascending and mountain biking. There were numerous midweek meets to the Avertical climbing wall in Dundee and the newly opened Perth Grammar School wall through the winter. During the summer months club climbers visited local crags including old favourites, Polney, Tulliemet, Bennybeg, Aberdour, and Black Crag at Loch Ordie.

The Annual Joint Lecture with the Perth Society of Natural Sciences was again well attended, and was given by Hon. Member Robin Campbell. His lecture was entitled 'How London Drew the Highlands' – an investigation into the way the Highlands were painted by London Artists in the late 18th century. The President's Evening was held in the Royal George Hotel, and took the form of a photographic competition with five sections. The evening proved to be very popular with club members keen to show off their photographic skills.

The weather for the start of the year was not kind to the club with many meets drowned in rain, or blown off course by high winds. Nevertheless, in January the club paid its first visit to Lagganlia Lodge, Feshiebridge for its annual Burns Supper. This was attended by 18 members and was a great success. Severe weather conditions limited mountaineering activities, but several members battled their way to complete a circuit of Sgòr Gaoith and others walked up Ben Rinnes.

Difficult weather patterns continued for the following meets to Raeburn, Ling and Elphin which allowed lots of socialising on low level walks, beach and cave explorations, and rock scrambles. The camping meet to Mull was all but washed away, but having made the ferry crossing, camped in persistent rain, ascents of Dun da Ghaoithe, and Ben More had to be made in the dreich weather. The June meet was held at Sleeperzzz railway carriages in Rogart and the attendees were rewarded with glorious sunny days on Ben Klibreck, Càrn Ban and Càrn Chuinneag, with a little aid from mountain bikes.

Invercroft, Steall and Lagangarbh hut meets were well attended, and long summer's days were enjoyed on Airigh Charr, Moruisg and Sgùrr Nan Ceannaichean; The Ring of Steall, Grey Corries; Ben Starav, Beinn Fionnlaidh and Bidean nam Bian.

High winds returned for the October trip to Milehouse, where four members pedalled and pushed their bikes up the track, through heather and rivers to the top of Carn na Saobhaidhe.

The Annual Dinner was convened at The Moorings Hotel, Corpach, a new venue for the club. This turned out to be very popular as it provided an excellent base for access to a huge selection of hills including the Mamores, Grey Corries, and the many hills out towards Glenfinnan.

Members continued to venture further afield in the quest for new experiences and challenges, visiting Finestrat- Alicante, Axarquia- Costa del Sol, Dobbiaco- South Tyrol, Murcia- South Costa Blanca, Tiennes, Majorca, Patagonia, Banff, Bhutan and Nepal.

Two members completed their circuits of Corbetts this year. Mel Nicoll, accompanied by family and friends celebrated in the sunshine in June on Beinn Tarsuinn, Arran. Several club members accompanied Jeff Harris up his final Corbett, Mount Battock, on a dry but rather windy November's day.

In April this year Pam Cain, a longstanding member of the club sadly passed away, aged 97. Pam was active in the 1960s and '70s and retained her membership till the end.

Des Basset has now edited over fifty quarterly newsletters, continuing to keep us informed of meets and events future and past, and of members' activities further afield.

Officials elected at the AGM in 2013 were: President, Janice MacDonald; Vice President, Karen Murray; Secretary, Rob Wright, Meet Secretary, Paul Grace; Treasurer, Pamela Dutton; Newsletter Editor, Desmond Basset. Web Master, Phil Taylor; Committee, Richard Bott, Jeff Harris.

To contact the club, e-mail Sue James; <secretary@perthmountaineering-club.co.uk>.

Janice MacDonald

SMC ABROAD

MONT BLANC RANGE 2014

In August 2013, Tom Prentice and I set out to climb the crest of the unclimbed pillar in the centre of the East Face of Mont Greuvetta on the Italian side of the Mont Blanc Range. It was a striking line, but in the event we were sucked into the prominent line of corners defining its left edge. Casa Dei Gracchi (TD+) turned out to be an excellent climb, but it wasn't the crest of the pillar itself, and we knew that we would have to return.

The pillar became the key objective of last season's two-week trip to the Alps. Unfortunately the weather was very poor during the last two weeks of July and we were confined to low-level routes around the Envers Hut and in the Aiguilles Rouges. Luckily at the end of our second week, the weather forecast magically changed and a three-day weather window emerged. Casa Dei Gracchi had taken a full three days the previous year (one day each for the ascent, climb and descent), so we planned on a similar period for the pillar. We walked up to the Comino Hut in the rain, and set off in deep fog early next morning (31 July). Fortunately the cloud lifted, and unlike 2013 when our approach to a bivouac at the foot of the pillar took a full day, we were able to reach a similar point in half the time, so just after midday we set off up the pillar itself.

The route links the two-stepped ramps to join the crest of the upper pillar. From directly below, these looked undercut and very steep, and the route appeared very intimidating. But fortune was on our side, because as soon as we started the technical climbing the rock quality became superb with many hidden incut holds and chicken heads on otherwise blank sections. The climbing up the ramps was sustained with Tom leading a memorable section up a thin finger crack. Where the second ramp faded, there was a long intricate pitch weaving through hanging slabs leading to the easier upper crest. These pitches were amongst the best alpine rock climbing we'd ever done. The upper pillar led naturally up the crest and then left on to the top section of Casa Dei Gracchi that leads to the SSE Ridge of Mont Greuvetta. We abseiled down the 2013 route to reach a cramped bivouac at the foot of the pillar by nightfall.

The next day was forecast to be good, but it soon clouded in and started to rain. We had no option but to carefully reverse our approach in the wet reaching Val Ferret early in the evening. Although it didn't feel like it at the time, we had been remarkably fortunate. Our three-day good weather forecast ended up being reduced to a single day, and if we'd known this at the outset we wouldn't have considered setting out on such a committing outing. We called our route La Solitaria Pilastro (The Lonely Pillar) and graded it TD+.

Simon Richardson

HIMALAYA

Nama Glacier Area Expedtion 2014, Eastern Kumaon, India

Members: Steve Kennedy, Andy Nisbet, Des Rubens.
First ascent of Concordia Peak, c. 5850m. 4 October 2014. Difficulty around Alpine AD.

Pastoral scene on Day 3 of approach march in Adi Kailash. *Photo: D.Rubens.*

Steve Kennedy, Andy Nisbet and I joined forces with an expedition to the Adi Kailash area of India organised by Moran Mountain. This business is a guiding company run by our member Martin Moran. The arrangement was that we would share costs to base camp but we would then operate independently of Martin's group. This allowed Martin's expedition to be viable and we benefited greatly from his knowledge of the area. In reality, there was some sharing of routes above base camp and therefore plenty of social mixing and sharing of information. Overall, the month away was a very enjoyable experience and we all got on very well with each other.

Adi Kailash (meaning 'Little Kailash') is situated in the Eastern Kumaon area of the Indian Himalaya. Like its more famous counterpart, Kailash, which is situated in Tibet, it is also a sacred mountain. However, despite the expedition's title including Adi Kailash, we were aiming to explore the Nama Valley which is about 10km south-east of the mountain.

The area is little visited by non-Indians, due to the complexity of the Indian bureaucratic system, as well as being behind the Inner Line, the visiting of which involves yet further paperwork and uncertainty. Martin doubted whether any one at all had visited, at least with a mountaineering objective, in the several years since he had last visited. Difficulty of access was compensated by travelling in a most unspoiled area. It felt a great privilege to be travelling and exploring in such an unfrequented area.

As expected, the organisation by Martin and Himalayan Run and Trek was extremely efficient. We arrived in Delhi on the morning of 19 September, had our

Indian Mountaineering Federation briefing and were on the night train to Kathgodam in the evening. Two days of driving from Kathgodam took us to Dharchula which is situated on the river valley forming the boundary between western Nepal and India. A highlight of the journey was seeing sun rise over Nanda Devi from the hill station of Chaukori.

After two nights in Dhurchala, we drove a further two hours up the familiar dusty mountain roads of India, culminating in a terminus where the road was being cut out of a near vertical cliff. There was the usual dearth of safety barriers. We had three days of delightful walking beginning up the lush green valley of the Sarda River. Higher up, the scenery was reminiscent of the Canadian Rockies, with blue green rivers and dense forests. Unlike the concrete villages and towns of the plains, the higher villages retained their lovely stone and wood built structures, many with ancient Tibetan style carvings which, in the more prosperous houses, were brightly painted.

As usual, I wore my well-used Shalwar Kameez made for me in Rawalpindi many years ago. However, few locals now wear this kind of garment, being generally dressed in the much less practical T-shirts and jeans. On the first day of our walk, we were passing an Indian tourist, who stopped me with a polite 'May I take your photograph, sir?' How times change.

Near Gunji, we bore away from the Indian Nepal frontier to follow the valley up to the village of Kuthi. Here we executed a left turn and walked for a few hours up the Nama Valley, establishing a base camp at 3990m and an hour or so below the Nama glacier. The steep slopes above the river were troublesome to the mules, but the skill of the drivers overcame the understandable reluctance of the beasts. It was a gorgeous spot, with a rare supply of non-glacial water and views over to Kunti Peak on the Tibetan border only a few kilometres away on the far side of the main valley.

We did a few acclimatising forays, enlivened by chilly early morning crossings of the main stream. The peaks around the large Nama basin were all unclimbed, reaching up to over 6000m. However, selection of a target was not easy as many of the peaks were threatened by seracs. While Martin and his clients, Aberdonian Gordon Scott and Michael Page targeted Cheepaydang, the SMC party decided to go for a peak at the head of a tributary glacier on the north side of the main basin. With the help of our two Sherpas, Thukpa and Pemba, we established a final camp above some difficult crevassed areas and out of the way of the salvos on the serac encrusted flanks. (On descent, we managed to avoid the crevassed area by keeping close under the flanks of Cheepaydang).

Unfortunately, Andy was feeling the altitude and elected to stay in camp for the following day. Steve and I and the two Sherpas made it to the col at the head of the Glacier where the Sherpas preferred to relax in the sun. The route from the col to the summit was along a fine steep snow arête, with some moderate rock climbing near the summit. The arête was very exposed on both sides.

We were fortunate with the weather. We had wonderful views of distant mountains such as Nanda Devi in India and Gurla Mandata in Tibet. Closer at hand, the remote and largely unvisited glacial areas of the Sela peaks and Yirjenagung peaks made a wild and desolate impression.

We were also lucky in having reasonable snow conditions on our peak. In contrast, Jonathan Preston and Dave King ground to a halt on a 6000m peak on the south side of the Nama Basin due to unforeseen deep graupel like snow and loose rock. Despite a strong attempt, the conditions defeated them.

Steve Kennedy approaches the summit of Concordia Peak *Photo: D.Rubens.*

The peak we climbed is the final one in a ridge which lies between the upper Nama Glacier and the glacier we had ascended. We reckoned the height at around 5850 metres but as we had no altimeter, verification by subsequent ascenders would be welcome. The adjacent peak on the ridge was around the same altitude. The main disincentive to further investigation in this direction was the extreme looseness of the rock and the route not appearing straightforward.

We named the peak Concordia Peak after the Concordia-like coming together of tributary glaciers on the Nama Glacier. The northern tributary glacier by which we accessed the peak we named Jasuli after a local woman who was famous for her charitable activities in the 18th or 19th centuries.

Meanwhile, Martin and his team made the first ascent of Cheepaydang, 6220m.

Regarding future exploration: although the number of unclimbed peaks in the Nama basin has only diminished by two, future pioneers would benefit from a study of photographs of the area. This is because, as stated, many (though not all) of the peaks are difficult of access, at least from the Nama Basin. At present, the only approach permitted by the Indian Mountaineering Foundation and Uttarakhand State Government is the one taken by our expedition, despite the fact that other approaches would actually be further from the Indian/Chinese frontier. Such other approaches might yield more feasible routes.

A final highlight of the trip for me was a visit to the temple and sacred lake below Adi Kailash itself, about a day's trek above Kuthi. We were now well above the treeline and the autumn colours garnished the shrubs and grasses around the ascent route in flaming reds. The view of Adi Kailash from above the sacred lake,

The sacred lake and the temple with Adi Kailash in the background. *Photo: D.Rubens.*

with the small Hindu temple, made a powerful impression, even among those with strongly atheistic tendencies, (such as me). The occasional inadequately dressed pilgrim, the close to freezing temperatures, the remoteness of the spot from the throbbing plains of India and the brown hills stretching away towards Tibet, made this place seem special in an otherwise crowded land.

I have glossed over the amount of effort put in by Moran Mountain and Himalayan Run and Trek in making the expedition run efficiently. It would be fair to say that we would have achieved little in the time available without the very professional efforts of these organisations. Finally, our Liaison Officer, Gajju, was first class, giving unstinting service to the expedition.

Des Rubens

ARCTIC SWEDEN

In March 2015, my wife Moira and I decided to combine a visit to our son, studying in Copenhagen, with a hut to hut Nordic ski tour in Arctic Sweden. The Kungsleden or Royal Trail was established at the end of the nineteenth century and now extends some 400km running south from Abisko near the Norwegian town of Narvik. Over the years the Svenska Turistforeningen (STF) have established a chain of huts covering much of the route though few people do it in one go, particularly in winter. We decided the more popular top section would be enough of a challenge, involving seven days of skiing. Leaving Copenhagen after breakfast, we caught a regular train to Stockholm and that evening boarded the

Arctic Express with comfortable sleeper berths to Abisko Turistation (385m) where we arrived at lunchtime next day. The STF accommodation here is more like a hotel, very popular with tourists enjoying a brief Arctic experience involving skidoo rides, snowshoeing, husky dogs and a chance to see the Northern Lights. We stayed in the adjacent Hostal Keron and enjoyed the fantastic smorgasbord breakfast next morning before finally setting off. The forecast was predicting some alarmingly mild temperatures, so we made a last minute purchase of a tube of klister, as a precaution in the event of a thaw, which thankfully we did not need to use. Waxless skis seem now to be universally popular but we were waxing and in the course of the day progressed from Blue Special to Purple then Red Special. The Trail gently undulated through pleasant dwarf birch forest and route finding was simplified by a line of substantial posts with a prominent red cross on top every 20 metres.

Under grey cloudy skies, the 13km to Abiskojaure was long enough to help us get our ski legs though on the final section across a frozen lake the wind in our faces picked up and we were relieved to see the group of huts with the Swedish flag flapping outside. Each STF hut is looked after by a 'host' who welcomes new arrivals with a cup of hot fruit juice. All the hosts we met were very welcoming, friendly and helpful and spoke excellent English. Paying online in advance gave a substantial discount and avoided messing about with large sums of money. The huts all have wood burning stoves in their kitchens and bedrooms, with the onus on guests to split and replace wood used from the large stock of logs. The other obligatory chore is collecting water through a hole in the ice in the nearest river or lake, which could be up to almost a kilometre away. Most huts had a small shop selling basic foodstuffs (and beer) at a reasonable price and a sauna. This was my fist experience of this traditional way of relaxing and keeping clean in the mountains. There was always some discussion about timing for male, female and mixed sessions, though the latter seemed the most popular. Each sauna hut is divided into three with a dry changing room and a wet middle room with buckets of ice cold water, scalding hot water on tap and plenty of basins and scoops to mix the two for bathing. In the hot room the wood burning stove roars away, with a bucket of water and wooden scoop to sprinkle onto the hot coals above and bump up the temperature. Thermometers and timers were rare and yes, I did roll naked in the snow!

The next 22km stage to Alesjaure (780m) was our longest, starting with a notorious climb, the only time we used our skins. Crossing the plateau above, the sun came out at last and we were surrounded by impressive Cairngorm-like mountains. As the wind picked up again we were treated to an unforgettable experience with a thin layer of spindrift blowing across the ground all around us and huge plumes blowing off the ridges above, giving the impression of skiing through a dynamic landscape. The Trail then dropped down to the end of a long narrow frozen lake where an empty hut enabled us to escape the wind for a welcome lunch break before following the lake shore to our destination, a windswept collection of huts. Next day the wind gradually moderated and we enjoyed the steady climb of 13km up to Tjaktja (1000m). The day had started cloudy, but by dusk the skies had cleared and we had a first glimmer of the Aurora Borealis. By prior agreement, someone looked outside just before midnight and woke the rest of the hut to enjoy a spectacular display of the Northern Lights, with bright shafts and curtains of light stretching across the night sky, though very little colour. Waking to a fine morning, after doing our wood and water chores we scraped off the sticky Red wax and put on more Blue Extra for the steady climb up to our highest point, the Tjaktja Pass (1150m), then enjoyed some downhill running for the rest of the 12km to Salka (835m). This was a hive of activity as next winter's fuel supply had just been sledged in, birch logs towed by a huge piste basher and gas cylinders towed by a Weasel tractor. We shared the huts with a variety of fellow travellers but very few Swedes. As well as skiers there were snow shoeers and commercial husky sledge groups. Many parties were pulling pulkas and seemed to have a lot of stuff, while we preferred to follow the Norwegian ethos and travel as light as safely possible. Moira started with about 10kg while I had about 12kg, including much of our food and enough equipment to survive an emergency night out.

Fine weather continued next day as we followed the widening Tjaktjavagge valley passing several snow choked side valleys on the 12km stage to Singi (720m). To the east, the dramatic Kebnekaise massif rises to 2100m, the highest point in Sweden. At various points on the Trail we passed extensive Sami villages, largely deserted during the winter when the reindeer herds are moved to lower grazing. It would certainly be an interesting walk in summer, with the locals we spoke to all recommending late August and early September when the mosquitos are starting to die out and the autumn colours intensifying. Our route now left the Kungsleden, skiing east over an 840m pass into the Laddjurvaggi valley leading in14km to Kebnekaise Fjallstation (690m). By now the conditions underfoot were getting distinctly icy, no problem for the long gentle descent, but we ended up taking skis off for the last few hundred metres up to our destination. The first hut here was built in 1907 and gradually extended and new buildings added. We slept in the oldest part of the main building, dating back to 1924, which had been done out as a small interesting museum. These were the cheapest beds and we were surprised to have the dormitory to ourselves. The modern sauna gave a fantastic panoramic view of the mountains after which, suitably spruced up we sat down at a communal table with 9 other Swedish guests and enjoyed a splendid three course dinner of mostly locally sourced produce, including some delicious Arctic Char as the main course. A regular skidoo taxi is available for the 19km to the road end, but we were looking forward to a final ski, fuelled by another sumptuous breakfast. Another fine sunny day, we were constantly stopping to look back at the dramatic mountain vista we were gradually leaving behind. One of our fellow diners sped past on skating skis but we arrived in Nikkaluokta (470m) with plenty of time before our bus to Kiruna where our driver kindly dropped us at the door of our hostel. A very early start enabled us to catch the busy morning flight to Stockholm, and then back to Copenhagen for a long weekend of sightseeing.

Dave Broadhead

***Opposite**: 'A bunch of oldies from Edinburgh' visited Calpe last autumn (2014). The Hon Secretary leads Synovial (5 *), Sector Echo 1.5, Echo Valley. Photo: David Stone.*

REVIEWS

The Fell and Rock Journal 2014: (FRCC, 287pp.)
With its large membership and frequent meets (about sixty per annum), the FRCC generate abundant material for their journal. The 2014 issue ranges as widely as Malawi, New Zealand, Ladakh and Antarctica, and even includes a useful little guide to The Irish Munros by Karl Nelson. Scottish interest is served by a piece on Seana Bhràigh (variously spelt) and an article entitled Changes at Culra Bothy.

The focus of the club remains however the English Lake District. Today any proposal for a large bronze plaque on a major British summit would attract outrage, and yet the hallowed war memorial on Great Gable ('In glorious and happy memory…') is not only tolerated but cherished. By way of commemorating the centenary of the Great War, the FRCC recently arranged for the battered old plaque to be removed by the Royal Engineers, copied and re-cast, then re-attached to the rock. A heart-warming piece by Peter Smith describes the whole painstaking process, culminating in a snowy service on Remembrance Day, 2013, at which Richard Hargreaves (himself a nephew of Geoffrey Winthrop Young) drew aside a white ensign from the Battle of Jutland to reveal the reinstated memorial.

Another centenary is celebrated by Ron Kenyon, who writes about Central Buttress on Scafell, which was first climbed in its entirety in 1914 by Siegfried Herford, George Sansom and Charles Holland. How poignant to learn that Herford's name would soon be graven in bronze on Gable, while Sansom would survive the trenches and live to be ninety-one.

Like mischievous schoolboys, the editors dare us to upbraid them for discarding the time-honoured serif and changing the font from Baskerville to Myriad Pro. In their iconoclastic excitement they have unfortunately neglected their proof-reading and offered up a text sprinkled with errors. Nothing however can detract from the photographs, which are the cream of a competition judged by Colin Prior: the cover shot, of a climber poised on North-West Arête, Gimmer Crag, is simply superb.

The Pinnacle Club Journal, No 29, 2012–2014: (Pinnacle Club, 104pp.)
Having sprung from an awkward rib of the mighty FRCC, the ladies of the Pinnacle Club have been shinning up the tree of montane knowledge for ninety-odd years. The exploratory urge takes them to Mexico, Morocco and even Mingulay, and such is their gushing enthusiasm that we fairly itch to follow them.

Within their host a heavenly muse once sang The Pinnacle Song, which is reproduced in this issue and may even bear excerption here. (We are enjoined to sing it to the tune of Father O'Flynn.)

> 'For our talk about "pitches" and "right and left tentacle",
> Why need we choke in the Smokeroom conventicle?
> We've our own gossip – not always identical! –
> Let us be free to talk "shop" by ourselves!
> Better to learn from our women who lead! –
> Women will write, too, what women can read –
> Cut our own caperings; puff our own vapour rings;
> Stuff our own paper things, on our own shelves!
> Chorus: Here's a health to our Pinnacle crew,
> All that we stand for, and all that we do!

Dames may be cynical,
Ladies are finical,
Women! here's luck to our Pinnacle crew!'

Ironically it is in the obituaries that their members are brought to life. Indeed, one recently deceased lady, whom we shall forbear to name, is given such a character that we feel we must quote in extenso: '…the epitome of upper class Englishwomen, born in India (of course) with an accent to match, tall with a commanding, not to say terrifying, presence. She told me of how when she went back to India, which she frequently did, she always carried a gun concealed in the folds of her cashmere shawl. "I fixed my eyes on the border guards and gave them a look that dared them to search me," she explained to me. This was obviously before the days of today's security at airports, but she would probably still get away with it. She had a delightful husband, smallish and somewhat cowed, who was always referred to as "bloody Hugo". Are you getting a picture of her? Formidable is not the word.'

Appropriately the pastel drawing on the cover depicts a pinnacle – the Inaccessible one.

Oxford Mountaineering Journal 2012 & 2013: (OUMC, 40pp & 70pp.)
The OUMC presents the paradox of a century-old club that has a young and transient membership. Apart from a brief but interesting survey of the club's archives by Dawn Jackson Williams, the editors favour the fresh and new, viewed wide-eyed by youngsters on the giddy edge of adulthood. A breathless piece entitled A Whistle-Stop Tour of Scottish Trad describes a five-day midge-bitten dash around the Buachaille, the Etive slabs, the Ben, Garbh Bheinn and Ardverikie, concluding with the remark 'It was just a shame we couldn't stay for longer!' In Peter Hill's Sugar & Ice: The Migot Spur, youthful bravado shares the page with engaging modesty, as sun-softened snow threatens the unbelayed party: 'All too easy, in the mountains, to rush yourself into these silly situations and realise suddenly that what you are doing is pretty serious.' This is just part of growing up, no doubt, but the reader of mature years may be forgiven for occasionally feeling some avuncular concern.

It is good to see the A C Irvine Fund, which commemorates Mallory's young companion and paid for my first pair of boots, still supporting adventurous activity. On his safe return to Oxford, the beneficiary is obliged to submit a report of his expedition, and in consequence the journal contains an assortment of 'Irvine Reports'. Thus Thomas Codrington provides an entertaining account of big-wall climbing in Kyrgystan, with 7b+ crux moves on Pik 4810 and Mount Asan, while Ian Faulkner and others describe sport climbing in Turkey.

Highlights of these numbers are the various articles about Norwegian climbing. In The Great Undiscovered Secret of Southern Norway Steve Broadbent praises unfrequented Setesdal, which he characterises as a 'genuine paradise for ice climbers seeking reliable, high-quality, low-commitment, classic water-ice routes.' There is also a piece about rock climbing in Lofoten (and falling off the Svolvaer Goat), while elsewhere Mary Sligo writes especially well about Stetind, which Slingsby unjustly called the 'ugliest mountain' he ever saw. Her article is accompanied by a spectacular silhouette of Stetind against the setting sun; so wonderful a photograph, indeed, that it is reproduced twice in successive pages.

Finally, there is a lively account by Peter Hill of the 2013 Oxford West Greenland Expedition, with the succinct title Granite, Midnight Sun & Icebergs.

SMC members may remember a recent Eastern District talk about this expedition, in which the gut-heaving outward yacht voyage, from Montreal by the St Lawrence seaway, caught the imagination as much as the 1000m granite E6. The observation that most drowned men are fished out trouserless should serve as a warning against defecating over the gunwales.

Graeme Morrison

The Avalanche Pocket Guide: A Field Reference: Bruce Tremper. (Mountaineers Books, 2014, folded laminate, 2pp, ISBN 978-1-59485-719-5, $8.99.)

This is a fold-out field reference written by Bruce Tremper. Having authored numerous book and papers about avalanches, as well as having been the Director of the Forest Service Utah Avalanche Centre for over 25 years, Bruce clearly knows his stuff. It is no surprise then that The Avalanche Pocket Guide is a well thought out, neat and informative reference for the North American audience.

As the name suggests it is a pocket guide, having a width of 8.5cm, a length of 17cm and a thickness of just a few millimetres. It folds out to eight panels of these dimensions, which total about 70cm long. The material is a laminated card. In many ways it is similar in size and scope to the SportScotland Be Avalanche Aware leaflet. A fair bit of thought has gone into the layout, and there is a good balance of text photos and diagrams. It is colourful and has a pleasant feel about it. It is packed with information and, for its size, gives a reasonable summary of all the main aspects of avalanche avoidance and rescue. Its aim was not to teach avalanche avoidance skills (other than perhaps the very basics), but to be used as a field reference, or a document to base a course or teaching day around.

The content and style is very North American. For example, right at the start there is a command in bold text saying 'Snowmobiles: keep rescue gear in a back pack on your body, NOT ON YOUR SNOWMOBILE'– not so relevant for Scotland. Also, point No 6 on the 'Outdoor Gear Checklist, The Ten Essentials' is 'matches or a lighter or firestarter'. I can't really imagine these items being too essential on your typical Ben Nevis day in January.

However, there were aspects of the style which I enjoyed. Personally I quite liked The Ten Commandments of low-risk travel, a list of good practices when travelling in avalanche terrain. Commandment 7 for example is 'Thou shalt communicate', and Commandment 4 'Thou shalt never trust a cornice'. However, Number 3, 'Thou shalt never go first', is less than practical in a Scottish environment (though perhaps it just means send your climbing partner first). However, some others that I showed the pocket guide to did not seem so impressed.

Of the fifteen sheets (excluding the cover) which make up the pamphlet, three are dedicated to stability tests, while observations that are considered very important to avalanche hazard evaluation in this country, such as whether or not there is blowing snow, are hardly mentioned. There is an emphasis in Scotland on moving away from stability tests and building up an avalanche hazard using general observations, and I felt that this guide did not reflect this change in approach.

So, overall a nice leaflet, but geared a bit more to the North American audience than a Scottish one.

Blair Fyffe

The Munro Society Journal No. 3: (2014, 123pp.)
Mountain Bothies: (Mountain Bothies Association, 2014, £10.00, 175pp.)
The Sweet Especial Scene: Robin Lloyd Jones. (Two Ravens Press, 2014, 196pp, ISBN: 978-1-906120-69-6, £9.99.)

These three slender paperbacks provided much interesting reading for me over the Festive Season. Although not a member, your Clerk of the List works closely with The Munro Society, enclosing a copy of their information flyer together with a similar one for the Scottish Mountaineering Trust in all Compleation and Amendment correspondence. Along with a fresh supply of flyers, I was pleased to receive a copy of their latest quarterly news-letter and Journal. Some years ago (SMCJ 199) I wrote an enthusiastic review of their first Journal, published in 2007 and noticed straight away that the Editorial Team had taken on board my comments about the cover and photos, with the latest Journal featuring a striking full colour front cover and an excellent mixture of colour and black and white illustrations throughout. Members of TMS are clearly eager to put pen to paper – their equally colourful A4 newsletter is packed with accounts of members activities while the A5 Journal features 24 articles ranging over a variety of topics of interest to anyone keen on the hills, by no means restricted to a narrow "Munros" remit. Spaces in the text are filled with short amusing "Best of Times/Worst of Times" features and Roderick Manson has contributed one poem per month to celebrate "2011-The Year of Big Walks' . All in all an excellent read.

Although no longer a member of the Mountain Bothies Association I was delighted to receive a copy of their publication "Celebrating 50 years of the MBA" from my wife, a long time member. Once again the Editorial Team has done a fantastic job, and this high quality production was a delight to read. Looking back over the years, there is plenty of information on the history of the MBA, some of its many personalities and many of the bothies they look after, including acknowledgement of the help received from the SMC in the early years of the Association. There are the inevitable accounts of work-parties and renovations and lots of brief entertaining comments gleaned from "bothy books". Short poems and a range of illustrations help to vary the content. Anyone who has ever spent a night in a bothy will enjoy this book and if you have never had that pleasure, find out what you have been missing. Copies available from Jill Dhanjal, 85 Hogarth Drive, Cupar, Fife, KY15 5YU, enclose a cheque for £10 payable to Mountain Bothies Association, includes p&p.

Robin Lloyd-Jones will be familiar to readers as the author of the excellent "The Sunlit Summit: the life of W. H. Murray" reviewed in last year's SMCJ. I remember many years ago being inspired by his Argonauts of the Western Isles when I started sea-kayaking. This latest publication is described as 'a collection of work, nature and outdoor writing…spanning nearly forty years.' The author has clearly lived an interesting life, having been brought up in India, schooled in Devon, graduating in Social Anthropology from Cambridge University and working in education before retiring early to Scotland to concentrate on writing. Twenty eight short pieces cover a wide range of his experiences and observations from close to home in the Arrochar hills to far flung corners the world such as Greenland and Colombia, interspersed with some poetry and fiction. All are carefully crafted and easy to read, with helpful notes on sources and inspiration and a small selection of colour photos. Those of us fortunate enough to be able to look back and reflect on similar memories and experiences will envy his easy but erudite writing style while younger readers will be inspired to value and appreciate their surroundings and their companions wherever circumstances may lead them. Highly recommended.

Dave Broadhead

The Climbing Chronicles: Harry Parker, compiled by John Parker. (Baton Wicks, 2014, paperback, 103pp, ISBN 978-1-898573-29-0, £7.99.)
This slim volume is more a work of filial piety than of literature but is none the worse for that. Harry Parker (born 1916) was an enthusiastic climber from Lancashire who, by reason of his occupation as an engineer in the armaments industry, was able to carry on climbing throughout the Second World War years. He kept a climbing diary – the Chronicles of the title – and his son has collected and published some sections from them. They do not appear to have been edited and a few mis-spellings of Scottish place names occur, but they are trivial and do not detract from the freshness of the narrative.

The Climbing Chronicles vividly describe an era in which climbers had to use public transport or bicycles to get to the hills, food was rationed and clothing primitive. It was the time of hemp ropes and tricouni-nailed boots. His list of equipment for a trip to Glencoe with his climbing partner Alan makes salutary reading – it lists one karabiner and no slings. A large component of enthusiasm was required for any climbing trip.

Two sections concern trips to Scotland – an Easter weekend in Glen Coe and a cross-country trek from Glenfinnan to Torridon. On the Glen Coe trip Harry and Alan encountered the members of a 'JSMC' meet, including the Honorary Secretary, one 'Alan' Small (surely Alec Small). The travails of the travel involved on this expedition make me admire their persistence in those days before widespread car ownership. Indeed, throughout the Chronicles more effort and ingenuity seem to have been required to get to the hills than were expended upon them.

The expedition to Torridon in 1945 also required complex logistics: a parcel despatched to Achnashellach Youth Hostel, long train journeys, an overnight hotel stop in Glasgow. At Crianlarich railway station Alan and his friend Bob encountered SMC members George Peat and Jimmy Stuart. There is also mention of a previously encountered 'good lad Archy Nendy' (Archie Hendry?).

Leaving Glenfinnan station they went north to Glen Dessary and to Glen Shiel, camping along the way. In 1945 upper Glen Dessary, Sourlies and Carnoch were still inhabited, and they were welcomed and supplied with milk – a welcome luxury in those days. (By the time the reviewer passed by Carnoch and Sourlies in 1953 the houses were deserted.) Reaching Torridon from Glen Shiel involved bus to Mallaig, train to Achnashellach then into the hills at Coulags to a camp in Glen Neimhe. From this curiously chosen spot they climbed Liathach by going back up to Lochan Neimhe, down by what was to become the Ling Hut, and an east-to-west traverse of Liathach. The expedition ended by walking back to Coulags and Achnashellach before taking various trains to the south. Throughout the account of this expedition two things are notable: the hospitality of the people living in the remote areas (I experienced the same in my stravaigings in the early 1950s) and the stamina of the pair.

The Climbing Chronicles were never written for a wide audience but give an interesting account of what it was like to be a climber in those times. It is unfortunate that more of Harry's diaries did not survive, as he was obviously not only an enthusiastic mountaineer but a more than competent rock climber.

Bob Richardson

Hanging On – A Life inside British Climbing's Golden Age: Martin Boysen. (Vertebrate Publishing, 2014, hardback, 265pp, ISBN 978-1-910240-00-7, £20.)

Martin Boysen was one of the most outstanding British rock climbers for over twenty years. Before he had even gone to university he had done far more hard climbs than mere mortals like me have achieved in a lifetime, and still now in his seventies he climbs at a level that many younger climbers can only aspire to. Additionally Martin was an important member of early expeditions to Cerro Torre and Torre Egger, the 1970 south face of Annapurna and 1975 south-west face of Everest expeditions, the Trango Tower ascent and the first ascent of Changabang. Thus his well crafted autobiography has a good story to tell.

As is often the case it is the early chapters that are of greatest interest. Martin was born in Germany during the war and had quite a hard time in his early years with his mother shuttling the family backwards and forwards between Kent and Germany while his father was stuck in a Soviet prisoner of war camp. Growing up in Tonbridge he discovered sandstone at the age of about fifteen and immediately recognised rock climbing as the love of his life. He was obviously an absolute natural. One of the notable aspects of the book is how time and again he knocks off classic hard climbs with no apparent difficulty. He clearly had the 'rock intelligence' that Geoff Francis talked of – the ability to spot very quickly the right combinations of holds to use.

Martin climbed with most of the famous British climbers of his generation. He has interesting remarks and anecdotes about Joe Brown, Chris Bonington, Nick Estcourt, Richard McHardy, Paul Nunn, Clive Rowland and scores of others. Like Richard, whose excellent autobiography is complementary to Martin's, he has a formidable memory. I was astonished for example that he recalled placing Baz Ingle's 'favourite brass nut' on the first ascent of Gogarth, and that Estcourt was wearing a striped rugby shirt when they first met.

There are some hilarious vignettes of his time as a biology student at Manchester University. It is a pity that with Martin's love of natural history and his knowledge as a biologist he didn't give more scope to his reactions to the varieties of landscape he has experienced. Occasionally we get brief sketches that convey some of the emotions he felt, as on his first visit to Patagonia when he could not resist just running off towards the mountains, or when he describes a misty Val di Mello as being like an old Chinese landscape painting. But these are few and far between.

The most memorable parts of climbing books are often the scary stories. Martin has his ration of these, especially in his early trips abroad. An escapade on the Cassin route on the Cima Ovest provides a horrendous tale, when his German companion (whom he hardly knew) hung in space for hours while held on a waist belay with only a questionable peg keeping them both from oblivion. A rock fall near the top of the Philip-Flamm broke Paul Nunn's leg and provided another stirring epic. And of course there was the famous episode on the Trango Tower when Martin having spent hours with his knee jammed in a crack, had almost given up hope of surviving but escaped by cutting the material of his breeches with a beaten peg.

There is an account of a typical Patey-led day on Creag Meagaidh. The party arrived on the summit plateau in the dark, in bad weather without a map and ignorant of the topography. They were not the last famous climbers to get into such a predicament! On another occasion he had a less than welcoming reception at the CIC from a club stalwart. Again shades of many similar incidents! He has enthusiastic descriptions of Parallel B and Jib, but there is relatively little overall about Scottish climbing. Sadly for those of us fascinated by it there is no mention of Gog, the climb on Ben Loyal that he once told the magazine Rocksport would be one of his 'desert island climbs'.

Interspersed with the fascinating accounts of both his early and latter climbing years are vignettes of life with his wife Maggie. He gratefully acknowledges her constant love and support, as well as describing a desperate car accident they were lucky to survive and some other close shaves.

His personal account of the ascents of Annapurna, Everest, Changabang and Trango are an important contribution to Himalayan history and shed a revealing light on the characters of Bonington, Whillans, Haston and the others. Of course Boysen himself would have to admit to being a prima donna too, and indeed he is honest enough to admit at times his impatience with lesser climbers. It was a combination of bad luck and illness that led to his not achieving the summit of either of the 8000ers. I was disappointed that he deals only briefly with his bold attempt with Bill Barker on the west face of Gasherbrum IV, which took place after he had been dropped from 'Team Bonington' for the 1978 K2 expedition.

The selection of photos is judicious: wonderful black and white shots redolent of the Welsh climbing scene of the '60s; stunning high mountain views; heart-warming family photos; and several from his Alpine filming escapades (e.g. with Clint Eastwood).

To sum up, this is a splendid book that will bring pleasure to a great many of Martin's contemporaries. I am perhaps not well placed to give an unbiased review. I knew quite a few of the characters and places that Martin describes, and though a little younger I lived through much of the same times; thus I found it pretty 'unputdownable'. The great climbs that were the acme of ambition for our generation, whether on grit, in North Wales or in the Alps were the stuff of my dreams; the only difference being that Martin achieved many of them and I did rather few! But I wonder how the book will be read by younger climbers or armchair mountaineers. I fear that to some it may read too much like a long list of climbs and climbers, spiced only to a degree by dramatic events and amusing anecdotes. In particular the last chapter reads too much like one of those circulated Christmas letters of the 'We did this and then we did that' variety. Perhaps the key to good writing is knowing how much to omit. Martin has done so much climbing in his life that there was only space for a brief mention of many of his ascents. Finally it is pretty unforgiveable that the publishers did not commission an index for a book so packed with people and place names.

Geoff Cohen

50 Shades of Hillwalking: Ralph Storer. (Luath Press, 2014, paperback, 186pp, ISBN 978-1-91002-65-1, £7.99.)
First, a disclosure. While aware that this gentleman has written other books, most notably ones about Munros, I have not read any. They may be good examples of their species, they may even be readable, informative and worthy of purchase, but I remain ignorant. So I have approached Ralph's (can I call you Ralph, Ralph?) collection of wee stories here with a mind unblemished by what he has written elsewhere.

Now I have finished this collection, a gallimaufrey of brief tales from the outerworld of someone who has long been infected by the windswept hillsides, frozen summits, blistering long approaches, and of course miserable and non-comforting Scottish pubs. Initially, I was taken by the apparent ease with which he seemed to find female company for his scampers. Christine, Anne, Wendy, Sandi, all lovely girls I am certain, who must have enjoyed his company, if not his apparel. Sandi was the stayer, as it turned out.

It was Tale #16 which finally cracked my wizened visage, the one entitled Nutty Deals a Face Plant, where Nutty was his mountain bike and a face plant was what you think it is. I believe now, with some retrospective analysis, that I laughed for the first time here because Ralph was being hurt, and it was written humorously with no sign of self pity. At the same time I was a little bit pleased as I was finding the tales a little bit, how should I put it, pedestrian, and I wished some punishment to be meted out to Ralph. Sorry Ralph.

Tale #34, Highpointers and Peakbaggers was of course a low point for me personally, as it contained list upon list of how and what those affected by the mountain ticking disease can tick. It read like something written for one of the comics, collated from a brief trawl through the internet, and indeed Ralph has been honest enough to mention at the start that half-a dozen of the Tales have appeared elsewhere in one version or another.

Moving quickly on, we meet a few contradictory essays, sorry Tales. #37, Leave No Trace, recommends a website that may help you traverse wild country leaving, er, no trace. Then #39, The Chain Gang, recommends building more via ferrata in perhaps the Cuillin, or Coire an t-Sneachda in the Cairngorms. Hmm.

Ralph confesses to having being born a Sassenach. Now we scholarly types are aware that originally this was a term of affection bestowed upon those Scots from the Lowlands who did not have the Gaelic. No matter, if Ralph is happy with that, so be it. However, his direct and somewhat brutal approach to delicate matters such as path building, access problems and so on, do not arise from any southern culture in my opinion, but from his sojourn in Dundee. So we must make some sympathetic allowances here.

His Tales concerning the Cairn Gorm funicular access to the summit debacle, and in particular the building of stony paths up the most popular sites such as Ben Nevis and Schiehallion, certainly for me represent the meat of this book, and left my head buzzing with their attacks on the so far disjointed PC approach to such matters. I am sure I am not the only one whose sensitive knee joints wince at the sight of one of these often lovingly crafted yet agonisingly jolting descents. Ralph states that he is happy to see the alternative sight on a hillside, even if it be a multi-tracked, wide sea of mud, such as grew on Ben Lomond, Schiehallion, above Glen Brittle and so on. And yet thus far we do not seem to have an answer which satisfies everybody.

I suspect this book will not satisfy everybody either. It is a Marmite™ collection of tales, with lots of added salt but no Vitamin B12. If the readers of his various Munro books enjoy his style (and here I assume they have a similar tone) then I dare say there may be much to enjoy here. I thank Ralph for making me think harder about path building and access problems. He obviously has a deep love for the hills and mountains, and for that matter he is a true and loyal friend, as his Tale #47, Lost Innocence shows, describing the death of a friend.

Ken Crocket

The Grahams and the Donalds – SMC Hillwalkers' Guide: edited by R. Anderson & T. Prentice. (Scottish Mountaineering Club, 2015, hardback, 336pp, ISBN 978-1-907233-19-7, £25.)

This is an extremely comprehensive, well-written and beautifully illustrated guide to the Grahams and Donalds. Whilst not every hillwalker or mountaineer feels that they need a guidebook in order to enjoy the hills and mountains of Scotland (and I probably include myself in this category), there is no doubt that more and more people are looking for challenges in the smaller mountains having finished their (first?) rounds of the Munros and Corbetts, and many of us do like to have a guidebook to dip into for inspiration and for help in choosing starting points and routes.

This guidebook is very much more than a list of hills and routes. It has clearly been written by a group of people with a real and in-depth knowledge and love of the hills they are writing about. The book begins with an introduction to the Grahams and Donalds and those who first listed them, and this is followed by a straightforward description of how to use the guide, read the maps and interpret the route descriptions. There are short but useful pages on mountain safety and other relevant information before the descriptions begin. The book is then divided into sections, the numbering of most of which will already be familiar to those who own the SMC Munros or Corbetts books. The hills in each section are described in detail, with a mixture of history, background information and useful detail which will help the walker decide on access points and routes.

The maps are truly excellent, easy to follow and clearly show which summits are Grahams, Graham tops, Donalds and Donald tops (or fall into more than one category, which many do). Munros, Munro tops, Corbetts and Corbett tops are also shown. I often choose to traverse a hill or visit from an unusual direction (rather than go in and out by the most commonly used paths) and, for this reason, really liked the fact that the maps often showed multiple route options, with descriptions of the advantages and disadvantages of each.

The book is illustrated by some excellent photographs of the mountains in all sorts of weather and seasons. I liked the honesty of the authors in admitting (both on maps and in some photographs) that pylon lines and wind turbines exist. Scottish mountain landscapes are currently under severe threat from industrialisation in some places, and too many tourist brochures and adverts are using old photographs to depict mountain scenes which are now disfigured by wind turbines, pylons or wide hill tracks. For example, it is now difficult to photograph Schiehallion from many northern and some north-eastern aspects without including the Beauly Denny powerline. By being honest and showing people what some of our spoiled mountains look like, we might help protect the remaining ones from industrial development.

I thoroughly enjoyed reading this guidebook, will certainly refer to it frequently from now on, and would love to have had it when I was first doing the Donalds and Donald Tops back in the early 1990s. I can't help smiling when trying to decide whether, if doing them now on wild wet and windy days (and I experienced plenty of those way back then), I'll be one of the 'purists' 'floundering along' (as described under Blackhope Scar, Bowbeat Hill and Dundreich) or one of the 'sensible' who choose to 'use the turbine access roads' for the much maligned wind-factories!

Audrey Litterick

The Great Mountain Crags of Scotland: G Robertson & A Crofton. (Vertebrate Publishing, 2014, hardback, 304pp, ISBN 978-1-906148-89-8, £35.) This is a coffee table book with the subtitle A Celebration of Scottish Mountaineering and is particularly appealing due to the many fine photographs. It is compiled by Guy Robertson and Adrian Crofton, with contributions from many of Scotland's leading climbers covering a wide range of summer and winter routes across mainland Scotland and the Scottish islands.

The crags are grouped into four sections as the South-West Highlands, the North-West Highlands, the Islands, and the Cairngorms & Central Highlands. The grouping of the Cobbler along with Glen Coe and Ben Nevis within a South-West Highlands section might appear unusual at first until it is remembered that this book is compiled from the perspective of climbers based in the Aberdeen area rather than the central belt. There is a short foreword by Andy Cave to give a non-Scottish based perspective on the subject, and ecological notes from Gareth Marshall. At the start of each section there is a poem by Stuart Campbell and an introduction, although these are very different in style and content for each section and therefore appear unclear as to their purpose.

By necessity the book is selective and very much reflects the areas where today's activists have concentrated most of their efforts and where recent climbing developments have been taking place. The climbs included for each crag tend therefore to be at the top end in both summer and winter, with little room for routes to which the average climber might aspire. As a result, there are only three cliffs from Ben Nevis included, and it seems strange that Aonach Mor and Aonach Beag are omitted.

The individual cliffs are described in each chapter under the headings of the Place, the Cliff, the Climbing, the Routes, and the Story, this last being an individual's account of a particular route or experience of the cliff over a period. This approach has allowed some very personalised accounts to be included, which provide a fascinating insight into the approach of today's activists following in the footsteps of past greats such Raeburn, Murray and Patey.

This is undoubtedly an impressive book with many excellent photographs of the outstanding cliffs and crags that continue to challenge today's climbers. It is unclear to me, however, to whom this book is addressed since its subject and detail may be too specialist for most. It is therefore unlikely that the routes and climbs will ever become a tick list as was the case in earlier times with books such as Classic Rock or Hard Rock. Perhaps this does not matter, since the essential point is that today's climbers continue to be challenged in summer and winter by the great diversity that is provided by the Scottish cliffs, and this book is a celebration of their experience. The final paragraph of the introduction to the book simply states that it is hoped that the reader enjoys reading the book and might use it for inspiration, for ideas or just for pleasure. The final sentence indeed states: 'Let the photos tell the story as much as the text itself, and indeed look closely and you will no doubt find some interesting gaps.'

Brian Shackleton

SMC Climbers' Guide to the Inner Hebrides and Arran: Colin Moody and Graham Little. (SMT, 2014, 320pp, ISBN 978-1-907233-17-3, £25.)
It is late March, the sky is azure, the temperature is ferocious and the view across the sea is dreamy. Whilst absorbing the idyll before me that is purely Caribbean, I am also reading through the new guidebook to the Inner Hebrides and Arran. I stop at the pages that describe the granite rocks of Erraid and my mind drifts; thinking back to the great times I had camping, and soloing over those lovely stones. To be honest, I wanted to be back there on the West Coast rather than in the Caribbean. Such is the lure of climbing on the Islands when the weather is good. No better place to be in the world.

OK, back to reality and a review of the book. I think this is the first SMC guide that is in a larger or wider format. I presume this is to make room for two columns of text, which is more economical for the information. Personally, I like it and it has a nice feel. The downside of course is the practicality of carrying it up climbs or in one's rucksack. Guidebooks used to be small and slender and could be carried on multi-pitch routes, but nowadays with the wealth and volume of routes in these guides, this isn't going to happen any more. The best thing to do for multi-pitch routes is to write out the description, or, dare I say it, photocopy the page. Anyway, information is probably more important than size, and you certainly get value for money with this guide.

Covering about sixteen islands from Muck to Cara, this guide is an absolute treasure trove of information for adventurous and armchair readers alike. It was certainly an 'open sesame' moment for me when I first started delving into it. Some of the islands have never been written up in a guide before, such as Canna, where there are a remarkable 200 routes to go at. Scotland just seems to have an endless supply of rocks and climbing – a lifetime's worth of adventure.

To me, it feels almost like a coffee table book with full-page photographs: I really like them; it gives the guide an air of quality. The front cover shot is a lovely composition of a relatively new crag with Ben More in the background; having said that, it does feel a little dull for a front cover. Inside, Dan Arkle's photos of an ancient Arran landscape add some class, and I love the historical photo of Anne Littlejohn pioneering in the '60s on Rum. There are a good variety of pictures to give a taste of what is to come. However, I felt that the quarter-page / thumbnail pictures were 'lost' and didn't add anything. In fact it would probably be better to have one half-page picture rather than two thumbnails. Almost all the pictures are found adjacent to the relevant text in the guide, which works really well.

The topos are a revelation: they are bright, clear and extremely informative. They are the working cogs of any modern guide and have been detailed superbly. There has been a lot of painstaking work over the maps too. In most cases they are full-page, colourful and more than adequate. There is even a 'map' for Muck, telling you which routes are beneath which stakes – spoon fed or what! The four-star system for the best routes is still in use, and for the first time this system has been used conservatively as there are only three four-star routes in the whole guide: two summer routes and one winter route. Personally, I prefer it that way –

it's more realistic.

The history section is concise and informative. Not too much, not too little. Sometimes guides have too much, and it takes up too much room. Getting the balance right is hard, and this has worked. In the future, historical accounts from SMC journals etc. could be referenced in the history section for those who want to read more. The First Ascent list is comprehensive, with the odd discrepancy here and there. What I like most about the list are the one-line anecdotes, such as the route Neanderthal which was 'cleaned with a sheep bone'.

All in all, it is a wonderful guide containing more than a lifetime's worth of adventure. I'll be petitioning Caledonian Macbrayne to make sure the authors, Colin and Graham get their share of the additional ferry profits. A good job well done. Now it is time to get out there.

Jules Lines

Reinhold Messner – My Life at the Limit: Thomas Hüetlin. (Mountaineers Books, 2014, paperback, 257pp, ISBN 978-1-59485-852-9, $19.95.)
The achievements of internationally renowned Tyrolean-born mountaineer Reinhold Messner are remarkable: the first person ever to ascend all of the fourteen 8000m peaks, ascents of each of the highest mountains on the seven continents, crossing Greenland, the Antarctic, the frozen Arctic Ocean to the North Pole, Tibet, and the Gobi and Takla Makan deserts on foot, to mention but a few. Much has already been well documented, so what do we learn from this latest addition? An autobiography in the form of an interview by Berlin- and London-based journalist Thomas Hüetlin, and translated into English by Tim Carruthers, this book offers a reflective account of his personal life and achievements.

Messner endeavours to set the record straight as well as putting his achievements into context with his early life and influences. The second child of eight brothers and one sister, the young Messner was raised in the South Tyrol hill-farming community of Villnöss by parents who eked out a modest living. By way of resistance to becoming Italianised in the immediate post-war period, each of the Messner children was given a name that was distinctively German.

Messner recounts his very early days of climbing with this father at the age of four, and then with his brother Günther. As expected, Messner is questioned about, and offers, his own version of events that led to Günther's death in an avalanche on Nanga Parbat, and the profound effect this has had on him. Messner's forthright views on the actions of Nanga Parbat-obsessed leader Dr Karl Herrligkoffer are unambiguous, as he describes his marginalisation by Herrligkoffer in the same way that Herman Buhl had been marginalised years earlier.

Messner defends other criticisms such as why his successful oxygen-free partnership with Peter Habeler on Everest ended acrimoniously. Taking exception to a particular passage in Habeler's book that the publisher refused to retract, Messner remains critical, arguing that Habeler took editorial responsibility. But the damage was done. Messner accepts that they are now older and wiser – and indeed still alive – so have developed a mutual respect for one another.

The same, however, cannot be said of Arved Fuchs, owing to a comment in Fuchs's book which was orthogonal to Messner's recollections of their unsupported 2800km transantarctic crossing. He, too, is off the Christmas card list. And there are others.

As one would expect, Messner is clearly fascinated by mountains generally. In particularly reflective mood, Messner says that the mountain is only a challenge before he climbs, which counts more than the success afterwards. The driver is the feeling of curiosity about the next challenge. He also describes his interest in the discovery of Mallory's body on Everest, and postulates his own credible theories as to whether the quintessential Englishman had both the equipment and capability to ascend the notorious Second Step and reach the then elusive summit. Messner remains dismissive of the Chinese claims of finding evidence above the Step.

Messner also describes his encounter with the legendary upright walking Yeti or Chemo, which he describes as a rare kind of nocturnal Tibetan bear. Indeed, most bears rear up on their hind legs when they meet people, as a gesture of curiosity or threat.

Beyond climbing, Messner describes his motivation for standing for– and winning–a seat in the European Parliament in 1999. Having served a single term, he left to work on developing his Messner Mountain Museums legacy, devoted to art, culture and religion. Today, at 71, Messner lives in South Tyrol with his partner, Sabine, and their children. In the final chapter, Tying up Loose Ends, Messner is asked about his friendship with past expedition partners. He accepts that they shared experiences together but fails to elaborate in any depth other than acknowledging that they each had their own strengths. Equally, there is a paucity of insight into his personal life. The breakdown of his first marriage to Uschi Demeter is attributed to his no-compromise attitude to climbing, while his affections for Sabine are again guarded and reveal little of his softer side.

The interviewing is somewhat stage-managed and does not drill down to what we have previously read of his life and times. Certain topics are either glossed over or simply avoided altogether. The style of interviewing can in no way be compared to that of Jeremy Paxman. Messner is asked for example about his egotistical character, which he does not deny, but the somewhat banal questioning does not attempt to explore his carefully worded replies. No doubt this will have been a cathartic experience for Messner, but the reader is often left disappointed not to learn more of his forthright views and opinions, which for example made his book K2: Mountain of Mountains such a compelling read.

What this book does achieve though is the opportunity for Messner to set the record straight in his own words. Indeed, there is nothing wrong with that. Few would dispute he is the greatest living mountaineer today, and this is an interesting read that reveals a little more about a man who, unlike many of his contemporaries, has had the good fortune to grow old.

Carl J.Schaschke

Higher Ground – A Mountain Guide's Life: Martin Moran. (Sandstone Press, 2014, 276pp, paperback, ISBN 978-1-908737-55-7, £14.99.)

It is a staple of ribald humour that every paragon of virtue has her price. Many of us pull a face at the suggestion we might take to climbing for money, but is our distaste truly a matter of high principle, or do we secretly fear that an amateur delight could eventually become a professional chore? More venally still, do we worry that the rewards will be paltry and hard earned, and we may not have what it takes to be une grande verticale, to borrow the language of courtesanship? In reading Martin Moran's absorbing account of his life as a guide, these are questions on which we inevitably reflect.

The first section of the book takes us episodically through Moran's upbringing on Tyneside, his eye-opening family holidays in the Lakes and Scotland, a spiritual revelation on Braeriach, a youthful ascent of the Eiger North Face, and an arduous novitiate as an aspirant guide. Presently, at the age of thirty, having satisfied such hard-hearted examiners as Bob Barton and Mick Tighe, he qualifies as a British Mountain Guide. Forsaking a secure career in accountancy he moves almost at once with his wife to Lochcarron, where he begins to establish a guiding business. 'Combining new-won climbing skills with my love of climbing, I wanted to take my clients out of their comfort zone to a new level of experience where the mountains would become as special for them as they were for me. Already I had seen guides in the Alps who merely went through the motions of mountaineering without a spark of passion. I was determined never to give in to the dread curse of tedium, and truly believed that I could inspire a genuine improvement in the ability, confidence and courage of each of my clients.'

Higher ground, indeed. Moran gives an account of his challenging winter courses, and the tough education undergone by guide as well as clients when snow-holes collapse, blizzards sweep in, testicles tangle in thigh-loops, and rooky leaders fall from ice pitches. Unfortunately the fine winters of the mid-80s were followed by lean years when '… for whole weeks there was continuous rain. My diary extracts lost their former verve and hinted at despair ' Though we might wonder why a geography graduate did not check the annual rainfall figures before settling in Wester Ross, it is difficult to remain indifferent to his account of these penurious early years of juggling daily guiding commitments with the demands of a wife and newborn children: 'A day after Alex's arrival I was up on Fuar Tholl with the first of our groups.' Eventually however his reputation spreads and bookings increase, boosted by publication of The Munros in Winter and by 'increasing consumer wealth as the boom of the later Thatcher years took off'. He takes on assistant guides and a cook, and settles into an annual cycle of winter courses in the north-west, spring forays to the Cuillin, summer guiding in the Alps, and post-monsoon expeditions in the Himalaya. Satisfied clients return for more, and there is even one wealthy enthusiast, David Litherland, who engages Moran year after year in pursuit of the Alpine four-thousanders. (It is to Litherland's camera and his lavish consumption of film-spools that we owe several of the fine photographs in the book.)

Unlike some continental professionals whose climbing memoirs have portrayed a surefooted superman endowed with heroic powers of endurance, Moran disarmingly describes many a minor slip and error of judgement, at least in his early days, and he even confesses to breaking one of 'the three golden rules in the etiquette of a guide' by losing his temper. Needless to say, these episodes give us more entertainment than many an uneventful climb. Moreover he engages the reader of merely average skill, who is gratified by a respectful account of the Mummery Crack on the Grépon ('… would have rated HVS or even E1 on Derbyshire gritstone') or Naismith's Route on the Tooth ('I grovelled across slimy gangways to the crux move, a bold pull on finger pockets without any nearby protection.'). For all his modesty, however, Moran is clearly a climber of great technical ability who keeps himself exceptionally fit: on an occasional day off, he puts up a new winter route (The Godfather, VII) or sets a record for running the Cuillin Ridge (3 hours 33 minutes).

The later sections of the book are arranged geographically, and deal in turn with Scotland (including two chapters on the Cuillin), the Alps, Norway and the

Himalaya. It is a special delight to find Moran writing so enthusiastically about Lyngen in a chapter entitled 'Midnight Mountains', and to behold two glorious photographs of Jiekkhevárri in midnight sunshine. There is also an account of an interminable ascent of Rulten in Lofoten: when Moran writes in his preamble that 'knowing Weir [who climbed it in 1951] as the lovable naturalist and broadcaster of his later life we felt that we could use his fifteen-hour time as the upper limit of likelihood' we should perhaps not be surprised it will take him and his party nineteen hours.

A chapter neutrally entitled 'Piz Badile' tells a harrowing tale. In June 2004 Moran was approaching the foot of the Cassin route with two clients, Neil Lindsey and Julie Colverd, and an aspirant guide, Jules Cartwright. Colverd and Cartwright, who were short-roped together, set off across a steep snow slope and (unseen by the other two) fell to their deaths on the slabs below. 'It happens every year,' according to the helicopter pilot who attended the accident. The circumstances are described in some detail by Moran, concluding with his return to the mountain seven years later.

The section on Himalyan expeditions, including an ambitious attempt on Kamet that failed just a hundred metres below the summit, is followed by a final chapter in which Moran reflects generally on his occupation. Taking issue with Mummery's 'jaundiced view' that a client pays a guide merely to get to the top, Moran writes: 'The true mountain guide offers companionship, the sharing of adventure, discovery of the natural world, the coaching of skills and the mastery of self-confidence, while generating an enormous amount of fun in the process.' He goes on to deplore 'the insidious creep of protectionism and legislation' but counts it lucky that 'the United Kingdom has retained a laissez-faire approach to mountain activities, and our civil court judges take the sane view that participation in mountaineering involves a wilful exposure to risk, irrespective of whether a guide is in charge of the party. Nevertheless, our profession faces a battle to preserve its freedom.'

If an aspiring youngster remains undeterred by this prognostication, and is willing to brush aside the observation that 'few mountain guides are rich', he will find that Moran has added a useful appendix on the BMG and IFMGA qualifications, and how to set about obtaining them. There is even a glossary of climbing terms, which the layman will doubtless find helpful.

One aspect of the book might attract adverse comment, not least from some of the clients named within it. In his nail-biting account of the SW face of the Täschhorn, Winthrop Young (whom Moran occasionally quotes) described how at one point the guide Josef Lochmatter became hysterical and was brought to his senses by Young's sharp reproach, this being 'an example of how the educated man plays up to the occasion.' It is a passage that has always made me uncomfortable. Moran, as a graduate of one of our ancient universities but hired by all manner of men, cannot resist turning the tables: 'Ian sank to his knees on reaching the arête and commenced the jabber of panic… After several minutes of inertia I ordered Ian to untie from the rope.' Elsewhere he describes his clients as variously 'shaking and weeping' or 'baulking and bolting'. This equally makes me uncomfortable. Carlos is 'a professional masseur with an unhealthy obsession for vertical lingams of rock.' Even Belle du Jour preserved the anonymity of her clients (or so I am told).

Moran has a crisp style and a keen eye, and some delightful word-paintings enliven the book. At the Old Man of Hoy he observes: 'Dressed in bright yellow

Destivelle flitted about the stack like a canary as she fixed her lines.' And at the Hörnli Hut: 'Only after the meal did the Zermatt guides emerge from their private dining area, looking like a bunch of desperadoes from a spaghetti western, an assortment of handlebar moustaches among the older specimens and thousand-yard blue-eyed stares among the younger ones.' He also has a gift for suspense, which he deploys adroitly in the chapter describing Andy Nisbet's rescue from Poacher's Fall on Liathach, after hanging there for twelve hours with a dangerously shattered leg. (Alright, we all know he survives, but the general reader just might be moved to worry about him.)

One thing only is missing, and may leave the purchaser unsatisfied. Here is a man who has led hundreds of clients up the Inaccessible Pinnacle, many of them wholly dependent on him for their security, and has taken some thirty groups to the Himalaya. He must know every technical trick of the trade, but divulges none. For that, presumably, monsieur must pay extra.

Graeme Morrison

Mountaineering in Scotland – The Early Years: Ken Crocket. (Scottish Mountaineering Trust, 2015, hardback, 354pp, ISBN 978-1-907233-20-3, £24.)
This book is much more than a forensic investigation into, and commentary on, what must be just about every rock and snow and ice climb done in Scotland before 1914, all 292 of the First Ascents recorded between 1890 and 1914. It certainly is that, and the author has trawled the available sources for his information and referenced these thoroughly, in a manner which I am sure would meet with the approval of a modern-day Sherlock Holmes. The book additionally provides evidence for the writer's argument that the standards of climbing set before 1914 in Scotland were not re-established until the 1930s, and not actually surpassed until the 1950s.

A number of English alpinists had already found Skye a challenging prospect in the 1880s, and climbers from south of the border played a large part in the exploration of the Cuillin. Skye aside, the great majority of the exploratory climbs were made by members of the Scottish Mountaineering Club Thus Ken Crocket's primary mother lode for his work has been the Journal of the SMC. The Club quickly developed from a Salvationist hillwalking club–which other clubs like the Cairngorm Club remained–into an Ultramontane one of climbers, and therefore it is inevitable and appropriate that the history of Scottish mountaineering in its early days is largely the history of the SMC.

Despite Scotland having about 90% of the British mainland's mountain mass, that Scottish mountaineering was a late developer is undeniable. Climbing in England's Lake District–largely from Wasdale Head–and to a lesser extent in North Wales from Pen-y-Gwryd had drawn aspirant alpinists well before Scotland's attractions were discovered and promoted. Crocket offers some possible explanations for this late development, including the difficulties of travel in pre-motor-car days (and largely pre-railway days, Fort William being connected to the iron road only in 1895). Another hindrance in the Victorian period was the growing use of Scottish Highland estates for sporting purposes, and the resultant attempted exclusion of mountaineers by landowners. (Scottish mountaineers, and the SMC itself, largely accepted this exclusion rather than challenging it, the Club distancing itself from any intentions of 'stravaiging and marauding'.)

The early mountaineers were also held back by lack of accurate maps in some areas such as the Cuillin, and by inadequate equipment. Crocket gives us the story of what was initially a group of (mainly) climbing novices who honed their skills through practice and debate, with discussions on ice-axe technique, footwear and rope work occupying much space in the pages of the Journal. These were people who treated the Scottish hills in winter as a comparable challenge to the Alps in summer, a point made by both Naismith (quoted on p33) and Raeburn (p234), who were thoroughly serious in their approach to their mountain craft, going through a rising curve of experience with each new climb. By 1903, for example, over one-third of SMC members were also members of the Alpine Club. They were also astonishingly fit, and some of the epics they undertook, such as that of Tough and Brown in their ascent of the North-East Buttress of Ben Nevis in 1895 (pp134–7), are staggering feats that few could equal today.

Crocket points out that there were no fatalities amongst Scottish mountaineers (or the English AC visitors) prior to 1914. Whilst this was partly owing to the growing skill of those participating in the sport, it might also be attributed to a combination of the small numbers frequenting the mountains–maybe a couple of hundred people at most? – and good luck. Crocket's book does give details of a surprising number of accidents that took place in the period—in more than one of which it looks as if the participants were fortunate to escape with their lives—including the mishap involving Raeburn himself on the aptly named Stuc a' Chroin (Peak of Danger) in 1910. The lack of any more effective belaying technique than the 'hitch' – throwing the rope over a nodule or passing it round the back of a rock – was the major objective danger at this period, and necessitated the golden rule that 'the leader must not fall.' (An excellent example of the 'hitch' is given in the illustration on the front cover of the book.)

Notwithstanding the difficulties faced by the pioneers, Crocket throughout his narrative reiterates and re-emphasises his view that the standard reached by the Scottish mountaineers (and by mountaineers in Scotland) at this period was unequalled until the achievements of the1930s generation associated with Bill Murray and his companions, who had the benefit of better transport facilities and better maps and guidebooks. Indeed one has an inkling that Crocket feels that such commentators as Murray and even guidebook writers like Macphee were at times ignorant and somewhat dismissive of the efforts of the pioneers who paved the way.

And one giant stands head and shoulders above the other pioneers. Harold Raeburn, and his galaxy of climbs, from Raeburn's Arête (1902) to Green Gully (1906) and beyond, would seem to validate, in at least his own person, that here we have a climber who set a standard unequalled and certainly not surpassed in Scotland for a quarter of a century or more. As Crocket states on p145: 'From joining the SMC in December 1896 until the Great War all but eclipsed such activities, Raeburn would be instrumental in expanding the known boundaries of Scottish mountaineering, raising the standards in icy gullies, and taking rock standards up to that so far only enjoyed in England and Wales.'

The appetite has been whetted for the forthcoming biography of this man who was a major figure, not only in the Scottish mountains but in the Alps and the greater ranges of the Caucasus and Himalaya. Not for nothing was Raeburn chosen to be on the first Everest expedition of 1921. Any who might have thought the possibly more celebrated Norman Collie to have been at the very forefront of Scottish mountaineering at this time, with ascents such as Tower Ridge on Ben Nevis in winter in 1894, and his climbs with Mackenzie (the latter generally leading) on Skye, will certainly have to reconsider who should wear the laurel crown.

An interesting point is that the meets and other social gatherings of the SMC before 1914 appear to have been worthy affairs but rather staid socially. When one thinks of the goings-on (recorded and unrecorded) at Pen-y-Pass before 1914, or even more so the uproarious high-jinks at Wasdale Head, detailed in Alan Hankinson's The First Tigers (1972), there appears to be a marked contrast with the social interaction of the members of the SMC at Sligachan or the Alexandra Hotel. Here the edgiest it would appear to have got was Munro playing his flute. Was this so–and if so, why? Presbyterianism? Or possibly the less widespread attendance at public schools by the Scottish haute bourgeoisie, where they would have had the benefit of learning the bad behaviour expected of upper class gentlemen at play, instilled in their English counterparts?

As well as a copy of the book in question, one of the privileges to which the reviewer is entitled is to let a bee out of his or her bonnet in the form of a few quibbles. Is James David Forbes deserving of the honour to be considered as 'Scotland's first known mountaineer' (p11)? Expert on mountains though he was, he was primarily a scientist who climbed in pursuit of his professional goals. Mountaineering has no ulterior purpose and therefore I would rather award this honour to his successor Sheriff Alexander Nicholson for his Skye climbs in the 1870s. Collie may have taken the first X-ray for medical purposes and may well have developed the first neon gas-discharge tube; but the claim which he himself made (verbally) that he discovered neon dies hard. Collie was not actually at UCL when neon was discovered in Sir William Ramsay's laboratory (he had left–though he came back later), and he himself did not repeat the claim in his 1927 pamphlet 'A Century of Chemistry at University College'.
[See http://www.ucl.ac.uk/chemistry/history/chemical_history/slides/neon]

Altogether this is a fine, thorough book, which adds to the growing corpus of works produced by the SMT on the history of Scottish mountaineering and will help to give our native mountains their proper place in the international pantheon. Specifically, Mountaineering in Scotland – The Early Years, dispels any ideas, should they ever have been held, that the period before 1914 constitutes simply the prehistory of the sport in this country, and it finally gives the doughty pioneers the credit they fully deserve.

Ian R Mitchell

In the Cairngorms – Poems: Nan Shepherd. (Galileo Publishers, 2014, hardback, 64pp, ISBN 978-1-903385-31-9, £14.99; also available in paperback, 80pp, £9.99.)
Nan Shepherd was born in 1893 in Cults, now on the outskirts of Aberdeen, and would live in that same house and occupy the same bedroom throughout her 88 years–continuity unimaginable today. The Cairngorms too would become another extension of her self-prescribed living space; she was an English Literature graduate of Aberdeen University and spent her 37-year Training Centre career teaching teachers how to teach–in Aberdeen. That she would write was perhaps inevitable, the North East of Scotland then enjoying a distinctive literary flowering based on a deep-rooted and distinctive culture based on the land.

Between 1928 and 1933 three novels set in this world were published: The Quarry Wood, The Weatherhouse and A Pass in the Grampians. Then in 1934 the

Moray Press published In the Cairngorms, a slim, attractive book of just over 40 poems, now re-issued in an equally attractive-looking volume through the enthusiasm of, and with a foreword by, Robert Macfarlane.

She turned from poetry to prose during World War Two and wrote what is a unique work, The Living Mountain, a sort of symphony to the Cairngorms, every aspect and nuance of the range coming in like different instruments. It, rightly, is the work she will be remembered by, yet, strangely, Neil Gunn voiced scepticism about finding a publisher and it sat in a drawer till 1977. It too is now back in print. In the Cairngorms is a poetic coda to the prose work.

Many of the poems, justifying a note in the journal, are about the Cairngorms and reflect thoughts expressed in The Living Mountain. In her own words she went 'not up but in' (echoes of John Muir), viewing both the widest scenes and tiniest details with 'undistracted eyes', perception and introspection connecting how the mind takes in the realities of storm and rock, wind and water. She knew these mountains in every mood: 'The granites and schists of my dark and stubborn country', 'the shining sides of Glen Guisachan/Wet with storm'. Water more than anything else, write into that what you may, appears constantly: 'Living water, / Like some pure essence of being, / Invisible in itself, / seen only by its movement', 'a burn with glass-white shiver / singing over stone', 'that loups like licht, / Caulder than mou can thole'. (Four short poems are in the Doric.)

Of the book's 53 pages, 30 are directly mountainy, there are 8 pages of other lyrics, and the last 14 pages are headed 'Fourteen Years', a more enigmatic sequence of eleven sonnets – but still with the most favoured 'ecstasy/ecstatic' appearing, though she knew darkness as well as light. The Cairngorms were her confessional where in the words of one poem, 'Nothing avails him here but the mind's own fineness'. Substitute her for him and we have Nan Shepherd.

Hamish Brown

One Day as a Tiger – Alex MacIntyre and the birth of light & fast alpinism: John Porter. (Vertebrate Publishing, 2014, hardback, 230pp, ISBN 978-910240-08-3, £20.)

A quick dip into Colin Wells's indispensible Who's Who in British Climbing reminded me that Alex MacIntyre, '…one of the legendary early '70s Leeds University group, epitomised the last hurrah of a macho era when climbers pursued birds'n'booze, sported big hair and persisted in calling each other "youth".' John Porter, an experienced American climber who moved to the UK to dodge being drafted into the Vietnam war, also found himself at Leeds University 'at the heart of the talented clique of climbers including Brian Hall, John Syrett, Roger Baxter-Jones and Alex MacIntyre. Porter took the latter under his wing for his first Alpine and Himalayan experiences.'

In the autumn of 1982 MacIntyre's life was cut tragically short on the south face of Annapurna by a single falling stone. The dust-jacket introduction reminds us that 'although only twenty-eight years old, Alex was already one of the leading figures of British mountaineering's most successful era. His ascents included hard new routes on Himalayan giants like Dhaulagiri and Changabang and a glittering record of firsts in the Alps and Andes.' Over thirty years later, with a unique personal knowledge of the places, climbs and people involved, Porter has made an absorbing and highly readable attempt to give a more rounded picture of

MacIntyre's short life and explain how it gradually became dominated by his passion for climbing. Equally interesting is his historical overview of this whole generation of inspirational climbers, and his objective analysis of MacIntyre's contribution to the development of climbing in the UK in his rôle as National Officer for the BMC. Porter ties these different threads together skilfully in twenty-nine short chapters, each one headed by the title of a popular song, as MacIntyre was seldom without some music blaring out from his favourite ghetto blaster. (I had already started this year's 'Munro Matters' before I opened this book, so obviously some convergent thinking by Porter and myself!) In fact, as the story does not unfold chronologically, when I came to prepare this review I did not find the chapter headings helpful. Sadly indexes seem to be going out of fashion, but this one could have been headed 'Easy as ABC'. Just a minor quibble on my part!

The title of course refers to Tipu Sultan's famous aphorism inscribed on Alex's memorial stone at Annapurna base camp: 'Better to live one day as a tiger than to live for a thousand years as a sheep.'

This memoir hit a few other personal chords with me. Alex was only a few months my junior, and while he was developing a love of climbing at Leeds University, I was going through a similar epiphany at Edinburgh University, though they sounded a much more anarchic bunch than the EUMC. I never met 'Dirty Alex' as he quickly became known, but we both survived our first alpine season in the summer of 1973. Many will recognise from first-hand experience the apprenticeship system described by Porter: 'Before the widespread popularity of climbing walls, sport climbing and mountain commercial tourism.

Walk in the hills and dales – observe mad people climbing rocks. Read books about climbing, get inspired.

Decide you are also mad and find someone with whom to go climb a rock.

Climb ice in winter, get thoroughly miserable and thoroughly hooked. Go to the Alps in summer, learn to function in thin air, to move fast.

Climb in the Alps in winter, have miserable epics and taste the joy of hard fought success.'

In looking back, Porter avoids putting on rose tinted spectacles. On the contrary, his personal accounts of significant climbs with Alex all make for gripping reading. Starting with the latter's first alpine route, the east face of Pointe Lepiney (1973) before moving on to greater things such as the north-east face of Bandaka (1977), the south buttress of Changabang (1978), and the east buttress of Tarke Kang (1982), Porter gives a convincing insight into the enormous physical and mental challenges involved in climbing at this level. These autobiographical chapters really make this book stand out from many of the recent climbing biographies I have read. MacIntyre's own accounts of a couple of climbs are also included, though their style now feels a bit dated.

Porter also introduced Alex to the active and resourceful Polish climbing community, which led to some strong and successful international partnerships, reiterating Roger Baxter-Jones summary of the 'essential dynamics of teamwork on a Himalayan climb: 1. Come back. 2. Come back friends. 3. Get to the top.' Things did not always go quite so smoothly, illustrated by some of the tensions which surfaced during the first ascent of the south west face of Shisha Pangma with a team of disparate skills and motivation, which the author ascribes to the changing nature of high altitude climbing at that time. On this climb they used a tent designed by MacIntyre, and Porter acknowledges his close involvement with several clothing and equipment manufacturers, though he was famously quoted as saying 'I don't want to play this game to have a rucksack named after me.'

The author also gives the reader a unique and sensitive insight into MacIntyre's personal life through the friendship and support of his younger sister Libby, his partner Sarah Richards, and particularly his late mother Jean, a down-to-earth Scot from Kintyre. Few mothers must welcome a developing passion for climbing in their children. Those of us whose mothers remained unquestioningly supportive have much to be grateful for. Other sources include Maria Coffey, partner of the late Joe Tasker and Alex's landlady for much of his time at the British Mountaineering Council. In analysing his contribution to this fledgling organisation, Porter gives a succinct overview of the pressures on the sport during the 1970s, which had been brought sharply into public focus by the Cairngorm tragedy of 1971. He concludes that 'he brought tremendous flair and creativity to the job at a turning point in British mountaineering when politicians were considering tampering with the basic freedoms of the sport.'

Stephen Venables contributes a short foreword, and there are lots of excellent, mostly colour, photographs of the climbs and characters involved. All in all a well researched and carefully crafted memoir covering a lot of topics, and a highly recommended read.

Dave Broadhead

A Passion for Mountains: edited by Hannah Burrows-Smith with foreword by Iain Peter. (Robert Hale, 2014, hardback, 208pp, ISBN978-0-719807-19-0, £25.)

Coming from the strongly amateur student mountaineering club tradition of the 1970s, I approached reviewing this anthology of writing by British Mountain Guides with a degree of trepidation. I have a number of good friends who guide for a living, and although they are all decent people, nonetheless I often feel rather unnerved when out in their company. My uncoiling of the rope inevitably leads to tangles, and it is not uncommon for a major item of gear to have been forgotten. Being tolerant types, they try hard not to show they have noticed, but they can't help it – their training lets them down.

So that caveat out of the way, let's get started. I very much enjoyed the entire book. Hannah Burrows-Smith has done a wonderful job of extracting writing out of the guides, and although we have many familiar writers, we read here others who are less well known but with good tales to tell. The book starts with a history of guiding in Britain reminding us of the trials and achievements of the early guides and, later, the struggle for international recognition.

We then have three major sections: Britain, the Alps and World Climbing. Beginning near home, accounts of ice climbing by Bruce Goodlad on Meagaidh and a November traverse of the Cuillin by Martin Moran with a client are examples of Scottish interest. I also particularly enjoyed Martin Burrows-Smith's account of extreme Scottish skiing, as it wasn't a story well-known to me. Wales is also well covered, and I particularly enjoyed elder guide Ron James's account of his life's calling. Richard McHardy, always a man for a great story, provides a gripping one on a snow-covered Idwal Slabs.

On the Alps, Mal Creasey provides a personal retrospective from the 1970s onwards; then there is a varied selection from big Valais ascents of such mountains as the Weisshorn, ski-touring in Italy, guiding classic '30s climbs on the Dru and the Eiger and steep descents on ski by the editor. All are a good read.

The final part of the book deals with world climbing. The Himalaya is in, of course, but also climbs in Spain, California, Jordan, Canada and Patagonia. Although we all know Alan Hinkes climbed the 8000 metre peaks, for 99.999% of us his nail-biting account of the final three brings immense relief that it was him, rather than you, who was attempting this feat. He really did have to dig deep on Kangchenjunga. Andy Perkins on Cerro Kishtwar tells of fifteen desperate days without reaching the summit – but ultimately a satisfying experience despite the disappointment. In Zanskar, John Barry has his own bluff writing style on Hagshu. Rob Collister, who was with myself and Geoff Cohen, describes a purist adventure, also in Zanskar, in the mid-1970s. This would be rather harder to replicate nowadays. Away from the Himalaya, things are not much easier in Patagonia with Tim Neill, but some less tremor-inducing – though still exciting – tales come from Rowland Edwards with the Bedouin and from Tania Noakes and Jonathan Preston in the Sierras.

Because they are highly competent individuals, there are also tales of adventures which run smoothly, and sometimes it is a bit of a surprise and relief to reach the end of a chapter without any major drama. But the stories are none the worse for that. And of course, working in a hazardous environment, there are casualties. The book is dedicated to Roger Payne, who lost his life on Mont Blanc du Tacul having done much for mountain exploration.

Finally, for those of us who still harbour ambitions, there is much useful 'beta' as I suppose we must call it these days. But beta or not, this is a very fine collection of writing.

Des Rubens

The Cairngorms – A Secret History: Patrick Baker. (Birlinn Ltd, 2014, paperback, 189pp, ISBN978-1-78027-188-0, £9.99.)

This fine wee book details one man's search and his explorations into the lesser known aspects of the Cairngorms, 'looking for the alter ego of these hills'. The contents vary from the Muckle Spate of 1829 to Landseer's liaisons with the Duchess of Bedford in Glen Feshie. The crash of a RAF aircraft on Beinn a'Bhuird in 1945 makes interesting reading and seems to have had a profound effect on him.

He clearly has a fascination with the area, and spends time sleeping out at numerous locations during his explorations, be it in caves, huts, the open air, or the Shelter Stone. Some of the locations such as The Cat's Den in Rothiemurchus were new to me, but most other chapters such as the Big Grey Man and the high Cairngorm bothies will be known to most folks, although his take on them makes fine stories.

There are numerous references to SMC members throughout the book, detailing their individual contributions to the development of mountaineering in the region.

If there is one slight criticism, it is his tendency to go off at a tangent before returning to his original story line, but this is him building up a picture of his quest for the truth. All in all, a worthwhile read.

Brian Findlay

Place Name Discoveries – Upper Deeside and the far Highlands: Adam Watson and Ian Murray. (Paragon Publishing, 2015, ISBN 978-1-78222-328-3, £24.99.)

This book is a follow on from The Place Names of Upper Deeside by Adam Watson and Elizabeth Allan (1984). It became apparent to Adam Watson and Ian Murray, while going to the hill and in conversation with locals, that there were many place names that they had not encountered and had not been previously published. The pair were excited by their small, but growing, list of nearly-extinct names and felt a responsibility to preserve them.

They discovered that by visiting the new-found names they could check if the name fitted the location because quite often the name describes the landscape or a significant feature. Also, this enabled the authors to translate Gaelic or Scots names into English. The list of pronunciations use the phonetic symbols of the International Phonetic Association.

Chapter 9 is particularly interesting as it lists nearly 200 misleading Ordnance Survey spellings of Anglicised names in Upper Deeside and the North-east – about time too!

The book is amply illustrated covering many of the named places and also featuring some of the folk who supplied them with valuable information. For me, two photographs stand out – both of Bob Scott o' the Derry. Bob with his pony, Punchie, ready to sledge from Luibeg to Inverey (the cover and page 13), and Bob standing at the edge of Coire an Dubh-lochain on Beinn a' Bhuird (page 17) – very atmospheric.

Derek Pyper

Wild Voices – Journeys through Time in the Scottish Highlands: Mike Cawthorne. (Birlinn, Edinburgh, 2014, paperback, 273pp, ISBN: 978-1-78027-192-7, £9.99.)

The author visits seven wild places in Scotland on foot or by canoe. He is usually accompanied by a friend and, more interestingly, by the author of a book on each area. He follows up the Findhorn in the company of Kenn, Neil Gunn's hero in Highland River, crosses by canoe the tangled loch system of Assynt with McCaig, Adnamurchan with Alasdair Maclean, the author of the evocative memoir Night Falls on Ardnamurchan (who was also a gifted poet). He explores the lands beyond Lairg, trying to find Rowena Farre's isolated croft. This lady published a book Seal Morning detailing the life she led for several years with an aunt and a tame seal who arrived from a neighbouring loch – all fantasy of course, even if an untrainable seal had been a trainable sea-lion. He canoes through a loch system in Lewis in the company of Alastair McIntosh, a local man who wrote a cogent book Soil and Soul dealing with environmental issues; then he walks through the wild country from Strath Carron to Glen Shiel accompanied by Iain Thomson, or rather Thomson's book Isolation Shepherd, and finally makes a circular tour through the western Cairngorms in the company of the works of Syd Scroggie, our legendary late Hon Member.

The author knows his literary material. The rough country he traverses is described in great detail with numerous reminiscences. He has thought about his subject and his observations are worthy of attention. I found the book interesting because I have a good visual memory and have empathy with someone who wanders off the conventional routes. Nevertheless, it is a difficult read, made easier if you have the relevant OS maps to hand to augment the ones supplied.

IHMS

The Way that We Climbed – A History of Irish Hillwalking, Climbing and Mountaineering: Paddy O'Leary. (The Collins Press, 2015, paperback, 324pp, ISBN 978-1-84889-242-2, £17.99.)

The author has savoured a life threaded into his mountain world. His span nears the end. He has lived its Irish story and so writes succinctly and knowledgeably of how it was in his past. The last pages in his epilogue reek of things changing and new souls pushing at the great outdoors. Where, he wonders, is mountaineering going in our shrinking world?

It brings on a sense of personal nostalgia for the high places, with its indelible memories of past days spent on rock, ice and snow. With our own store of experiences, we can find in Paddy O'Leary a kindred spirit who is reliving his days on the hills. He wrote this book under some provocation. Frequently he had complained that someone should write the history of Irish mountaineering, so his pals challenged him to do some research and just get it written. This he has done, providing sustained interest with thoroughness, and with spice on every page.

O'Leary wrote an epilogue, and its gist is as follows. Three elderly walkers were descending from a snow-capped Lugnaquilla, the sole Munro in the Wicklow hills. They had just fought through the debris of a felled forest. The oldest remembered when there was no forest there, and marvelled that he had outlived an entire ecosystem.

Out of a side path emerged a youthful trio. 'How far is it now?', one asked. They claimed that they had been misdirected by 'them', whoever they were. They were participants in an annual walk that followed vaguely a section of the escape route followed by two Donegal princes fleeing from incarceration in Dublin Castle in January 1592, and the walk was now one of many such popular events. All this may be commendable but it is a faint echo of the endurance trek made by the redoubtable H.C.Hart to win a wager. He was a Victorian gentleman walker who in 1886 had hoofed its 75 miles there-and-back in ten minutes short of a target of 24 hours.

Onward went the old people, stabbing the ground with their walking poles, to the big car park. All was hubbub: welcoming faces appeared but turned away when they realised these weary walkers were not participants in the sponsored walk. Scores of onlookers were here to greet the compleaters as they staggered into the big tent for soup and certificates. No one seemed aware it should be two hours more to the stronghold that had been the true destination of the 16th century fugitives. This big car park was good enough for their outing. The walkers passed the commemorative boulder inscribed with the names of the rebellious fighters of 1798 who had lived in the glen, and they stopped by the waiting car to remove their boots. Cheers broke out for the three tired youngsters who had followed them down.

Thus the tenor of the book is set with its background of history through the centuries, and it reaches into a global spread of the high places attainable now for anyone with money, motivation and time. The text is abundantly leavened with appropriate incidents, some notable, others facetious or even ultimately sad. There is the risk that unless you are au fait with the welter of peaks and valleys that exist in the world, you may get overwhelmed by the catalogue of routes done on familiar Alpine peaks or virgin ridges, and the faces struggled up upon unsung Himalayan or Andean mountains. Such a book grows tedious with people you have never heard of even if you are currently involved in this zeitgeist, but don't worry for the tale is full of interest and can mirror your own experience.

Paddy O'Leary has given a well-balanced and historical account with selected anecdotes of deeds of daring-do done by the activists that came and went in the Irish climbing scene. They began on their nearest rocks before extending to mountains outside their home ground and eventually to the top of Everest. This reviewer has undertaken to look at the earliest fraction of the history on its journey to the conclusion at the millennium date.

Here is the story of a small semi-isolated climbing fraternity from its beginning to its maturity. Maybe it began in the south when some cultured gentlemen of means and leisure, all members of a high-spirited, non-sectarian, non-political, social club in Dublin, began to look for sublime experiences with like-minded gentlemen across the water. Conor O'Brien used his yacht to give passage for members to cross to North Wales to join G.W.Young's famous gatherings in Snowdonia. Young was somewhat discomforted about the possibility that the poet W.B.Yeats, if invited and if he climbed, would in mid-pitch lose concentration in some poetic or metaphysical reverie with disastrous consequences for all.

Up north there were sporadic sallies to the granite tors of the Mournes. These playful efforts owed nothing to what was going on across the border. Probably they were unaware of similar activities in the hills of Wicklow and Kerry, but then all this was brought to a sudden halt by the outbreak of WWII. An era had passed, never to return.

In 1948 a mountaineering club was revived in Dublin with the stravaiging naturalist Lloyd Praeger, the author of The Way that We Went [sic], as its first president. Three years later the club embraced all Ireland when a Belfast section was born, a rare example of a shared interest crossing boundaries in a troubled land. Both sections had reasonable access to local rocks and soon developed their own style and skills, and with different philosophies and attitudes. For example, at the end of a tram-ride out of Dublin was the very accessible abandoned granite Dalkey quarry, full of wonderful problems for a summer's evening, perched on a hillside overlooking the sea, and it was not too hard to penetrate into the Wicklow hills, where there were steep buttress walls with interesting cracks and stimulating exposure. Up north the slabby sheets and frictionful grooves imposed an essential stay-in-contact requirement, although their harsh abrasive surfaces did little for sartorial elegance. Somehow the top climbers both south and north thought of themselves as daringly unconventional, there being an unspoken belief that the grottiness of one's britches was directly related to one's climbing ability. This shrugging off of societal norms required some spirit, especially in a republic that lived with narrow religiosity and lack of enterprise. It is rumoured that once upon a time any female members of the University College climbing club going to Dalkey quarry had to be chaperoned by the lady dean of residence.

However, this hardly accounted for the extraordinary abilities and dominance of the Dublin climbers like Frank Winder and Peter Kenny. It is necessary to say that the names of those scattered over these pages will normally be omitted to avoid telephone directory abundance. They and nameless others as in those earlier days could cross by ferryboat to Wales to test their mettle on the hard routes being pioneered in Llanberis and elsewhere. On their return it drove their ambition to ferret out an impressive tally of climbs on the steep Wicklow buttresses at Camaderry, Luggala and elsewhere.

On a June day in 1953 the apotheosis of Camaderry climbing came with the first ascent of Spillikin Ridge, when after several previous attempts and some top-rope inspections Kenny led the crux pitch of this spectacular prow route up the buttress edge with its twin overhangs. With Winder belaying from the Spillikin, a 6m semi-detached pinnacle of dubious stability, later to topple off the cliff, Kenny made a long stride to gain a shallow quartz crack leading to the first overhang. An old piton protected a tricky move on a short diversionary parallel line that outflanked the second overhang to reach a very airy stance. Using combined tactics 'even the use of Kenny's stubbly face as a hold and a wobbly move atop his shoulders along with the use of a stirrup, helped Winder to move up until the angle and their tension eased'….and it is remarked also that those who have stood on one foot when balanced so precariously at this last stance will testify to the poor prospect of holding a fall in those days without harnesses, nuts, friends, and with the ropes too short to avoid stopping higher up but still on the edge of airy space.

Things were less passionate up north. This reviewer once wrote that 'we didn't dash at it; if we could put up one new route, and maybe repeat an earlier route, we were satisfied. There was no rush, we had the scene to ourselves, there was no competition from other climbers. We were content with what we climbed within our limits, and were well aware that our standard fell well below that of our fellow Dubliners.'

Both sections acquired huts in their hills that became social centres for weekend outings, before in later years day visits to the hills became standard practice, and the enthusiasm for club activity and sociability waned. For example, a tiny cottage on the slopes of Binnian was rented at £13 per annum as a refuge for the impecunious Affables, as they styled themselves. It was known as the Bloathouse after McMurray's culinary speciality 'the bloat, an evil concoction of rice, pom, onions and whatever was handy and could be lived off for a whole weekend and even the following one if it survived the intervening days in the drawer to which leftovers had been confined.'

Affluence came slowly; motorbikes and then unreliable bangers were acquired and gave access to other crags. In the north-west, Donegal attracted pioneers to Poisoned Glen, Belshade and Lough Barra. The Dubliners were to the forefront and were often joined by enthusiastic climbers first met on the Welsh visits; some of whom 'fell deeply, blindly, helplessly under the spell of the country.' New routes grew like fungi, but after a few years of intense activity there was the inevitable drop in enthusiasm until a fresh cliff was discovered and the rush was on to fill in the blanks. One such find in 1969 was Fair Head, the closest chunk of Ireland to the Mull of Kintyre, which provided 4km of steep parallel dolerite columns overlooking the sea. Later the western Ailladie sea cliffs in Clare were exploited: they were close to the road, with adjacent wild camping, pubs with trad musicians, and Reiff-like routes.

The sixties too was a time when more climbing clubs were born: they were the gathering point for the more dedicated and talented climbers who considered the older clubs had become rather socially and culturally moribund. One such was the Spillikin Club, who in looking for fresh lines travelled north braving the

'Troubles' to penetrate the check-points. Although not too happy to meet armed patrols in the dark the opportunity for virgin climbing won their day.

Developments grew apace. Climbing began separately in Kerry, where some hopefuls acquired ropes 'like something you'd use for tying down bales of hay' from a local hardware shop, and took to their crags. New clubs multiplied for ramblers, walkers, orienteers, fell runners, and mountain rescuers. Alongside came the back-up bureaucracy with hopeful access legislation, mountaineering councils, codes of behaviour, health and safety standards, introductory training, aspirant courses, guide books, log and journal publications, and lecture nights close to hostelries, all satisfying the need to backup the sport.

Paddy O'Leary writes on, carefully covering his subject in this comprehensive, absorbing and compact account. Perhaps it was possible to cover such a full history because it deals with a specialised small active group of adherents inhabiting a flat boggy land fringed with rugged wee hills dripping on the western edges of Europe. However what was happening was in no ways unusual, because they were matching step by step what occurred in Britain. What may be remarkable was that such a small number of mountaineers could achieve such high standards and take their activities across the world. Think of routes they got up: the Bonatti Pillar on the Dru, the Central Pillar of Freney on Mount Blanc, the Eiger Nordwand in winter, and big hills like Ama Dablam, Denali, Kenya and others too numerous to enumerate, and of course in 1987 the first Irish bagging of all the Munros. Expeditions were going everywhere; in Asia they failed unceremoniously on Manaslu, but succeeded when Dawson Stelfox continued up alone to make the first Irish and incidentally British ascent of the north ridge of Everest in 1993.

What now about the technicalities of this paperback? Thirteen compact chapters ranging from 'Comrade Lysenko and The Affables' to 'Distant Ranges and Domestic Strife.' There are 600 individual references to back up the text, over 60 contributors acknowledged, a bibliography listing as many books, articles, journals, magazines, newspapers, memoirs, and selected guide books from the 100 or so versions or editions published. The index is very good, even if there are 77 references to the Irish Mountaineering Club. A glossary of arcane mountaineering terminology is offered, and a grading list too: the rock standards go to a series of numbered E-grades, but the ice grades stop at VI, and this poses the question: is the octogenarian author behind the times or has he got something here?

However the biggest regret is the poor quality of many of the numerous B&W photos, a mixture of individual and group portraits with a sprinkling of mountain landscapes and climbing shots; they lack fine detail, contrast, and clarity, are often muddy and indistinct, but at least they do cover the personalities featured in the text and so help to add some more genuine character to them. This scattering of B&W photos is redeemed by a central block of good colour photos, perhaps selected at random for being already available due to previous publication.

What more can be said about this history except to fling a bit of the real stuff…

In March 1997 two climbers are tackling the steep Exit Cracks on the Eiger Nordwand. They are on their fourth day, and they are wondering how much harder they could actually climb. 'I had to swing diagonally across my right to get a placement. I swung and the ice shattered. At this stage of the climb the pick was blunted and with the awkward angle I couldn't grip as firmly as normal. I aimed again a little higher and saw the ice fall away. There was no good ice left within arm's reach. The walls on either side of the groove were bare. Featureless. I envisaged desperate moves. Above protection, as on the ramp or access to the Gods, this is reasonable. Fifteen metres out from the belay, with nothing in between, it's not. I looked down and saw little hope of successfully reversing the moves. Besides there was no point. There was no other way out. I knew I couldn't risk moving up with only a couple of pick teeth biting in the ice. I placed my hammer firmly, a few centimetres below my axe. I mantelshelfed up on both tools, keeping my body as close to the ice as possible. I removed the axe and reached high above the hammer. The body was alive! My arteries and veins felt like the walls of a gorge trying to restrain a raging torrent. Adrenalin was surging through me. I picked my spot, held the axe firmly and struck carefully. I heard a dull thud. The placement was solid. I was back on course. The spirit was on fire. It burned strongly. It burned brightly. It danced beautifully. It danced like never before. We had almost cracked the route. The Exit doors were opening.'

Phil Gribbon

Scottish Rock, Volume 2 North, 2nd Edition: Gary Latter. (Pesda Press, 2014, paperback, 480pp, ISBN 978-1-906095-46-8, £23.)

The second edition of Scottish Rock, Volume 2, is a reprint of the 2009 first edition with a few small amendments but no major changes. This volume describes well over 2000 routes in the area north of the Great Glen while its sister, Volume 1, covers the area further south. It is well laid out with an abundance of photographs and clear photo diagrams to inspire the reader. Opening the book reveals a clear overview map of both volumes to help you plan your expeditions, but don't use it to locate Creag Ghlas (Easter Ross) which is too far south and should surely be included in this volume rather than Volume 1.

In addition to some grade revisions this edition includes some more 'deep water soloing' routes at Foghorn Cove, Neist, on Skye. While these are probably very worthwhile inclusions, an explanation of their graces is hidden inside the back cover and is not easy to find. DWS is not yet a mainstream climbing activity in Scotland and there may be the odd unsuspecting climber who sees the grade F6a+ SO and expects to find some bolts!

The use of full names for first ascentionists gives the book a more personal feel, and the inclusion of some obscure quotes about some of the crags and climbs adds further to the character. Route selection is also refreshingly different in some areas so if you pick up this book, even with a thorough knowledge of Scottish rock climbing, you will almost certainly discover some quality routes of which you were unaware. There is more comprehensive cover of the Hebrides than other selected guides and it includes the spectacular climbing on Pabbay and Mingulay. While route selection for a book like this is always going to be subjective and down to the whim of the author, I do feel an opportunity has been missed to include Moy Rock near Contin, which has become a popular venue and is a very handy retreat when conditions are unfavourable further north. (Perhaps these are the obsessive ramblings of a conglomerate addict.)

Overall the guide is very well presented, inspiring, and has a great selection of routes. If you have not got a copy of the previous edition, I would thoroughly recommend this book as it may take you somewhere new.

Andy Tibbs

Crystal Mountains - Minerals of the Cairngorms: Roy E. Starkey. (British Mineralogy Publications, 2014, softback, 229 col photos, 4 col maps, 184pp, ISBN 978-0-9930182-1-3, £25.)
Books about minerals can be fairly dull. I have numerous such books and most of them are just reference books that I dip into from time to time. This book is different because it concentrates on the minerals found in one mountain massif – The Cairngorms.

Quartz is an extremely common mineral, in fact one of the most abundant of all rock forming minerals. The main mineral that the Cairngorms are famous for is a special form of quartz called 'smokey quartz'. Pure quartz is colourless, but smoky quartz ranges in colour from pale grey-brown to almost black. The colour is attributed to trace contamination by aluminium and low level gamma radiation over a prolonged period of time. Specimens of smoky quartz found in the Cairngorms are often referred to simply as 'cairngorms'. I will shamelessly name drop for a moment and mention meeting the Queen and Prince Philip at an event in Glen Nevis a few years ago. Prince Philip was telling my colleague about having 'a huge cairngorm at home'. He raised his hand above a table to indicate the height. My colleague had never heard the term cairngorm for a mineral before and thought Prince Philip was losing it. I was able to save my colleague from embarrassment.

This is a remarkably well researched and very interesting book. The author has hunted out details of, and photographed, all the enormous specimens found in the Cairngorms including the one at Balmoral which is 38cm high and 21.3kg in weight. This is thought to have been discovered in a pothole on the Fèith Buidhe around 1851 and presented to Queen Victoria. However, this isn't quite the largest specimen found in the Cairngorms. The Invercauld cairngorm, formerly displayed in Braemar Castle, is slightly bigger at 46cm high and 23.8kg. You would be very lucky to discover specimens one tenth of this size today. At one time the extraction of minerals specimens was a small industry. A 5m-long tunnel can still be seen on Beinn a' Bhuird where a pegmatite vein was exploited.

As well as cairngorms, there are more than two dozen other minerals to be found in the Cairngorms, notably among them are beryl and topaz. The author also covers these in a very comprehensive manner. I highly recommend this book to anyone who wants to find out more about these 'crystal mountains'. If you keep your eyes peeled when out in the 'Gorms, with the aid of this book, you could still make some interesting discoveries.

Matthew Forster Heddle - Mineralogist and Mountaineer: Hamish H. Johnston. (NMS Enterprises Ltd, 2015, paperback, 270pp, ISBN 978-1-905267-98-9, £14.99.)
Another book about minerals, or more accurately the life of a man who was a phenomenal collector of minerals in the nineteenth century. Matthew Forster Heddle was a giant in his field and his treatise on *The Mineralogy of Scotland* (1901), which was published in two volumes only after his death, is still regarded as a magnificent work. Although first editions of this book are hard to get hold of electronic copies can be downloaded from <archive.org>.

This is the first full biography of a larger-than life-figure. It has been written by his great-great-grandson. He has done a huge amount of research into the personal and professional life of his relative. It makes a fascinating tale.

I well remember how as a young teacher I first came across Heddle's name. An adult in my geology evening class brought in a highly unusual form of calcite that he'd found at the mines near Strontian. I hadn't seen this sort of crystal growth before and thought it was sufficiently interesting to send to the National Museum in Edinburgh. They replied remarkably quickly and said that it was due to secondary growth and was called coronetted calcite. It had been described by Professor Heddle and specimens were in his collection at the museum. The secondary growth was particularly well picked out under ultraviolet light.

The story of how Heddle's mineral collection came to end up in the National Museum of Scotland is told in some detail at the end of the book. In order to amass his collection of over 7000 specimens Heddle walked vast distances in the hills carrying a 4-lb hammer, a 14-lb sledge hammer, blasting powder and wedges. He then walked back with a sack weighed down with samples. There seems little doubt that if Munro had published his Tables a little earlier, then Heddle would have been the first to complete the list of summits. As it was he climbed at least '350 of the 409 hills over 3000ft'. He couldn't get at most of the others because William Winans forebade access to his land at that time. Some of the routes Heddle took in the hills are marked on 86 early Ordnance Survey maps which are held in the Club archives. A number of maps signed by Heddle are also held in the National Museum of Scotland Geology and Zoology Department archives

Heddle took particular delight in the Cuillin and made a very early ascent of Sgùrr a' Ghreadaidh (1871), possibly pipped to its first ascent by a 14-year-old John Mackenzie the year before. (See Ashley Abraham's *Rock-Climbing in Skye.*) He also visited by boat a remarkably inaccessible mineral location in the sea-cliffs beneath Sgùrr nam Boc on the south-west coast of Skye. (I chickened out of descending 200m of steep, wet grass to visit the site on the Skye Meet last year.)

In 1879 Heddle was invited to become a member of the Royal Society of Edinburgh's Boulder Committee. This had been set up in 1871 to record the position and type of glacial erratic boulders across the country. Over the next few years Heddle walked long distances checking out these features. His excellent knowledge of the hills helped pinpoint where they might have come from. (Now that we have GPS technology there's a strong case for reviving this committee!)

Heddle first met Munro in 1883 when they shared the box seat of the mail from Kingussie to Fort William. Heddle was on his way to Ben Nevis for the opening of the Observatory. Munro was extremely impressed by Heddle and his knowledge of the hills. Eventually Heddle was made one of the early Honorary Members of the Club.

I can strongly recommend this book. It tells the story of a most interesting character who in the course of his epic collecting got to know the Scottish hills better than anyone else of his day.

Noel Williams

ERRATA

In the SMC Abroad section of the 2014 Journal (p.299), the article entitled 'Too Old for Mount Blanc?' was written by Geoff Cohen.

ORDERING THE SMC JOURNAL

Members should automatically receive a copy of the Journal when it is published. Members wishing to order extra copies or non-members wishing to place a regular order should contact the Distribution Manager, Roger Robb, by **e-mail** <journal.distribution@smc.org.uk>.

SMC JOURNAL BACK NUMBERS

Back numbers of the Journal may be obtained from Clifford Smith:
16 House o' Hill Gardens, Edinburgh, EH4 2AR.
e-mail: <journal.archive@smc.org.uk>
tel: 0131-332 3414 mob: 07748 703 515

The following years are available:

	Year
£5.00	1972
	1977
	1978
	1979
	1980
	1983
£5.50	1985
£5.70	1986
	1987
	1989
	1990
	1991
	1992
£6.95	1993
	1994
	1995
£8.95	1996
	1997
	1998
£11.95	1999

	Year
£12.95	2000
	2001
	2002
	2003
	2004
£13.95	2005
	2006
	2007
	2008
£14.95	2009
	2010
	2011
	2012
	2013
	2014

Post & Packaging is extra.

SCOTTISH MOUNTAINEERING CLUB HUTS

Bookings can be made to stay at any of the five Club Huts by contacting the relevant Custodian.

CHARLES INGLIS CLARK MEMORIAL HUT, BEN NEVIS

Location: (NN 167 722) On the north side of Ben Nevis by the Allt a' Mhuilinn. This hut was erected by Dr and Mrs Inglis Clark in memory of their son Charles who was killed in action in the 1914–18 War.
Custodian: Robin Clothier, 35 Broompark Drive, Newton Mearns, Glasgow, G77 5DZ.
e-mail <cic@smc.org.uk>

LAGANGARBH HUT, GLEN COE

Location: (NN 221 559) North of Buachaille Etive Mor near the River Coupall.
Custodian: Bernard Swan, 16 Knowes View, Faifley, Clydebank, G81 5AT.
e-mail <lagangarbh@smc.org.uk>.

LING HUT, GLEN TORRIDON

Location: (NG 958 562) On the south side of Glen Torridon.
Custodian: John T Orr, 8 Fleurs Place, Elgin, Morayshire, IV30 1ST.
e-mail <ling@smc.org.uk>.

NAISMITH HUT, ELPHIN

Location: (NC 216 118) In the community of Elphin on the east side of the A835.
Custodian: Andrew Tibbs, Crown Cottage, 4 Crown Circus, Inverness, IV2 3NQ.
e-mail <naismith@smc.org.uk>.

RAEBURN HUT, LAGGAN

Location: (NN 636 909) On the north side of the A889 between Dalwhinnie and Laggan.
Custodian: Clive Rowland, Inverene, Links Place, Nairn, IV12 4NH.
e-mail <raeburn@smc.org.uk>.

SCOTTISH MOUNTAINEERING CLUB GUIDEBOOKS

Published by THE SCOTTISH MOUNTAINEERING TRUST

HILLWALKERS' GUIDES

The Munros
Munros GPS data sets – from <www.smc.org.uk/>
The Corbetts and other Scottish hills
The Grahams & The Donalds
The Cairngorms
Central Highlands
Islands of Scotland including Skye
North-West Highlands
Southern Highlands

SCRAMBLERS' GUIDES

Highland Scrambles North
Skye Scrambles

CLIMBERS' GUIDES

Scottish Rock Climbs
Scottish Winter Climbs
Scottish Sports Climbs
Inner Hebrides & Arran
Ben Nevis
The Cairngorms
Glen Coe
Highland Outcrops
Lowland Outcrops
North-East Outcrops
Northern Highlands North
Northern Highlands Central
Northern Highlands South
Skye The Cuillin
Skye Sea-Cliffs & Outcrops

OTHER PUBLICATIONS

Ben Nevis – Britain's Highest Mountain
The Cairngorms – 100 Years of Mountaineering
A Chance in a Million? – Scottish Avalanches
Hostile Habitats
The Munroist's Companion
Scottish Hill Names – Their origin and meaning

e-BOOKS

Cairngorms Scene and Unseen
A Century of Scottish Mountaineering
A History of Glenmore Lodge

APPLYING FOR MEMBERSHIP OF THE SCOTTISH MOUNTAINEERING CLUB

The following notes are provided outlining the principles by which climbers may be admitted to membership of the Club.

The Committee does not lay down any hard and fast rules when considering applications but considers each case on its own merits. Candidates must be over 18 and have experience of mountaineering in Scotland in both summer and winter. This experience should have extended over a period of at least four years immediately prior to application and should not be confined to just a single climbing district.

The normally expected climbing standards include:

- Experience of winter climbing including several routes of around Grade IV standard and the ability to lead climbs of this level of difficulty.
- Rock climbing experience including climbs of Very Severe (4c) standard and the ability to lead routes of this level of difficulty. In considering applications, emphasis will be placed on multi-pitch climbs in mountain locations.
- The ascent of at least 50 Munros of which at least one third should have been climbed in snow conditions.

In short, the candidate should be able to show – by producing a detailed list of climbs – that they are competent to lead a variety of outings in the mountains of Scotland in both summer and winter. The technical standards specified refer to applicants currently active and may be varied at the discretion of the Committee for older candidates provided that the applicant's routes reflect a reasonable standard for their time. Climbing in the Alps and elsewhere is taken into consideration. Candidates who do not fulfil the normal qualifications listed above but who have made special contributions to Scottish mountaineering in the fields of art, literature or science may receive special consideration.

It is essential that each candidate, before applying, should have climbed with the member proposing the application. It is also desirable that a candidate should be introduced to a member of the Committee before the application is considered. Application forms must be obtained on behalf of candidates by members of the Club who may not propose or support candidates for election during their own first two years of membership. The annual membership fee is £40.00 (£30.00 for those aged 65 and over) which includes the Club Journal.

A fuller version of these notes for members wishing to propose candidates is available from the Club Secretary who is happy to advise candidates and members on any aspect of the application process. Please contact John R R Fowler, Honorary Secretary at:

e-mail: <jrrfowler@tiscali.co.uk>
tel: 0131 226 4055.

OFFICE BEARERS 2014–2015

Honorary President: Iain H.M. Smart
Honorary Vice-Presidents: Neil Quinn and Bob Richardson
President: D. Noel Williams
Vice-Presidents: Roger J.C. Robb and Derek A. Bearhop.

Honorary Secretary: John R.R. Fowler, 4 Doune Terrace, Edinburgh, EH3 6DY. **Honorary Treasurer**: John A. Wood, Spout Close, Millbeck, Keswick, CA12 4PS. **Honorary Membership Secretary**: Geoff Cohen, 198/1 Grange Loan, Edinburgh, EH9 2DZ. **Honorary Meets Secretary**: John R.R. Fowler. **Honorary Editor of Journal**: Peter J. Biggar, Hillhead, Craigton, North Kessock, Inverness, IV1 3YG. **Honorary Librarian & Honorary Archivist**: Robin N. Campbell, Glynside, Kippen Road, Fintry, Glasgow, G63 0LW. **Honorary Custodian of Images**: David Stone, 30 Summerside Street, Edinburgh, EH6 4NU. **Honorary Reporter on Accounts**: David Small, 5 Afton Place, Edinburgh, EH5 3RB. **SMC Website Manager**: Tony Stone, 36 Huntingtower Road, Sheffield, S11 7GR. **Convener of Publications Sub-Committee**: Rab Anderson, 24 Paties Road, Edinburgh, EH14 1EE. **Convener of Huts Sub-Committee**: Andrew M. James, 41 Urquhart Road, Dingwall, IV15 9PE. **Representative to the MCofS**: Brian R. Shackleton, 4A Campbell Road, Edinburgh, EH12 6DT. **Committee**: Richard K. Bott, Simon Fraser, Helen G.S. Forde, Adrian Hart, Graeme N. Hunter and Ruth Love.

Journal Information

Editor:	Peter Biggar, Hillhead, Craigton, North Kessock, Inverness, IV1 3YG. **e-mail** <journal@smc.org.uk>
New Routes Editor:	Andy Nisbet, 20 Craigie Avenue, Boat of Garten, PH24 3BL. **e-mail** <newroutes@smc.org.uk>
Photos Editor:	Ian Taylor, 15, Pulteney Street, Ullapool, Ross-shire, IV26 2UP. **e-mail** <itandtf@hotmail.com>
Reviews Editor:	Graeme Morrison, 42 Orchard Drive, Edinburgh, EH4 2DZ. **e-mail** <g.d.morrison@btopenworld.com>
Distribution:	Roger Robb, Blaven, Upper Knockbain Road, Dingwall, IV15 9NR. **e-mail** <journal.distribution@smc.org.uk>
Back Numbers:	Cliff Smith. **e-mail** <journal.archive@smc.org.uk>

INSTRUCTIONS TO CONTRIBUTORS

The Editor welcomes contributions from members and non-members alike. Priority will be given to articles relating to Scottish mountaineering. Articles should be submitted **by the end of April** if they are to be considered for inclusion in the Journal of the same year. Material is preferred in electronic form and should be sent by e-mail direct to the Editor. Most common file formats are acceptable – PDF, Open Document Format (odt), Rich Text Format (rtf), Plain Text (txt) or MS Word (doc/docx).

Those without access to e-mail can send hard copy (typewritten and double-spaced) by post to the Editor's home address. Illustrations not relating to an article should be sent to the Photos Editor. All photographs should be accompanied by appropriate information, including the name of the photographer.